my World Social Studies

We Are Texas

SAVVAS
LEARNING COMPANY

It's my story, too!

You are one of the authors of this book. You can write in this book! You can take notes in this book! You can draw in it, too! This book will be yours to keep.

Fill in the information below to tell about yourself. Then write your autobiography. An autobiography tells about you and the kinds of things you like to do.

Name _____

School _____

City or Town _____

Autobiography _____

_____

SAVVAS
LEARNING COMPANY

Built for Texas

Savvas *Texas myWorld Social Studies* was developed especially for Texas with the help of teachers from across the state and covers 100 percent of the Texas Essential Knowledge and Skills for Social Studies. This story began with a series of teacher roundtables in cities across the state of Texas that inspired a program blueprint for *Texas myWorld Social Studies*. In addition, Judy Brodigan served as our expert advisor, guiding our creation of a dynamic Social Studies curriculum for TEKS mastery. Once this blueprint was finalized, a dedicated team—made up of Savvas authors, content experts, and social studies teachers from Texas—worked to bring our collective vision into reality.

Savvas would like to extend a special thank you to all of the teachers who helped guide the development of this program. We gratefully acknowledge your efforts to realize the possibilities of elementary Social Studies teaching and learning. Together, we will prepare Texas students for their future roles in college, careers, and as active citizens.

Program Consulting Authors

The Colonial Williamsburg Foundation
Williamsburg VA

Armando Cantú Alonzo
Associate Professor of History
Texas A&M University
College Station TX

Dr. Linda Bennett
Associate Professor, Department of
   Learning, Teaching, & Curriculum
College of Education
University of Missouri
Columbia MO

Dr. James B. Kracht
Byrne Chair for Student Success
Executive Associate Dean
College of Education and Human
   Development
College of Education
Texas A&M University
College Station TX

Dr. William E. White
Vice President for Productions,
   Publications and Learning
   Ventures
The Colonial Williamsburg
   Foundation
Williamsburg VA

Reviewers and Consultants

ACADEMIC REVIEWERS

Kathy Glass
Author, *Lesson Design for
   Differentiated Instruction*
President, Glass Educational
   Consulting
Woodside CA

Roberta Logan
African Studies Specialist
Retired, Boston Public Schools/
   Mission Hill School
Boston MA

Jeanette Menendez
Reading Coach
Doral Academy Elementary
Miami FL

Bob Sandman
Adjunct Assistant Professor of
   Business and Economics
Wilmington College—Cincinnati
   Branches
Blue Ash OH

PROGRAM CONSULTANT

Judy Brodigan
Former President, Texas Council
   for Social Studies
Grapevine TX

Padre Island National Seashore

CONNECT

Master the TEKS with a personal connection.

myStory Spark

The **myStory Book** writing strand in the program begins with a **myStory Spark** activity. Here you can record your initial ideas about the **Big Question**.

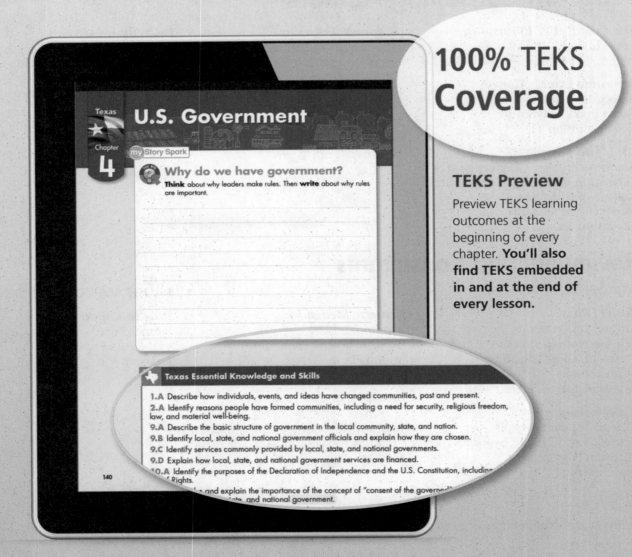

Texas
Chapter
4

U.S. Government

my Story Spark

Why do we have government?
Think about why leaders make rules. Then **write** about why rules are important.

Texas Essential Knowledge and Skills

1.A Describe how individuals, events, and ideas have changed communities, past and present.
2.A Identify reasons people have formed communities, including a need for security, religious freedom, law, and material well-being.
9.A Describe the basic structure of government in the local community, state, and nation.
9.B Identify local, state, and national government officials and explain how they are chosen.
9.C Identify services commonly provided by local, state, and national governments.
9.D Explain how local, state, and national government services are financed.
10.A Identify the purposes of the Declaration of Independence and the U.S. Constitution, including
 Rights.
 and explain the importance of the concept of "consent of the governed"
 and national government.

140

100% TEKS Coverage

TEKS Preview

Preview TEKS learning outcomes at the beginning of every chapter. **You'll also find TEKS embedded in and at the end of every lesson.**

myStory Video

Move seamlessly from **the Student Worktext** to technology! Watch the myStory Videos to explore the **Big Question** and key ideas in the chapter.

Lesson 1 America's First Peoples
Lesson 2 Early Explorers
Lesson 3 Early Spanish Communities
Lesson 4 Early French Communities
Lesson 5 Early English Communities
Lesson 6 Creating a New Nation

Mission San Luis
A Multicultural Community

From about 1560 to 1690, there were more than 100 Spanish missions built throughout Florida. A mission is a settlement that has a church where religion is taught. One of the most famous missions is Mission San Luis. Located in Tallahassee, it is one of the last remaining mission sites today. "It's also the only place where both the Apalachee and the Spaniards lived together," says Grace. The Apalachee are Native Americans and Spaniards are people from Spain. "I love learning about other cultures," she adds. No one lives at the mission anymore, but it has been rebuilt. Visitors can tour the mission and watch people act out what life was like there hundreds of years ago.

"Native Americans and Spaniards shared this mission," Grace explains. At that time, Native Americans and European settlers usually did not live together. Mission San Luis was special.

Grace was excited to visit one of the last remaining missions.

Mission San Luis

Access the TEKS

Texas *myWorld Social Studies* covers the TEKS in all formats. Access the content through the printed worktext, eText, or online with the digital course on Realize.

 **Go online at:** SavvasTexas.com

Every lesson is supported by digital activities, myStory Videos, vocabulary activities, and myStory Book on Tikatok.

EXPERIENCE

Enjoy social studies while practicing the TEKS.

Student Interactive Worktext

With the Texas *myWorld Social Studies* worktext, you'll love writing, drawing, circling and underlining in your own book.

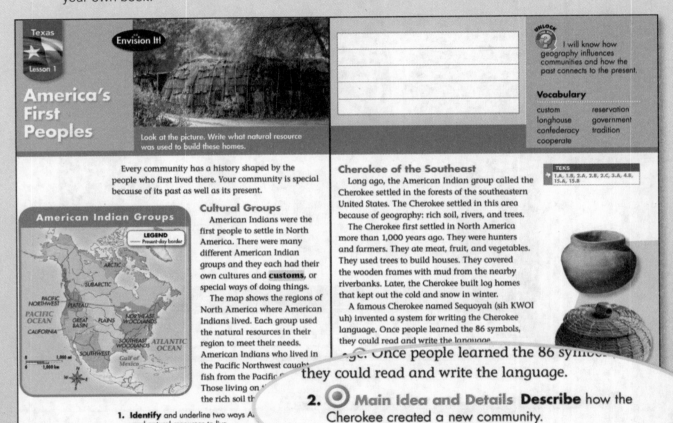

Texas

Lesson 1

America's First Peoples

Envision It!

Look at the picture. Write what natural resource was used to build these homes.

Every community has a history shaped by the people who first lived there. Your community is special because of its past as well as its present.

Cultural Groups

American Indians were the first people to settle in North America. There were many different American Indian groups and they each had their own cultures and **customs**, or special ways of doing things.

The map shows the regions of North America where American Indians lived. Each group used the natural resources in their region to meet their needs. American Indians who lived in the Pacific Northwest caught fish from the Pacific Those living on the rich soil th

American Indian Groups

LEGEND
— Present-day border

ARCTIC

SUBARCTIC

PACIFIC NORTHWEST
PLATEAU
PACIFIC OCEAN
CALIFORNIA
GREAT BASIN
PLAINS
NORTHEAST WOODLANDS
SOUTHEAST WOODLANDS
SOUTHWEST
ATLANTIC OCEAN
Gulf of Mexico

1,000 mi
1,000 km

1. **Identify** and underline two ways A used natural resources to live.

UNLOCK
I will know how geography influences communities and how the past connects to the present.

Vocabulary

custom   reservation
longhouse   government
confederacy   tradition
cooperate

Cherokee of the Southeast

Long ago, the American Indian group called the Cherokee settled in the forests of the southeastern United States. The Cherokee settled in this area because of geography: rich soil, rivers, and trees.

The Cherokee first settled in North America more than 1,000 years ago. They were hunters and farmers. They ate meat, fruit, and vegetables. They used trees to build houses. They covered the wooden frames with mud from the nearby riverbanks. Later, the Cherokee built log homes that kept out the cold and snow in winter.

A famous Cherokee named Sequoyah (sih KWOI uh) invented a system for writing the Cherokee language. Once people learned the 86 symbols, they could read and write the language.

TEKS
1.A, 1.B, 2.A, 2.B, 2.C, 3.A, 4.B, 15.A, 15.B

...ge. Once people learned the 86 symbols... they could read and write the language.

2. **Main Idea and Details** **Describe** how the Cherokee created a new community.

Target Reading Skills

The worktext enables you to practice important **Target Reading Skills**—essential skills you'll need when reading informational texts. Reinforce your ELA TEKS during the social studies block of time.

 **Go online at:**
SavvasTexas.com

Every lesson is supported by digital activities, myStory Videos, vocabulary activities, and myStory Book on Tikatok.

Leveled Readers

Engaging leveled readers are available in print and digital formats on Realize.

Digital Activities

Every lesson includes a **Digital Activity** that helps support the Big Idea.

UNDERSTAND

Assess TEKS and demonstrate understanding.

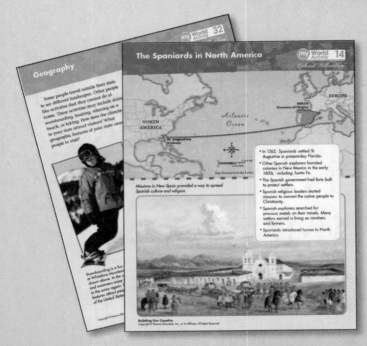

myWorld Activities

Work together in small groups on activities that range from mapping, graphing, and role playing, to read-alouds and analyzing primary sources. Digital versions of innovative hands-on activities for each chapter can be found on Realize.

Find **TEKS practice** at the end of every chapter.

myStory Book

The **myStory Book** final writing activity gives you the exciting opportunity to write and illustrate your own digital book. Go to **www.Tikatok.com/myWorldSocialStudies** to learn more.

 Go online at: SavvasTexas.com

Every lesson is supported by digital activities, myStory Videos, vocabulary activities, and myStory Book on Tikatok.

Texas

Celebrating Texas and the Nation

The Geography of Texas

How does geography affect our lives?

realize. Go online at:
SavvasTexas.com

- ▶ **Interactive eText**
- ▶ **Big Question Activity**
  How does geography affect our lives?
- ▶ **myStory Video**
  Big Bend National Park, a Natural Treasure
- ▶ **Vocabulary Preview**
- ▶ **Lesson Introduction**
- ▶ **Digital Got it? Activity**
- ▶ **21ˢᵗ Century Learning Tutorials**
  Identify Main Idea and Details
  Interpret Physical Maps
- ▶ **Vocabulary Review**
- ▶ **myStory Book on Tikatok**
  www.tikatok.com/
  myWorldSocialStudies
- ▶ **Chapter Tests**

Texas ocelots are an endangered species.

The Geographic Regions of Texas

The Cross Timbers area in the North Central Plains region of Texas has good soil.

THE BIG ? What makes a good community?

The Early History of Texas

Go online at:
SavvasTexas.com

- ▶ **Interactive eText**
- ▶ **Big Question Activity**
  How do people adapt to where they live?
- ▶ **myStory Video**
  Ysleta del Sur Pueblo, a Place of Culture
- ▶ **Vocabulary Preview**
- ▶ **Lesson Introduction**
- ▶ **Digital Got it? Activity**
- ▶ **21ˢᵗ Century Learning Tutorials**
  Compare and Contrast
  Conduct Research
- ▶ **Vocabulary Review**
- ▶ **myStory Book on Tikatok**
  www.tikatok.com/
  myWorldSocialStudies
- ▶ **Chapter Tests**

How do people adapt to where they live?

*Some American Indian groups
lived in teepees in the mountains
and plains of West Texas.*

Texas

Chapter 4

Exploration and Colonization of Texas

 Why do some people leave their homelands?

realize Go online at:
SavvasTexas.com

- ▶ **Interactive eText**
- ▶ **Big Question Activity**
  Why do some people leave their homelands?
- ▶ **myStory Video**
  Henry and Nancy Jones, Early Texas Pioneers
- ▶ **Vocabulary Preview**
- ▶ **Lesson Introduction**
- ▶ **Digital Got it? Activity**
- ▶ **21ˢᵗ Century Learning Tutorials**
  Analyze Cause and Effect
  Use Primary and Secondary Sources
- ▶ **Vocabulary Review**
- ▶ **myStory Book on Tikatok**
  www.tikatok.com/
  myWorldSocialStudies
- ▶ **Chapter Tests**

In the 1400s, conquistadors took gold jewelry similar to this piece from the Americas back to Spain.

Revolution and the Republic of Texas

 How does the past shape our present and future?

Texans fought Mexican soldiers, dressed in uniforms like these, for independence in the 1830s.

The Road to Statehood

 When does change become necessary?

Today, Texans celebrate holidays from their past such as Cinco de Mayo which honors the heritage of Mexico.

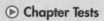

New Challenges for Texas

 What is worth fighting for?

SAVVAS realize. **Go online at:**
SavvasTexas.com

- ▶ **Interactive eText**

- ▶ **Big Question Activity**
  What is worth fighting for?

- ▶ **myStory Video**
  Juneteenth, a Celebration of Freedom

- ▶ **Vocabulary Preview**

- ▶ **Lesson Introduction**

- ▶ **Digital Got it? Activity**

- ▶ **21ˢᵗ Century Learning Tutorials**
  Distinguish Fact and Opinion
  Resolve Conflict

- ▶ **Vocabulary Review**

- ▶ **myStory Book on Tikatok**
  www.tikatok.com/
  myWorldSocialStudies

- ▶ **Chapter Tests**

United States President Abraham Lincoln was against the spread of slavery, unlike many white Texans who believed slavery was important to the economy during the 1800s.

A Growing State

SAVVAS  **Go online at:** SavvasTexas.com

- ▶ **Interactive eText**
- ▶ **Big Question Activity**
  How does economic growth provide opportunity?
- ▶ **myStory Video**
  The Cattle Ranching Industry, Longhorns Change Texas
- ▶ **Vocabulary Preview**
- ▶ **Lesson Introduction**
- ▶ **Digital Got it? Activity**
- ▶ **21st Century Learning Tutorials**
  Draw Conclusions
  Interpret Graphs
- ▶ **Vocabulary Review**
- ▶ **myStory Book on Tikatok**
  www.tikatok.com/
  myWorldSocialStudies
- ▶ **Chapter Tests**

THE BIG **?** **How does economic growth provide opportunity?**

The longhorn, a Texas symbol, is the official state large mammal.

Hard Times at Home and Abroad

 How do people respond to good times and bad?

In October 1929, the
stock market crashed.
Many people across
the nation lost all of
their savings.

Texas

Chapter

10

Texas Today

SAVVAS **realize.** **Go online at:**
SavvasTexas.com

▶ **Interactive eText**

▶ **Big Question Activity**
What goals should we set for our state?

▶ **myStory Video**
The Johnson Space Center, Learning About the Space Program

▶ **Vocabulary Preview**

▶ **Lesson Introduction**

▶ **Digital Got it? Activity**

▶ **21ˢᵗ Century Learning Tutorials**
Draw Conclusions
Compare Viewpoints

▶ **Vocabulary Review**

▶ **myStory Book on Tikatok**
www.tikatok.com/
myWorldSocialStudies

▶ **Chapter Tests**

THE BIG ? **What goals should we set for our state?**

Texas farmers normally raise more cotton than do farmers in any other state.

Texas Government

Go online at:
SavvasTexas.com

- ▶ **Interactive eText**
- ▶ **Big Question Activity**
  What should be the goals of
  government?
- ▶ **myStory Video**
  A Visit to the Capital: The Texas
  Capitol
- ▶ **Vocabulary Preview**
- ▶ **Lesson Introduction**
- ▶ **Digital Got it? Activity**
- ▶ **21ˢᵗ Century Learning Tutorials**
  Classify and Categorize
  Solve Problems
- ▶ **Vocabulary Review**
- ▶ **myStory Book on Tikatok**
  www.tikatok.com/
  myWorldSocialStudies
- ▶ **Chapter Tests**

*Citizens work together to improve their community and
affect how their government is run.*

21st Century Learning
Online Checklist

You can go online to SavvasTexas.com to practice the skills listed below.
These are skills that will be important to you throughout your life.
After you complete each skill tutorial online, check it below.

◉ Target Reading Skills

☐ Main Idea and Details   ☐ Generalize

☐ Cause and Effect   ☐ Compare and Contrast

☐ Categorize   ☐ Sequence

☐ Fact and Opinion   ☐ Summarize

☐ Draw Conclusions

Collaboration and Creativity Skills

☐ Solve Problems   ☐ Resolve Conflict

☐ Work in Cooperative Teams   ☐ Generate New Ideas

Graph Skills

☐ Interpret Graphs   ☐ Interpret Timelines

☐ Create Charts

Map Skills

☐ Use Longitude and Latitude   ☐ Interpret Economic Data on Maps

☐ Interpret Physical Maps   ☐ Interpret Cultural Data on Maps

Critical Thinking Skills

☐ Compare Viewpoints   ☐ Make Decisions

☐ Use Primary and Secondary Sources   ☐ Predict Consequences

☐ Identify Bias

Media and Technology Skills

☐ Conduct Research   ☐ Evaluate Media Content

☐ Use the Internet Safely   ☐ Deliver an Effective Presentation

☐ Analyze Images

Keys to Good Writing

The Writing Process

Good writers follow five steps when they write.

Prewrite
- Choose a topic, gather details about it, and plan how to use them.

Draft
- Write down all of your ideas, and don't worry about making your writing perfect.

Share
- Share your writing with others.

Edit
- Check your spelling, capitalization, punctuation, and grammar.
- Make a final copy.

Revise
- Review your writing, looking for the traits of good writing.
- Change parts that are confusing or incomplete.

The Writing Traits

Good writers look at six qualities of their writing
to make it the best writing possible.

Ideas	Share a clear message with specific ideas and details.
Organization	Have a beginning, middle, and end that are easy to follow.
Voice	Use a natural tone in your writing.
Word Choice	Choose strong nouns and verbs and colorful adjectives.
Sentence Flow	Vary your sentence structures and beginnings to create writing that is easy to read.
Conventions	Follow the rules of spelling, capitalization, punctuation, and grammar.

TEKS 15.C, 16.A, 16.B, 16.C, 21.C

Vocabulary

colonist

constitution

culture

amendment

ethnic group

Celebrate Freedom

The United States of America has always been a nation of people who fought for and celebrated freedom. Before the United States existed, many colonists from Great Britain saw the need for an independent government. A **colonist** is a person who lives in a settlement far from the country that rules it. Three documents played an important role in establishing this freedom: the Declaration of Independence, the United States Constitution, and the Bill of Rights.

The Declaration of Independence

In 1775, the 13 colonies began a war with Great Britain. They were fighting for their rights. By 1776, a group of colonists, including Thomas Jefferson, decided to write a formal statement declaring that the colonies were free from British rule. This official statement was called the Declaration of Independence.

The Declaration of Independence was the first step in gaining freedom for the United States. Today, we celebrate Independence Day on July 4 every year.

1. **Recite** the following paragraph from the Declaration of Independence, in the box below, with your class.

Three main parts of the Declaration of Independence are: the preamble, or introduction; a list of charges against King George III of Great Britain; and a conclusion.

We hold these Truths to be self-evident, that all Men are created equal, that they are endowed by their Creator with certain unalienable Rights, that among these are Life, Liberty and the Pursuit of Happiness—That to secure these Rights, Governments are instituted among Men, deriving their just Powers from the Consent of the Governed.

The United States Constitution

The United States finally won its independence from Great Britain in 1783. Four years later, the leaders of the new country wrote a **constitution,** or written plan for the nation's government. It was called the Constitution of the United States.

The introduction to the Constitution is called the preamble. The first three words of the preamble, "We the People," are very important. They declare that the United States is ruled by the people and not by a king. Who are the people? They are a diverse group representing many cultures. They bring their skills, experience, and culture to Texas and the nation. **Culture** is the way of life of a group of people.

Today, people of many different cultures live in Texas.

The Bill of Rights

Over the years the United States Constitution has been amended, or changed. The first ten **amendments** of the Constitution are known as the Bill of Rights. The Bill of Rights was approved in 1791. It outlines the basic rights and freedoms of Americans. These rights include the freedom of speech, religion, and press, as well as the right to a fair and speedy trial for those accused of crimes.

2. **Locate, identify,** and write the purpose, meaning, and importance of the Declaration of Independence, the United States Constitution, and the Bill of Rights on another sheet of paper.

   A State of Many Cultures Today our nation and our state are made up of people from many different **ethnic groups.** This means that they can be grouped together by similar national origin and culture.

3. **Choose** an ethnic group that is part of Texas. **Find out** more about the contributions this group has made to Texas. **Create** a short presentation to share what you learn with the rest of the class.

The American Flag

The flag of the United States of America is an important symbol of our country. A symbol is a thing that stands for or represents something else. We treat our flag with care and respect. There are rules and laws about how to display the flag. For example, the American flag should be flown near public buildings, such as schools, every day.

When facing the flag, you should show it respect. Stand at attention with your right hand over your heart. This rule in particular should be followed when reciting the Pledge of Allegiance. To show **allegiance** is to show loyalty.

4. **Read** the Pledge of Allegiance below and complete the activity that follows.

The Pledge of Allegiance
I pledge allegiance to the flag of the United States of America and to the Republic for which it stands, one Nation under God, indivisible, with liberty and justice for all.

5. **Analyze** the Pledge of Allegiance. Then rewrite the pledge in your own words. Use a dictionary to help you define any unknown words.

....

....

....

....

....

The Texas Flag

Each state also has its own flag. The flag of Texas is an important symbol of the state. The Texas flag also has its own Pledge of Allegiance. The pledge speaks to the state's values. It may be recited at all public and private meetings at which the Pledge of Allegiance to the United States flag is recited. It may also be recited at state historical events and celebrations.

Like the United States flag, the Texas flag has rules and laws about how it should be displayed and honored. For example, when reciting the Pledge of Allegiance to the Texas state flag, follow these rules:

- **Stand at attention.** Face the flag with your right hand over your heart.
- **Recite after the pledge to the United States flag.** If both the Pledge of Allegiance to the state flag and the Pledge of Allegiance to the United States flag are being recited at an event, the pledge to the United States flag should always be recited first.

6. **Recite** the pledge to the Texas flag below.

> **Pledge to the Texas Flag**
> Honor the Texas flag; I pledge allegiance to thee, Texas, one state under God, one and indivisible.

7. **Explain** one way the meaning of the pledge to the Texas flag is similar to the meaning of the pledge to the United States flag.

....

....

....

"Texas, Our Texas"

William J. Marsh of Fort Worth wrote the song "Texas, Our Texas" in 1924. He wrote the words with Gladys Yoakum Wright. Marsh won a state song contest, and Congress made "Texas, Our Texas" the official state song in 1929.

8. The following page shows the lyrics and music for the state song. **Sing** or **recite** "Texas, Our Texas" as a class. Then **compose** a new verse that could be added to the song to update it for today. For example, you may choose to write about a recent event in Texas history or about a favorite place in your state. Then **sing** or **recite** the state song, including your new verse, to a partner.

"Texas, Our Texas"

Words by Gladys Yoakum Wright and William J. Marsh

Music by William J. Marsh

1. Tex - as, our Tex - as! All hail the might - y state!
2. Tex - as, O Tex - as! your free - born sin - gle star
3. Tex - as, dear Tex - as! From ty - rant grip now free.

Tex - as, our Tex - as! So won - der - ful, so great!
Sends out its ra - diance to na - tions near and far.
Shines forth in splen - dor your star of des - ti - ny!

Bold - est and grand - est, With - stand - ing ev - 'ry test;
Em - blem of free - dom! It sets our hearts a - glow
Moth - er of he - roes! We come, your chil - dren true.

O Em - pire wide and glo - rious, You stand su - preme - ly blest.
With thoughts of San Ja - cin - to and glo - rious A - la - mo.
Pro - claim - ing our al - le - giance, Our faith, our love for you.

REFRAIN

God bless you, Tex - as! And keep you brave and strong,

That you may grow in pow'r and worth, Through-out the ag - es long.

God bless you, Tex - as! And keep you brave and strong,

That you may grow in pow'r and worth, Through-out the ag - es long.

Texas Landmarks

Texas has many famous landmarks. Some are **monuments,** or structures, built to show respect for a past event. Others are **missions,** or religious communities. Each landmark played an important role in Texas history. Today, visitors can tour many of these landmarks and experience history firsthand. Here are some well-known examples.

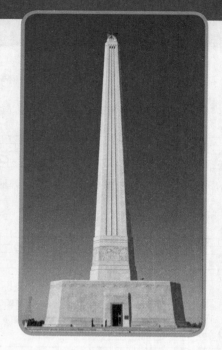

Washington-on-the-Brazos is known as the birthplace of Texas. It is at this location in Independence Hall, in 1836, that Texas's Declaration of Independence from Mexico was signed. It also was the site of the capitol of the early years of the Republic of Texas.

The San Jacinto Monument is located on the site where the Battle of San Jacinto was fought in 1836. This famous battle led to Texas's independence from Mexico. Standing 570 feet tall, the monument is the tallest war memorial in the world.

The Point Isabel Lighthouse is located in Port Isabel, one of the oldest towns in Texas. Built in 1852, it guided ships along the Texas coast during the Civil War and into the 1900s.

The Mission San Antonio de Valero was founded in 1718. It was the site of the famous Battle of the Alamo in 1836. At this battle, a small group of fighters for Texas independence held off a large group of Mexican troops. Ever since, the Alamo has been a symbol of heroism.

Vocabulary

monument
mission
presidio

Mission Espíritu Santo was founded in 1722. It was moved to its current location on the north bank of the San Antonio River near present-day Goliad in 1749. Across the river is the Presidio La Bahía. A **presidio** is a Spanish military fort. The chapel in Presidio La Bahía has been left almost unchanged since 1749.

The Mission of Corpus Christi de la Isleta (Ysleta) was among the first missions in Spanish Texas. It was founded in 1680 near present-day El Paso. Mission Ysleta is Texas's oldest continuously operated Christian church.

The Mission San José y San Miguel de Aguayo was founded in 1720. Known as the "Queen of the Missions," it is the largest of the San Antonio missions.

Founded in 1716, the Mission San Juan Capistrano was moved to San Antonio in 1731. This mission had a thriving community with orchards and gardens that provided food to other missions and settlements in the region.

9. Choose one of the landmarks discussed on these pages and **explain** more about it. **Research** when the landmark was founded, its meaning to the state, and at least two other interesting facts about it. Then **create** a fact card with this information.

State Symbols

Southwestern plants, animals, and other natural elements make Texas a special place. Many of these have become official symbols of the state. How many of these state symbols have you seen where you live?

State Small Mammal
Armadillos use their sharp sense of smell to find food.

State Tree
The pecan tree earned its title in 1919.

State Flower
Bluebonnet blossoms look like blue sunbonnets.

State Plant
The prickly pear cactus displays colorful flowers in spring and summer.

State Bird
Mockingbirds copy the calls of other songbirds.

State Gem
Blue topaz is a common gemstone found in central Texas.

State Large Mammal
In 1927, a herd of official state longhorns was formed to protect the breed.

10. Did you know that Texas also has many other state symbols, including a state vegetable, state shoe, and state insect? Choose a symbol not shown on this page and **create** a poster. Include a drawing of your symbol and at least four facts about it on your poster. Then **present** your poster to the class.

Good Citizenship

People show they are good citizens of Texas and the nation by the way they act. Read about the qualities of good citizenship. Then do the activity below.

Responsibility means being trustworthy. It means doing what you say you will do. When you are trustworthy, people can count on you.

Responsibility

Respect means being considerate of others' feelings and beliefs. It means not hurting others or their property.

Respect

Fairness means playing by the rules. It means taking turns and giving others their fair share.

Patriotism means love of country. It means working for the good of your country.

Courage means bravery. It takes courage to do what is right and stand up for what you believe.

Tolerance means accepting that others have different beliefs and opinions. It means respecting differences.

Fairness

Patriotism

11. Think about the qualities of good citizenship and the social studies words above that express this. Then choose one and write about why you think that quality is important and how you can show that quality in your life. Share what you have written with a classmate.

Courage

....

....

....

....

....

....

Tolerance

Texas Timeline

This timeline shows some of the events that have contributed to Texas's unique history. Review the events on the timeline.

1685–1690
The Kingdom of France

1685
La Salle brings French colonists to present-day Texas.

1519–1685
The Kingdom of Spain

1541
Coronado's Spanish expedition passes into present-day Texas in search of gold.

1690–1821
The Kingdom of Spain

800
Mound Builders (Caddo) farm in present-day Texas. *Texas* comes from the Caddo word for "friend."

800 **1600** **1700**

More than 12,000 years ago
The first people live on plains in present-day Texas.

1528
Spanish explorer Cabeza de Vaca reaches present-day Texas.

1680
Spaniards build the first mission, Corpus Christi de la Isleta, in present-day Texas.

1700s
Spaniards begin ranching in what is today Texas.

1821–1836
The Mexican Federal Republic

1836–1845
The Republic of Texas

March 1836
Texas declares independence and sets up a new government. Texas loses the Battle of the Alamo.

1852
The first locomotive comes to Texas.

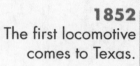

1824
Stephen F. Austin founds San Felipe de Austin.

April 1836
The Battle of San Jacinto

1820

1835

1850

1821
Stephen F. Austin brings 300 American colonists to settle what is today Texas.

1835
Texans battle Mexican troops at Gonzales and Goliad. Texas troops force Mexican army out of San Antonio.

1845
Texas becomes the 28th U.S. state.

September 1836
Sam Houston elected president of the new Republic of Texas.

1846–1848
United States and Mexico go to war.

1861–1865
The Confederate States of America

1901
Oil is discovered at Spindletop.

1911
Texas has more miles of railroad track than any other state.

1929
Stock market crashes and Great Depression begins.

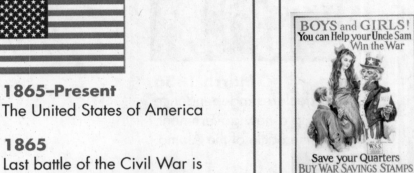

1865–Present
The United States of America

1865
Last battle of the Civil War is fought, and slaves are freed in Texas. Civil War ends.

1861
Texas secedes from the Union.

1914–1918
World War I

1860 | **1875** | **1900** | **1930**

1860
Abraham Lincoln elected president of the United States.

1870
Texas rejoins the United States.

1900
Farming becomes an important industry in Texas.

1925
Miriam A. Ferguson becomes first female governor of Texas.

1928
Texas becomes the leading oil-producing state.

1874
Joseph Glidden develops an improved barbed wire.

1969
Neil Armstrong walks on the moon. Mission Control at what is now called the Johnson Space Center in Houston directs this flight.

1973
Barbara Jordan becomes the first southern African American woman to serve in the U.S. Congress.

2008
Texan Dr. Michael E. DeBakey awarded the Congressional Gold Medal for his innovations in the field of heart surgery.

1941
United States enters World War II.

MS. JORDAN

1940　　　　**1960**　　　　**2000**　　　　**2020**

1945
World War II ends.

1963
Lyndon B. Johnson becomes president of the United States.

2000
George W. Bush elected president of the United States.

2013
George W. Bush Presidential Library opens near Dallas.

Our Land and Regions
Five Themes of Geography

Geography is the study of Earth. This study can be divided into five themes that help you understand why Earth has such a wide variety of places. Each theme reveals something different about a place, as the example of Big Bend National Park shows.

Where is Big Bend National Park located?
Big Bend National Park is located at about 29°N, 103°W.

Big Bend National Park

SANTIAGO MOUNTAINS

385

118

N
W E
S

Texas

Rio Grande

CHISOS MOUNTAINS

Big Bend National Park

Rio Grande

LEGEND
— U.S. highway
— Texas highway
— Other road
▢ Park area

0   10 mi
0   10 km

29°N

MEXICO

103°W

Place

How is this area different from others?
Big Bend has mountains, desert, and the largest river in Texas.

How people have changed a place is only part of the human/ environmental interaction. The other part is how people have adapted to the place.

How do people interact with the place?

People enjoy hiking the natural landscape of Big Bend, which is protected by its status as a national park.

Human/Environmental Interaction

Movement

How has movement changed the region?

Population growth and tourism have led to an increased use of the area.

Region

What is special about the region that includes Big Bend?

The park is in an area of Texas where the Rio Grande "bends" around dry lands.

Reading Globes

This is an image of Earth. It shows some of Earth's large landforms, called continents. It also shows Earth's large bodies of water, called oceans.

Atlantic Ocean

North America

Pacific Ocean

South America

1. **Interpret** the information on the globe. Then **identify** the two continents shown in this photo of Earth.

....

2. **Identify** the two oceans shown.

....

To the right is a **globe,** a small round model of Earth that you can hold in your hands. It shows the true shapes and locations of Earth's continents and oceans.

A globe often shows two lines that divide Earth. These two lines are called the prime meridian and the equator. You can see the equator on this globe.

NORTH ATLANTIC OCEAN

Earth's Hemispheres

The equator and the prime meridian divide Earth into halves called **hemispheres.** The **prime meridian** is a line drawn from the North Pole to the South Pole that passes through Europe and Africa. It extends only halfway around the globe. That line divides Earth into the Western Hemisphere and the Eastern Hemisphere as shown below.

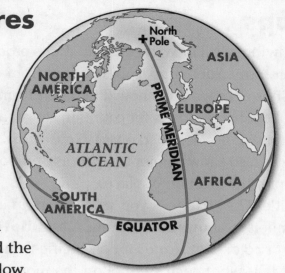

Vocabulary

globe
hemisphere
prime meridian
equator

The **equator** is a line drawn around Earth halfway between the North Pole and the South Pole. It divides Earth into the Northern and Southern Hemispheres.

Because Earth is divided two ways, it has four hemispheres.

Western Hemisphere	Eastern Hemisphere	Northern Hemisphere	Southern Hemisphere

3. **Interpret** the information on the globes. Then **identify** the two hemispheres in which North America is located.

....

....

4. **Identify** whether Asia is located north or south of the equator.

....

Political Maps

A map is a flat drawing of all or part of Earth. Maps organize information in a visual way. Each map shows a place from above.

There are many kinds of maps that show different information. A map that shows political boundaries for counties, states, or nations, as well as capital cities, is called a **political map.** This kind of map sometimes also shows major landforms and bodies of water to help interpret the location of places.

Each map has a title. The **title** tells you what the map is about. Maps use symbols to show information. A **symbol** is a small drawing, line, or color that stands for a specific thing. The map **legend,** or key, tells what each symbol on the map stands for. On this political map, a star stands for the state capital. Lines show the state boundaries, or borders. Color is used to show the area that is Texas. The surrounding states and the country of Mexico are a lighter color to show that they are not the subject of the map.

5. **Interpret** the information on the map. Use the legend to **identify** the symbol for the state capital of Texas. Then circle the city name on the map.

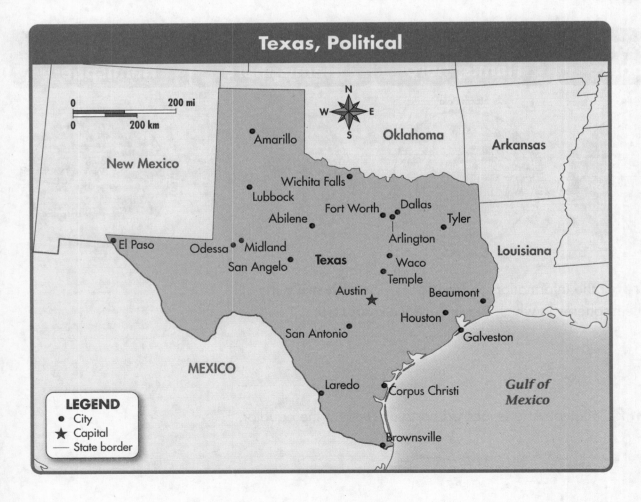

Texas, Political

LEGEND
- • City
- ★ Capital
- — State border

Physical Maps

A **physical map** shows landforms, such as mountains, plains, and deserts. It also shows bodies of water, such as oceans, lakes, and rivers. Physical maps often show borders between states and countries to help locate these landforms. A good place to look for political and physical maps is an atlas. An **atlas** is a collection or book of maps.

This physical map of Texas includes labels for many special landforms found in Texas. An escarpment is a long, steep slope or cliff. A plateau is a level area higher than the surrounding land. An island is land that is completely surrounded by water. Texas also has basins, or large bowl-shaped depressions.

6. **Interpret** the information on the map. Circle an escarpment on the map. Draw an X through a plateau on the map.

Vocabulary

political map
title
symbol
legend
physical map
atlas

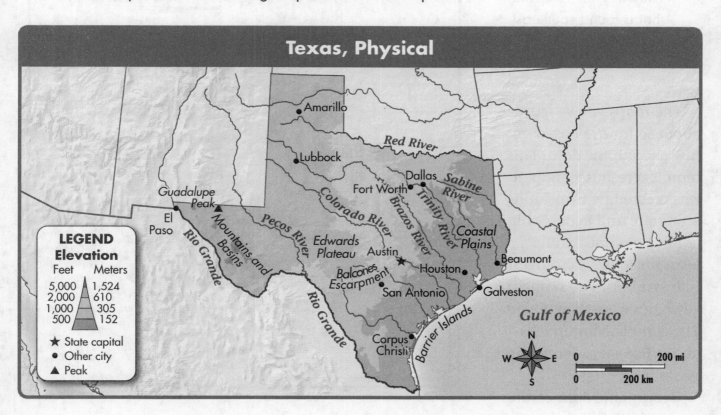

Maps Show Direction

Maps show directions. A **compass rose** is a symbol that shows directions on a map. There are four **cardinal directions:** north, south, east, and west. North points toward the North Pole and is marked with an *N*. South points to the South Pole and is marked with an *S*.

Look at the compass rose on the map. In addition to showing the cardinal directions, it shows directions that are midway between them. These are the **intermediate directions.** They are northeast, southeast, southwest, and northwest.

7. Use the legend and compass rose to **interpret** the map. **Identify** the resource that is found southeast of Houston.

....

The maps you've learned about so far are based on raw geographic data. This map is a resource map. It was created by translating economic and geographic data (the names and locations of key resources) into symbols. The names of key cities were then added. The completed map tells about Texas's economy and geography.

Geographic data can be translated in other formats, such as graphs. For example, temperature data can be translated into a bar graph.

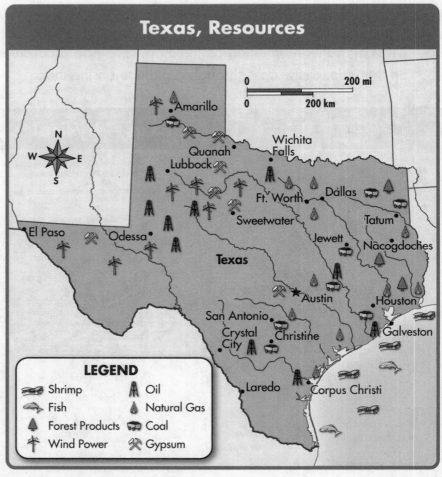

Texas, Resources

LEGEND
- Shrimp
- Fish
- Forest Products
- Wind Power
- Oil
- Natural Gas
- Coal
- Gypsum

8. Research and **analyze** the average yearly rainfall of a city in Texas. Then, on a separate sheet of paper, **translate** the data into a graph.

Maps Show Distance

A map is a very small drawing of a large place. However, you can use math skills to find real distances in miles or kilometers from one point to another on Earth by using a map scale. A map **scale** shows the relationship between distance on the map and distance on Earth. One way to use the scale is to hold the edge of a scrap of paper under the scale and copy it. Then place your copy of the scale on the map to measure the distance between two points.

The map below is a cultural map. You can use it to find distances between some of Texas's cultural attractions.

9. **Use** the scale and math skills to **interpret** and **identify** about how many miles Dinosaur Valley State Park near Fort Worth is from Big Bend National Park on the Mexican border.

....

10. **Identify** if King Ranch is more or less than 100 miles from the Alamo.

....

....

....

Vocabulary

compass rose
cardinal direction
intermediate
  direction
scale

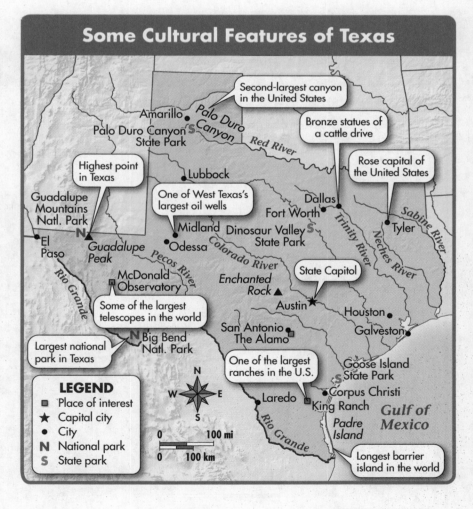

Some Cultural Features of Texas

Second-largest canyon in the United States

Bronze statues of a cattle drive

Rose capital of the United States

Highest point in Texas

One of West Texas's largest oil wells

Amarillo
Palo Duro Canyon State Park
Palo Duro Canyon
Red River
Lubbock
Dallas
Fort Worth
Tyler
Sabine River
Guadalupe Mountains Natl. Park
El Paso
Guadalupe Peak
Midland
Odessa
Dinosaur Valley State Park
Trinity River
Neches River
Pecos River
Colorado River
State Capitol
McDonald Observatory
Enchanted Rock
Austin
Houston
Some of the largest telescopes in the world
San Antonio
The Alamo
Galveston
Largest national park in Texas
Big Bend Natl. Park
One of the largest ranches in the U.S.
Goose Island State Park
Corpus Christi
Rio Grande
Laredo
King Ranch
Gulf of Mexico
Padre Island
Longest barrier island in the world

LEGEND
- ▪ Place of interest
- ★ Capital city
- • City
- N National park
- S State park

N
W — E
S

0   100 mi
0   100 km

21

Elevation Maps

An elevation map shows you how high the land is. **Elevation** is height above sea level. A place that is at sea level is at the same height as the surface of an ocean's water.

Elevation maps use color to show elevation. To read this kind of map, first look at the map legend. Note that there are numbers next to each color on the map legend. The numbers show the range of elevation that each color represents. On this Texas map, dark green represents the lowest elevation. The range for dark green is between 0 and 500 feet above sea level.

11. Use the legend to **interpret** information on the map. **Identify** the elevation range of the Edwards Plateau.

....

....

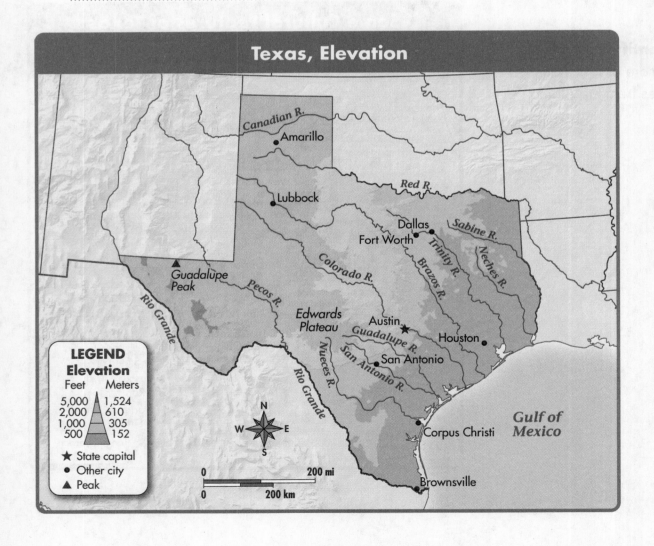

Texas, Elevation

LEGEND
Elevation
Feet   Meters
5,000   1,524
2,000   610
1,000   305
500   152
★ State capital
● Other city
▲ Peak

0   200 mi
0   200 km

Use a Grid System

Vocabulary

elevation

grid

A city map shows the streets of a city. It might also show points of interest and natural features. To help locate places more easily, this city map has a grid. A **grid** is a system of lines that cross each other, forming a pattern of squares. The lines are labeled with letters and numbers. These squares give every place on the map a location.

To find a specific location, the map has an index. An index is an alphabetical listing of places. The index gives the letter and number of the square in which the place is located.

12. Apply the geographic tool, grid system, to **interpret** information on the map. Then **organize** the information and add the number and letter set for the Alamo to the index.

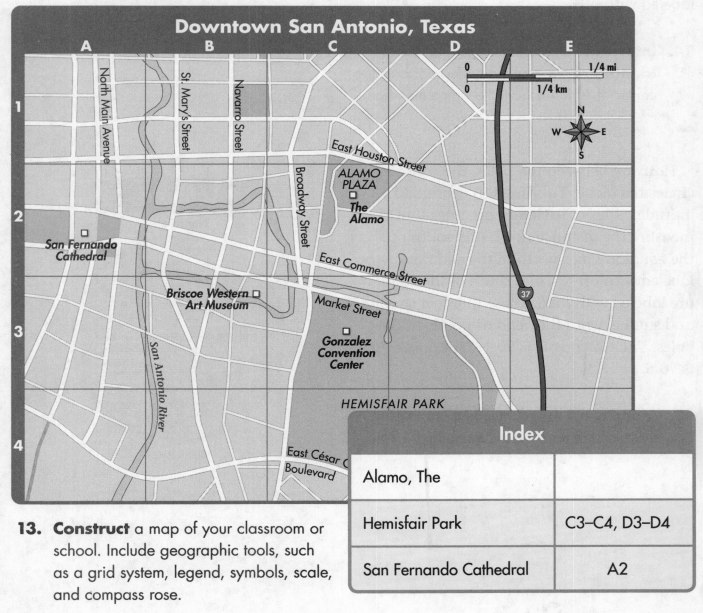

Downtown San Antonio, Texas

Index	
Alamo, The	
Hemisfair Park	C3–C4, D3–D4
San Fernando Cathedral	A2

13. Construct a map of your classroom or school. Include geographic tools, such as a grid system, legend, symbols, scale, and compass rose.

Use Latitude and Longitude for Exact Location

Long ago, mapmakers made a system for locating exact places on Earth. The system uses two sets of lines that form a grid around the globe. These lines are numbered in units of measure called **degrees.**

One set of lines extends from the North Pole to the South Pole. These are lines of longitude. Lines of **longitude** measure the distance east and west of the prime meridian. The prime meridian is labeled 0 degrees (0°) longitude. Lines of longitude are labeled from 0° to 180°. Lines east of the prime meridian are labeled with an *E*. Lines west of it are labeled with a *W*.

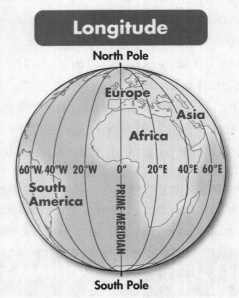

Longitude

14. Interpret the information on the globe. **Identify** about how many degrees east the center of Africa is from the prime meridian.

....

Halfway between the poles, the equator circles the globe. This line is 0 degrees (0°) latitude. Lines of **latitude** are lines that measure the distance north and south of the equator. Lines north of the equator are labeled with an *N*. Lines south of the equator are labeled with an *S*. These lines get smaller and smaller until they end as points at the poles. The North Pole is 90°N. The South Pole is 90°S.

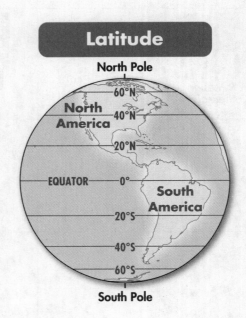

Latitude

15. Identify the line of latitude that is closest to the southern tip of South America.

....

....

....

Maps Show Events

Some maps are used to show historic events. You can use the legend on this map to locate important events that happened long ago.

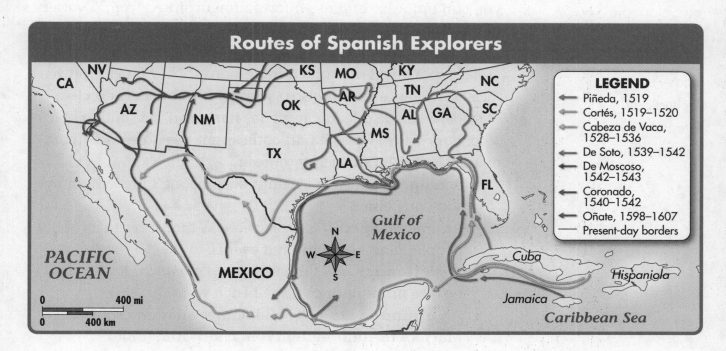

16. **Identify** and retrace the route of the explorer who traveled across present-day Texas in 1528.

Vocabulary

degree

longitude

latitude

Routes of Spanish Explorers

LEGEND
- Piñeda, 1519
- Cortés, 1519–1520
- Cabeza de Vaca, 1528–1536
- De Soto, 1539–1542
- De Moscoso, 1542–1543
- Coronado, 1540–1542
- Oñate, 1598–1607
- Present-day borders

Maps are used to show current events, too. You can use the compass rose and timetable on this map to track the path of Hurricane Ike through Texas.

17. **Identify** the direction that Hurricane Ike traveled though Texas.

....

....

....

....

Path of Hurricane Ike

1:00 P.M. Sunday

1:00 P.M. Saturday

1:00 P.M. Friday

4:00 P.M. Thursday

Gulf of Mexico

TEKS 15.A, 21.A, 21.C, 22.C, 22.D, 22.E

Vocabulary

secondary source
biography
encyclopedia
dictionary
almanac
atlas
technology
Internet
primary source

Research Skills: Our Amazing State

Types of Resources

When you do research for a written or oral report or a project, you can organize and use information acquired from a variety of valid sources. For example, you might locate valid sources in print, electronic technology, or within your community.

Reference books are valid print resources. They provide proven facts. A reference book is also a **secondary source**, or a piece of evidence made after an event has happened. The author of a secondary source was not part of the event. Here are a few more examples of valid secondary sources:

- A **biography** is an account of someone's life written by someone else.
- An **encyclopedia** is a set of books that gives facts about people, places, things, and events.
- A **dictionary** gives the meanings of words. It also shows how to pronounce and spell each word.
- An **almanac** has facts and figures on many subjects. Much of the information is in charts and tables.
- An **atlas** is a collection or book of maps.

Today, many reference resources also have electronic technology components. **Technology** is the use of scientific knowledge, skills, and tools to help people meet their needs. For example, an encyclopedia might offer sound and video clips on computer software or the Internet. The **Internet** is a global network connecting billions of computers around the world. The collection of sites on the Internet is called the World Wide Web. Individual sites are called Web sites. Some sites contain factual information organized in databases. It is a good idea to check that the information in any Web site is valid. One way to do this is to find at least two other sources with similar information.

In addition to reference resources, you can interview people in your community to acquire information about the United States and Texas. For example, a person who works at a history museum can provide you with primary source information. A **primary source** is a piece of evidence created by someone at the time of an event. Primary sources might be print resources such as letters, diaries, or government records. They can be visual resources, such as photographs, artifacts, or art. They also can be oral resources, such as songs and speeches. You can hear oral resources by using electronic resources, such as television and radio recordings.

The Texas Constitution is one of the most important documents of our state and is a primary source in print. The Texas Constitution gives a plan for the state's government. Because the state has been ruled by many different nations, the Constitution has been revised many times. Today, the Texas Constitution reflects the state's history and outlines the basic rights of Texas citizens. You can find an electronic version of the Texas Constitution on Texas's government Web site.

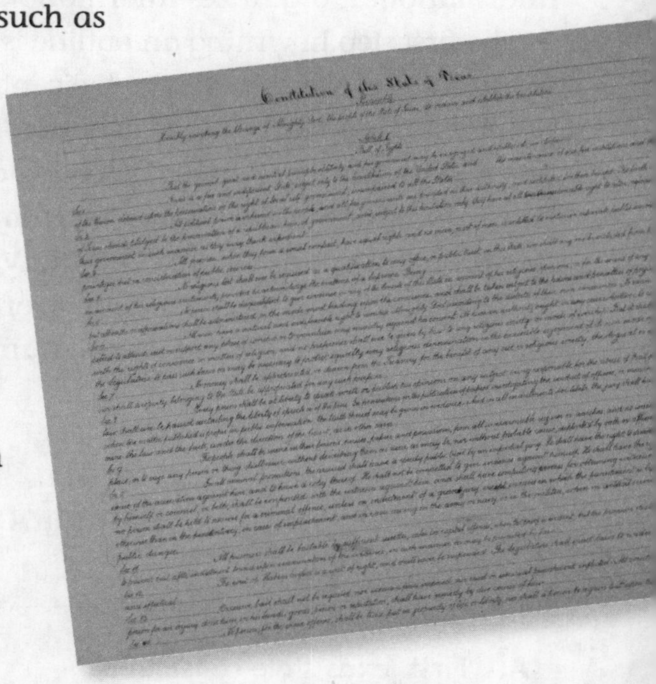

The Texas Constitution is a primary source.

1. Prepare a written or oral research report about Texas on a topic of your choice. **Locate, interpret,** and **use** one technology source, such as a database, one print, and one community resource. Keep a record of your resources in the second column of the chart below. Then **differentiate** and label in the third column whether or not that source is a valid primary or secondary source.

Resource	Example	Primary or Secondary
Technology		
Print		
Community		

Write an Outline

Good writers organize their ideas. Writing an outline is a good way to do this. An **outline** is a written plan to interpret information. It organizes information and ideas about a topic.

The first step in writing an outline is to identify the topic in the title of the outline. Next, divide the topic into main ideas, or subtopics. Use Roman numerals to list each subtopic. **Roman numerals** were first used in ancient Rome. They use a combination of letters from the Latin alphabet to show values. The numbers 1 to 10 can be shown in Roman numerals as follows: I, II, III, IV, V, VI, VII, VIII, IX, X.

Under each subtopic, list details, or supporting ideas, that tell more about it. Use capital letters, numbers, and lowercase letters to list these details.

Constitution of 1845

I. Basic Facts

A. **First Texas state constitution**
    1. Required for admission to the United States

B. **Based on common constitutional principles in the United States**
    1. Popular sovereignty
        a. Power comes from the people
    2. Individual rights
    3. Republican form of government
    4. Separation of powers

2. **Interpret** the information. **Identify** and underline the topic of the outline above. Then **identify** and circle the subtopic. Finally, **identify** the Roman numeral you would use if you wanted to add another subtopic: .... Now **organize** and **interpret** an outline for a topic about Texas on a separate sheet of paper. Include at least two subtopics and supporting details for each subtopic.

Write a Research Report

Vocabulary

outline
Roman numeral
research report

A **research report** is an in-depth essay based on detailed information on a topic. Reports help you interpret information. Choosing a topic is the first step in writing a research report. Suppose your assignment is to write a 500-word research report about the Texas Constitution. You need to narrow down the topic to something more specific.

3. **Identify** a specific topic about the Texas Constitution.

....

Once you have a topic, write down questions about the topic. Then use different sources to answer your questions and take notes about your topic. It is important to organize and list your sources. Keep a list of the book title, author, and the page numbers as well as Internet addresses of every source. Be sure to reword any information in your own words. If you use information exactly as it appears in a source, put quotation marks around the text.

Write a first draft of your report. Use your notes to organize your information into paragraphs. Then reread your work. Does it make sense? Do you need to add more information? Be sure to check your report for any errors in grammar, spelling, sentence structure, and punctuation. Make all corrections before neatly writing or typing a final copy of your report.

4. On another sheet of paper, **organize** and write a first draft of a research report about a specific topic related to Texas or the United States. Be sure to incorporate the main idea and supporting ideas, and to organize the information so it can be interpreted. Use standard grammar, spelling, sentence structure, and punctuation in your report. Also, include visual materials you created to add interest to your report.

Create a Bibliography

Giving proper credit is a key to good research. A carefully written bibliography is an essential part of that research. A **bibliography** is a written list of sources used in preparing a research report.

Most bibliographies sequence all sources in alphabetical order according to the author's last name. If no author is listed, the first letter in the title of the source is used. Read the list of sources for a research paper on the Texas Constitution below. Which source would be listed first in a bibliography? The last name of the author of the newspaper article begins with the letter *B*, so this source would be first.

Some bibliographies list sources in groups of different types of sources. First, all of the books are listed in alphabetical order. Next, all of the magazine articles are arranged in alphabetical order, and so on.

5. **Identify, analyze,** and **sequence** the sources in the order that they would appear in a bibliography.

Book	May, Janice C. *The Texas State Constitution.* pp. 5–45. Oxford University Press, 2011.
Magazine article	Sager, Ryan. "10 Reasons Texas is America's Future." *Time Magazine.* http://ideas.time.com/2013/10/17/10-reasons-texas-is-our-future/. October 17, 2013.
Newspaper article	Blumenthal, Ralph. "Hue and Cry Replaces Yawns in Vote on Texas Constitution." *New York Times.* September 15, 2003.
Web site	Texas Politics: The Constitution. http://texaspolitics.laits.utexas.edu/7_1_0.html

Publish Your Report

Vocabulary

bibliography
visual materials

You have now spent time planning, gathering information for, writing, and revising your research report. What is the next step? It is to publish and present your report to an audience.

When presenting your report, keep these tips in mind:

- Always keep your audience in mind. Think about the clearest way to express your information. For example, if your report is about geography, use the correct social studies words to express your ideas.
- Speak clearly and use eye contact. Try not to look at your notes often.
- Show enthusiasm about your topic. If you are bored, your audience will be, too!

Visual materials can add interest to written reports and oral presentations. **Visual materials** include pictures, maps, charts, and graphic organizers. These help you organize and interpret information. There are many audio and visual resources on the Internet. You may be able to download photographs, charts, or parts of videos or movies. Keep track of the sources for all media you download and use in your presentation. Then you can include the media sources in the bibliography.

6. **Plan** an oral presentation for your topic about Texas or the United States. Before you begin, **identify** at least three examples of visual materials you plan to use in your presentation. Make sure to incorporate the main idea and supporting ideas of your report in your oral presentation.

The Geography of Texas

my Story Spark

How does geography affect our lives?

Analyze your surroundings. **Identify** how your surroundings influence what you do every day. **Describe** how they affect you and the way you live.

....

....

....

....

....

Texas Essential Knowledge and Skills

6.A Apply geographic tools, including grid systems, legends, symbols, scales, and compass roses, to construct and interpret maps.

6.B Translate geographic data, population distribution, and natural resources into a variety of formats.

7.B Identify, locate, and compare the geographic regions of Texas (Mountains and Basins, Great Plains, North Central Plains, Coastal Plains), including their landforms, climate, and vegetation.

8.B Describe and explain the location and distribution of various towns and cities in Texas, past and present.

8.C Explain the geographic factors such as landforms and climate that influence patterns of settlement and the distribution of population in Texas, past and present.

9.A Describe ways people have adapted to and modified their environment in Texas, past and present, such as timber clearing, agricultural production, wetlands drainage, energy production, and construction of dams.

9.B Identify reasons why people have adapted to and modified their environment in Texas, past and present, such as the use of natural resources to meet basic needs, facilitate transportation, and enhance recreational activities.

9.C Compare the positive and negative consequences of human modification of the environment in Texas, past and present, both governmental and private, such as economic development and the impact on habitats and wildlife as well as air and water quality.

12.B Explain how geographic factors such as climate, transportation, and natural resources have influenced the location of economic activities in Texas.

12.C Analyze the effects of exploration, immigration, migration, and limited resources on the economic development and growth of Texas.

13.B Identify oil and gas, agricultural, and technological products of Texas that are purchased to meet needs in the United States and around the world.

13.C Explain how Texans meet some of their needs through the purchase of products from the United States and the rest of the world.

21.B Analyze information by sequencing, categorizing, identifying cause-and-effect relationships, comparing, contrasting, finding the main idea, summarizing, making generalizations and predictions, and drawing inferences and conclusions.

21.C Organize and interpret information in outlines, reports, databases, and visuals, including graphs, charts, timelines, and maps.

22.B Incorporate main and supporting ideas in verbal and written communication.

Big Bend National Park

A Natural Treasure

my Story Video

"I've always said *everything's big in Texas,* but wow, you can really tell in this park!" exclaims Connor as he enters Big Bend National Park for the first time. This national park, in the Mountains and Basins region of Texas, has some very impressive geography.

"It would take as long to drive across Texas as it would to drive across several states in the Northeast," says David, Connor's travel guide at Big Bend today. "And we're not only big, we're diverse, too!" From the mountains and canyons to the flat plains and beaches, Texas has many different landforms and climates. Because of this and the history and culture found here, Texas is a popular place to visit. "At Big Bend we receive about 350,000 visitors every year," David declares proudly. Tourism is big business in Texas, and Connor can easily see why.

Many tourists enjoy exploring Big Bend. The Rio Grande flows about 110 miles on the park's southern boundary.

The Chisos Mountains are in the center of Big Bend National Park.

Many of the over 1,000 species of plants in Big Bend are cacti covered in spines or barbs.

Turtles live along the bank of the Rio Grande.

"Here at Big Bend National Park," explains David, "you'll see a variety of wildlife, flowers, and plants. Many of these species are endangered. This means that there are very few left of their kind. Because they are endangered, they are protected by both the government of the United States and the government of Texas. "If you look closely, you might just see some turtles along the bank of the Rio Grande!" says David. Some of the plants you find at Big Bend can't be found anywhere else in Texas. The giant yucca dagger is one sight you might see only in Texas and New Mexico.

Texas is the second-largest state in the United States and is bordered by four other states. It's probably the easiest state to spot on a map. "People from all over take Texas-shaped souvenirs home with them," says David. "Texas's shape is recognized all over the country."

Big Bend covers more than 800,000 acres of land and is famous for its natural resources and spectacular geology. Geology is the science that studies the composition and history of Earth. The various elevations you find throughout our park create microclimates that give us diversity, or variety, with plant and animal life, too" explains David.

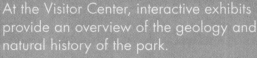

At the Visitor Center, interactive exhibits provide an overview of the geology and natural history of the park.

The roadrunner is one of the 450 species of birds that call Big Bend home.

"I'm surprised there aren't more people living in this area," Connor notes. "Is it tough to live here?" he asks. "Well," David answers, "while this land is beautiful and holds a lot of history, it's not easy to live here. This region is dry and rocky, and mountains separate towns." The nearest town is more than 20 miles from park headquarters, and its population is pretty small. Early settlers relied on the Rio Grande for water and transportation, and they built homes nearby. You can still find remnants, or remains, of their homes around the park today. But, as with many old civilizations, these settlers probably found they had to move on and settle in cities and towns that would be easier to live in. While this tucked-away land is a wonderful place for scientists to explore, learn, and discover, its geography isn't the best for settlements.

"I'm glad the area remains like it did hundreds of years ago," exclaims Connor. "There's a lot to learn about all kinds of geography right here at Big Bend!"

Think About It How do you think it might have been to live in a place such as Big Bend? As you read the chapter ahead, think about how geography affects people's lives. Then think about how people affect the world they live in.

Much of Big Bend's beauty was created by volcanic activity, earthquakes, and erosion over millions of years.

SAVVAS realize™ Go online to access your interactive digital lesson.

35

Locating Texas

Envision It!

From space, planet Earth looks like a giant blue sphere.

To walk around the border of Texas would take you at least one thousand hours of nonstop movement. But the journey would be exciting because Texas is not only big—it is varied, too. That means it is not all plains or hills, mountains or deserts. Texas has all those landforms and more. Today you begin your journey learning about the geography of Texas. Geography is the study of Earth, including its physical features and the ways humans use them. An important part of Texas's geography is its location.

Where Is Texas?

Every place on planet Earth has a global address that describes its location. The address begins by locating Earth's hemispheres. The word *hemisphere* describes half of Earth's land and water. You find the Eastern and Western Hemispheres by dividing Earth from the North Pole to the South Pole along the prime meridian. Texas is located in the Western Hemisphere. You can find the Northern and Southern Hemispheres by dividing Earth at the equator. Texas is located in the Western and Northern Hemispheres. Next you identify the continent. A continent is one of Earth's seven great bodies of land. Texas is located on the continent of North America. The country follows, and as you know—that is the United States.

A **region** is an area with common features, people, and ways of living that set it apart from other areas.

The Rio Grande in Santa Elena Canyon in Big Bend National Park is one of the many places to explore in Texas.

Look for the United States in the view of Earth from space.
Draw your own map of the United States.

Vocabulary

region   escarpment

groundwater   plateau

spring   basin

barrier island

To locate Texas within the United States, geographers divide the country into regions. There are many types of regions. They can be based on any shared feature, from crops grown or language spoken to music played! The map below shows the United States divided into five geographic regions.

TEKS
6.A, 6.B, 7.B, 8.B, 8.C, 12.B, 13.C

1. **Interpret** the map. In which geographic region is Texas located? Circle the region's name on the map legend.

Regions of the United States

LEGEND
- Northeast region
- Midwest region
- Southeast region
- Southwest region
- West region

The Port of Houston is the largest port in Texas.

Texas in North America

North America is the third largest continent on Earth. It stretches from the Arctic Ocean in the north all the way south to South America. The vast continent has 37,000 miles of coastline dotted with inlets and bays. These geographic factors give the continent many good ports for ships that can cross the Pacific Ocean to Asia or the Atlantic Ocean to Europe and Africa. Ships can also sail both those oceans south to South America. Ships from port cities in Texas sail these oceans to trade with people on every continent in the world.

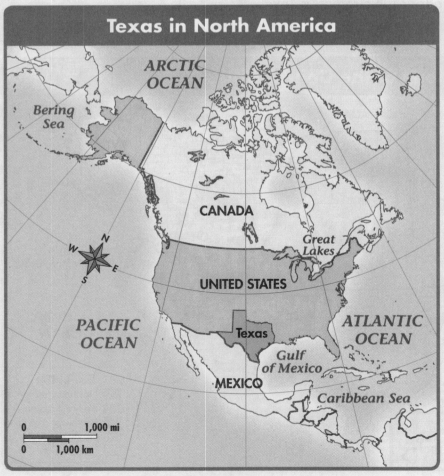

Texas in North America

ARCTIC OCEAN

Bering Sea

CANADA

Great Lakes

UNITED STATES

PACIFIC OCEAN

Texas

ATLANTIC OCEAN

Gulf of Mexico

MEXICO

Caribbean Sea

0   1,000 mi
0   1,000 km

2. Look at the map to **identify** the places and write in the blanks below. The ocean that borders North America to the east is the

....

The ocean that borders North America to the west is the

....

The country that borders the United States to the north is

....

The country that borders the United States to the south is

....

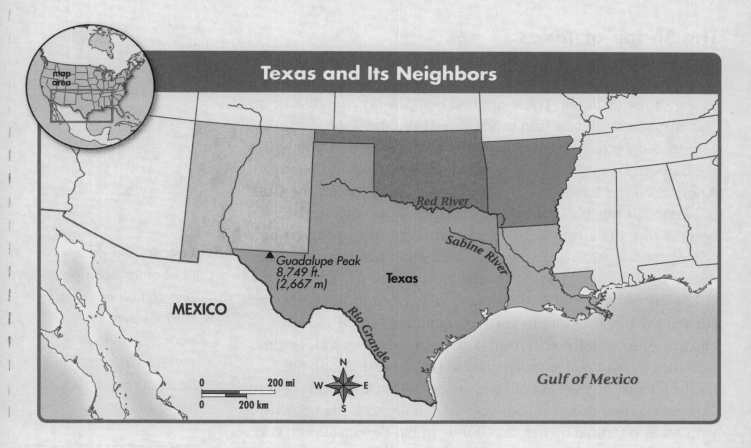

Texas and Its Neighbors

map area

Guadalupe Peak
8,749 ft.
(2,667 m)

MEXICO

Texas

Red River

Sabine River

Rio Grande

Gulf of Mexico

0   200 mi
0   200 km

N W E S

Texas also trades with its neighbors in North America. Texas has five neighbors. Four of them are U.S. states and the fifth neighbor is a country. To the west, Texas is bordered by the state of New Mexico. The land in this border region is dry and rocky with mountains such as Guadalupe Peak. This mountain is the highest peak in Texas.

To the north of Texas is the state of Oklahoma. Part of this border is formed by the Red River. The northeast corner of Texas is bordered by the state of Arkansas. And to the east, Texas is bordered by the state of Louisiana. The Sabine River forms part of this border. To the south, across the Rio Grande, is the country of Mexico.

3. On the map, **locate** and label the four states that border Texas.

4. **Explain** how the geography of Texas has influenced the location of economic activities in the state.

....

....

....

The Shape of Texas

Texas is not only big and diverse but also it has a unique shape that people recognize. Think about all the objects made in the shape of Texas. There are belt buckles, serving dishes, and charms; you can even find macaroni in the shape of Texas.

How did Texas get its shape? Look at the map and you will see borders formed by rivers. These borders curve and bend. Another border formed by water is the coastline along the Gulf of Mexico. It has bays, inlets, and islands. Now look at the borders that are straight lines. Sometimes people use rivers or other physical features as borders, and other times they decide that a straight line is a good border.

Use the pictures and map below to take a tour of Texas's borders. Start at the highest point in Texas, Guadalupe Peak. Follow the border of Texas, going east until you reach Lake Texoma. Texoma is named for its location in **Tex**as and **O**klaho**ma**. Along the border formed by the Gulf of Mexico, see the big shipping port of Galveston. Then relax on Padre Island. Finally, visit the border with Mexico formed by the Rio Grande in Big Bend National Park.

5. **Locate** and draw a symbol for each place pictured on this page. Add the symbols to your map in their correct locations. Then add your symbols to the map legend.

LEGEND

Guadalupe Peak

Big Bend National Park

Padre Island

Touring Texas Borders

Lake Meredith
Amarillo
Red R.
Lake Texoma
Pecos R.
Lubbock
Dallas
Ft. Worth
Tyler
Sabine R.
Midland
Colorado R.
Trinity R.
Toledo Bend Reservoir
El Paso
Guadalupe Peak
Odessa
Texas
Brazos R.
Rio Grande
Big Bend Natl. Park
Austin
San Antonio
Houston
Galveston
Amistad Reservoir
Nueces R.
MEXICO
Crystal City
Laredo
Corpus Christi
Gulf of Mexico
Padre Island
Falcon Reservoir

0   200 mi
0   200 km

Lake Texoma

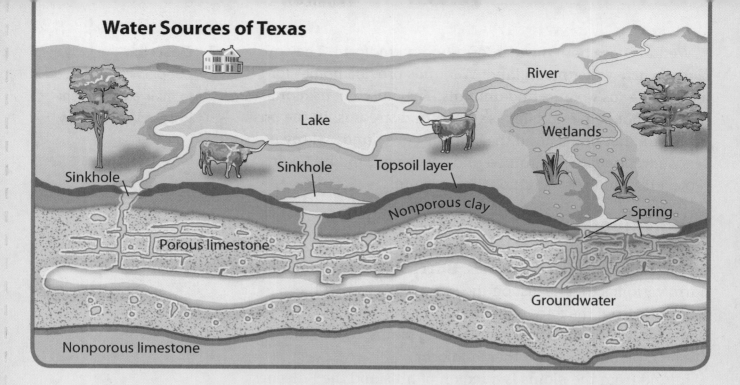

Water Sources of Texas

Labels in the diagram:
- River
- Lake
- Wetlands
- Sinkhole
- Sinkhole
- Topsoil layer
- Nonporous clay
- Spring
- Porous limestone
- Groundwater
- Nonporous limestone

Water

In Texas, water comes from different sources. There is groundwater and surface water. **Groundwater** is located below the surface, out of sight. The water you see, such as lakes and rivers, is called surface water.

Wherever water comes from, people need it for farming, ranching, and industry. We even use it for transportation. Boats can move people and goods easily on water. That is one reason early Texans chose to live by waterways. They especially looked for river valleys. Early Texans knew that floods made river valleys fertile, and that is good for growing crops. Many rivers flow across Texas from the higher lands in the west to the Mississippi River or the Gulf of Mexico.

Springs are another source of surface water. A **spring** is a place where groundwater comes to the surface. Many Texans use water from springs.

There are places in Texas that are dry, such as West Texas. Where do farmers in these areas get the water their crops need? Underground! Large amounts of water are held in the spaces in between the underground rock formations. One of the largest, the Ogallala Aquifer, begins under the surface of West Texas and stretches north to South Dakota. All across Texas, water from aquifers is pumped up and used by agriculture, industry, and homes like yours. Pumping groundwater to the surface changes the land, making it more useful.

6. Identify the details and underline the different sources of water in Texas described on this page.

Wetlands are both a water form and a landform. They are places where water meets land. Wetlands provide homes for many of Texas's plants and animals. They also act as giant sponges that help clean Texas's rivers and streams. In the past, people did not understand the benefits of wetlands. Many of Texas's wetlands were drained and developed. Today, Texans protect the valuable wetlands that remain.

Landforms

As you have read, Texas has a variety of landforms. Along the Gulf Coast are barrier islands. **Barrier islands** are long, narrow islands that lie just off the coast. They protect the mainland from the force of ocean waves. Move inland and you find a large area of flat or gently rolling plains. More Texans live on a plain than any other landform.

Inland from the plains is a region of hills and the Balcones Escarpment. An **escarpment** is a long steep slope or cliff. The Balcones Escarpment cuts across Texas from north to south. Farther inland is the Edwards Plateau, another large landform. A **plateau** is a level area higher than the surrounding land. The Edwards Plateau was formed when the area was covered by ocean millions of years ago.

7. **Describe** the ways people have adapted to their environment in Texas.

....

....

....

....

....

....

....

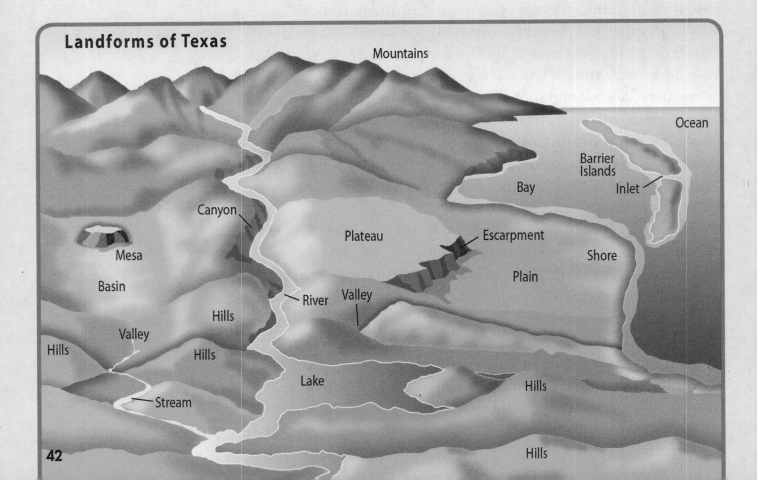

Landforms of Texas

Mountains

Ocean

Barrier Islands

Bay

Inlet

Canyon

Plateau

Escarpment

Mesa

Shore

Basin

Plain

River

Valley

Hills

Valley

Hills

Hills

Lake

Hills

Stream

Hills

42

The North Central Plains of Texas extends from the Red River to the Colorado River. It's dotted with many hills and mesas, or flat-topped hills. Parts of the North Central Plains have a large cattle-raising industry, with many of the ranches in the state located here.

The highest land is in West Texas where the mountains are. The highest mountain in Texas is Guadalupe Peak. It reaches 8,749 feet (2,667 m) above sea level. Guadalupe Peak is part of the Guadalupe Mountains National Park. Texas also has **basins**, large bowl-shaped depressions.

8. **Compare** the landforms on the map. On the legend, circle the type of landform that covers most of Texas.

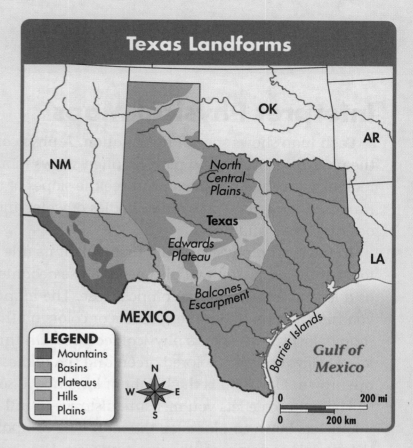

Texas Landforms

LEGEND
- Mountains
- Basins
- Plateaus
- Hills
- Plains

OK
AR
NM
North Central Plains
Texas
Edwards Plateau
LA
Balcones Escarpment
MEXICO
Barrier Islands
Gulf of Mexico

0 200 mi
0 200 km

N W E S

Got it?

TEKS 6.A, 6.B, 7.B, 8.C

9. **Main Idea and Details** **Using evidence** from the lesson, write details that support the following main idea: Texas has a variety of landforms.

....

....

10. Suppose you were among the first people who came to settle Texas. **Describe** the landforms and bodies of water you would want near your new home.

my Story Ideas

....

....

11. Think of three places you would like to visit. **Apply** geographic tools, and on a separate sheet of paper, construct a map and **locate** the three places. First copy the map of Texas on page 40. Be sure to construct your map the same size so you can copy the distance scale. Add the locations you would like to visit using symbols. Add a compass rose, a title, and a map legend.

Interpret Physical Maps

Each map shows special information. A physical map shows the physical features of a place. It often shows mountainous regions with shadows so you can see the slopes of the mountain ranges. It may also show major bodies of water, including oceans, lakes, and rivers.

To interpret a physical map, first look at its title to learn the topic of the map. You will also need to use geographic tools such as a legend, map scale, or compass rose. The map legend gives you information about the symbols or colors on the map. The map below shows Texas's physical features. On this map, the lowest elevations are colored green and the highest elevations are brown. Elevation is the height of land above sea level.

The map scale lets you measure distance in miles or kilometers between places on the map. The compass rose shows the directions north, south, east, and west. Use the information you gain from looking at the map to interpret the map.

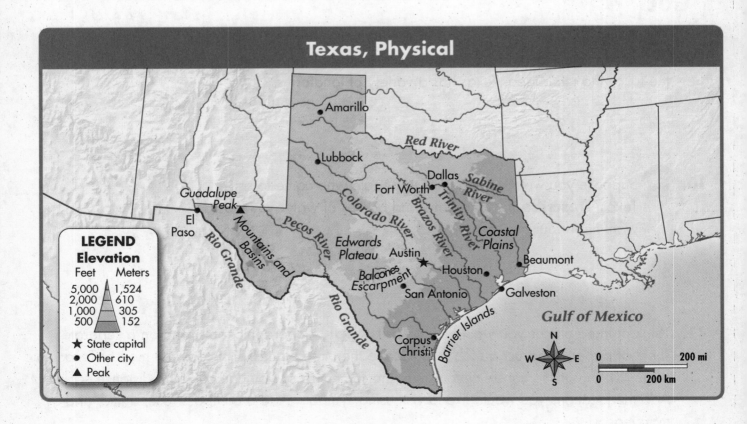

Texas, Physical

LEGEND
Elevation

Feet	Meters
5,000	1,524
2,000	610
1,000	305
500	152

★ State capital
● Other city
▲ Peak

TEKS

ELA 13.B Explain factual information presented graphically.

SS 6.A Apply geographic tools, including grid systems, legends, symbols, scales, and compass roses, to construct and interpret maps.

SS 6.B Translate geographic data, population distribution, and natural resources into a variety of formats.

SS 21.C Organize and interpret information in visuals, including maps.

Suppose you are taking a trip from Beaumont to El Paso. **Identify** these cities on the map. Then answer the following questions about your trip **applying** geographic tools such as the legend, map scale, and compass rose.

1. **Identify** and list the landforms you see along the way.

   ....

   ....

2. **Apply** the geographic tool, map scale, to **interpret** the map and write the number of miles you travel.

3. **Apply** the geographic tool, compass rose, to **interpret** the map and write in which direction you go.

4. **Locate** and list the major rivers you cross.

   ....

   ....

5. **Identify** the geographic tools you used to **interpret** the map.

   ....

6. **Apply** Now take a trip from Austin to some other city in Texas. **Decide** on any place you like. Keep a record of this trip, too. Name the major landforms you cross. Also list the directions you travel and the distance you cover.

   ....

   ....

   ....

   ....

SAVVAS realize Go online to access your interactive digital lesson.

45

Texas Resources

LEGEND

 Cattle
 Corn
 Fish
 Fruit

Goats
 Natural gas
 Pecans
Petroleum

Sheep
Shrimp
Water

Texas resources are from three places: underground, above ground, and in the water.

Shrimp are an important natural resource in Texas. These fishers want to protect the environment where shrimp live.

Look around you. Much of what you see began as a natural resource. Much of what you see around you is either a resource or something made from resources.

Natural Resources

A **natural resource** is anything found in nature that is useful to people. Water, minerals, soil, and most plants and animals are all natural resources. Any material from the environment that helps people meet their needs is a natural resource. So, a place with many natural resources is a good place to live.

Texas has many natural resources, which brought people to the state. For example, many people moved to Texas to use the soil and water to grow crops. They modified the environment by clearing land or draining wetlands to make farms. They dammed rivers to store water for their crops. People also modified the environment to facilitate transportation. They built railroads and roads on the land to help farmers get their goods to market. Texas resources are shipped to other states and around the world. People used natural resources and modified the environment. They helped develop Texas.

Sometimes, however, development damages the environment or uses up valuable resources. Today Texans look for ways to protect their environment and resources. As you read, think about ways you can help.

1. In the paragraphs above, **identify** and circle the resources people used and underline ways that **describe** how people modified the environment.

Look at Texas's natural resource symbols. Draw symbols for and label three resources found underground.

UNLOCK THE BIG ?

I will know how Texas's natural resources affect how we live.

Vocabulary

natural resource

renewable resource

nonrenewable resource

reservoir

drought

conserve

pollution

Renewable Resources

Fishers gather tons of shrimp from the Gulf of Mexico every year. As long as they don't take too many, the shrimp reproduce, making more shrimp. Shrimp and trees are **renewable resources** because their numbers can be restored naturally over time.

Americans use a lot of wood. We use it to make paper, furniture, homes, and even clothing! That means we need to cut a lot of trees down. But when we cut down too many trees, the forest floor is changed. There is no more shade from the sun so the soil gets dry. Plants that grew on the forest floor die. Then when the rains come, there are no plant roots to hold the soil in place, so it washes away. Local streams and rivers fill with mud. As you can see, cutting down too many trees not only uses up a resource but changes the environment.

However, people in the lumber industry have found a solution. Now when they cut trees, they plant new ones! By renewing the resource, we protect the environment.

TEKS
6.B, 9.A, 9.B, 9.C, 12.C

2. **Cause and Effect** In the text, **identify** and underline some effects of cutting down trees.

The lumber industry is important to the economy of Texas.

Nonrenewable Resources

Many of Texas's natural resources, such as oil, natural gas, and coal, are fossil fuels. They are valuable energy sources used by everything from power plants to lawn mowers. Fossil fuels are limited, or nonrenewable resources. **Nonrenewable resources** are available in limited supply and cannot be replaced or renewed. If Texans do not protect these resources, it may harm the state's economic development. Texans are already looking for renewable energy sources such as solar power or wind energy.

For now, however, Texas still has a good supply of fossil fuels. Texas has other nonrenewable resources too, such as gypsum. This mineral has many uses, from construction materials to fertilizers and even shampoo. The map shows where some of Texas's natural resources are located.

3. **Apply** geographic tools. **Translate** what you know about natural resources in Texas into symbols on the map.

- Draw symbols for oil on the map. **Locate** three near Odessa. Add the fourth oil symbol west of Houston.

- Draw symbols for natural gas on the map. **Locate** one north of Amarillo, one north of Nacogdoches, and one east of Wichita Falls.

- **Analyze** where you might find shrimp and draw those symbols on the map.

- Draw symbols for gypsum on the map. **Locate** them at Quanah, Sweetwater, and west of Austin.

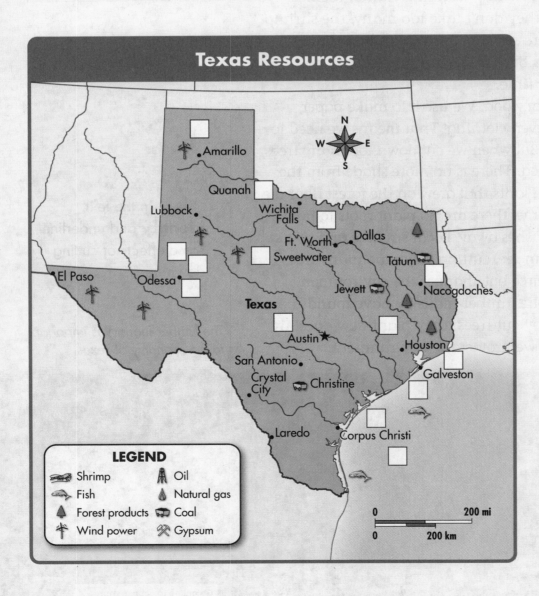

Texas Resources

LEGEND

🦐 Shrimp   🛢 Oil

🐟 Fish   ⛽ Natural gas

🌲 Forest products   🚃 Coal

🌀 Wind power   ⛏ Gypsum

0   200 mi

0   200 km

Amistad National Recreation Area Dam on the Rio Grande in Del Rio, Texas

Water

People cannot live without water. We need lots of water for drinking, cooking, washing, growing food, raising animals, and more. We use it for fun things such as swimming and boating, too! So Texans both need and enjoy their water.

Government has modified the environment so that all Texans have the water they need. One example is reservoirs from which we get much of our water. A **reservoir** is a natural or artificial lake used to reserve, or store, water. Texans have built about 200 large reservoirs and thousands of small ones.

Another example is damming rivers. It is a great way to store water. Dams also control the flow of water, preventing floods. This protects homes and businesses. They make lakes for swimming, boating, and fishing. Some dams, called hydroelectric dams, generate power. However, dams have negative consequences for the environment. Dams flood the habitats where wildlife live.

Texas needs many reservoirs because people are using the underground water faster than rainfall can replace it. Water shortages are increased by droughts. A **drought** is a period of time with little rain. During droughts, the water level of aquifers and lakes lowers. Sometimes local governments ask people to **conserve,** or limit, their water use.

Businesses also modify the environment. This helps create jobs. But it also creates pollution. In communities where pollution has affected the air and water quality, people are working to clean it up. **Pollution** is chemicals and other harmful substances that can damage the water, air, or land. Reservoirs can become polluted over time. This harms the people and animals that use the water.

4. **Compare and contrast** the positive and negative consequences of modification of the environment by government and businesses in Texas. Underline the positive effects. Circle the negative effects.

Using Resources Wisely

Once, the place that is now Texas had pure air and water. When people moved here, they made changes. Some of these changes were good. Dams and fossil fuels brought power. Fishing and agriculture provided food. And the clearing of land created land for people to live on and wood that could be turned into things that people needed.

Using the land in this way, however, also caused some harm to the environment. For example, too much logging causes harm to the environment and the plants and animals that live there. Pollution is also a problem. Texans today are looking for ways to undo the harm they have done to the environment.

One way they are doing this is by reusing and recycling. Recycling means using something again instead of throwing it out. Recycling also saves energy. Recycling one aluminum can saves enough energy to run a computer for three hours.

5. ◎ **Categorize**
Analyze the art below of a home that recycles. In the art, circle three ways to save water. Then draw a box around three ways to save energy.

Reuse and Recycle!

- Use energy-efficient bulbs and turn lights off.
- Wash full loads of laundry.
- Turn water off.
- Use ceiling fan for cooling.
- Reuse and recycle.
- Use your bike.
- Plant native plants that need less water.

Conservation is another way Texans are helping the environment. That means we are learning how to use our natural resources carefully. For example, if a tree is cut down, a new one is planted. In this way we keep renewing our natural resources.

Some Texans are building green homes that use energy from the sun to power lights or make hot water. Some homes use cooler air from deep underground to cool the home in summer. Together, these people are making Texas a cleaner, more energy-efficient, and beautiful place.

Fort Worth Botanic Garden

Got it?

TEKS 9.A, 12.C

6. **Main Idea and Details** **Describe** how people have modified their environment to supply their water needs.

....

....

7. **Explain** what people can do to protect the environment and the state's resources.

my Story Ideas

....

....

8. Describe what local governments sometimes ask people to do during droughts. **Explain** why they do this.

....

....

....

Main Idea and Details

A **main idea** is the most important idea about a topic. **Details**, or supporting ideas, support the main idea. Main ideas and supporting details can be found in written materials as well as in verbal communication. Identifying the main idea will help you better understand what you read.

Finding the main idea is not always easy. Here are some tips.

- Often a main idea is stated at the beginning of a passage or speech, but not always.

- Main ideas can be stated or not stated. When it is not stated, the reader must use the important details to figure out the main idea.

- Details give supporting information about the main idea.

Read and analyze the following passage about Texas wetlands. Then analyze the chart below to identify the main idea and supporting details.

In the past, some Texas wetlands have been drained, covered over, and filled with dirt or garbage. People thought they were making useless land useful. But wetlands are not useless. They are home to many Texas plants and animals. Migrating birds use them to stop and rest. During floods they hold soil and pollutants. This keeps rivers and streams clean. Texas wetlands are an important resource.

Main Idea

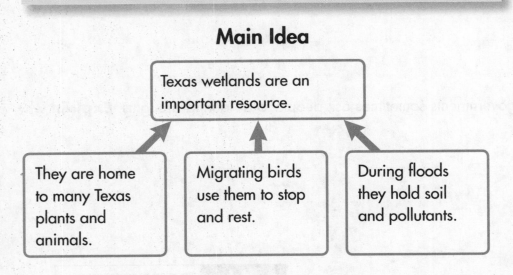

Texas wetlands are an important resource.

| They are home to many Texas plants and animals. | Migrating birds use them to stop and rest. | During floods they hold soil and pollutants. |

TEKS

ELA 11.A Summarize the main idea and supporting details in text in ways that maintain meaning.
SS 21.B Analyze information by finding the main idea.
SS 22.B Incorporate main and supporting ideas in verbal and written communication.

Reread the section titled "Using Resources Wisely" on page 50. Then answer the following questions about the main idea and supporting details.

1. **Analyze** the information and identify the main idea.

   ....

   ....

   ....

2. Was the main idea stated in the beginning of the passage, or did you use supporting details to identify the main idea?

   ....

   ....

   ....

3. **Identify** the supporting details of the main idea.

   ....

   ....

   ....

4. **Examine** the section titled "Landforms" on pages 42–43. On a separate sheet of paper, **organize** the information in a main idea and details chart for this section. Interpret your chart by sharing it with a classmate.

Texas Climate

Is it raining today? Or is it sunny? The answer depends on where you live.

Weather and Climate

The **weather** describes the air at one time and place. **Climate** describes the patterns of weather in a place over a long period of time. It takes many years for climates to change. Climate can influence the distribution of the population in an area. In Texas this means that more people choose to live in areas where the climate is mild.

The weather in Texas includes hot days, freezing days, heavy rains, and long periods of no rain at all. The climate in Texas varies by location, but many areas have a mild climate. Do you know what makes the climate mild in these areas? Location.

Vocabulary

weather	norther
climate	blizzard
tornado	precipitation

When you step outside in the morning, what might surprise you, the weather or the climate?

At the North Pole, the climate is cold all year long. Generally, the closer a place is to the North Pole, the colder the climate is. Northern states, such as Alaska, have longer and colder winters. Because Texas is much farther south, it has mild winters.

Places near the equator are hot all year. Texas is not close to the equator, but it is nearer than most states. So Texas is generally warmer than other states. Because of its location, Texas has four seasons: hot summers, mild winters, spring, and fall.

Climate influenced patterns of settlement in Texas in the past and still does today. More people settled in areas where the climate was mild. South Texas is warmer than the rest of the state. East Texas has more rain than drier West Texas. That is one reason more Texans live in East Texas.

TEKS
6.A, 7.B, 8.C, 21.C

1. **Compare** the two photographs on these pages. Using what you learned about the climate, label one photograph *East Texas* and the other *West Texas*.

This scientist was keeping an eye on Hurricane Rita as it came ashore near the Texas-Louisiana border in 2005.

Extreme Weather

The Texas climate may be mild, but the state has extreme weather, too. Think of these record-breaking events. Hail eight inches wide fell in Winkler County in 1960! The town of Follett was buried under 25 inches of snow in 24 hours! And back in 1900, the deadliest storm in the history of the United States hit Galveston, Texas.

A hurricane is a violent storm with high winds and heavy rains. There is a saying that in Texas there are two types of rain: too little and too much. Hurricanes often bring too much.

The hurricanes that have the greatest impact on Texas develop over the Atlantic Ocean and the Gulf of Mexico. They weaken over land. So the coast is often the hardest place hit. When the Galveston hurricane hit in September 1900, it left about 8,000 people dead. Today, Galveston has a seawall to protect it from high tides and flooding. It has something else to protect it too: information. Government scientists use technology to track storms and warn people. When Hurricane Rita hit in September 2005, people were warned and prepared.

2. **Describe** how the people of Galveston are protected from hurricanes today.

....

....

....

Tornadoes are another form of extreme weather. A **tornado** is a fierce swirling funnel of wind created by thunderstorms. The very high wind of tornadoes can rip apart houses. Tornadoes occur more often in west-central Texas. Several tornadoes went through Granbury, Texas, in 2013 with high winds and hail the size of grapefruits. Sheriff Roger Deeds described it simply as a "nightmare."

Hurricanes and tornadoes are typically warm-weather events. But Texas gets winter storms, too. Cold air masses called **northers** blow into North, West, and Central Texas. These storms can drop temperatures by 50 degrees quickly. Sometimes they bring blizzards. A **blizzard** is a storm with high winds and lots of snow.

3. In the paragraph above **identify** and underline the warm-weather events. Circle the cold-weather events.

On March 28, 2007, a large "elephant trunk" tornado crossed Prairie Dog Fork on the Red River in the Texas Panhandle.

Temperature and Precipitation

What causes the climate in one part of Texas to be so different from other parts? You know that places located farther south are warmer. Elevation affects temperature, too. High elevations, such as mountains, are colder than low areas. Texas is like a series of steps that get higher as you go north and west. Look at the map showing Texas temperatures below. The coldest temperatures are in the higher elevations in the west.

But why aren't the highest temperatures along the coast where the land is lowest? Bodies of water affect temperatures as well. The temperature of water does not change as fast or as much as air. So the water helps keep the land cooler in the summer and warmer in the winter. The milder climate of the coast brings a lot of people to the area.

West Texas gets less rainfall than East Texas. Rain, hail, sleet, and snow are all forms of **precipitation.** Now look at the precipitation map. It shows how much drier the west is.

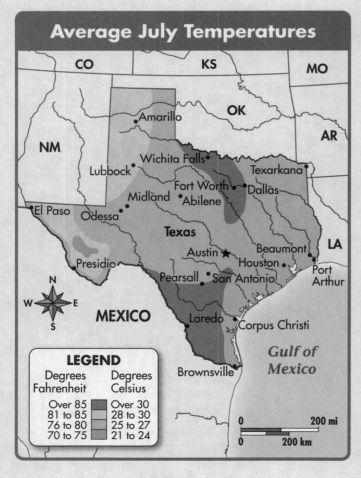

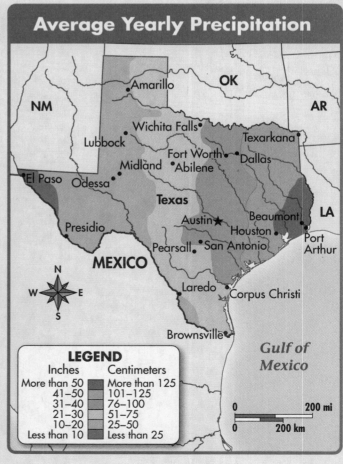

4. **Examine** the map to find average annual precipitation for Beaumont, Fort Worth, Lubbock, and El Paso. Locate these cities on the graph. **Organize** the information from the map into a graph. **Translate** the data and complete the graph by adding bars that show how much rain each city receives.

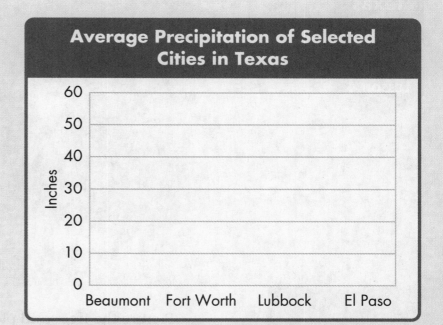

Average Precipitation of Selected Cities in Texas

Got it?

 TEKS 8.C

5. **Compare and Contrast Compare** how hurricanes and tornadoes are the same. **Contrast** how they are different.

....

....

....

6. **Describe** how your local climate differs from other places in Texas. **my Story Ideas**
   List ways that your community is prepared for extreme weather.

....

....

....

7. Think about all you know about geographic factors such as climate in Texas. **Draw conclusions** about patterns of settlement in Texas. **Identify** and **explain** where people live in the state and why?

....

....

....

SAVVAS realize. | Go online to access your interactive digital lesson.

59

Texas Plants and Animals

In Big Bend National Park you might see coyotes, a mother bear, or a herd of collared peccaries such as these.

Picture the trees and plants growing in your area. Do you think what grows in other parts of Texas looks the same? You have read how Texas's landforms, elevation, and climate vary. These factors and the soil cause Texas's vegetation to vary, too. **Vegetation** includes all the trees and plants growing in an area, even farmers' crops. Plants that have grown naturally in an area for a long time without being planted or watered are the area's **natural vegetation**.

Natural Vegetation

In some places, where crops or homes cover the land, it is hard to picture the natural vegetation. It has been removed or cleared to use the land for other things. In other places, people have planted trees and flowers from far-away places. For example, people planted elephant ears, a pretty plant from Asia. Today this plant has spread and grows freely in Texas wetlands, crowding out the natural vegetation.

Bald cypress trees grow in Cypress Swamp in Caddo Lake, Texas.

List two wild plants and two wild animals seen in your area.

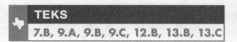

I will know how geography affects what plants and animals live in different parts of Texas.

Vocabulary

vegetation

natural vegetation

endangered

habitat

threatened

The natural vegetation of the Coastal Plains includes thick pine forests that are cut for timber. Marsh grasses and other wetland plants also thrive in this wetter region. In South Texas where freezing temperatures are rare, palm trees grow naturally.

In the North Central Plains' drier and cooler climate supports smaller trees and more grasses. And farther west, where it is drier still, the trees are shorter and fewer. In this dry, mountainous region, you will see plants such as cactus.

As you have read, the soil in river valleys is especially fertile. Along the lower Rio Grande in an area Texans call "The Valley," the soil is rich and the climate warm. This makes it a good place for farming. However, people enjoy the climate, too, so homes cover much of this fertile land today.

TEKS
7.B, 9.A, 9.B, 9.C, 12.B, 13.B, 13.C

Guadalupe Mountains

Texas Crops

There are more farms in Texas than any other state in the country. All these farms and the agricultural products grown there help feed people in the state, the country, and the world. They also help clothe people by growing lots of cotton. Cotton is the most valuable crop in Texas and is worth about $2.2 billion. Cotton from Texas is shipped to other states and around the world. At first, cotton was grown in East Texas where there was enough water. Today, most of it is grown in the drier plains of the northwest. The water needed is pumped from aquifers now. Irrigation systems then push the water through sprinklers to spray the crops or through pipes to water the ground.

The next biggest crop is corn. Corn accounts for about 14 percent of the total crop receipts in Texas. Other important cash crops include sorghum, wheat, and hay.

1. **Identify** the agricultural product grown in Texas. **Explain** why this valuable crop is shipped to other states and around the world.

....

....

....

Cotton accounts for 30 percent of the crop receipts in Texas.

Oranges were once an important crop in Texas, but freezing weather has reduced the crop. Freezing weather destroys oranges. Now, they are grown in the warm Rio Grande Valley. Grapefruits such as the official state fruit, the Texas Ruby Red, are grown there, too. Texas is also known for its peaches, peanuts, pecans, watermelons, cantaloupes, and carrots. It takes a lot of water to grow rice, so it is grown near the northern Gulf Coast.

A fast-growing business in Texas is growing flowers and potted plants. Homeowners and businesses buy these plants to keep indoors or plant outside. Sometimes potted plants are rented for special events. If you go to a shopping mall or public building and see potted plants, they were probably grown in Texas.

2. **Explain** how climate affects where oranges are grown.

....

....

....

....

Some Texas animals, such as this cactus wren, make their home in more arid West Texas.

Texas Animals

Picture yourself on a tour of Texas wildlife. Notice that the wild animals you see change as you travel around the state.

Start in the western mountains. You will see black bears. They used to live throughout the state, but today most live in this quiet area. There are antelope, mountain lions, and jackrabbits, too. Look for cactus wrens. These birds make nests in cacti that only grow in this dry area.

Next, travel north onto the plains of the Panhandle. You will enjoy watching the large towns of prairie dogs. Scientists recently found out these animals are not just barking: they are talking to each other! There are unusual birds such as the big sandhill cranes and the lesser prairie chickens to see. And if you look for it, you might find a Texas horned lizard.

3. Explain why the cactus wren does not live in eastern Texas.

....

....

....

....

....

Next stop are the grasslands and forests of Northeast Texas. The region's many lakes and rivers are home to fish and river otters.

Texas, and especially the Gulf Coast, is the best place in the country for bird watching. More than 600 types of birds have been recorded in the state. Some live in Texas year-round. Many others cross the state as they migrate to homes far away. During the spring and fall migrations, you can even see beautiful birds resting in a nearby park.

Monarch butterflies also migrate across the state. Every fall, tens of millions of them fly south across the state to a forest in Mexico. So many land on each branch and leaf of the forest that you can't see the tree at all. In the spring, the butterflies fly back across Texas to their homes farther north. So many monarchs cross Texas that they were named the state insect!

4. ◉ **Compare and Contrast** **Describe** the difference between a bird that migrates and other Texas birds.

....

....

....

Texas is home to more than 600 types of birds. Some of these birds live in Texas year-round. Others stop over as they migrate or live in the state during the summer or winter.

Endangered Species

In 2013, 63 animals and 25 plants were listed as endangered in Texas. **Endangered** species are in danger of disappearing forever. When a species such as the passenger pigeon disappears forever, it is extinct. Once huge flocks of these birds flew over Texas. Now they are gone forever.

Today the government protects endangered plants and animals. Laws make it illegal to kill or harm the animals. Laws protect important habitats, too. **Habitats** are places in nature where a plant or animal lives. These laws prevent people from using the land in ways that harm the natural habitat. This helps the animals survive but limits how people use the land.

Endangered animals in Texas come in all sizes. There are big ones, such as ocelots and jaguars. The whooping crane is the tallest bird in North America. There are tiny ones, such as minnows and even some spiders. Some, like bats, live in caves. Others, like sea turtles, live in the Gulf.

Remember the lesser prairie chicken you saw on the plains? They are becoming hard to find and may be added to the list of threatened animals. **Threatened** plants and animals are close to becoming endangered.

5. **Describe** how government laws protect endangered species but also limit development.

....

....

....

....

....

....

Texas is the winter home of North America's endangered whooping cranes.

Government laws protect these plants and animals. However, there are things you can also do. First, find out what species need help in your area. Find out all you can about why the species is threatened. A big threat to many species is loss of habitat. You can help protect the environment by keeping it litter-free.

You can help birds by putting out a bird feeder. If there is a place you can plant things, choose plants native to your region. Native animals often use native plants for food or shelter. Lastly, talk to people about what they can do to help Texas plants and animals stay healthy.

6. **◉ Main Idea and Details** In the paragraphs above, **identify** the ways you can help protect endangered plants and animals and underline them.

Texas ocelots are an endangered species.

7. **◉ Cause and Effect Describe** the effect of pumping water from aquifers on how land in Northwest Texas is used today.

....

....

8. **❓ Describe** what plants and animals live in an area in Texas and write what people can do to protect them.

my Story Ideas

....

....

....

....

....

9. **Explain** how people can protect the plants and animals found in Texas.

....

....

Lesson 1  TEKS 8.C

Locating Texas

1. Identify Texas's location by filling in the blanks.

Hemispheres:

....

....

Continent:

....

Country:

....

Region:

....

2. Today, people are settling in the lower Rio Grande Valley for the climate. **Explain** how river valleys were geographic factors that influenced where people settled in the past.

....

....

....

....

Lesson 2 TEKS 9.A, 9.B, 9.C

Texas Resources

3. ◉ **Compare and Contrast** Building dams and reservoirs is too big a job for individuals. It is a job for governments and businesses. **Compare** and **contrast** the positive and negative effects of modification of the environment by government or businesses through the building of dams.

....

....

....

....

....

4. Describe how Texans use four resources: two that are nonrenewable and two that are renewable.

....

....

....

....

....

....

....

5. List ways in which people have modified their environment to meet their basic needs. **Identify** reasons why they modified the environment. How have these modifications helped or harmed the people of Texas and the environment?

....
....
....
....
....
....
....
....
....
....
....
....
....
....
....
....
....

Texas Climate

6. ◎ **Main Idea and Details** In the chart below, **identify** and list the missing details that support the main idea.

Main Idea

> Texas has many kinds of severe weather.

Detail 1 ....
Detail 2 tornadoes
Detail 3 northers
Detail 4 ....
Detail 5

7. On a separate piece of paper, **apply** geographic tools and **construct** your own map of Texas. Shade the map to show the landforms of Texas. Write the title of your map below. Add the following geographic tools to your map: title, symbols, compass rose, scale, legend, a grid system, and a locator map showing Texas's location in the world.

....

8. **Explain** how climate influences the distribution of population in Texas.

....

Lesson 4 ➜ TEKS 9.B, 12.B

Texas Plants and Animals

9. Read the question carefully. Determine the best answer to the question from the four answer choices provided. Circle the best answer.

How did cotton farmers change the environment in the plains of the northwest of Texas?

A Wetlands were drained and the land cleared for farming.

B Water from aquifers was pumped to the surface for irrigation.

C Dams and reservoirs were built to store water for irrigation.

D Forests were cut and the land cleared for farming.

10. **Explain** two geographic factors that make the lower Rio Grande Valley a good place to grow oranges.

....

....

....

....

....

....

11. ❓ **How does geography affect our lives?** ➜ TEKS 13.C

Think about where the things you wear and use are from. Look at the picture and **explain** how geography affects the goods that your family needs and purchases.

....

....

....

....

....

....

....

....

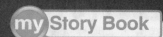

Go online to write and illustrate your own **myStory Book** using the **myStory Ideas** from this chapter.

 THE BIG ?

How does geography affect our lives?

TEKS
SS 9.B
ELA 15

Texas has a variety of landforms, bodies of water, natural resources, and climates. This varied geography affects people in different ways, depending on where they live. Geography influences the kinds of homes we live in, what we wear, and what we do for fun and work. How does geography affect you?

Think about where you live and the activities you do.
Explain how geography affects your life.

....

....

....

....

Now draw a picture to illustrate your writing.

The Geographic Regions of Texas

 my Story Spark

What makes a good community?

Think about what you like most about where you live. **Describe** why someone would want to live in your community.

....

....

....

....

....

....

Texas Essential Knowledge and Skills

6.A Apply geographic tools, including grid systems, legends, symbols, scales, and compass roses, to construct and interpret maps.

7.A Describe a variety of regions in Texas and the United States such as political, population, and economic regions that result from patterns of human activity.

7.B Identify, locate, and compare the geographic regions of Texas (Mountains and Basins, Great Plains, North Central Plains, Coastal Plains), including their landforms, climate, and vegetation.

7.C Compare the geographic regions of Texas (Mountains and Basins, Great Plains, North Central Plains, Coastal Plains) with regions of the United States and other parts of the world.

8.B Describe and explain the location and distribution of various towns and cities in Texas, past and present.

8.C Explain the geographic factors such as landforms and climate that influence patterns of settlement and the distribution of population in Texas, past and present.

9.A Describe ways people have adapted to and modified their environment in Texas, past and present, such as timber clearing, agricultural production, wetlands drainage, energy production, and construction of dams.

9.B Identify reasons why people have adapted to and modified their environment in Texas, past and present, such as the use of natural resources to meet basic needs, facilitate transportation, and enhance recreational activities.

21.B Analyze information by sequencing, categorizing, identifying cause-and-effect relationships, comparing, contrasting, finding the main idea, summarizing, making generalizations and predictions, and drawing inferences and conclusions.

21.C Organize and interpret information in outlines, reports, databases, and visuals, including graphs, charts, timelines, and maps.

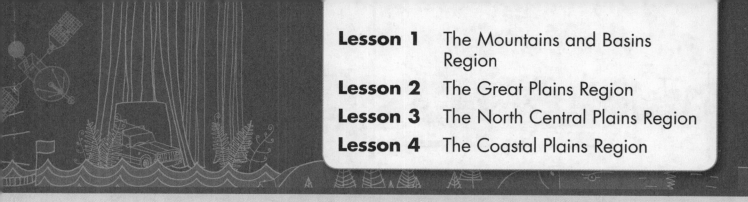

Texas
A Varied State

my Story Video

"Snow?" thinks Connor as he looks at pictures on the Big Bend National Park Web site. The 11-year-old from Midland has just returned home from his trip to Big Bend National Park. "It was pretty warm down there by the river," he says.

Big Bend National Park is located in the southeastern portion of the Mountains and Basins region of Texas. It's pretty dry in this area; in fact, much of the region has desert conditions. But in some areas, especially at higher elevations, there is snow. The Mountains and Basins region, as the name suggests, has mountains. Those areas can have cold winters and are where you might see snow. Because of the arid climate and dry land, this region is not very good for agriculture. It is also not very populous, which means that not a lot of people live there. The Mountains and Basins region is known for its beauty and wildlife.

These are some of Connor's pictures of his trip to Big Bend National Park, located in the Mountains and Basins region.

Midland is a city in the Great Plains region. It has a large oil and gas industry.

Palo Duro Canyon is a popular tourist destination in the Great Plains region.

A dinosaur footprint at Dinosaur Valley State Park.

Gabrielle would like to visit Dinosaur Valley State Park.

Not too far away from Big Bend, just a little east, is the border of an entirely different region of Texas. "Midland is in the Great Plains region," Connor says. "It's different here." This region has a few different climates, which vary based on their elevations. The region overall gets about 10 to 15 inches of rainfall every year. This makes for good agriculture, so cattle and grains are big business in the Great Plains. And, because Texas Tech University is in Lubbock, the biggest city in the Great Plains, education plays a big role in the economy here, too. "Dad and Mom both went to Texas Tech," Connor shares. "Maybe I will, too. I still have some time to think about that."

Thinking about college is something Gabrielle is doing, too. Gabrielle lives in Abilene, in the North Central Plains region, and the city has three universities. "I'm not sure which I'll choose, but I think I'll stay close to home when the time comes," she says. Gabrielle's dad has worked in the oil business for more than a decade, and she learns the business from him when she can. "A lot of families work in oil here," she explains. "But there's a lot of agriculture in Abilene, too. And of course, there are many jobs at the universities." Some of the state's largest ranches are found in the Rolling Plains area of the North Central Plains region. "And you know what else?" Gabrielle chirps in. "Dinosaur Valley State Park is in the Grand Prairie area of this region. I've never been there, but I'd love to see those dinosaur footprints!" she says.

Fort Worth is in the North Central Plains region. It is home to many museums and several universities.

San Antonio is in the Coastal Plains region. The city has a beautiful River Walk.

"Do you know what region the state capital of Austin is in?" Lauren asks her mother. Lauren and her mom have just visited the State Capitol in Austin. "I do, but why don't you tell me, Lauren?" her mother answers. "The Coastal Plains region," she proclaims.

With a long coastline facing the Gulf of Mexico, the Coastal Plains region is the largest region in Texas. Five smaller areas make up the region, and each area's climate is a little different. One thing they all have in common is that they are fairly flat and close to an ocean. "We don't get to the ocean that often," says Lauren, "but it's just a few hours away."

Some of the biggest and most well-known cities in the state can be found in this region. San Antonio, Dallas, Houston, and Austin are all in this region. Padre Island is a popular tourist beach in Texas. Warm weather and plenty of sunshine bring tourists here all year round.

Texas is one of the biggest states in the country, so it's no surprise that the four geographic regions here have a lot of variety. Even with differing climates, elevations, populations, and traditions, there's one thing all these regions have in common, and that is Texas pride.

"Thanks for visiting!" Lauren exclaims. "Y'all come back soon, all right?"

Lauren lives near Austin, in the Coastal Plains region.

Think About It Based on this story, what is special about each region of Texas? As you read the chapter, think about what makes a good community.

SAVVAS realize Go online to access your interactive digital lesson.

75

The Mountains and Basins Region

The Guadalupe Mountains of Texas are the highest of the mountain ranges in this region.

1. **Describe** how the economy of this region changed as a result of human activity.

Texas can be divided into four major geographic regions. These regions are determined by their major landforms. The region located in the far west of Texas is the Mountains and Basins region, also known as the Basin and Range region. Find this geographic region on the map.

The Land

The basins in the western part of this region make up part of the Chihuahuan (chih WAH wun) Desert. Texas shares this desert with New Mexico, Arizona, and the country of Mexico. Mountain ranges run through the center of the region. The Guadalupe Mountains run from New Mexico into Texas. This is the highest mountain range in the state. Guadalupe Peak is the highest point in Texas. It stands 8,749 feet above sea level. The second-tallest mountains are the Davis Mountains. South of these, the Chisos Mountains are the third-highest range in the state.

The climate in this geographic region is very dry. In fact, much of this region is a **desert**, or an area that gets less than 10 inches of rain per year. The vegetation in the desert includes the creosote bush, cacti, and yucca, agave, and sotol plants. It is very hot in the summer, but because of the mountains, the region can have cold winters. There can even be snow here.

Because this region is dry and rocky, it is not good for farming. Most of the population lives along the Rio Grande, where they have access to water. In the rest of the region, communities are small, and the mountains separate towns.

Vocabulary

desert   border

time zone   landmark

Identify the landforms on the left. Above, draw and label a picture of a landform you see in your community.

People have adapted to the rugged environment of this geographic region by creating parks. Every year, about one half million people visit the Guadalupe Mountains National Park and Big Bend National Park. Mountain lions, peregrine falcons, and other wildlife make their homes in these parks. Many people work in these parks, protecting the animals and the land and helping visitors. This is an example of human activity creating an economic region. In this case, the economy is based on tourists visiting parks.

TEKS

7.A, 7.B, 7.C, 8.B, 8.C, 9.A

2. **Identify** the landforms of this geographic region. On the map, circle the Chihuahuan Desert and the tallest peak in Texas.

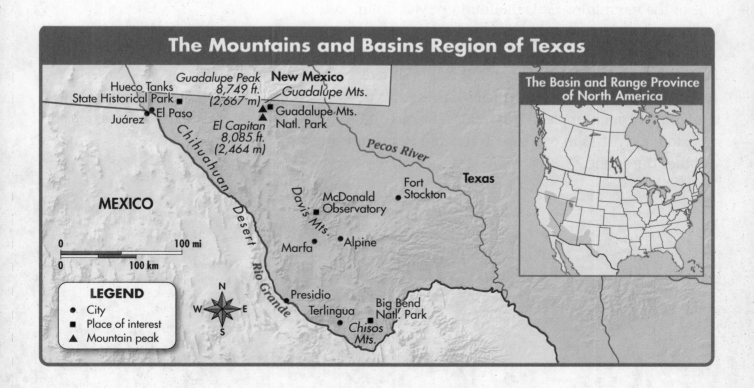

The Mountains and Basins Region of Texas

The Basin and Range Province of North America

Hueco Tanks State Historical Park

Guadalupe Peak 8,749 ft. (2,667 m)

New Mexico

Guadalupe Mts.

Juárez   •El Paso

Guadalupe Mts. Natl. Park

El Capitan 8,085 ft. (2,464 m)

Chihuahuan Desert

Pecos River

Texas

MEXICO

Davis Mts.

McDonald Observatory

Fort Stockton

0   100 mi

0   100 km

Marfa   •Alpine

Rio Grande

Presidio

Terlingua

Big Bend Natl. Park

Chisos Mts.

LEGEND

• City

■ Place of interest

▲ Mountain peak

Compare Geographic Regions

Texas is not the only part of North America to have mountains and basins. The Mountains and Basins region of Texas is part of a larger region known as the Basin and Range Province. This larger region extends from Mexico and covers much of New Mexico, Arizona, and Nevada.

Long, narrow mountain ranges separated by flat valleys or basins cover much of the region. This is one of the driest areas in the United States. In fact, it includes parts of four different deserts: the Chihuahuan, the Sonoran, the Mojave, and the Great Basin.

The Basin and Range Province is home to three national parks. While there are a few large cities, most towns have small populations and are often isolated. Many people work in recreation and tourism, ranching, or mining.

Major Cities

Most of the towns in the Mountains and Basins region are small. Often, they are separated from other towns by mountains. However, there is one major city in this geographic region: El Paso. *El Paso* is Spanish for "the pass." The city is located near a mountain pass, an area lower than the surrounding mountains that makes it easy to get to the other side of the mountains. This mountain pass is an important landform in the geographic region.

El Paso is the fifth-largest city in Texas. It is so far away from other major Texas cities that it is in a different time zone. A **time zone** is an area in which all the clocks are set to the same time. For example, if it is 4:00 in El Paso, it is 5:00 in Houston. El Paso is in one time zone, and Houston is in another time zone.

3. ⊙ **Draw Conclusions**
Explain why the location of El Paso was important to its growth.

....

....

....

....

....

....

....

El Paso is the largest city in the Mountains and Basins region.

El Paso is located on the Rio Grande, a river that marks the border between Texas and Mexico. A **border** is a boundary line. On the other side of the Rio Grande is the Mexican city of Juárez (HWAH res). More than two million people live in these two cities.

A Natural Landmark

A **landmark** is an object, such as a mountain, that stands out from the area around it. Early settlers needed a landmark to help them find their way through the Guadalupe Pass. The mountain known as El Capitan was perfect for the job! It was tall enough to be easily seen. It was different enough to be easily recognized. Even today, people use this mountain as a landmark when traveling in this part of Texas.

El Capitan helped early travelers to find their way.

Got it?

TEKS 7.B, 8.C, 9.A

4. ◉ **Make Generalizations** **Identify** and **describe** the climate of the geographic region known as the Mountains and Basins region.

....

....

5. ❓ **Explain** how geographic factors such as landforms in this geographic region influence patterns of settlement.

my Story Ideas

....

....

....

6. **Describe** how people have adapted to the region so that people can enjoy its beauty.

....

....

....

The Great Plains Region

Envision It!

The northwest part of Texas is often called the Panhandle.

Moving east from the Mountains and Basins region, we come next to the Great Plains region of Texas.

The Land

The Great Plains region has four sections. The High Plains section is separated from the North Central Plains region by a long, steep slope called the Caprock Escarpment. The Edwards Plateau is hilly. In fact, the eastern part of the Edwards Plateau is called the Texas Hill Country. The Toyah Basin is a broad, flat area located in the Pecos River Valley. The Llano Basin sits on the eastern edge of the Edwards Plateau.

The vegetation in this geographic region includes different grasses. The Great Plains region has some forests with very tall trees.

The natural resources of the High Plains include oil, natural gas, and good soil. Farmers use underground water to irrigate the land. Farmers grow wheat, cotton, and sorghum in the Great Plains region. The Edwards Plateau is ideal for raising angora goats. The hair of these goats is called **mohair.** Mohair can be spun into fine yarn. Almost all of the mohair made in the United States comes from Texas.

The climate depends partly on elevation. Higher elevations usually mean cooler temperatures. This geographic region has hot summers and cool winters. Sometimes cold weather can blow in from the Rocky Mountains. The western part of this region gets about 10 inches of rain and the eastern part gets about 30 inches of rain annually.

1. **Compare** the vegetation of the geographic regions of Texas. How is the vegetation in the Great Plains region different from the vegetation in the Mountains and Basins region?

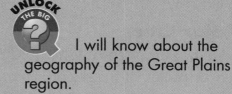
Vocabulary

mohair

helium

tourism

Look at the pictures on the left. **Explain** why the northwest part of Texas is called the Panhandle.

Compare Geographic Regions

The Great Plains stretch from the Rio Grande northward, across Texas, across the center of the United States and up into Canada. You can see this on the map. People moved to this geographic region because it is a good place to graze cattle and grow grains. There are a few cities, but it is largely a rural area.

In South America, there is a large area called the Pampas, which is similar to the Great Plains. In fact, the word *pampas* means "plains." As with the Great Plains in the United States, the Pampas is great for agriculture and cattle raising.

TEKS
7.A, 7.B, 7.C, 8.B, 9.A, 9.B

2. **Locate** the Great Plains region. Circle the area where angora goats are raised. **Locate** and underline the name of the slope that separates the High Plains from the next geographic region.

The Great Plains Region of Texas

LEGEND
- City
- Place of interest

0   100 mi
0   100 km

New Mexico

Canadian River

Oklahoma

High Plains

Amarillo
Palo Duro Canyon

White River

Caprock Escarpment

Red River

Lubbock

Odessa
Midland

Texas

Brazos River

Colorado River

Pecos River

Toyah Basin

Llano Basin

Edwards Plateau

MEXICO

Rio Grande

Nueces River

The Great Plains Region of the U.S. and Its Neighbors

Major Cities

Lubbock is often called Hub City because it is the economic hub, or center, of the region. Founded in 1890, Lubbock grew quickly after the Santa Fe Railroad built a line through the town in 1909. There are many schools, including Texas Tech University. Many people have jobs related to education and healthcare. People also work in agriculture and manufacturing.

Amarillo is the largest city in the Texas Panhandle. It was founded in 1887 by business owners who built stores there. The business owners thought it was a good location for a town because a railroad was going to be built there. Amarillo quickly became a booming cattle town, with cattle being sent by rail to distant markets. People still raise cattle here. Amarillo is also a center for agriculture, healthcare, and the natural gas industry. One of the products found with natural gas is helium. **Helium** is a gas that is lighter than air with no color or smell.

Tourism is also important in Amarillo. **Tourism** is the industry that serves people who are visiting an area for pleasure. People come to enjoy learning about the history of the Old West. They can go to the outdoor musical *Texas* at Palo Duro Canyon. The musical is performed every year and tells about the past.

Neighboring cities Midland and Odessa have large oil and gas industries. They also have businesses and stores that meet the needs of farmers and ranchers.

3. 🎯 **Cause and Effect**
Explain how the railroad helped the economy of Amarillo.

....

....

....

....

....

....

....

Horses are important to Texas cattle ranching. This museum in Amarillo honors the American Quarter Horse.

AMERICAN QUARTER HORSE HALL OF FAME & MUSEUM

A Natural Landmark

Palo Duro Canyon is about 120 miles long, 20 miles wide, and as great as 800 feet deep. It was carved by the Prairie Dog Town Fork, a river that feeds into the Red River. The vegetation in the canyon includes mesquite and juniper, which are hardwood shrubs. *Palo duro* means "hard wood" in Spanish.

Sometimes people adapt to an environment. This means that they change their behavior instead of changing the land. In the 1930s, people decided to protect Palo Duro Canyon. One reason people adapted to the land rather than change it was so that future generations could enjoy its natural beauty. Today, about 300,000 people visit Palo Duro Canyon State Park each year.

The Palo Duro Canyon is the second-largest canyon in the United States. Only the Grand Canyon is larger.

Got it?

🔶 TEKS 7.B, 9.B

4. ⦿ **Cause and Effect** **Identify** the climate of the Great Plains region. **Explain** how the higher elevation affects the climate of this geographic region.

....

....

5. ❓ **Identify** and record two or three details about each city.

my Story Ideas

City	Details
Amarillo	
Lubbock	

6. **Identify** reasons why people adapted to the environment in Palo Duro Canyon.

....

....

The North Central Plains Region

Envision It!

Pecans are shaken from the trees and harvested after they fall to the ground. This tractor is gathering pecans that have fallen.

The West Texas Rolling Plains (top) and Cross Timbers (bottom)

1. **Identify** the vegetation found in this geographic region. In the text, underline the trees that grow in the Cross Timbers.

Continuing east from the Great Plains, we come to the North Central Plains region of Texas. Locate this geographic region on the map.

The Land

The North Central Plains region starts at the Caprock Escarpment and stretches east. A **plain** is a large area of flat land with gently rolling hills and few trees. The elevation of this region rises from about 400 feet in the east to 2,000 feet in the west. This geographic region is broken into three smaller areas: the West Texas Rolling Plains, the Grand Prairie, and the Cross Timbers. The Cross Timbers is divided into eastern and western sections by the Grand Prairie. The Cross Timbers area has soil that is good for growing tall trees, such as pecans, oaks, and elms.

Like the rest of Texas, the climate in this geographic region offers hot summers. Depending on the elevation, winters can be cool or cold. Compared to the Mountains and Basins region, the North Central Plains region is much wetter. The annual rainfall ranges from 30 inches in the east to 20 inches in the west.

Compare Geographic Regions

The North Central Plains of Texas cross the state border and sweep upward across the United States and into Canada. Most of this is good farming land. However, as one moves north, the climate changes. Farther north, there are more clearly defined seasons with more rain and colder winters.

List other Texas crops you can think of that grow on trees.

UNLOCK THE BIG ? I will know what communities are like in the North Central Plains region.

Vocabulary

plain
cultivate
livestock

The North Central Plains of the United States are located near the Great Lakes. This geographic region is more commonly known as the Midwest. It is also sometimes called the country's breadbasket because so much grain (especially corn and wheat) is grown there.

There are large plains in other parts of the world as well. The European Plain covers much of Europe. As with the Central Plains of the United States, agriculture is important on the European Plain.

TEKS
7.A, 7.B, 7.C, 9.A

2. **Compare** the North Central Plains region of Texas to the European Plain. How are they alike?

....

....

....

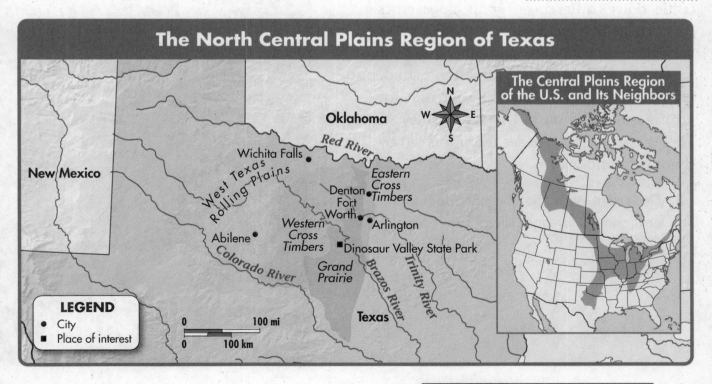

The North Central Plains Region of Texas

Oklahoma

Red River

New Mexico

Wichita Falls

West Texas Rolling Plains

Eastern Cross Timbers

Denton
Fort Worth

Arlington

Western Cross Timbers

Abilene

Colorado River

Dinosaur Valley State Park

Grand Prairie

Brazos River

Trinity River

Texas

LEGEND
● City
■ Place of interest

0 ——— 100 mi
0 ——— 100 km

The Central Plains Region of the U.S. and Its Neighbors

Farming and Industry

The Eastern and Western Cross Timbers may look like two different areas, but the areas are connected along the Red River. The name *Cross Timbers* comes from the strips of forest that cross the prairies. People have modified this geographic region by cutting down trees to clear land so it could be used to meet their basic needs. Some of the reasons they cleared land was to make room for farms, ranches, houses, or businesses. However, this is still the best area in the North Central Plains for growing trees. People have adapted to the environment by planting crops that grow on trees, such as pecans and a variety of fruits. Area ranches raise cattle, sheep, and goats. Other resources include oil, gas, clay, sand, stone, and gravel.

The West Texas Rolling Plains area has an important cattle-raising industry. It is the site of some of the state's largest ranches. There is also flat land that farmers can **cultivate,** or use to raise crops. Unlike the Mountains and Basins region, which is dry and rocky, this geographic region has rich soil. Farmers here grow wheat, cotton, and sorghum. There are oil fields in this area, too.

The Grand Prairie area is a grassy land, which makes it good for raising livestock, such as beef cattle, dairy cattle, sheep, goats, hogs, chickens, and turkeys. **Livestock** are animals that are raised by farmers. Corn and other grains, as well as cotton, are grown here. Limestone, sand, and gravel are among the area's resources. Grand Prairie is also the site of Dinosaur Valley State Park. Here, visitors can see footprints left by dinosaurs long ago.

Dinosaur footprints from Dinosaur Valley State Park

3. **Describe** ways that people adapt to the environment for agricultural production.

   ....

   ....

   ....

   ....

Cities in the Region

The chart shows some of the cities in this region. Most of these cities were first located near railways or grew larger once the railways arrived.

Abilene was founded in 1881 as a railway town along the Texas and Pacific Railway. Originally focused on agriculture, Abilene now has an economy that is based on oil, agriculture, and business. In addition, there are three universities in Abilene.

Fort Worth was a fort established by the United States War Department in 1849. However, the town didn't really grow until after the Civil War. Then it became an important center of the cattle industry and was soon known as Cowtown. Today, Fort Worth is home to many museums and universities. Meatpacking and aircraft building are also important industries.

City	Population
Abilene	117,063
Arlington	365,438
Denton	113,383
Fort Worth	741,206
Wichita Falls	104,553

Source: Bureau of the Census, 2010

4. **Identify** and circle the city that began as a railway town and now has three universities. What is the population of this city?

....

Got it?

TEKS 7.B, 7.C

5. ◉ **Compare and Contrast** **Compare** the geographic regions of the North Central Plains of Texas and the Central Plains of the United States. **Explain** a difference.

....

....

6. Both Abilene and Fort Worth benefited from railroads. **Explain** why you think transportation is important to the growth of a town or city.

my Story Ideas

....

....

7. On a separate sheet of paper, create a Venn diagram comparing the North Central Plains and the Mountains and Basins regions. **Identify** and **compare** the vegetation, landforms, and climate of these geographic regions of Texas.

Using a Cultural Map

Texas gets millions of visitors each year. They come to explore what Texas offers. Even people who live here like exploring the state's many attractions. One way to find these attractions is to use a cultural map. **Cultural maps** identify sites that are related to an area's culture or history.

The map below is a cultural map of Texas. Suppose you wanted to use it to find out what there is to see or do in or near Corpus Christi. First, look at the map legend and interpret the symbols. It shows what each symbol on the map stands for. Then, locate Corpus Christi on the map. Look for symbols nearby. Read the labels. They show that Goose Island State Park is near Corpus Christi.

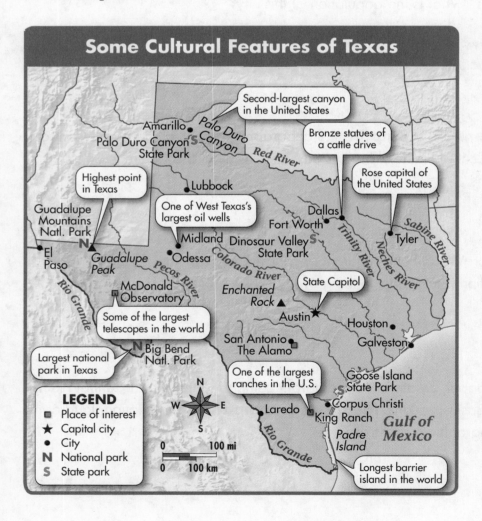

Some Cultural Features of Texas

Second-largest canyon in the United States

Bronze statues of a cattle drive

Rose capital of the United States

Highest point in Texas

One of West Texas's largest oil wells

Palo Duro Canyon State Park

Amarillo

Palo Duro Canyon

Red River

Lubbock

Dallas

Fort Worth

Tyler

Sabine River

Trinity River

Neches River

Guadalupe Mountains Natl. Park

El Paso

Guadalupe Peak

Midland

Odessa

Dinosaur Valley State Park

Colorado River

Pecos River

Rio Grande

McDonald Observatory

Enchanted Rock

State Capitol

Austin

Houston

Galveston

Some of the largest telescopes in the world

Big Bend Natl. Park

San Antonio The Alamo

One of the largest ranches in the U.S.

Goose Island State Park

Corpus Christi

Largest national park in Texas

Laredo

King Ranch

Gulf of Mexico

Padre Island

Longest barrier island in the world

LEGEND
- Place of interest
- ★ Capital city
- City
- N National park
- S State park

N W E S

0   100 mi
0   100 km

Learning Objective

I will know how to interpret cultural features on a map of Texas.

TEKS

ELA 13.B Explain factual information presented graphically.

SS 6.A Apply geographic tools, including grid systems, legends, symbols, scales, and compass roses, to construct and interpret maps.

SS 21.C Organize and interpret information in visuals, including maps.

Your cousins from Michigan are coming to visit. What do you want to show them while they are here? Use the cultural map to locate some interesting places that will help them learn more about Texas.

1. **Locate** Austin on the map. Draw a circle around it. This is where your cousins will be arriving.

2. What could you take your cousins to see in Austin?

   ....

3. From Austin, you could visit Enchanted Rock for a day of hiking. **Examine** the map and tell in what direction you would travel to get there.

   ....

4. **Identify** and draw an *X* on Enchanted Rock.

5. One cousin has always wanted to see the Alamo. **Interpret** what you see on the map and decide what city you would need to visit in order to see the Alamo.

   ....

6. After you visit the Alamo, you could drive southeast to visit a state park. **Apply** the geographic tool, map legend, to find the symbol for state parks. What state park would you reach?

   ....

7. Use the compass rose and **identify** the direction you need to travel to visit the longest barrier island in the world.

   ....

8. You can visit one more place. On a separate sheet of paper, **organize** a list of four cultural features and how far you are from each of them. Choose one place and **construct** a map showing that location and other major features of Texas.

The Coastal Plains Region

Ships are a common sight at the many harbors along the coast of Texas, like this one in Houston.

The final geographic region, moving east, is the Coastal Plains region. It is the largest region of Texas.

The Land

As in the Mountains and Basins region and Great Plains region, the Rio Grande marks the southern border between this region and Mexico. The Rio Grande is one landform that these regions have in common. Some of their landforms are very different. For example, this region does not have mountains or deserts like the Mountains and Basins region. The Coastal Plains region has a long coastline that faces the Gulf of Mexico.

The Coastal Plains region stretches **inland,** or away from the coast toward land, for about 250 miles. The region has the Piney Woods, the Coastal Prairies, the South Texas Plain, the Post Oak Belt, and the Blackland Prairie.

The climate is not the same throughout the region. There is more rain along the coast and in the north. The Piney Woods gets the most rain with about 50 inches per year. The South Texas Plain gets the least rain (about 20–30 inches per year). Still, the Coastal Plains region gets more rain than the other three geographic regions of Texas. Temperatures are generally warm in this region all year.

1. ◎ **Compare and Contrast Compare** the landforms of the geographic regions of Texas. **Identify** and underline the landform that is found in the Coastal Plains and other geographic regions. **Identify** and circle the landform that is only found in this region.

Vocabulary

inland	trading post
lignite	port
bayou	mainland

Explain the kinds of economic activities that take place in locations like the one pictured at left.

Compare Geographic Regions

The Gulf of Mexico helps define the Coastal Plains region of Texas and the larger geographic region known as the Gulf Coastal Plains. The Gulf Coastal Plains stretches all the way from Florida to Mexico. This geographic region has a climate that is hot with a lot of rain. The plant life, soil, and natural resources are similar throughout the region. This is one reason their industries are the same. The Coastal Plains region of North America continues to the north, along the East Coast, bordered to the east by the Atlantic Ocean.

TEKS
7.A, 7.B, 7.C, 8.B, 9.A, 9.B

2. **Locate** the Coastal Plains region. Circle the Gulf Coast of Texas. **Infer** What are two industries that would require being near water?

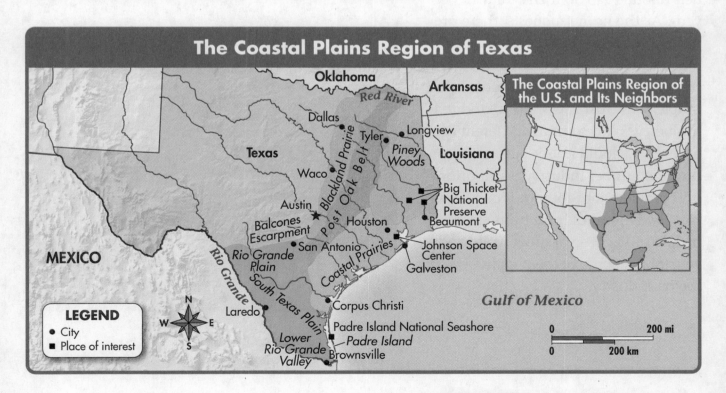

The Coastal Plains Region of Texas

The Coastal Plains Region of the U.S. and Its Neighbors

LEGEND
• City
■ Place of interest

SAVVAS realize — Go online to access your interactive digital lesson.

91

All coastal plains in the world are fairly flat and are next to an ocean. However, they are not all hot like the Coastal Plains region of Texas. Alaska has coastal plains with cool and very cold climates.

Blackland Prairie, Post Oak Belt, and Piney Woods

The Blackland Prairie gets its name from the rich, dark soil, which is good for farming crops and raising livestock. Grains and cotton are grown here.

The Post Oak Belt is named for the post oak tree that grows there. Like the Blackland Prairie, the Post Oak Belt has many farms. There are mines for **lignite,** a type of soft coal. Oil and gas are also found here. People adapt to the environment by using these natural resources for energy production. People need the energy to meet their basic needs. For example, heating oil can keep their homes warm and electricity can keep their food from spoiling.

East of the Post Oak Belt is the Piney Woods area. The Piney Woods gets about 40 to 50 inches of rain per year. As the name suggests, there are many pine trees. But the vegetation also includes many other trees, such as the southern red oak, water oak, red maple, white ash, sweetgum, and red mulberry. With so many different types of trees, it should not be surprising that the lumber industry is important and provides jobs for many people. In places where trees have been cleared, people raise cattle or grow fruits and vegetables. Some of the people work in the oil industry.

3. Identify reasons why people adapt to the environment. Underline the basic needs people meet with energy production.

Coal mined in the Post Oak Belt can be burned to create electricity.

92

Coastal Prairies and South Texas Plain

South of the Piney Woods are the Coastal Prairies. This is where most of Texas's major rivers empty into the Gulf of Mexico. This marshy area has bays and slow-moving streams called **bayous.** Fishing and shipping are important industries here.

Farther inland, the land is flat and fertile. It is good for ranching and for raising crops, such as cotton and sorghum. Oil is an important industry as well. Oil wells don't stop at the coast, however. There are oil rigs on platforms in the Gulf of Mexico.

The South Texas Plain, made up of the Lower Rio Grande Valley and the Rio Grande Plain, is drier than the other areas in this geographic region. Much of the land is covered with thorny brush. Many large cattle ranches, such as the famous King Ranch, are found here.

Since the South Texas Plain is dry, farmers need to modify the environment in order to farm. They use irrigation to get water from the Rio Grande and use it to water their crops. The soil is rich and the weather is mild. This ideal combination is one reason Texas is a top vegetable-producing state in the country.

4. ◉ **Compare and Contrast** How would you **compare** and **contrast** the vegetation of the South Texas Plain to that of the Piney Woods?

....

....

....

....

....

....

....

Bayous support lush vegetation and abundant wildlife.

Houston is the largest city in Texas.

Major Cities

Austin is the state capital. Many people in Austin have government jobs. Like all cities, there are many different jobs, but a lot of people work in education or the computer industry.

People come to San Antonio to visit the Alamo and to enjoy the famous River Walk. People can learn about Texas and its people at the Institute of Texan Cultures. Government, medical research, and tourism all offer jobs to the people of San Antonio.

Dallas began in 1841 as a **trading post,** or small frontier store. People traded local crops or products for the supplies they needed. Today Dallas is a leading business center.

Houston is a port city on the Gulf of Mexico. A **port** is a place where ships can dock to load or unload cargo. The Port of Houston is a major center for trade with foreign countries. Houston is famous for its aerospace industry. It is home to the Johnson Space Center. The Texas Medical Center is also found here.

Some other large cities in the Coastal Plains region are Longview, Galveston, Brownsville, Laredo, Bryan/College Station, and Waco.

5. Identify a detail about each city and add it to the chart.

Austin	
San Antonio	
Dallas	
Houston	

94

A Natural Landmark

Padre Island is a barrier island and a natural landmark in the Coastal Plains region. Padre Island protects the mainland from the full force of hurricanes and tropical storms in the Gulf of Mexico. The **mainland** is the main part of the continent.

Padre Island is about 110 miles long and up to 3 miles wide. It runs along the south coast of Texas. It has the longest sand beach in the United States. Most of the island's beachfront is now part of the Padre Island National Seashore.

Padre Island has the longest beach in the United States.

TEKS 7.B, 9.A, 9.B

6. ● **Main Idea and Details** **Describe** two ways people modify the land to make it better for farming.

....

7. ❓ **Explain** how the place where people live affects the work they do in different parts of the Coastal Plains region.

my Story Ideas

....
....
....
....

8. **Identify** the climate in this geographic region and **describe** how it is different in the north and south.

....
....
....

SAVVAS realize. Go online to access your interactive digital lesson.

95

Make Generalizations

A **generalization** is a broad statement or rule that applies to many examples. These clue words are often part of a generalization: *all, most, many, some, sometimes, usually, seldom, few,* or *generally.* An example of a generalization is *Many people here work in the computer industry.*

Readers can make generalizations based on main ideas, details, and their own knowledge. Making generalizations helps you see similarities between ideas and facts that may appear different at first. A good generalization is supported by facts and examples. Read the chart and compare the information for each region.

The Geographic Regions of Texas

Region	Landforms	Climate	Economic Activity and Resources
Mountains and Basins region	rocky soil mountains basins Rio Grande desert	very dry very hot summers cool to cold winters	tourism wildlife Guadalupe Mountains National Park Big Bend National Park
Great Plains region	high, flat grasslands Rio Grande Caprock Escarpment plateau	fairly dry very hot summers cool to cold winters	ranching farming mohair production oil and gas *Texas,* the musical
North Central Plains region	flat and rolling elevation from 400 to 2,000 feet	fairly dry hot summers cool to cold winters	farming ranching building materials
Coastal Plains region	wet and dry land Gulf of Mexico Rio Grande bayous forests barrier islands	30 to 50 inches of rain temperatures generally warm all year	farming ranching forests fishing shipping oil and gas building materials

Learning Objective

I will know how to analyze information by making generalizations.

TEKS

ELA 11.A Summarize the main idea and supporting details in text in ways that maintain meaning.

SS 7.B Identify, locate, and compare the geographic regions of Texas (Mountains and Basins, Great Plains, North Central Plains, Coastal Plains), including their landforms, climate, and vegetation.

SS 21.B Analyze information by making generalizations.

SS 22.C Express ideas orally based on experiences.

When you want to make a generalization, you start by gathering information. Then you analyze the facts and details. Finally, you make a verbal or written statement that brings the information together. Make sure the facts or examples support your generalization. Use a clue word such as *many, seldom,* or *generally* to make it clear you are making a generalization.

You can make generalizations about the four geographic regions of Texas. Read the table on page 96. Think about how the regions are similar. Use the similarities to help you make a generalization. For example, the Rio Grande is a landform in three of the four geographic regions. A generalization might be this: *Most regions in Texas have the Rio Grande as a border.*

Use the chart and what you know about these regions to answer the questions.

Try it!

1. **Identify** a resource that is found in two of the regions. Write the resource and the regions.

   ....

2. **Analyze** the information above and make a generalization.

   ....

3. Based on your experience, **express** a generalization about summers in Texas to a classmate.

   ....

   ....

4. What **generalization** can you make about farming and ranching?

   ....

   ....

5. What generalization can you make to **explain** why irrigation is needed?

   ....

Lesson 1 TEKS 7.B, 7.C, 8.B

The Mountains and Basins Region

1. Read the question carefully. Determine the best answer to the question from the four answer choices provided. Circle the best answer.

   Identify the vegetation you would most likely find in the geographic region known as the Mountains and Basins region.

   A pine trees

   B cacti

   C pecan trees

   D orange trees

2. **Explain** and **describe** the location and distribution of cities in this geographic region.

   ....

   ....

   ....

3. **Compare** the Mountains and Basins region of Texas to the Basin and Range Province of the United States.

   a. How are the populations of the towns similar?

   ....

   ....

   b. **Explain** how the economies are alike.

   ....

   ....

4. How would you **locate** this geographic region on a map?

   ....

   ....

   ....

5. **Examine** the photo.

   Why was this landmark important to early settlers in this geographic region?

   ....

   ....

   ....

Lesson 2 TEKS 7.B, 7.C, 9.A

The Great Plains Region

6. **Explain** how people use underground water supplies in this geographic region.

   ....

   ....

7. Identify how the vegetation in Palo Duro Canyon helps **explain** its name.

....

....

....

8. Identify the climate of this geographic region. How does elevation affect the climate?

....

....

....

....

9. ◎ **Compare and Contrast Describe** what the Great Plains regions of Texas and the United States have in common.

....

....

....

Lesson 3 ⬅ TEKS 7.A, 7.B

The North Central Plains Region

10. Identify and **compare** the climate in the North Central Plains region of Texas and the Great Plains region.

....

....

....

11. Identify one thing that is raised or grown in each area of this geographic region.

Cross Timbers ....

West Texas Rolling Plains ....

Grand Prairie ....

12. Describe why the North Central Plains of the United States is sometimes called the country's breadbasket.

....

....

....

13. Describe one thing that helped determine the location of Abilene when it was founded.

....

14. On the map below, **locate** the geographic regions of Texas. Color in the North Central Plains region.

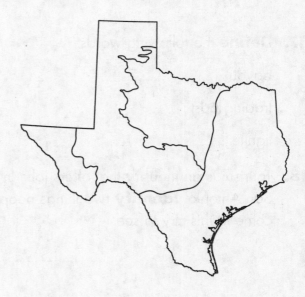

The Coastal Plains Region

15. **Make Generalizations Compare** the geographic regions of Texas. How does the climate of the Coastal Plains compare to the other three regions?

....

....

....

....

16. **Draw Conclusions Compare** the regions of Texas with regions of the United States. Why do people in Florida and other places along the Gulf of Mexico grow some of the same crops as people in the Coastal Plains region of Texas?

....

....

17. **Define** the following words:

bayou ....

trading post ....

lignite ....

18. Tourism is an industry that offers jobs in San Antonio. **Identify** two things people come to this city to see.

....

....

19. **Explain** why the landform of Padre Island is important.

....

....

....

....

20. **What makes a good community?** TEKS 7.B, 8.B, 8.C

Use this photo of the Mountains and Basins region to think more about what you learned about this geographic region in Chapter 2.

Suppose you live in this region. What might your community be like? How would the region's geography affect your community?

....

....

....

....

....

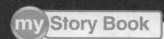

Go online to write and illustrate your own **myStory Book** using the **myStory Ideas** from this chapter.

What makes a good community?

TEKS

SS 7.B
ELA 15

Communities come in many sizes. They are located in different regions. However, all communities have things in common. One thing all communities must have, no matter how small or large, is a way for people to make a living.

Think about the community where you live. **Identify** and write the name of the region where your community is located. **Describe** one or two jobs available in your community, and **explain** why these jobs are located in your community. Draw a picture showing someone working at one of the jobs.

....

....

....

....

....

realize. Go online to access your interactive digital lesson.

101

The Early History of Texas

my Story Spark

THE BIG ? How do people adapt to where they live?

Analyze the environment around your home. **Identify** the weather, land, and things people have built there. **Describe** ways you have adapted to your environment.

....

....

....

....

....

....

Texas Essential Knowledge and Skills

1.A Explain the possible origins of American Indian groups in Texas and North America.

1.B Identify American Indian groups in Texas and North America before European exploration.

1.C Describe the regions in which American Indians lived and identify American Indian groups remaining in Texas.

1.D Compare the ways of life of American Indian groups in Texas and North America before European exploration.

8.A Identify and explain clusters and patterns of settlement in Texas at different time periods.

9.A Describe ways people have adapted to and modified their environment in Texas, past and present.

9.B Identify reasons why people have adapted to and modified their environment in Texas, past and present.

10.A Explain the economic activities various early American Indian groups in Texas used to meet their needs and wants.

14.A Compare how various American Indian groups governed themselves.

21.A Differentiate between, locate, and use valid primary and secondary sources to acquire information about the United States and Texas.

21.B Analyze information by comparing and contrasting.

22.C Express ideas orally based on research and experiences.

22.D Create written and visual material.

Ysleta del Sur Pueblo

A Place of Culture

my Story Video

Amanda is visiting the Ysleta del Sur Cultural Center, in El Paso, to learn about the history and traditions of the Tigua Indian tribe. As she walks into the courtyard to watch a traditional Eagle dance performed by Tigua tribal social dancers, she's excited at what she sees. "Did you see all those feathers?" asks Amanda. "That dancer really does look like an eagle!" she exclaims. "My ancestors have been performing that dance for centuries," explains Samantha, the lead dancer. "It's a tribute to the great American eagle, which is respected and honored by our Pueblo people."

Rafael, Amanda's museum guide today, is a council member of the Tigua tribe. "We are Pueblo Indians," he explains, "and we have been here for over 330 years. We established Ysleta del Sur in 1682, after the Great Pueblo Revolt of 1680. My people are originally from the Pueblo of Quarai and Pueblo Isleta, both in New Mexico."

With Rafael's help, Amanda is learning all about the native people who had to fight for the land to make this area of Texas their home.

Amanda gets ready to watch a traditional Eagle dance.

103

The Pueblo people used adobe bricks to make their homes.

Tigua tribal dancers used to perform the Buffalo dance before a buffalo hunt, in order to bring success.

The Tiguas settled near the Rio Grande. In this dry and windy region they built pueblos and farmed. "*Pueblo* is the Spanish word for village," Rafael explains. The Pueblo people made extensive irrigation ditches in order to water their crops. Rafael tells Amanda that early Pueblo farmers grew corn, pumpkins, squash, beans, melons, and gourds. Many of those crops are still grown by the Pueblo today. "We are still farming this land," he says, "and you can see what we grow all around you."

Amanda wants to know more about the types of food the Tiguas eat. "Do you also bake bread?" she asks. "Yes, we do still bake bread today in Pueblo adobe ovens called *hornos*, just like our ancestors have done for over 300 years," says Rafael. "There is bread-baking going on now in the courtyard. Let's take a break and go outside to see the process."

After tasting some bread, Amanda wanders back into the museum to finish her tour with Rafael. She sees display cases with beautiful pottery. Rafael explains that the Pueblo people still have traditional artists who use red clay from nearby mountains to make pottery and paint original designs on each one. Baskets are made from the grasses in the area, and cups and bowls are made from gourds.

"What type of homes did your people live in?" Amanda asks Rafael. "The Pueblo people made large buildings from available resources," says Rafael. "We made adobe bricks from clay mixed with water and dried grass or twigs. We also used rocks and logs to build walls, which were then covered and sealed with mud."

Tigua Indian pottery is becoming very rare. This traditional painted pottery is created without pencil lines or templates.

The Tigua Indians use ovens called *hornos* to bake bread. These beehive-shaped ovens are made out of adobe bricks.

Amanda learns that the Tigua Indians are part of a rich culture.

Amanda wonders out loud, "These homes must be very old." Rafael responds, "Some are, but we've had to fight for this land." He explains that many native tribes in the area fought with Europeans, Americans, and even other American Indian groups for use of land. Many groups native to Texas were moved to reservations in other states, including Oklahoma and New Mexico.

"The Ysleta del Sur Pueblo is one of only three reservations located in Texas today," Rafael tells Amanda. "And we are still thriving, still using our land to produce food, and still making authentic artwork." "And still performing amazing dances!" Amanda interrupts. On that note, Amanda goes outside to the courtyard and picks up a loaf of freshly baked Indian bread. She settles down to watch another dance, catching a glimpse of a rich and fascinating American culture.

Think About It What adaptations did American Indian groups make to strengthen their communities? As you read this chapter, think about choices people make to adapt to where they live and who they live with.

Ysleta del Sur Pueblo is located near El Paso.

SAVVAS realize Go online to access your interactive digital lesson.

105

The First Texans

Envision It!

The first Americans hunted huge animals that died out and became extinct long ago.

Little is known about the possible origins of the American Indians who first lived in North America. Some scientists say they arrived tens of thousands of years ago during an Ice Age. An **Ice Age** is a time when huge sheets of ice and snow cover parts of Earth's land and sea. During the last Ice Age, the oceans shrank. People from Asia could walk to North America across a strip of land that linked the two continents. This land bridge is called Beringia.

The First Americans

These ancient people were hunter-gatherers. A **hunter-gatherer** is a person who collects plants and hunts wild animals for food. They may have followed herds of huge animals, such as woolly mammoths and giant bison, across the grassy plains of Beringia.

Scientists have other theories, or ideas, about possible origins of the first people who may have come to North America. Some think that ancient people from Europe crossed a part of the ocean that was frozen, hunting seals. Or perhaps people sailed along the coasts in small boats.

Routes of First Americans

ASIA

Bering Strait

Beringia Land Bridge

NORTH AMERICA

PACIFIC OCEAN

ATLANTIC OCEAN

0   2,000 mi
0   2,000 km

SOUTH AMERICA

LEGEND
- Dry land during the Ice Age
- Ice cap
- → Route of first people

N W E S

1. **Identify** and circle on the map the strip of land people used to cross from Asia to North America.

Draw a picture of an animal that still lives wild on the Texas plains. Write the animal's name on the line.

UNLOCK THE BIG ?

I will know the possible origins of the first people to arrive in North America and Texas.

Vocabulary

Ice Age	archeologist
hunter-gatherer	quarry
descendant	culture
artifact	agriculture

Possible Origins of the Earliest Texans

The first American Indians of present-day Texas were descendants of the earliest people who came to North America. A **descendant** is a relative, such as a person's children and grandchildren. The ancient Texans probably reached the Texas plains more than 15,000 years ago. They, too, followed and hunted huge animals—mastodons and mammoths.

These ancient Texans adapted to their environment. To adapt means to adjust or change. Bones, ashes, spear points and other artifacts provide clues about how they lived. An **artifact** is an object made and used by people. Scientists called **archeologists** study the culture and artifacts of early people. They say that hunters in Texas threw darts or spears, using atlatls, or long sticks, to kill large game. Back at camp, people used the animal's meat to feed many families. They used the animal's skin to make clothing and tents. Tools were made from the animal's bones.

2. **Summarize** four ways people adapted to their environment and used the animals they hunted.

....

....

....

TEKS
1.A, 9.A, 9.B, 10.A

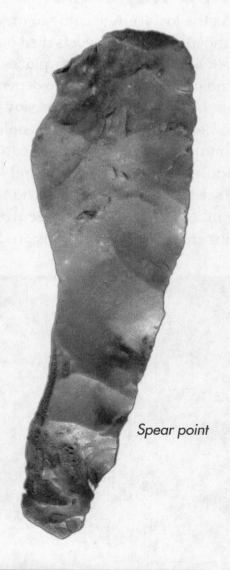

Spear point

SAVVAS realize Go online to access your interactive digital lesson.

107

The Ancient People Trade Resources

As the people followed the great herds across Texas, they discovered resources that they could modify. In the red mesas of the Texas Panhandle, they found flint. Flint is a hard rock that people shaped into points for spears and arrows. At first they gathered the flint from the hillsides. Later they mined it from **quarries**, or open pits where people mine, or dig up rocks. Today the area is known as the Alibates Flint Quarries National Monument.

Tools made from Alibates flint have been found across the Southwest and the Great Plains. Archeologists say this shows the people traded Texas flint far and wide. Trade made it possible for people to have access to resources that could not easily be made or found where they lived.

A New Way of Life

As the last Ice Age came to an end, life in ancient Texas changed. The great beasts died out. Smaller animals such as elk and bears took their places. This changed the culture of the people who had once depended on mammoths and giant bison. **Culture** means way of life.

A new culture took hold. People continued to hunt animals, but they turned more to plants for food. They modified their environment and learned to save and plant the seeds to grow food. This change to agriculture began about 2,000 years ago. **Agriculture** means farming. The main crops were corn, beans, and squash.

3. **Identify** and underline two details on this page that **explain** why ancient people modified and used flint to meet their basic needs.

At the Alibates Flint Quarries National Monument, archeologists found artifacts that showed how the earliest Texans once lived.

People settled in small clusters to be near their fields. They dried food for later use and stored it in woven baskets and clay pots. They traded their baskets, pots, and food for other goods.

4. **Contrast** life for ancient American Indians before and after the last Ice Age.

....

....

....

....

Corn, beans, and squash were the most important crops for early Texans.

Got it?

⬥ TEKS 1.A, 9.A, 9.B, 10.A

5. ◉ **Compare and Contrast Explain** the possible origins of the American Indian groups of North America and Texas. **Compare** where they came from and how they got here.

....

....

....

....

6. ❓ **Describe** how ancient Texans adapted to their environment.

my Story Ideas

....

....

7. Suppose you could send an e-mail to a child who lived in Texas 2,000 years ago. Write the e-mail to share how your life is different from their life. Give at least three examples.

....

....

....

Compare and Contrast

How are things alike? How are things different? These two questions will help you compare and contrast. To **compare** means to tell ways in which things are alike. To **contrast** means to tell ways in which things are different.

Writers often use comparisons and contrasts to make information clearer. They use clue words.

- *Like, both, similar to, as, in common* and *also* show comparisons.
- *Unlike, different, yet, however instead,* and *but* show contrasts.

Sometimes writers let readers make comparisons for themselves.

You can use a Venn diagram to analyze and sort out information to see how things are alike and different. Read the paragraph below about animals of the Ice Age and then look at the diagram.

Ancient American Indian groups in North America might have seen woolly mammoths and saber-toothed cats in their travels. The mammoths looked a bit like elephants but had thick hairy coats. Their tusks were curved. The saber-toothed cats also had thick coats, but they looked something like tigers. Their saber-like teeth were also curved. Mammoths ate grasses, but saber-toothed cats ate ancient horses.

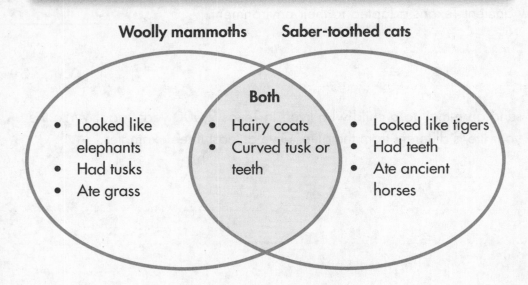

Woolly mammoths   **Saber-toothed cats**

Both

- Looked like elephants
- Had tusks
- Ate grass

- Hairy coats
- Curved tusk or teeth

- Looked like tigers
- Had teeth
- Ate ancient horses

Learning Objective

I will know how to analyze information by comparing and contrasting.

TEKS

ELA 11.C Describe explicit and implicit relationships among ideas in texts organized by comparison.

SS 1.D Compare the ways of life of American Indian groups in Texas and North America before European exploration.

SS 10.A Explain the economic activities various early American Indian groups in North America used to meet their needs and wants such as farming.

SS 21.B Analyze information by comparing and contrasting.

SS 22.D Create written and visual material such as graphic organizers.

Read about the lives of ancient American Indian groups. Then answer the questions.

During the last Ice Age, hunter-gatherers appeared in North America. Some say they followed great herds of giant beasts over a land bridge from Asia. Others say they came by boat or crossed the ice fields from Europe. They spread across the land, hunting woolly mammoth and giant bison for food.

Then the Ice Age ended. The glaciers retreated. The giant beasts died out. Smaller animals, such as elk, buffalo, bear, and deer flourished. The hunter-gatherers had to adapt to a different way of life. Instead of following great mammoths, they hunted the smaller animals and gathered more plants for food than before. They learned to save the seeds and plant them to grow crops for food. Agriculture became important. Instead of traveling all the time, people settled into small villages near their fields. But they still hunted game for meat and gathered wild plants, just like the earliest people.

1. **Analyze** the information. Then circle the clue words in the paragraphs above that show contrast.

2. **Analyze** the information by **comparing** in what ways the lives of the first hunter-gatherers were similar to the lives of the people who learned to farm.

   ....

3. **Analyze** the information by **contrasting** the ways in which the two groups of American Indians were different.

   ....

   ....

   ....

4. On a separate sheet of paper, **create** a Venn diagram to **compare** and **contrast** what you had for breakfast this morning with what you had for dinner last night.

SAVVAS realize Go online to access your interactive digital lesson.

111

American Indians of the Coastal Plains

Envision It!

The Caddo modified their environment and used materials from nature to build their homes.

Three thousand years ago in the river valleys of the eastern and central parts of what is now the United States, an ancient culture built great mounds to honor their gods and the dead. Over time these Mound Builders moved south. They settled in East Texas more than 1,200 years ago. Today we call these descendants of Mound Builders the Caddo (KAD oh).

The Caddo

The Caddo lived in clusters of settlements along the Red River near what is today Nacogdoches. Their community was arranged as a **confederacy**, or a union of people or groups who work together for a common goal. The Caddo confederacy protected settlements from attack. They also organized food for the whole community.

The Caddo were farmers. Each spring, they gathered to plant clearings in the woods. They sowed corn, beans, and squash until every bit of farmland was planted. Groups of men traveled to the plains each year to hunt buffalos for meat and hides. Caddos also fished the rivers of East Texas and gathered acorns, pecans, and walnuts from the forests.

American Indians of Texas

0 200 mi
0 200 km

Kiowa
OK
AR
Red R.
NM
Comanche
Wichita
Trinity R.
Cherokee
LA
Colorado R.
Brazos R.
Caddo
Neches R.
Jumano
Mescalero Apache
Pecos R.
Tonkawa
Atakapa
Alabama-Coushatta
Concho
Lipan Apache
Guadalupe R.
San Antonio R.
Karankawa
Nueces R.
Coahuiltecan
Gulf of Mexico
Rio Grande
MEXICO

LEGEND
- Central Plains
- Great Plains
- Mountains and Basins
- Coastal Plains
— Present-day state borders

1. On the map, **identify** and circle the region in which the Caddo lived. Then **explain** why you think the Caddo settled in clusters along the Red River.

....

UNLOCK THE BIG ?

I will know what life was like in East Texas for American Indians long ago.

Vocabulary

confederacy
reservation
nomad
dugout canoe

Identify three materials from nature used to build your home. Write them in the lines above.

The Caddo modified their environment and used natural resources to make shelter. The houses in Caddo settlements were shaped like cones. Framed with wood, each house was covered in mats made of dried grasses. Beds and chairs inside made them comfortable places. Several families might live together in the same large house.

Today, most Caddo people live in Oklahoma near the town of Binger. In the 1850s, the United States forced the Caddo to leave East Texas and move to Oklahoma to a reservation. A **reservation** is land set aside as a place for American Indians to live. Nearly 5,000 Caddo, direct descendants of the early Mound Builders, live in the United States today. From the Caddo word for "friend" comes the name of our state—Texas.

TEKS
1.B, 1.C, 1.D, 8.A, 9.A, 9.B, 10.A, 14.A, 22.C

2. **Describe** the region in Texas in which the American Indian group called the Caddo lived.

....

....

....

....

....

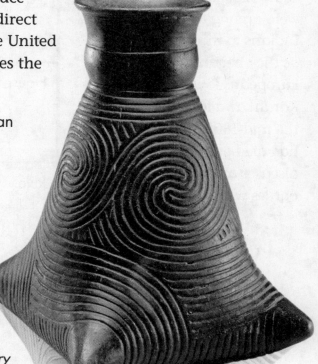

Caddo pottery

SAVVAS realize™ Go online to access your interactive digital lesson.

113

The Karankawa

Along the coast of the Gulf of Mexico, south of the Caddo, lived the Karankawa (kah ran KAH wah). Although they sometimes dwelled in villages, the Karankawa did not have permanent homes. They were nomads. A **nomad** is someone who travels from place to place at different seasons.

In the summer, small bands of family groups roamed inland, hunting deer, small animals and birds. They also gathered wild plants. They took their houses, made of woven grasses and animal skins, with them. The Karankawa governed themselves. Each band had its own leader. In winter, the bands gathered into larger villages along the shore and on islands off the coast. Hundreds of people lived together in wood-frame houses. Each village had its own chief.

The Karankawa traveled the waters of the coast in **dugout canoes,** or boats made by hollowing out long logs. Whole families might travel in a single canoe with their belongings. They fished from the canoes, shooting fish with bows and arrows. They also caught shellfish to eat.

Because they lived on the coast of Texas, the Karankawas were among the first American Indians to meet Europeans as they began to arrive. The Europeans fought the Karankawa for their land. By the mid-1800s the Karankawa had died out from European diseases and from many battles with European groups.

3. ◎ Compare and Contrast Complete the chart to **compare** the ways of life of American Indian groups in Texas before European exploration.

Two Coastal Plains American Indian Groups

	Caddo	Karankawa
Region	....	inland areas, gulf shore
House	permanent, cone-shaped, made of wood and grass	....
Rule	....	family bands led by a chief
Food	squash, beans, buffalo meat, nuts	....

Other American Indians of the Coastal Plains

Many other American Indians lived in East Texas before Europeans came. For a few thousand years, a people called Atakapa (uh TAK uh puh) roamed the coasts and bayous near modern-day Houston and east into Louisiana. To meet their needs and wants, they were hunter-gatherers who caught game, fished, and gathered plants. They ate alligator meat and used alligator oil as an insect repellant. When Europeans came, the Atakapa were exposed to new diseases. Their bodies had not built up any natural defenses, nor did they have medicine to fight them. Therefore, the Atakapa Indians all died.

At the Museum of South Texas History, this display shows how the Coahuiltecan lived during the 1200s.

Compared to the Atakapa, the Coahuiltecan (koh uh WEEL tek un) lived in southern Texas. Hundreds of small bands of these nomadic hunter-gatherers traveled the area. Today, their descendants live throughout South Texas.

The Wichita (WIH chih taw) had a different way of life. They began arriving in Texas in the 1700s. They called lands near the Red River their home. In winter, they hunted as nomads. The rest of the year they farmed in villages. Today the Wichita live near Anadarko, Oklahoma, on a reservation.

Another group, the Tonkawa (TAHNG kuh wuh), probably migrated to central and eastern Texas during the 1600s. Nomadic hunters, they relied on the buffalo for meat and materials. They lived in small teepees. The Tonkawa were moved to Oklahoma in the 1800s. Very few live on the reservation today.

4. Underline three economic activities of the American Indians of the Coastal Plains. Then choose an American Indian group and one activity and **explain** how it helped them meet their needs and wants.

....

....

115

American Indians in East Texas Today

As Europeans moved deep into Alabama in the 1700s, the peoples known as the Alabama and Coushatta began moving to Texas. They were farmers and hunters. In Texas, they joined together, settling in the southeast. Today, the Alabama-Coushatta reservation is the oldest in Texas and the only one in East Texas. Though small in number, they proudly honor their culture.

Cherokee Indians first arrived in East Texas in the late 1700s. They were an agricultural people, living in towns and farming fields. They also hunted game. Many Cherokee still live in Texas today. More than 300,000 Cherokee live throughout the United States.

Many thousands of American Indians live and work in East Texas today. They are farmers, ranchers, teachers, business people, and government officials. However, they still seek to preserve and continue their traditional cultures.

Alabama-Coushatta American Indians live and work in East Texas today.

5. ⊙ **Compare and Contrast** **Analyze** the information about East Texas's American Indian culture in the past and today. Then fill in the Venn diagram.

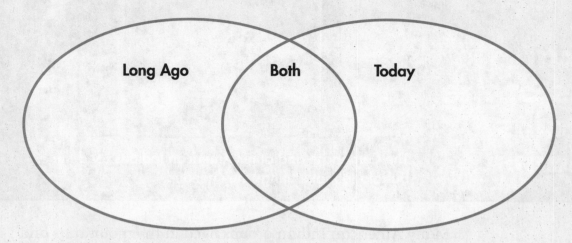

Long Ago   Both   Today

Got it?

🔶 TEKS 1.C, 8.A, 10.A, 14.A, 22.C

6. ⊙ **Compare and Contrast** Write two sentences about the life of the Caddo and Karankawa before European exploration. In one, **compare** how they were alike. In the other, **contrast** how they were different.

....

....

....

7. ❓ **Identify** American Indian groups that lived in Texas before European exploration. Write two questions you would like to ask them.

my Story Ideas

....

....

....

8. Use library and Internet sources to **research** one of the American Indian groups in this lesson. Choose one area of their culture, such as their way of governing, as your focus. Using your research, express your ideas orally to the class about the culture.

....

....

American Indians of the Mountains and Plains

Envision It!

1

2

The Comanche and other American Indians used the buffalo to make things they needed.

Many American Indian groups lived in the mountains and plains of West Texas. Some groups were nomads who roamed the region with striped faces, painted or tattooed. Other American Indian groups settled in communities.

The Jumano

More than 500 years ago, the Jumano (hoo MAH noh) were a well-known American Indian group in the region. One branch of the Jumano lived near the Rio Grande. In this dry, windy region, they built pueblos and farmed. **Pueblo** is the Spanish word for "village." Because there was little rain, the Jumano irrigated their crops. They dug ditches from nearby streams to bring water to their fields.

Each Jumano pueblo had its own government. A **government** is a system by which a group of people are ruled. A chief governed each village. Pueblo buildings were made of **adobe**, a brick made from mud and straw, as well as stone and wood.

Some Jumano people did not live in pueblos. They were nomadic buffalo hunters and traders. They moved east when hunting on the plains was best. **Teepees,** or large tents made of hide, were their homes.

Life at a Jumano hunting camp

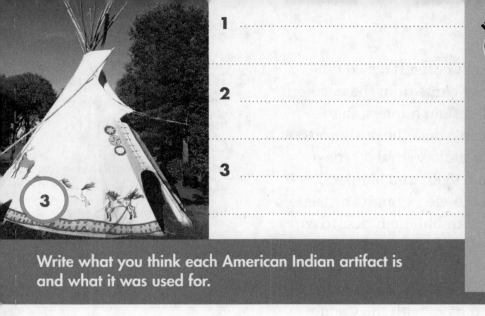

1 ....

2 ....

3 ....

Write what you think each American Indian artifact is and what it was used for.

UNLOCK THE BIG ?

I will know what life was like in West Texas for American Indians long ago.

Vocabulary

pueblo	teepee
government	travois
adobe	ally

In winter, nomadic Jumano returned to be near communities with which they traded. This pattern of settlement allowed Jumanos to get things they did not grow or make themselves. To meet their needs and wants, Pueblo Jumano traded dried beans, squash, and corn. Nomadic Jumano traded buffalo hides and meat. Other goods that were traded included feathers, turquoise, shells, salt, and items from other faraway American Indian groups.

The Jumano had a special way of cooking food. They placed water in a hollow gourd and added hot stones until the water boiled. A Spanish explorer wrote about Jumano cooking:

"As soon as it [the water] boils they put into it what they want to cook, always taking out the stones as they cool off and throwing in hot ones to keep the water boiling steadily."

TEKS

1.B, 1.C, 1.D, 8.A, 9.B, 10.A, 14.A

1. **Identify** and **explain** the Jumano's pattern of settlement.

....

....

....

....

The Comanche

In the 1700s, a powerful group of nomads called the Comanche moved into Texas. They came from the northern Great Plains. Strong fighters and buffalo hunters, the Comanche followed the great herds across the grasslands. They modified every part of the buffalo so that it served them as food or supplies. Clothing, tools, and blankets could be fashioned from skins and bones. Comanche teepees were made of long poles covered with buffalo hides. To carry their teepees and belongings, the Comanche built travoises (truh VOY ziz). A **travois** was a kind of wooden sled dragged by dogs or horses. One economic activity of the Comanche was the trade of buffalo meat and hides with the Caddo and the Wichita.

Horses first came to North America on Spanish ships. When the Comanche people obtained horses, it changed their way of life forever. They became expert riders and trainers. They hunted and fought on horseback, moving more swiftly than ever before.

The Comanche quickly took control of the Great Plains and North Central Plains regions of Texas. They roamed the open land in bands. The bands joined together to fight other American Indians and Europeans for control of their lands. At those times, the Comanche chose a war chief.

By 1875, the United States forced most Comanche people onto a reservation in what is now Oklahoma. Today there are about 15,000 Comanche in the United States. About half of them still live in southwest Oklahoma where they own land and have an organized government that offers many services to tribal members.

2. Think about the geography and natural resources of the Great Plains and North Central Plains region. **Identify** how and why the Comanche modified their environment to help transport their belongings.

....

....

....

....

....

A Comanche horseback rider

120

Members of the Lipan Apache tribe continue to live in Texas today.

The Lipan Apache

The Lipan Apache arrived in the Southwest more than 600 years ago. They were also nomads whose culture depended on buffalo. Dressed in hides and dwelling in hide tents, they followed the herds in family groups. Dogs carried their belongings until the arrival of the horse. The Lipan Apache quickly became expert riders. Pueblo Indians and the Spanish feared the raids of Lipan Apache warriors on horseback.

Over time, groups of Lipan Apache began to farm. They returned twice a year to their fields to plant or to harvest. This made them easy targets for their enemy, the Comanche. The stronger and better-armed Comanche pushed the Lipan Apache south and west to the West Texas plains. There they fought with the Spanish, and later, Mexicans and Americans. By the early 1900s, most of the surviving Lipan Apache lived on the Mescalero Apache reservation. Today Lipan Apache continue to live in Texas.

3. **Sequence** these events in the order they occurred.

_____ Lipan Apache began farming.

_____ The Comanche gained control of the plains and pushed their enemies out.

_____ Horses arrived in North America.

121

Other American Indians of the Mountains and Plains

The Mescalero (mes kuh LAYR oh) Apache nomadic way of life was comparable to the Lipan Apache's ways. They lived along the Rio Grande. They hunted and gathered plant materials. Today their reservation is in New Mexico.

The Concho (KAHN cho) people once lived in what is now southwestern Texas and Mexico. Their bands roamed the arid lands around the Rio Concho and Rio Grande. Near the rivers, they could farm and fish. Away from the rivers, they hunted small animals and gathered roots, nuts, and seeds. The Spanish forced the Concho people to work in mines. Many died. The surviving Concho people joined the Jumano in the 1700s.

The Kiowa (KYE oh wah) lived in the Texas Panhandle. They had come from the north and adapted to living on the plains. Nomads on horseback, they followed the herds. They also raided and fought with other American Indians. They became allies with the Comanche. An **ally** is someone who helps you. Today there are about 12,000 Kiowa.

American Indians in West Texas Today

Today American Indians from different groups live in West Texas. For example, the Tigua live in Ysleta del Sur (is LET uh del soor) near El Paso. They are part of the Pueblo culture and have lived in Texas for about 350 years. The Tigua have kept their traditional government practices and ceremonies.

A band of Kickapoo who have deep roots in Texas received reservation land in the 1980s. The land is near Eagle Pass, in the far western part of the Coastal Plains, a landscape much like that of West Texas. The Kickapoo have held fast to their culture. Each year they travel in family bands to work fields in Mexico and the United States. In the fall, they return to their winter homes to farm, hunt, and take part in ceremonies.

Beaded moccasins of the Kiowa people

American Indian Reservations of Texas

N W E S

0 — 100 mi
0 — 100 km

El Paso 🏠

Alabama-Coushatta
Reservation
Livingston 🏠

Austin ★

Eagle Pass 🏠

Gulf of Mexico

LEGEND
- City
★ Capital
🏠 American Indian reservation

4. 🎯 **Compare and Contrast Identify** and label on the map where the Tigua people and Kickapoo people live in Texas. Then **compare** a way that these American Indian groups keep their culture alive.

....

....

....

Got it?

🪶 **TEKS 1.B, 1.C, 1.D, 10.A, 14.A**

5. 🎯 **Compare and Contrast** Make a list **comparing and contrasting** how the Comanche and the Pueblo Jumano groups governed themselves.

....

....

6. ❓ Think about the life of West Texas Indians who lived near the Rio Concho and Rio Grande. **Describe** how they adapted to life in that arid land.

my Story Ideas

....

....

7. **Identify** three American Indian groups that have lived in West Texas and an economic activity that met the group's needs or wants.

....

....

SAVVAS realize™ Go online to access your interactive digital lesson.

123

Conduct Research

You have just learned about American Indians who have lived in Texas. How can you find more information? You can generate a plan and conduct research. When you do research, you investigate and study primary and secondary sources. You follow the plan, collect information and sometimes come to new conclusions.

Reference sources

One way to learn more is to use reference sources. These are secondary sources that contain facts about subjects. Dictionaries and encyclopedias are reference sources. So are almanacs and atlases. They're available as library books, e-books, and CD–ROMs.

Internet sources

Another way to research a subject is to search the Internet. The Internet is a huge network of computers. The collection of sites on the Internet is called the World Wide Web. Individual sites are called Web sites. These can provide information on the topic you're researching.

A search engine, or browser, can help you acquire information quickly. The search engine usually gives you the title of the Web site and a little information about it.

Step 1 Type in keywords for your search.

Step 2 Click on the word "Search."

Step 3 Click on the title of the Web site you think will be best. Web sites that end in .edu and .gov are usually valid Web sites.

| Lipan Apache Indians in Texas | Search |

About 6,540,000 results (0.21 seconds)   Advanced search

Apache Indians—Texas State Historical Society
Lipan Apache people of Texas
www.tshs.edu/handbook/online/articles/

Lipan Apache Tribe of Texas
Site dedicated to the preservation of the Lipan Apache Tribe of Texas
www.lipanapache.org

Ms. Brown's Lipan Apache Home Page—Travels
Last summer, I traveled across the traditional homelands of the Lipan Apache …
www.blogspot.com/MsBrown/travel.html

I will know how to conduct research using reference and Internet sources.

 TEKS

ELA 23.B Generate a research plan for gathering relevant information about the major research question.

ELA 24.A Follow the research plan to collect information from multiple sources of information both oral and written.

ELA 25 Improve the focus of research as a result of consulting expert sources.

SS 21.A Differentiate between, locate, and use valid primary and secondary sources such as computer software; interviews; biographies; oral, print, and visual material; documents; and artifacts to acquire information about the United States and Texas.

SS 22.C Express ideas orally based on research and experiences.

Suppose a student wanted to find out more about American Indians in the United States or Texas. First, the student visited the library. Next, the student did an Internet search. The first part is on the screen on the opposite page. Use it to answer some of the questions below.

1. What valid secondary reference source might the student **locate** and **use** to find out more about his or her subject?

....

2. Underline the keywords the students used. What is another term or phrase the student could have used to search?

....

3. Why is it important to use keywords in a search of the Internet?

....

....

4. **Locate** the Web sites which seem most valid. Circle one valid Web site. **Explain.**

....

....

5. Suppose you want to learn more about the Caddo. First, generate a research plan. Next, write keywords you would use to search. Then, **locate** and use valid primary and secondary sources. Finally, on a separate sheet of paper, write your report and present your findings in a brief oral report to the class.

....

....

....

Other Civilizations of the Americas

The food that people eat comes from their environment.

North American Culture Areas

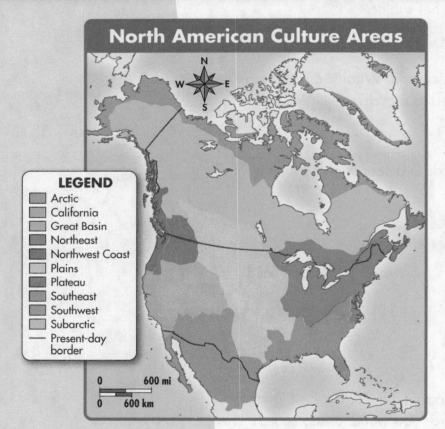

LEGEND
- Arctic
- California
- Great Basin
- Northeast
- Northwest Coast
- Plains
- Plateau
- Southeast
- Southwest
- Subarctic
- — Present-day border

0   600 mi
0   600 km

1. Outline modern-day Texas on the map. **Identify** the culture areas found there.

....

....

....

The ancient American Indians who originated in North America thousands of years ago spread out across the continent. While each American Indian group was different, people in the same area often shared ways of doing things. Experts call these culture areas.

Possible Origins of Other North American Indians

The Inuit (IN oo it), who continue to live in Alaska and Canada, may have been the last of the ancient people to arrive in North America nearly 4,000 years ago. Some scientists think they sailed by boat in the Pacific Ocean. Others believe they traveled across the ice fields that once linked North America and Europe.

The Inuit settled in the icy far north and adapted to the cold. They kept warm and dry in the water in **kayaks,** or canoes with watertight coverings. On land, they rode dogsleds. They used harpoons, spears attached to long ropes, to hunt seals and whales. They also hunted caribou, walrus, and fish.

The center of Inuit culture was the family. They shared the food they hunted. They built winter homes called igloos from blocks of snow. In summer, people lived in animal skin tents.

_____

_____

Write the names of the foods that are shown. Then write where American Indians would have found these foods.

UNLOCK THE BIG ?

I will know what life was like for American Indian groups in North America.

Vocabulary

kayak

import

civilization

empire

Mound Builders

Far to the south of the Inuit in a region around the Mississippi River, an American Indian group had a comparatively different way of life before European exploration. They began to build mounds. Once they had been simple hunters and fishers, growing a few plants. The Mound Builders, as we call them today, were known for their huge earthen structures.

Building huge earthen structures took skill and organization. It is likely that leaders directed many workers at a time. Some of the mounds they built served as graves. Others served as temples. The largest community, the city of Cahokia, may have had 20,000 people. Farmers grew maize, or corn, to support the people. Cahokia served as a marketplace for trade. People could get shells from distant places, or special stones for making tools. The Mound Builders traded for goods and resources throughout much of North America.

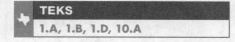

TEKS

1.A, 1.B, 1.D, 10.A

Mound Builders

Problem
To build huge earthen structures was a complex and difficult task.
People needed resources from distant places.

Solution

2. Assess the problems of the Mound Builders. Add their solutions to the organizer.

SAVVAS realize. Go online to access your interactive digital lesson.

127

Puebloans

About 2,000 years ago, groups of hunter-gatherers in the Southwest began to farm corn. They lived in the dry canyon country of what is today Arizona, Colorado, New Mexico, and Utah. The early Puebloans wove baskets and lived in caves or pits.

A Puebloan cliff dwelling in Mesa Verde

Over time they began to grow beans and raise turkeys for food. They built small dams to provide water for their crops. They still hunted game and gathered wild plants for food, but farming grew in importance. They also mastered the art of making pottery.

Some of the Puebloan communities grew very large. Using stone or clay for bricks, people built multistory apartments tucked into the overhanging canyon cliffs. At Mesa Verde in Colorado, villages might have more than 150 rooms. People farmed the mesa tops. In Chaco Canyon in New Mexico, the Puebloans built villages out in the open. Some buildings soared five stories high.

Agriculture was difficult in the harsh desert of Chaco Canyon. To get the things they needed and wanted, the people traded. Chaco became an important center of long-distance trade. Trade routes reached from Chaco to Mexico and the Gulf of California. Chert and obsidian, used to make tools such as points, knives, and scrapers, were common imports. An **import** is a product brought from a different place to trade or sell. Traders also brought in turquoise, used to make beads and to decorate objects. Shells came from the seacoasts. Macaws from distant jungles were kept for their feathers. Pueblo Indians are thought to be the modern descendants of these ancient people.

3. ⊙ **Compare and Contrast** The Inuit, Mound Builders, and Puebloans were not the only American Indians to live in North America before European exploration. The chart identifies other American Indian groups that lived in North America. **Complete** the chart with information about the Puebloans. Then write a sentence comparing and contrasting two of the culture areas in Texas.

....

....

....

....

American Indian Culture Areas of North America

Culture Area	Location	Lifestyle
Arctic	Canada, Alaska	Hunters and gatherers who followed the seasons; traded fur with Russians and later with Europeans
Subarctic	Canada, Alaska	Hunters and gatherers who followed the seasons; traded fur with Europeans
Northeast	Southern Canada to northeastern United States	Mainly farmers, also hunted game in woods and fished in streams and sea; traded fur with Europeans
Southeast	North Carolina to eastern Texas	Mainly farmed corn, beans, and squash, hunted, fished, ate shellfish; forced to work by Spaniards in 1500s
Plains	Central Canada to southern Texas	Followed and hunted bison; farmed corn, beans, and squash along rivers; traded over long distances
Great Basin	Utah, Nevada, Oregon, Wyoming, Colorado, Arizona, California	Hunters and gatherers, mostly ate wild plants and small game; then introduction of horses led to bison hunting
California	California to Mexico	Hunted, fished, collected wild plants; colonized by Spaniards in 1700s
Northwest Coast	Coastland from Oregon to Alaska	Plentiful fish and game led to complex societies; traded with Russians and later with Europeans
Plateau	Parts of Montana, Idaho, Oregon, Washington, Canada	Mainly fished, ate wild plant foods; traded with Europeans in 1800s
Southwest		

Mayan and Aztec Worlds

Great civilizations arose throughout the Americas. A **civilization** is a highly developed human society. In Central America, the Maya cleared the jungle and planted squash, beans, and corn. With plenty of food, they began to build centers to hold religious ceremonies. The centers became cities. Over time the Maya developed an empire. An **empire** is a group of countries under the control of one ruler.

Mayan cities consisted of stone temples, pyramids, palaces, plazas, and courts for playing ball. Skilled artists turned clay into pottery, made jewelry, and wove fabric for clothing. Most people lived in wood and thatch houses. The people developed a writing system. By watching the sky carefully, they created accurate calendars. They also had an advanced system of mathematics.

Although the great cities tumbled into ruin more than a thousand years ago, the Maya people still remain. Today there are more than one million people in Central America who speak Mayan languages.

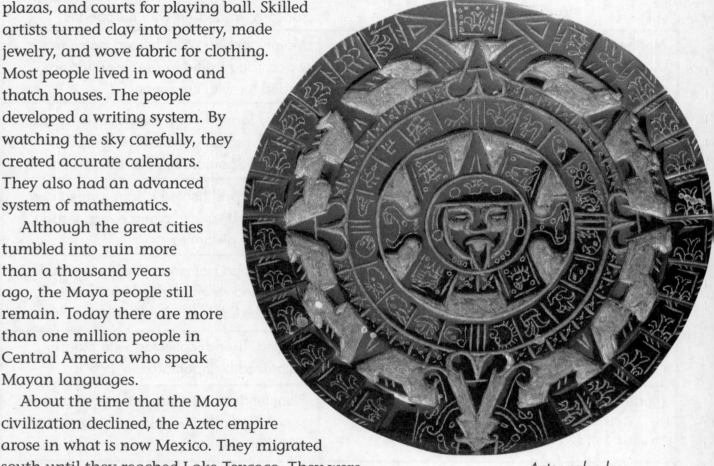

Aztec calendar

About the time that the Maya civilization declined, the Aztec empire arose in what is now Mexico. They migrated south until they reached Lake Texcoco. They were skilled farmers and used irrigation to bring water to dry fields. They grew crops on man-made islands in swamps. Like the Maya, they also developed complex calendars.

By 1325, they had begun to build their great city, Tenochtitlán (tay nawk tee TLAN), on an island in the lake. Stone temples soared high above great plazas, canals, and markets. Perhaps as many as 400,000 people lived there by the early 1500s.

The Aztecs ruled a large territory in central Mexico. They made allies of their trading partners. They fought and conquered enemies. They grew wealthy and powerful, ruling over many other Indian groups from whom they demanded gifts.

Nearly six million people were under Aztec control when Spanish explorers arrived in 1519. In 1521, the Aztec empire ended. Today, Mexico City lies atop the ruins of Tenochtitlán. Descendants of the Aztecs still live in Mexico.

4. **Explain** a great achievement of either the Maya or Aztec.

....

....

....

Teotenango Pyramid in Mexico

TEKS 1.B, 1.D, 10.A

5. **Compare and Contrast Compare** and **describe** a way of life of the Inuits, Mound Builders, and ancient Puebloans before European exploration.

....

....

....

6. **Summarize** how two American Indian groups in this lesson adapted to their environment.

my Story Ideas

....

....

....

7. Suppose you meet a descendant of one of the groups you've read about in this lesson. Think about a conversation in which he or she tells you about the lives of his or her ancestors. Write the conversation on a separate sheet of paper.

....

....

Lesson 1 — TEKS 1.A, 8.A, 9.B

The First Texans

1. Write T for true or F for false next to the following statements about the possible origins of American Indians in North America.

    _____ a. by crossing a land bridge

    _____ b. across ice fields

    _____ c. by boat

    _____ d. from South America

2. **Identify** one reason that ancient Texans stopped traveling as much and settled in small clusters.

    ....

    ....

    ....

3. **Identify** the reasons why ancient American Indians in Texas modified their environment with the use of the natural resource flint. Write an X next to each correct answer.

    _____ a. for protection

    _____ b. for hunting food

    _____ c. for clothing

    _____ d. for transportation

Lesson 2 — TEKS 1.B, 1.C, 1.D, 9.A, 10.A

American Indians of the Coastal Plains

4. ⦿ **Compare and Contrast**
   Identify a similarity and a difference between the Caddo way of life and the Karankawa way of life.

   ....

   ....

   ....

5. Read the question carefully. Determine the best answer to the question from the four answer choices provided. Circle the best answer.

   Which of the following American Indian groups remains in Texas today?

   A Alabama-Coushatta

   B Caddo

   C Karankawa

   D Wichita

6. **Identify** the Caddo and where they settled in Texas. **Describe** the region briefly.

   ....

   ....

   ....

   ....

   ....

   ....

7. Write T for true or F for false next to the following statements about the economic activities of the Karankawa.

_____ a. They roamed in small bands to hunt in summer.

_____ b. They built dugout canoes to use in fishing.

_____ c. They tended small fields of corn.

_____ d. They traveled to the Atlantic coast to trade.

8. **Explain** why the Caddo modified their environment for farming.

....

....

....

....

Lesson 3 🟥 TEKS 1.C, 1.D, 10.A

American Indians of the Mountains and Plains

9. **Describe** the region in Texas in which the Comanche lived.

....

....

....

10. **Compare and contrast** how the Caddo and the Comanche groups governed themselves.

....

....

....

....

11. **Compare** the ways of life of the Jumano and the Lipan Apache before European exploration.

....

....

....

....

Lesson 4 🟥 TEKS 1.A, 1.B, 1.D, 9.A, 10.A

Other Civilizations of the Americas

12. According to scientists, what are the possible origins of the Inuit?

....

....

....

....

....

....

13. **Identify** the Mound Builders, where they lived, and what they are best known for.

....

....

....

....

14. Write an X next to each statement that describes an economic activity of the Puebloan people.

_____ a. raising turkeys

_____ b. raising horses

_____ c. building dams to water fields

_____ d. trading for chert and shells

15. **Compare** the ways of life of Maya and Aztec civilizations before European exploration by listing two things they had in common.

....

....

....

....

....

16. **Identify** one way the Aztecs changed their environment. **Infer** how this change helped them.

....

....

....

....

....

17. **How do people adapt to where they live?** TEKS 9.A

Analyze the picture of the Caddo village below and answer the question.

How did the Caddo adapt to and modify the environment when they came to Texas?

....

....

....

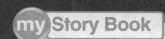

Go online to write and illustrate your own **myStory Book** using the **myStory Ideas** from this chapter.

How do people adapt to where they live?

TEKS
SS 9.A, 9.B
ELA 15

For thousands of years the first Texans found inventive ways to adapt to their environment. Whether they were nomads or villagers, hunters or farmers, they created rich cultures based on the resources they could find, use, or trade for.

Think about the ways people adapt to or modify their environments today. **Identify** and **describe** at least three examples.

....

....

....

Draw an image that shows one of your examples.

Exploration and Colonization of Texas

 my Story Spark

Why do some people leave their homelands?

Describe a time when you or someone you know moved from one country or community to another. **Explain** why you or they moved.

....

....

....

....

....

Texas Essential Knowledge and Skills

2.A Summarize motivations for European exploration and settlement of Texas.

2.B Identify the accomplishments and explain the impact of significant explorers on the settlement of Texas.

2.C Explain when, where, and why the Spanish established settlements and Catholic missions in Texas.

2.D Identify Texas' role in the Mexican War of Independence and the war's impact on the development of Texas.

2.E Identify the accomplishments and explain the economic motivations and impact of significant empresarios.

6.B Translate geographic data, population distribution, and natural resources into a variety of formats.

8.A Identify and explain clusters and patterns of settlement in Texas at different time periods.

8.B Describe the location of various towns and cities in Texas, past and present.

8.C Explain the geographic factors such as landforms and climate that influence patterns of settlement and the distribution of population in Texas, past and present.

12.A Explain how people in different regions of Texas earn their living, past and present.

12.B Explain how geographic factors have influenced the location of economic activities in Texas.

12.C Analyze the effects of exploration, immigration, migration, and limited resources on the economic development and growth of Texas.

14.B Identify and compare characteristics of the Spanish colonial government and the early Mexican governments and their influence on inhabitants of Texas.

16.A Explain the meaning of various patriotic symbols and landmarks of Texas.

17.D Identify the importance of historical figures and important individuals who modeled active participation in the democratic process.

19.C Summarize the contributions of people of various racial, ethnic, and religious groups in the development of Texas.

20.A Identify famous inventors and scientists and their contributions.

21.A Differentiate between, locate, and use valid primary and secondary sources to acquire information about the United States and Texas.

21.B Analyze information by identifying cause-and-effect relationships.

22.D Create written and visual material.

Henry and Nancy Jones

Early Texas Pioneers

my Story Video

"Wow, this log cabin is huge!" exclaims Leigha as she walks up to an old structure. "You're right. This is a huge cabin, and it's a replica of one built in the early 1800s," says volunteer J. R. "This style of home is called a Dog-Trot Cabin and is located on one of the park's oldest farms," he explains.

Today, Leigha is getting a tour of George Ranch Historical Park in Richmond, Texas. She is accompanied by her guide, J. R., who has worked at the park for many years. He loves sharing the park's history and explaining why this area became a popular spot for early Texas colonists. "The park is more than just wide open space; it's a real working ranch with lots of history," says J. R.

Leigha is visiting George Ranch Historical Park to learn more about the lives of Texas pioneers.

George Ranch Historical Park is located just 30 miles from downtown Houston and sits on more than 20,000 acres of land. J. R. explains, "The farm was established in 1824, when Texas was still part of Mexico, and has been handed down for generations." Leigha asks who the first people were to live there. "The farm was originally owned by the pioneers Henry and Nancy Jones. They came down here in 1822," says J. R. "They were part of Stephen F. Austin's Old Three Hundred colonists."

Austin's colony settled near the Brazos River.

The interior of the log cabin takes you back in time and gives you a glimpse of what life was like in 1830s Texas.

Austin was an empresario, or land agent, whose job was to find an area and attract settlers to move to Texas, where they received land grants from the Mexican government. "Austin chose this area because of its proximity to the Brazos River," explains J. R.

Like the Jones family, many people jumped at the opportunity to own a large piece of land. "Henry and Nancy moved here from Arkansas Territory in 1822 and claimed 4,428 acres of land in 1824," adds J. R. "What did they do with all this land?" asks Leigha. "Well, some people grew crops, some raised livestock, and some people did both."

To fully understand what life was like for the colonists, Leigha tries her hand at tilling, or preparing, the field. Without modern-day farming tools, Leigha quickly realizes how difficult it must have been to run a farm in the 1830s. "How old were the children when they started to work?" asks Leigha. "Well, in those times, if you could walk you could work. You could be three years old and help Mom and Dad out in the fields," explains J. R. "The Jones family had lots of help. They had 12 children to help share the chores."

Children of Texas pioneers used to help out in the fields. Leigha is trying her hand at tending the field with old tools.

At the farm, interpreters recreate the conversations and daily chores of early Texas pioneers.

At George Ranch, sunflowers grow tall in the warm Texan sun.

Next, J. R. leads Leigha to the outbuildings surrounding the farm. The outbuildings include the smokehouse, barn, hog pen, and chicken coop. "The outbuildings were very important extensions of the family's home," says J. R. "These buildings provided support for the family's daily operations," he adds. "I like the chore of feeding the animals, especially the chickens," says Leigha. "These ones are my favorite," she says, petting the grey and white hen.

As Leigha's tour comes to an end, she is happy that she had the chance to see and experience how the Jones family lived back in the 1830s.

"I'm amazed that the Jones family moved here and that they were able to build all of this," says Leigha, "because life sure wasn't easy back then." J. R. smiles and says, "Well, we like to say that in order to succeed in the future, you have to understand the past."

Think About It What does the story of the Jones family tell you about why people may have wanted to leave their homelands and come to a colony in Texas? What did they hope they would find there?

Leigha would have liked the chore of feeding the animals, especially the chickens.

Europeans Explore Texas

Explorers from Spain came to the Americas. When they arrived, they met many American Indian groups.

The conquistadors took gold jewelry similar to this piece back to Spain.

In the 1400s, powerful kings and queens in Europe were competing with each other. Each had a strong desire to expand and wanted more lands to rule and riches to spend than the others. The economic opportunities were great. There were spices worth a fortune in Asia. However, the overland trade route was long and controlled by others. So the king and queen of Spain backed the plan of a sea captain and trader named Christopher Columbus. He would reach Asia by sailing west around the world.

Spain Reaches the Americas

In 1492, Columbus reached an island near Florida. He was certain it was near Asia when he claimed the land for Spain. He didn't find the rich Asian cities he had heard of or the spices he sought. He did see good land, many people, and some gold.

Soon Spain sent explorers to find the gold and conquer the land and its people. It was the explorers who learned the land was not part of Asia at all. It was a land off their maps and unknown to them. It was a new land.

Spain sent an expedition of 500 soldiers led by Hernán Cortés. An **expedition** is a journey made for a special purpose. Cortés was a **conquistador** (kohn KEES tah dohr), which means "conqueror." In 1519, Cortés landed in Mexico and set out to conquer the Aztecs, the richest and most powerful people there. It took two years and the help of other American Indians, but the Aztec empire finally fell and became part of New Spain. Aztec gold, silver, and pearls were sent to Spain.

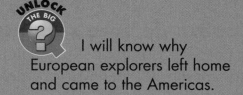

I will know why European explorers left home and came to the Americas.

Vocabulary

expedition
conquistador
slavery
colony

Write about what you think may have happened when American Indians and Europeans first met.

In 1519, Alonso Álvarez de Piñeda (uh LAHN zoh AL vuh rez deh pih NYAY dah) became the first explorer to reach present-day Texas. He sailed along the Gulf Coast making the area's first map.

TEKS
2.A, 2.B

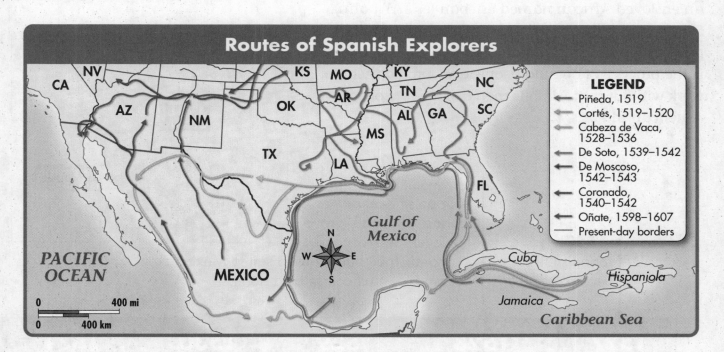

Routes of Spanish Explorers

LEGEND
← Piñeda, 1519
← Cortés, 1519–1520
← Cabeza de Vaca, 1528–1536
← De Soto, 1539–1542
← De Moscoso, 1542–1543
← Coronado, 1540–1542
← Oñate, 1598–1607
— Present-day borders

PACIFIC OCEAN

MEXICO

Gulf of Mexico

Cuba

Hispaniola

Jamaica

Caribbean Sea

0   400 mi
0   400 km

1. **Identify** and circle on the map legend the names of the explorers who passed through Texas or along the Texas coastline. Then **summarize** Spain's motivations for sending explorers to America.

....

....

Cabeza de Vaca's Journey

In 1528, a Spanish expedition landed in what is today Florida. Among the 600 men was Álvar Núñez Cabeza de Vaca (AHL vahr NOO nyes kah BEHZ suh day VAH kah). He was one of the few to live and return home. De Vaca wrote about his experiences in a journal. That is how historians know about his accomplishments.

Upon landing, 300 men went inland to explore. They got lost. Months later they found the shore again but had no ships and few supplies. Desperate, the men built rafts. The sails were made out of shirts and pants. They headed west toward Mexico. They sailed safely close to shore until a storm carried the rafts out to sea. For two weeks the men feared they would never see land again. Then early one morning Cabeza de Vaca heard the sounds of waves breaking on a shore.

Some historians believe the men came ashore near present-day Galveston Island. Then they separated, and many died during the winter. Years later, Cabeza de Vaca found two of the Spaniards and an enslaved African named Esteban (es TAY bahn). Slavery was an accepted practice among Spaniards and many American Indian groups, as well. **Slavery** is the practice of owning people and forcing them to work without pay. All four men became prisoners of American Indians.

Cabeza de Vaca's journal

TEXAS

Area of detail

Galveston Island

Gulf of Mexico

1527
Spanish fleet leaves Spain.

A Spanish fleet arrives in Florida. The main group, however, gets lost and stranded. They build rafts to sail to Mexico but are blown off course by a storm.

1527   **1528**   **1529**   **1530**   **1531**

Fall 1528
Cabeza de Vaca survives the storm and lands near Galveston Island after weeks at sea with 80 men.

Eventually, the four men escaped and walked across present-day Texas and much of the Southwest. They walked for more than 2,000 miles on bare feet, looking for other Spaniards. Finally in 1536 they were reunited with Spanish soldiers and reached Mexico City. It was eight years after their journey had begun.

Once back in Spain, Cabeza de Vaca told Spanish officials about seven cities of gold called Cíbola (SEE boh lah). He had not seen these cities himself but had heard about them from American Indians.

Spain wanted these cities of gold, so they sent an exploring party to find them. Fray Marcos de Niza led the group. Esteban was forced to guide them north. When they neared a Zuni Indian village said to be one of the golden cities, Esteban went ahead of the others and was killed. Hearing of his death, Niza quickly left without ever seeing the golden cities. But in Mexico he spoke of them as if he had.

2. Use the text to **identify** the missing dates on the timeline. Then **identify** the accomplishments of Cabeza de Vaca and **explain** why he was a significant explorer.

....

....

1534
Cabeza de Vaca escapes the island with two other Spaniards and an enslaved African named Esteban. They travel along the Texas coast hoping to reach Mexico.

1537
Cabeza de Vaca returns to Spain and tells stories about the seven cities of gold he heard about from American Indians.

| 532 | 1533 | 1534 | 1535 | 1536 | 1537 |

1533
Cabeza de Vaca and the other survivors struggle to live with American Indians in eastern Texas for four years.

1535
The four men meet different American Indian groups along their journey.

1536
The four men are reunited with Spanish soldiers in Mexico.

This replica of a 16th-century Spanish galleon is similar to the one Coronado captained.

Francisco Coronado Explores Texas

If there were seven cities of gold, Spain wanted to find and conquer them. So another great expedition was planned. In 1540, Francisco Vásquez de Coronado (frahn SEES koh VAHS kez day kor oh NAH doh) gathered more than 300 Spaniards and about 1,000 American Indians. Along with cattle, sheep, horses, and mules, they set out for the golden cities.

When they reached a Zuni village, Coronado attacked. He won that battle but found no gold. Coronado was determined to find some, so he kept going.

Coronado sent some men west to explore. He led the others east. They searched village after disappointing village. Then a captive of the Pawnee Indians named the Turk said he could take them to a land of great riches called Quivira (key VEHR uh). They followed this man across the area known today as the Texas Panhandle and then north to Quivira. They traveled a long way to find a village with houses made of grass. When Coronado realized he had been fooled, he had the Turk killed. After two years, the great expedition returned to Spanish Mexico. They had no gold, but they had made an impact on future settlement in Texas. They had learned about a vast land and its people.

3. ◎ **Cause and Effect Identify** and underline one accomplishment of Coronado's expedition.

More Spanish Explorers in Texas

Two years before Coronado set out looking for the golden cities of Cíbola, an expedition left Spain with ten ships and about 600 men. It was led by Hernando de Soto. Like Coronado, he heard the stories told by Cabeza de Vaca and wanted to conquer cities filled with gold. Both De Soto and Coronado traveled with Franciscan missionaries. The missionaries gave spiritual help on the expeditions. They also tried to teach their Christian religion to American Indians.

De Soto never reached what is today Texas. He led his expedition through present-day Florida all the way to the Mississippi River, where he died. It was Luis de Moscoso (loo EES deh moh SKOH soh) who led the group through what is today eastern Texas. They did not find the riches they were looking for, but Moscoso saw oil shimmering on the water near the coast.

Juan de Oñate (hwan deh oh NYAH teh) led an expedition into present-day New Mexico in 1598. His mission was to conquer the people, claim the land for Spain, found a colony, and look for gold. To get there he crossed the Rio Grande at a place he called *El Paso del Norte*, "the pass to the north." Today this site is named El Paso.

4. **Identify** and write the correct name for each explorer.

Led an expedition to present-day New Mexico through what is today El Paso

....

....

Led an expedition in search of gold; found the Mississippi River

....

Led an expedition in search of gold; saw oil

....

La Salle Comes to Texas

While Spain was exploring to the south, France sent explorers north to what is today Canada. At first the French were looking for furs to buy and sell. Soon they had the desire to expand. They were looking for new lands to claim and settle, too.

In 1682, fur trader René-Robert Cavelier, Sieur de La Salle, explored the Mississippi River all the way down to the Gulf Coast. He claimed the huge river valley for France and named it Louisiana. The name honored the king of France, Louis XIV.

To protect the claim, La Salle wanted to start a French colony at the mouth of the Mississippi River. A **colony** is a settlement of people who have moved to another country but are still ruled by their home country. La Salle went back to France for men and supplies. Then, in 1684, he and his crew set sail for Mississippi. La Salle's ships missed the site by 500 miles. They landed on the shore of Matagorda Bay on the Texas coast, land claimed by Spain.

La Salle's men built a fort on a marsh. Settlers there did not fare well. Many died, some from disease and others from attacks by American Indians. La Salle, meanwhile, continued to explore the area. He was eventually killed by one of his own men.

By the time Spanish soldiers arrived, the fort was empty and in ruins. The message to Spanish officials, however, left a strong impact. The French were interested in competing with Spain by setting up a colony near Spanish territory. Spain's claims had to be defended or they would be lost.

5. Locate and circle the spot where La Salle landed in 1684. Then **explain** why he landed there.

....

....

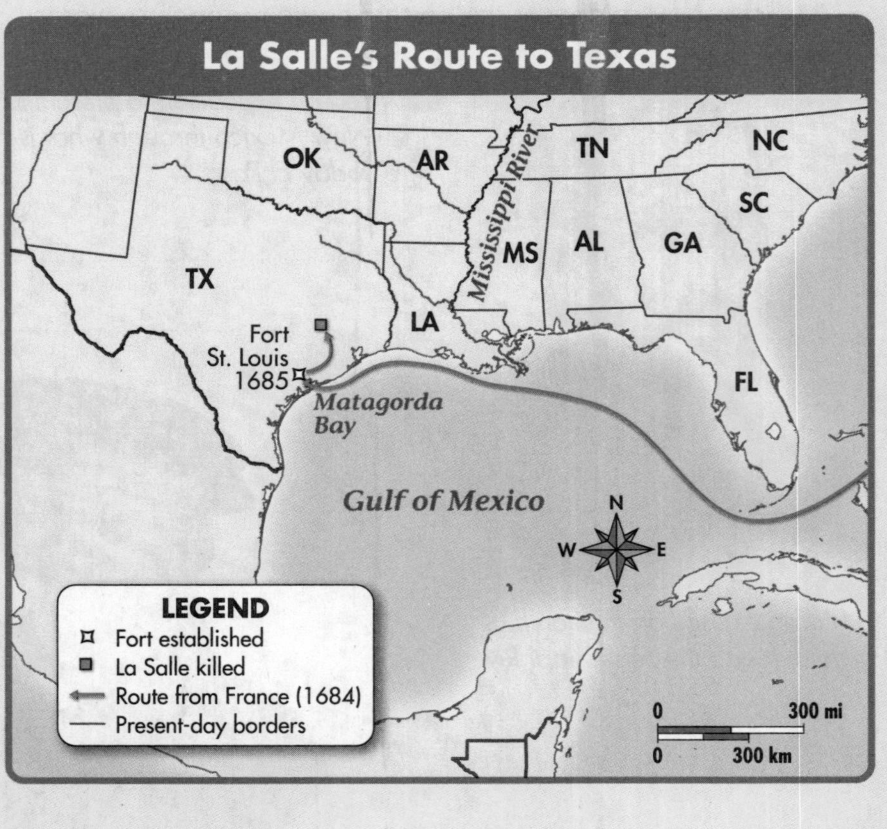
La Salle's Route to Texas
OK
AR
TN
NC
SC
GA
AL
MS
Mississippi River
TX
LA
FL
Fort St. Louis 1685
Matagorda Bay
Gulf of Mexico
N
S
E
W
LEGEND
Fort established
La Salle killed
Route from France (1684)
Present-day borders
0 300 mi
0 300 km

6. ◉ **Cause and Effect** **Analyze** the impact of French colonization of Spanish Texas. Then complete the graphic organizer.

French Colonization of Spanish Texas

Cause

Entry of the French into Spanish territory

Effect

⬤ TEKS 2.A, 2.B

Got it?

7. ◉ **Cause and Effect** **Explain** the impact of Cabeza de Vaca's stories about the seven cities of gold on the settlement of Texas.

....

....

8. ❓ **Think** of people you know who have moved to Texas. Maybe your family has moved, or the family of a classmate. **Identify** and write why you think they left their homes and moved to Texas.

my Story Ideas

....

....

....

9. **Summarize** the motivations, or reasons, why European explorers came to Texas. Then on a separate piece of paper, create a chart **identifying** the accomplishments of Cabeza de Vaca, Francisco Coronado, and René-Robert Cavelier, Sieur de La Salle, including economic opportunity, the land they explored, and their impact on the settlement of Texas.

....

....

....

Cause and Effect

Analyzing a cause and its effects helps us understand what we read. A **cause** tells why something happened. An **effect** is what happened. Sometimes writers use the words *cause* and *effect* to show readers how events are related. Other times, you have to look for clue words such as *because, if, then, so,* and *changed* to help you identify the causes and effects. Follow the tips below as you read.

- First, read the title to know the topic.
- Identify a change or effect for that topic and circle it. A cause can have more than one effect.
- To find the causes, underline the order of events or a description of how things were before the change.

Read the following passage. Then read the chart to identify the cause and effect.

The Spanish Settle East Texas

In 1685, La Salle brought French settlers, soldiers, and skilled workers to what is today considered southeastern Texas. They built a fort on land claimed by France's enemy, Spain. La Salle explored west toward the Rio Grande. He didn't see any Spaniards. Then he went east. He still didn't see any Spaniards. He must have wondered where the Spanish were. In fact, there were no Spanish settlements in the area. La Salle changed that, however. As soon as Spanish officials heard of his colony, they sent soldiers, priests, and settlers to the region, because that would help defend their land claims. The Spanish settlement of East Texas began.

Cause

France built a fort on land claimed by Spain. France and Spain were enemies.

→

Effect

Spanish officials sent soldiers, missionaries, and settlers to settle East Texas.

TEKS

ELA 11.C Describe explicit and implicit relationships among ideas in texts organized by cause-and-effect.

SS 2.A Summarize motivations for European exploration and settlement of Texas, including economic opportunity, competition, and the desire for expansion.

SS 2.B Identify the accomplishments and explain the impact of significant explorers, including René Robert Cavelier, Sieur de la Salle, on the settlement of Texas.

SS 21.B Analyze information by identifying cause-and-effect relationships.

Try it!

Reread the first paragraph on page 140 and answer the following questions about analyzing cause and effect.

1. What change is explained?

....

....

2. How were things in Europe before the change explained in question 1?

....

....

....

....

3. **Analyze** the information in the paragraph to identify a cause-and-effect relationship.

Causes → **Effect**

4. Reread the section titled **Spain Reaches the Americas** on page 140 to complete the following cause-and-effect chart.

Cause → **Effect**

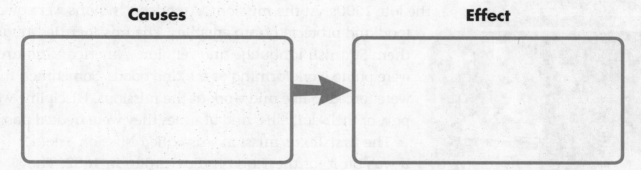

Spanish Settlements in Texas

Envision It!

Cities change over time. This picture shows what El Paso looked like hundreds of years ago.

The Spaniards occupied the land, setting up missions and towns. A **mission** is a settlement where religion is taught. The Spanish missions were home to missionaries and American Indians. The Spanish government was motivated to build missions in order to expand and protect their territory, and claim and develop land. They also wanted to teach Catholic beliefs and work skills to native people.

Building Missions

The Spanish began to build Catholic missions in Texas in the late 1600s. At the missions, American Indians were given food and protected from enemies. The missionaries taught them Spanish language and religion. American Indians were put to work farming or making goods. Sometimes, they were forced to live and work at the missions. Discipline was part of their daily life, and at times they were treated poorly.

The first Texas mission was called Mission Ysleta. It was built for the Tigua Indian group in 1682. The settlement that grew nearby is now the city of El Paso. The mission's church is open to this day.

In East Texas, missions were built near French Louisiana to establish settlements and a claim to the land. These settlements could discourage the French from competing for land and coming into the area and along the coast.

People still worship in Mission Ysleta, the first mission of Texas, in El Paso.

1. **Explain** when and why the Spanish established Caholic missions and settlements in Texas.

....

UNLOCK THE BIG ?

I will know why Spanish missions and other communities were established in Texas and what life was like then.

Vocabulary

mission	vaquero
presidio	*quinceañera*
villa	

It is 1682 and you just moved to El Paso. Write about what you see around you.

Other missions were founded on the San Antonio River. The largest is Mission San José, built around 1720 near present-day San Antonio. The American Indians in the mission developed a large piece of land as they learned ranching and farming skills. By 1749, they were herding 2,000 cattle and 1,000 sheep. They irrigated the farmland and grew corn, beans, lentils, potatoes, sugar cane, cotton, melons, and fruit. They built flour mills run by water power, a granary (for storing corn and wheat), and workshops. They also built houses on the grounds of the mission, creating a community. This allowed for the economic development and growth of this community. Today the mission is called the Queen of the Missions. It is part of the San Antonio Missions National Historical Park.

TEKS
2.A, 2.C, 8.A, 12.C, 16.A, 19.C

2. **Analyze** the illustration of the mission. **Identify** and circle two places where there were economic opportunities.

San José Mission in Texas

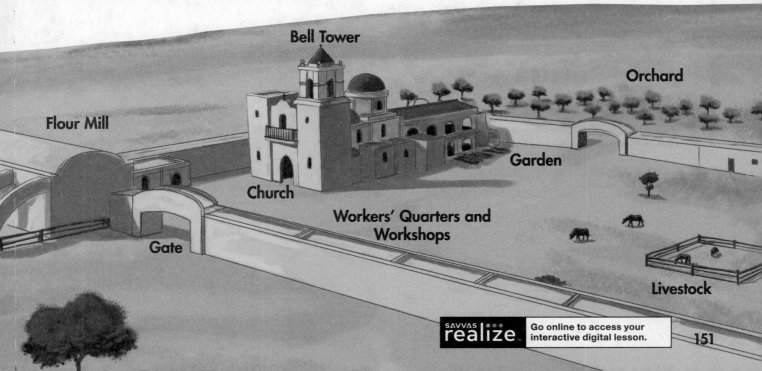

Bell Tower

Orchard

Flour Mill

Garden

Church

Workers' Quarters and Workshops

Gate

Livestock

Presidios and Villas

Some American Indians did not want missions built on their lands. For example, in 1680, not far from Texas, in what is now Sante Fe, New Mexico, the Pueblo Indians fought and drove the Spanish from their lands.

To protect missions from attack, the Spanish sent soldiers. They established forts called **presidios** near the missions. The arrival of soldiers helped develop an area because they carried news and mail. They protected supply wagons and travelers to the region. Some soldiers and their families built homes near the presidio. Soon merchants came to sell them goods from Spain. **Villas,** or towns, often grew near the presidios.

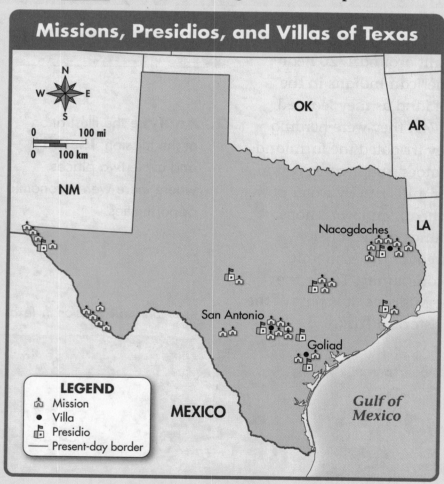

Missions, Presidios, and Villas of Texas

OK

AR

NM

LA

Nacogdoches

San Antonio

Goliad

MEXICO

Gulf of Mexico

LEGEND
- Mission
- Villa
- Presidio
- Present-day border

3. **Locate** and circle the presidios with nearby villas. **Explain** where the Spanish established villas in Texas and why they did so.

Villas also grew around successful missions. But the Spanish government worried that those villas were not enough. They needed more Spaniards to expand their territory and claim the land. So Spanish officials offered people land, livestock, tools, and weapons to move to Spanish Texas. Settlers came from Mexico and from other parts of the world. For example, in the 1730s, 55 people came from Spain's Canary Islands, a group of islands off the west coast of Africa. They settled around San Antonio and founded the town in 1731. In the villas, both men and women planted and harvested crops. Everyone helped with the animals. Some people in the villa offered services, like trading or blacksmithing. For enjoyment, the people had dances, concerts, and fiestas, or celebrations.

In 1747, José de Escandón had a plan to establish a settlement. He said the lower Rio Grande was a good place for settlers to establish towns and start ranching and farming businesses. Spanish officials granted his plan and made him governor. A few years later, the colony had 23 villas. A few of them, such as Laredo, were in present-day Texas. The others were south of the river in Mexico. Today Escandón is called Father of the lower Rio Grande Valley because of his important work in developing the area. In fact, a statue of Don José de Escandón exists in Alice, Texas, which grew to become one of the largest cattle-shipping centers in the United States in the late 1800s.

Don José de Escandón

4. In the paragraph above, underline when and where José de Escandón settled a colony. Then **explain** why Escandón is an important individual in Texas history.

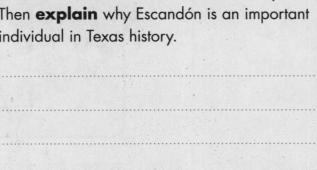

A Mix of Cultures

All the people who came to Texas brought their culture with them. The American Indians who first came brought their knowledge of America's plants and animals. When the Spanish arrived, they also learned how to grow and use these plants that were new to them, such as corn, squash, beans, tomatoes, and potatoes. Spaniards also learned about animals such as the American turkey and buffalo.

The Spanish also brought new plants and animals to the area. They brought the first horses to Texas. Knowledge of how to raise and ride horses spread and changed the lives of the Plains Indians. The Spanish also brought the first cattle for beef as well as sheep, goats, pigs, and chickens. They brought new fruits and vegetables such as lettuce, grapes, apples, and oranges. The mix of people and their cultures changed how people cooked and what they ate.

5. ◉ **Categorize Identify** and write some of the things that the Europeans and American Indians exchanged.

American Indian and European Exchange

From the Americas to Europe	From Europe to the Americas

American Indians shared plants and animals that were new to Europeans.

Europeans brought many plants and animals that were new to the Americas.

American Indian musical instruments

The mix of cultures changed music too. American Indians played their music on flutes and drums. At the missions they heard string instruments such as guitars, violins, and harps. Soon they learned how to play the new instruments, and their music changed. Here is what a Spanish priest wrote in 1761:

"Most of [the American Indians] play some musical instrument, the guitar, the violin or the harp. All have good voices, and on feasts . . . a choir of four . . . with musical accompaniment, sings so beautifully that it is a delight to hear it."

—Spanish priest, 1761

Some of the mission Indians converted, or changed, to the Catholic religion. Many converted while still keeping some of their traditional beliefs. For example, they would ask spirits for help before a hunt. Still others refused to change their religion at all.

6. **Cause and Effect Analyze** the effects of Spanish exploration on the economic and cultural development and growth of Texas.

....

....

....

Spanish Heritage in Texas

Spain ruled what is now Texas for more than one hundred years. You can still find Spanish heritage wherever you look. You can hear it, see it, taste it, live in it, and even wear it.

Many Texans speak Spanish at home, and others learn it in school. Everyone uses Spanish words to locate places. Look at a Texas map and you will see many Spanish names, from the Guadalupe Mountains to Padre Island.

Spain greatly influenced the art and architecture of Texas. Visit an art museum and you will see the Spanish influence on many of the paintings and sculptures. You can see dance that has a Spanish flair, too. Many homes and public buildings today are built in the old Spanish Mission style. The missions themselves are important symbols of Texas's rich heritage and history. For example, the Alamo, a mission church, was restored for visitors. Today this famous landmark is a symbol of patriotism for Texans and the nation.

Spanish culture influenced ranching and the rodeo. It was the Spanish cowboys called **vaqueros** (vah KAYR ohz) who developed skills such as roping and branding cattle. The spurs and chaps worn by later cowboys were from the vaqueros, too. Even the word *rodeo* is Spanish.

A team of cowboys roping steer at a rodeo in Llano, Texas

Some traditions that began in Mexico have also become a tradition in Texas. The Day of the Dead is a Mexican tradition when families celebrate loved ones who have died. The *quinceañera* is another Mexican tradition. It is a celebration that girls have when they turn 15.

7. **Identify** and underline a Mexican tradition in Texas. Then **summarize** the contributions of the Spanish people in the development of Texas.

....

....

....

A quinceañera is an important family tradition for many Texans of Mexican American heritage.

Got it?

TEKS 2.A, 2.C, 12.C

8. ⊙ **Cause and Effect** **Analyze** and **explain** the effects of Spanish exploration on the economic development and growth of Texas.

....

....

9. Suppose you are a Spanish Catholic priest who has been sent to build a mission in Texas in the 1600s. **Summarize** the motivations of the Spanish government for sending you.

my Story Ideas

....

....

....

10. **Explain** when, where, and why the Spanish established settlements by building the following Catholic missions in present-day Texas.

Mission Ysleta ....

....

Mission San José ....

....

Primary and Secondary Sources

A **primary source** is made or written by a person present at an event. It can be an artifact, such as an American Indian spear point. Primary sources are also oral material, such as a recorded interview or speech, or print material, such as a document, photograph, letter, or journal. A journal is a daily record of news and events in a person's life. Sometimes it is called a diary. The excerpt below is a primary source from a journal written by Marqués de Rubí in 1767. Rubí was sent to Spanish Texas by the king of Spain to inspect the area's defenses.

> [Mission], Rosario...is located on the south side of the river....Its possessions and property are...[not great] and the number of its Indians is [not] certain, for they frequently desert and flee to the coast.
>
> — Marqués de Rubí (1767)

A **secondary source** is a secondhand account of history. It comes from someone who was not present at an event. A biography or a textbook, either in print or on computer software, is a secondary source. The writer collects information about a time, place, or person and describes it in his or her own words. Here is an example:

> Mission Rosario was begun in 1754 to make peace with the American Indians in the area. The Spanish feared the French would settle their lands. Usually the Indians spent the winter in the mission but would leave in the spring when they could produce their own food.

To know how to differentiate between and use a valid primary or secondary source, ask yourself questions such as the following:

- Is this source from the event itself? Does the writer use the present tense to describe what he or she sees?

- Does the writer of this source draw conclusions about a past event? Does the writer use the past tense?

Learning Objective

I will know how to differentiate between and use primary and secondary sources.

 TEKS

ELA 24.A Follow the research plan to collect information from multiple sources of information both oral and written.

SS 2.C Explain when, where, and why the Spanish established settlements and Catholic missions in Texas.

SS 21.A Differentiate between, locate, and use valid primary and secondary sources such as computer software; interviews; biographies; oral, print, and visual material; documents; and artifacts to acquire information about the United States and Texas.

SS 22.D Create written and visual material such as journal entries.

 **Try** *it!*

Use the quotations on the previous page to **differentiate** between valid primary and secondary sources and **acquire** information about the United States and Texas.

1. **Locate** and underline an example of present tense in the first quotation. **Explain** how this information validates this source as primary.

   ....

   ....

2. **Identify** an example of a conclusion drawn by the writer in the second text. **Explain** how this information validates this source as secondary.

   ....

   ....

   ....

3. Now, use both quotations to **draw your own conclusions** and **acquire** information about the United States and Texas. **Use** examples from the quotations to support your answer.

   ....

   ....

   ....

   ....

4. **Apply** **Create** your own primary source record of an event from your life that shows how you are from Texas or the United States, such as a journal entry, interview, or a video recording. **Locate** and **use** visual materials, artifacts, and drawings to add interest and information to your work. **Express** your ideas orally by presenting your finished product to the class.

Mexican Texas: A New Era

These items are used by cowboys in Texas.

A parade celebrates Mexican independence in Freeport, Texas.

In the early hours of September 16, 1810, Father Miguel Hidalgo rang the church bells in Dolores, Mexico. The people gathered. "Death to bad government!" he cried.

Mexico's Independence From Spain

Hidalgo's cry for freedom began a revolution against the Spanish colonial government in Mexico. A **revolution** is the overthrow of one government and its replacement with another. September 16, or *Diez y Seis de Septiembre* in Spanish, is celebrated as the birth of Mexican independence in Mexico and the United States. On that day in 1810, Hidalgo led an army of rebels. Many of them were poor peasants and farmers. The rebels were tired of being mistreated by the Spanish colonial viceroy. A **viceroy** rules a country as the representative of his king and is empowered to act in the king's name. The viceroy collected taxes from the Mexicans to pay for the wars it fought with other European powers. Spain feared foreign expansion. The viceroy also took most of the food that the rebels farmed. This became a particular hardship because the region had been experiencing poor harvests.

1. **Identify** characteristics of the Spanish colonial government and its influence on inhabitants of Texas.

....

....

....

160

UNLOCK THE BIG ?

I will know how big changes in the government affected Texans.

Vocabulary

revolution   empresario
viceroy
frontier

Circle two items. Then **explain** how they are used.

Hidalgo's rebels, largely untrained and poorly armed, fought trained Spanish soldiers who had the best weapons of the time. After a terrible loss of life in battle, Hidalgo retreated north into Spanish Texas. There he gained supporters, and more battles were fought. But the rebels were soon defeated. Hidalgo was captured, sent to trial, and killed.

However, the war continued. In January 1811 a man named Juan Bautista de las Casas led a revolt of Mexicans living in San Antonio against the Spanish governor of Texas. Casas seized power and held it, but not for long. People who were loyal to Spain captured Casas. He, too, was tried and killed.

Mexican rebels continued to fight Spanish loyalists in Texas. Finally, in 1821, the war ended, and Mexico won its independence. A Spanish king no longer ruled Mexico.

2. Use the text to **identify** and circle on the map the location of Juan Bautista de las Casas's revolt. Then **identify** Texas's role in the Mexican War of Independence.

....

....

....

....

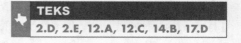

TEKS
2.D, 2.E, 12.A, 12.C, 14.B, 17.D

Texas Under Spanish and Mexican Rule

LEGEND
Spanish Texas (1810–1821)
Mexican Texas (1821–1836)

N W E S

0   200 mi
0   200 km

San Antonio (Spanish capital)

Saltillo (Mexican capital)

Gulf of Mexico

Tejanos and Tejanas

Mexico's War for Independence had a strong impact on the development of Texas. During the war, many lives were lost and homes destroyed. Cattle and crops dwindled. After the war the Mexicans in Texas began to rebuild their communities. The men, called Tejanos, and women, called Tejanas, got to work. Many Tejanos were ranchers. They lived in south Texas where the natural grasses grew abundantly in the river valleys and plains. Others lived on ranches and in the towns of San Antonio, Nacogdoches, and Goliad. Tejanos near the Nacogdoches settlement also made a living trading with the French in Louisiana.

The Tejanos lived on Mexico's frontier. A **frontier** is where settled land ended and American Indian land began. They also lived very far from Mexico's capital, Mexico City. When independence was declared the news had to travel many miles of rough trails to reach San Antonio. At that time news traveled at the speed of a horse and rider.

Tejanos and Tejanas had a strong sense of family and community. Each community had its own *comisario*, or leader. Groups of local citizens were appointed to take care of the community. One group made laws about the use of water, a most valuable resource. Another collected money and made all the arrangements for festivals. There was a group to hire teachers and build schools. When settlers began to come from the United States, it was a group of Tejanos who helped the new Mexican government write the laws allowing them to come.

3. **Explain** how most Tejanos earned a living. **Identify** the resources they needed and the areas in which they found those resources.

....

....

....

....

....

Empresarios

Compared to the Spanish colonial government, early Mexican governments ruled by an elected president and a congress. Money gained by taxes stayed in Mexico. Early Mexican governments feared U.S. expansion. Therefore, to develop Mexican Texas, the Mexican government made agreements with empresarios. An **empresario** was a land agent who brought settlers, divided up the land, and kept the law. In return, they could earn fees from the settlers and a large grant or gift of land from the government.

Martín de León was an empresario who made a significant impact on the settlement of Texas. He moved from Nuevo Santander in Mexico to Texas and founded a colony in 1824. Today the town is called Victoria. Martín de León and his wife, Patricia de León, accomplished many improvements to the community. For example, there was no school there, so Patricia de León started one. Then she helped found a church. Martín de León helped the colony to grow as a Tejano center for raising and transporting livestock.

Martín and Patricia de León

Lorenzo de Zavala also became an empresario. As a young man in Mexico, he was sent to jail for speaking out against the Spanish government. A well-known political leader, he supported a democratic government. After the Mexican revolution, de Zavala went to Mexican Texas. The new government gave Zavala the right to settle 500 settlers on a large piece of land northeast of Austin. He became an important supporter of Texan independence.

4. **Explain** the economic motive for someone such as Martín de León or Lorenzo de Zavala to become an empresario. Then **explain** how empresarios impacted the settlement of Texas.

Lorenzo de Zavala

....

....

....

....

....

This painting shows Tejano ranchers in the 1800s.

Ranchos and Vaqueros

The earliest Spanish explorers brought the first cattle, horses, sheep, and goats to Texas. They also brought the Spanish tradition of ranching. Ranching was part of the economy of the early days of the missions. By the late 1700s, mission herds of cattle and sheep numbered in the thousands. It was mission Indians who learned to care for the cattle. Cattle on missions were raised for their meat, hides, and tallow, or fat. The hides were made into leather items, and the tallow was used to make candles.

Tejanos continued the tradition on ranchos, or ranches. They settled in south Texas, where enough grass grew naturally to feed large herds of animals. Vaqueros, or cowboys, herded the cattle from the ranchos to markets as far north as Nacogdoches to those hundreds of miles away in Louisiana and south to Coahuila in Mexico.

During the 1830s, new settlers began to come to Mexican Texas from the United States. They were mostly farmers. They learned how to ranch from the Tejanos. For example, the words *rodeo, lasso, bronco, corral,* and *stampede* all come from Spanish.

5. **Cause and Effect Examine** the painting to **analyze** the effects of and contributions of the Spanish explorers on the development and growth of Texas.

....
....
....
....
....
....
....

Like most Tejanos, Erasmo Seguín was a rancher. He was also a statesman, businessman, and postmaster. He served the new government of Mexico and helped write its constitution in 1824. In Mexico City he pushed the interests of the people back home in San Antonio. When new settlers from the United States began to enter Mexican Texas, Seguín made the government welcoming to them. He became an important friend to the new settlers.

6. **Summarize** the accomplishments of Erasmo Seguín.

....

....

....

Got it?

TEKS 2.E, 14.B, 17.D

7. **Cause and Effect Identify** why the Spanish government jailed Zavala. Then **explain** how Zavala modeled active participation in the democratic process.

....

....

....

8. Your family has moved to the early settlement of Victoria. **Identify** how the accomplishments of significant empresarios Martín and Patricia de León encouraged you to move there.

my Story Ideas

....

....

....

9. **Identify** characteristics of early Mexican governments and their influence on inhabitants of Texas.

....

....

Empresarios and New Settlers

In the early 1800s, most kids in Texas had lots of chores to do.

Today Stephen F. Austin is known as the Father of Texas.

In the last days of Spanish rule, a United States businessman named Moses Austin had a bold plan. He would make money and obtain good land by starting a colony in Spanish Texas. No American had done this before, but he headed for San Antonio.

The Austin Colony

When he got there, Moses Austin bumped into an old friend. It was lucky he did because his Spanish friend knew the officials. With his help Austin's plan was accepted. The government would make a grant, or gift of land, if Austin brought 300 families, later called the Old Three Hundred.

Moses Austin died soon after returning home. It was his son Stephen F. Austin who carried out his plan. When Stephen F. Austin arrived in Mexican Texas, a whole new government was in place. So the young Austin had to go all the way to Mexico City. It took a year, but he convinced the new officials that settlers from the United States would be good for Mexico. They would help make Mexican Texas a safe and productive place again.

Austin chose the land for his colony carefully. He wanted land along rivers with good soil for economic activities, such as farming and raising cattle. He found what he wanted between the Colorado and Brazos rivers. There was plenty of good land, fresh water, and trees for building homes.

1. **Cause and Effect** In the paragraph above, **identify** and underline a significant accomplishment of Stephen F. Austin in the development of Texas.

UNLOCK
THE BIG
?

I will know why people moved to Texas and what life was like for them when they got here.

Vocabulary

militia
immigrant
cash crop

List the chores you do.

Then Austin set out to recruit settlers. He needed hard workers who would develop their plots of land. It was a good time to find United States settlers, as many of them wanted to move west where land was cheaper. In Austin's colony they could get a large piece of land for a small fee. As the first colonists began to arrive, Austin had a lot to do. He divided the land. He governed as a judge. He protected the colony as head of the **militia**, or volunteer soldiers. And what did Stephen F. Austin gain? He got money for his services and also received 197,000 acres of land. That was his bonus for bringing United States settlers to Texas.

TEKS
2.E, 8.A, 8.B, 8.C, 12.B, 12.C, 20.A

2. **Locate** the Colorado and Brazos rivers on the map. Circle the areas on those rivers within Austin's colony. Then **explain** Austin's economic motivation for locating his settlement in that geographic location.

....

....

....

....

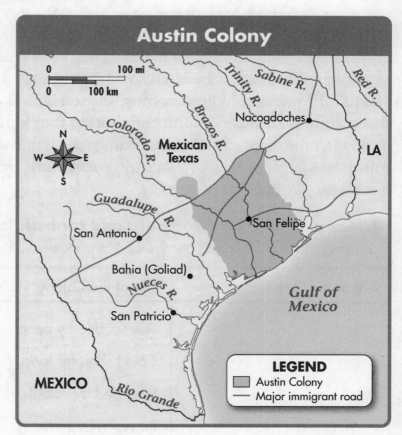

Austin Colony

0 ——— 100 mi
0 ——— 100 km

Trinity R.
Sabine R.
Red R.
Colorado R.
Brazos R.
Nacogdoches
Mexican Texas
LA
Guadalupe R.
San Antonio
San Felipe
Bahia (Goliad)
Nueces R.
Gulf of Mexico
San Patricio
MEXICO
Rio Grande

LEGEND
□ Austin Colony
— Major immigrant road

The First Colonists

The settlers who moved to Austin's colony were English-speaking immigrants. An **immigrant** is a person who moves to a new country. The Anglo American settlers who moved to Texas were called Texians. Most of them were planters from southern states, such as Louisiana, Alabama, Arkansas, Tennessee, and Missouri. Planters in these states grew cash crops such as cotton and tobacco. **Cash crops** are grown to sell at a market. When some planters came to Mexican Texas, they brought African American slaves with them. The African American slaves worked the cotton fields.

The first settlers needed a town, so Austin founded San Felipe de Austin near the center of the colony. In 1824 the site was just woods and grasslands. Only four years later there was a hotel, a blacksmith shop, three stores, and some 40 to 50 log cabins. The Texas colony was growing fast.

A woman named Jane Long moved to the colony in 1837. She had first moved to Mexican Texas with her family and a young servant girl named Kian in 1819. In the winter of 1821, Jane's husband, a soldier, left, promising to return in one month. Jane waited for him at Fort Las Casas. As the winter grew worse, everyone left the fort, even the guards. But Jane still waited with her family and Kian. She had no idea her husband had been killed.

Without food, Jane fished and shot birds to eat. Fearful of American Indians nearby, she sometimes shot a cannon. It was not until early spring that Jane finally left the empty fort. For her courage she is often called the Mother of Texas. At Austin's colony Jane ran a hotel with Kian's help.

Jane Long fired a cannon to make American Indians nearby think soldiers were still defending the fort.

3. Complete the chart to **compare and contrast** Jane Long's life at the fort to her life at Austin's colony.

Life at the Fort	Life at the Colony
	Surrounded by people
	Could shop for food
	Protected by colony
	Ran own business

Many settlers traveled to Texas in covered wagons.

Settlers Get to Texas

People across the United States began to hear about the cheap, fertile land in Mexican Texas. As thousands of people began to leave for the area, they were given nicknames. They were called the GTTs, for "Gone to Texas," or Go-Aheads.

The immigrants came any way they could. Some simply walked or rode a horse with their belongings strapped to the saddle. Most filled a covered wagon with as much as it would hold. Then they slowly bumped over dirt roads or trails west. People in Missouri piled their belongings and livestock on flatboats and floated down the Mississippi River. When they got to New Orleans, they took a ship to Mexican Texas.

The newcomers settled in clusters on the traditional land of the Karankawa Indians. The Karankawa were angry about their lands being taken. They sent raiding parties to attack the newcomers.

In 1830 a man named Gail Borden arrived at Austin's colony. He started an English-language newspaper so settlers could get the information they needed. Years later Borden became a successful inventor. One of his inventions that we still use today is condensed milk. Borden made so much money with his invention that he gave money away for schools and other good causes.

Gail Borden

4. In the paragraph above, **identify** and underline a way that Gail Borden helped improve life for early colonists.

This diagram shows the inside of a dogtrot cabin, named for the "trot" or open hallway that ran through the middle. The rooms on either side had fireplaces. One was the kitchen fire. The other was for heat during winter.

Daily Life in Austin Colony

When settlers got their plots of land, they had to do two things fast. They had to build a shelter to live in and plant a garden. They built their shelters and most of their furniture using the materials available to them: stones, mud, and wood. The shelter was often a log dogtrot cabin. It had two rooms with a covered opening or "trot" between them. Dogs liked the shaded trot, and the breeze through it cooled the rooms. An early Texan colonist, Frances Van Zandt, once wrote:

"When our need for things was pressing, we usually found a way for making them…"

—the Van Zandt letters, 1905

There were many everyday chores. Cooking was done over a fire, so a lot of firewood had to be chopped up. Children gathered the kindling. Everyone helped to provide food. The boys and men hunted wild turkey, deer, and geese. They caught fish in the streams. Women and small children worked in the garden and picked berries and nuts. The whole family worked in the corn and cotton fields. These crops had to be planted, weeded, and picked. There were chores around the house, too. Children might milk the cows, feed the livestock and chickens, and gather eggs. There was always sewing, cooking, washing, and candle making to be done.

At first, San Felipe was the only town in the colony, and many settlers did not live near it. Families had to wait for traveling peddlers to buy goods, such as material for clothing. Likewise, there were few doctors. Disease was a common threat to colonists.

Did children need to go to school? Away from town, parents taught their children at home. In San Felipe, the first school was built in 1829. There were 40 students, mostly boys. But the following year, there were four schools in the community, and the amount of students nearly doubled.

Cooking was done on an open fire.

5. **Summarize** what a typical day might be like for someone your age living in a community far from San Felipe.

....

....

 Got it?

🔹 TEKS 2.E, 8.C, 12.C

6. ◉ **Cause and Effect** **Explain** the impact of Stephen F. Austin on the settlement of Texas.

....

....

7. ❓ Suppose it was 1829. Your family just moved to San Felipe de Austin from a city in Missouri. Write a letter to a friend back home. **Describe** how immigrants like yourself have affected the economy.

 my Story Ideas

....

....

8. On a separate sheet of paper, construct a map of Mexican Texas showing the Brazos and Colorado rivers. Then **locate** and color the areas in Austin's colony settled by 1834. **Identify** and **explain** the geographic factors that influence patterns of settlement in Texas, past and present.

Lesson 1 🖐 **TEKS 2.A, 2.B**

Europeans Explore Texas

1. **Identify** the explorer according to his accomplishments or impact in the settlement of Texas.

....

was the first explorer to reach Texas in 1519 and map the coastline.

.... led a Spanish expedition across Texas looking for gold and returned to Spanish Mexico with knowledge about the area.

.... was a French explorer who built a fort and caused Spanish officials to strengthen their claims.

2. **Cause and Effect** In the chart, **describe** two effects.

Cause

> Cabeza de Vaca reported hearing about cities of gold called Cíbola.

Effect

a.

b.

3. **Summarize** the motives of France and Spain as they sent explorers to settle the Americas and Texas.

....

....

....

Lesson 2 🖐 **TEKS 2.A, 2.C, 8.A, 12.C, 16.A, 19.C**

Spanish Settlements in Texas

4. **Explain** where and why the Spanish established the following Catholic missions in present-day Texas. The first one has been done for you.

Eastern Texas, 1600s, near Louisiana, to protect Spanish land claims from the French

South Texas, Mission San José, 1720

....

....

West Texas, Mission Ysleta, 1682

....

....

5. **Analyze** the effects of Spanish exploration on the economic development and growth of settlements in Texas.

....

....

....

....

....

....

6. Summarize the contributions of people of the Catholic religion in the development of Texas.

....

....

....

....

....

Lesson 3 ✦ TEKS 2.D, 12.C, 14.B, 17.D

Mexican Texas: A New Era

7. Identify the impact of the Mexican War of Independence on the development of Texas.

....

....

....

....

....

8. Analyze the effects of Mexican immigrants during the 1830s on the economic development and growth of Texas.

....

....

....

9. Complete the chart to **identify** and **compare** characteristics of the Spanish colonial government with those of early Mexican governments and **identify** their influence on inhabitants of Texas.

Spanish Rule	Mexican Rule
Ruled by the king of Spain through a	Ruled by an elected president and a ....
Money from taxes sent to Spain.	Money from taxes stayed in Mexico.
Feared .... expansion.	Feared U.S. ....

10. Read the question carefully. Determine the best answer to the question from the four answer choices provided. Circle the best answer.

Why is Lorenzo de Zavala an important historical figure?

A He modeled active participation in the democratic process during the Spanish era.

B He helped make the Spanish era more democratic.

C He spoke out for the rights of American Indians in the missions.

D He founded a colony and a town called Victoria in 1824.

Lesson 4 TEKS 2.E, 6.B, 12.A, 12.B, 21.A

Empresarios and New Settlers

11. Explain how most of Stephen F. Austin's settlers earned a living. **Explain** the geographic factors that influenced their choice of settlement location.

....

....

....

....

....

12. To complete the map, use color or shading to **translate** what you know about the distribution of the Tejano population and the U.S. immigrant population in Texas during the 1800s.

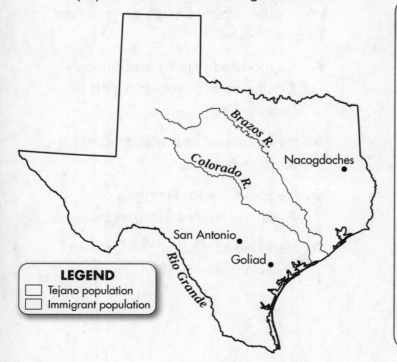

LEGEND
☐ Tejano population
☐ Immigrant population

13. Analyze the primary source below, written by a visitor to Austin's colony. Then answer the question.

"[Thomas Bell lived] in a little pole-cabin in the [middle] of a small clearing. . . . His wife, every inch a lady, welcomed me with as much . . . [politeness] as if she were mistress of a mansion. The whole family were dressed in buckskin, and when supper was announced, we sat on stools . . . around a clapboard table."
—Noah Smithwick, 1900

Stephen Austin sought good settlers for his colony. Did he succeed? **Explain.**

....

....

....

....

14. ❓ **Why do people leave their homelands?** TEKS 2.A, 2.C, 2.E

People left their homelands and came to Texas for many different reasons. **Identify** the most common reason for the following groups.

a. Explorers ....

b. Missionaries ....

c. Tejanos ....

d. Empresarios ....

e. Immigrants from the United States

....

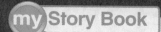

Go online to write and illustrate your own **myStory Book** using the **myStory Ideas** from this chapter.

Why do people leave their homelands?

 TEKS

SS 2.A, 2.C, 2.E, 22.D

ELA 15

People who left their homelands to settle in Spanish or Mexican Texas came for many different reasons. Their journeys, however, were always slow and dangerous. Today, people move quickly and safely on jets, cars, and trains. It is easier to move for a new job, to be near family, or to go to college.

Think about a place you might like to move to someday. Write a journal entry in which you **describe** what the place is like and your reasons for choosing it.

....

....

....

....

Now draw a picture of what you like most about the place.

Revolution and the Republic of Texas

How does the past shape our present and future?

Describe some of the holidays people celebrate in your community. Then, **explain** how those holidays connect us to the past.

....

....

....

....

....

Texas Essential Knowledge and Skills

3.A Analyze the causes, major events, and effects of the Texas Revolution, including the Battle of the Alamo, the Texas Declaration of Independence, the Runaway Scrape, and the Battle of San Jacinto.

3.B Summarize the significant contributions of individuals such as Texians William B. Travis, James Bowie, David Crockett, George Childress, and Sidney Sherman; Tejanos Juan Antonio Padilla, Carlos Espalier, Juan N. Seguín, Plácido Benavides, and José Francisco Ruiz; Mexicans Antonio López de Santa Anna and Vicente Filisola; and non-combatants Susanna Dickinson and Enrique Esparza.

3.C Identify leaders important to the founding of Texas as a republic and state, including José Antonio Navarro, Sam Houston, Mirabeau Lamar, and Anson Jones.

3.D Describe the successes, problems, and organizations of the Republic of Texas such as the establishment of a constitution, economic struggles, relations with American Indians, and the Texas Rangers.

6.A Apply geographic tools, including grid systems, legends, symbols, scales, and compass roses, to construct and interpret maps.

7.A Describe a variety of regions in Texas and the United States such as political, population, and economic regions that result from patterns of human activity.

15.A Identify the purposes and explain the importance of the Texas Declaration of Independence, the Texas Constitution, and other documents such as the Meusebach-Comanche Treaty.

16.A Explain the meaning of various patriotic symbols and landmarks of Texas, including the six flags that flew over Texas, the San Jacinto Monument, the Alamo, and various missions.

16.D Describe the origins and significance of state celebrations such as Texas Independence Day and Juneteenth.

17.A Identify important individuals who have participated voluntarily in civic affairs at state and local levels such as Adina de Zavala and Clara Driscoll.

17.B Explain how individuals can participate voluntarily in civic affairs at state and local levels through activities such as holding public officials to their word, writing letters, and participating in historic preservation and service projects.

17.D Identify the importance of historical figures and important individuals who modeled active participation in the democratic process such as Sam Houston, Barbara Jordan, Lorenzo de Zavala, Ann Richards, Sam Rayburn, Henry B. González, James A. Baker III, Wallace Jefferson, and other local individuals.

18.B Identify leadership qualities of state and local leaders, past and present.

21.B Analyze information by sequencing, categorizing, identifying cause-and-effect relationships, comparing, contrasting, finding the main idea, summarizing, making generalizations and predictions, and drawing inferences and conclusions.

21.C Organize and interpret information in outlines, reports, databases, and visuals, including graphs, charts, timelines, and maps.

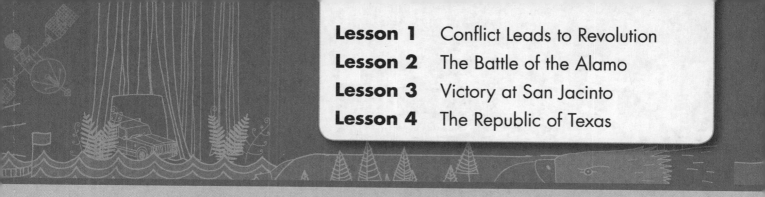

The Alamo
A Symbol of Texas's Freedom

my Story Video

Amir is visiting one of the most famous landmarks in Texas: the Alamo. "I can't believe that it's right in the middle of downtown San Antonio!" he exclaims. "It's strange that a historical site is surrounded by so many modern buildings." Amir knows that the Alamo has played an important role in Texas history. "I'm excited to be here!" he says.

Amir is greeted by Sherri, a museum educator, just outside the Alamo's main entrance. "Is that the mission?" he asks. "Yes, it's the most recognizable building here at the Alamo," chuckles Sherri, "but the Alamo is more than just a mission. The site sits on 4.2 acres and includes a mixture of historic and modern buildings." Sherri has worked at the Alamo for many years. Today, she is giving Amir a tour of the grounds and explaining why this landmark holds such special meaning in the hearts of Texans.

Amir and Sherri stand in front of the mission at the Alamo.

The city of San Antonio grew around the location of the Alamo.

Visitors to the Alamo can walk through these archways as they learn about Texas history and the fight for Texas independence.

The bell at the Alamo

"The mission was built in 1744 and became an important site to Christianize and educate American Indians," she explains. "Not only was it one of the first Spanish missions in the San Antonio area, but it also played a major role in battles fought here." During the Texas Revolution, the mission acted as a place of refuge for the Texas fighters. "After the Texian rebels gained control of San Antonio and the Alamo, they made a decision to defend the Alamo from the returning Mexican army," she says. "So they took to the safety of this old fortified mission. Even though they were protected by the walls of the mission, the Texas fighters were no match for the Mexican army." On March 6, 1836 the Mexican troops stormed the walls of the mission and flooded the compound. The battle lasted only 90 minutes as the Texians and Tejanos made their last stand.

An important building on the complex is a long limestone structure named the Long Barrack. "It was originally built as a two-story *convento*," says Sherri. "It served as both quarters and offices for the Spanish missionaries." While the building has gone through some changes over the years, its significance in the 1836 Battle of the Alamo still remains. "This building is another site where the Alamo defenders made their stand against the Mexican troops," says Sherri. "I can see why they decided to fight from here," replies Amir. "These stone walls would provide a lot of protection."

The period of the Republic of Texas was very trying for San Antonio and the Alamo, but the events that took place here were never forgotten. "*Remember the Alamo!* served as the battle cry when the Texians finally defeated General Antonio

Texians and Tejanos fought from behind the thick stone walls of the Alamo.

The mission at the Alamo is lit up at night.

López de Santa Anna's troops at the Battle of San Jacinto," says Sherri. "Oh yeah, that's when Texas defeated Santa Anna and won its independence," Amir adds.

After Texas joined the United States, the United States Army decided to fix up the abandoned mission and convert it into a warehouse to supply forts across Texas. "The Alamo was damaged in battle," says Sherri. So when the army decided to rebuild some of the structures in 1847, it helped the mission. It also helped the city of San Antonio. "As more and more people moved to the area, the city's needs grew," explains Sherri. "And that's why the Alamo is right in the heart of San Antonio. The city built up around it!"

As Amir's visit comes to a close, he now has a greater appreciation for the Alamo and its role in the history of Texas. "The Alamo not only represents our state's fight for independence," says Amir, "but it also symbolizes our pride and sacrifice."

This monument is sometimes called The Spirit of Sacrifice. It shows and names many of the people who fought and died at the Alamo.

Think About It Based on this story, how did events in the past affect the Alamo and the city of San Antonio? As you read this chapter, think about the events that occurred and how they affected people living in Texas then and also people today.

Conflict Leads to Revolution

Envision It!

Every citizen shall be at liberty to speak, write or publish his opinions on any subject.

This statement is found in Texas's first constitution, or plan of government. *Liberty* is another word for freedom.

At first, life for the Texas colonies did not change much under Mexican rule. Under the Constitution of 1824, leaders agreed to organize Texas as a part of the state of Coahuila and Texas. To help Texas grow, the government passed laws to allow more immigrants to move to Texas.

Trouble in the Texas Colonies

During the 1820s and 1830s, immigrants who moved to Texas from the United States became Mexican citizens. However, there were some problems. One issue was the fact that new citizens had to become Roman Catholic. But many of the immigrants were Protestants, who held different beliefs and practices from Catholics. Since they did not want to change religions, these newcomers often ignored the law.

Other problems arose. Settlers from the United States did not learn to speak Spanish. They also did not change their culture, or way of life.

Another issue was slavery. Slavery was still legal in some parts of the United States. But it was illegal in Mexico. Still, the government of Coahuila and Texas let slave owners from the United States come to Texas and bring slaves. The owners called the slaves "indentured servants" in order to go around the law. Settlers feared the Mexican government might change its mind.

Immigrants moved to Texas from the United States, and they opened businesses such as this general store.

Describe something in your life today that has to do with your right to free speech.

UNLOCK THE BIG ? I will know why and how the Texas colonies revolted against Mexico and gained their independence.

Vocabulary

tax	delegate
convention	republic
dictator	petition
right	

In 1830, Mexico passed a law to slow immigration from the United States. Slaves could no longer come. The law also created a new tax on goods. A **tax** is money a government charges in exchange for services. The people of Texas worried that their businesses would be hurt.

In 1832 and 1833 the colonists held conventions in San Felipe de Austin to talk about these matters. A **convention** is a formal meeting. The colonists wanted Texas to become its own state in Mexico so they could decide matters for themselves.

In 1833, Mexico elected Antonio López de Santa Anna, a well-known military hero, as president. He quickly became a dictator. A **dictator** is a ruler who does not answer to the people. Santa Anna's actions while he was the Mexican president contributed to Texas's independence. The Texas convention chose Stephen F. Austin to travel to Mexico City to talk to Mexican officials. Austin went to Mexico City, but waited for months to meet with Mexican officials. At last he wrote to Texas officials telling them to go ahead and set up a state government. When Santa Anna heard this, he thought the people of Texas were about to revolt. He had Austin arrested and put into prison.

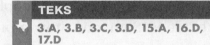

TEKS
3.A, 3.B, 3.C, 3.D, 15.A, 16.D, 17.D

1. **Summarize** a significant contribution of Antonio López de Santa Anna in Texas history.

....

....

....

....

....

....

General Antonio López de Santa Anna

 SAVVAS realize Go online to access your interactive digital lesson.

181

The Texas Revolution Begins

The people of Texas were angered by Austin's arrest. This was one of the early causes of the Texas Revolution because Santa Anna was trampling on the **rights,** or freedoms, of Mexican citizens. The settlers believed that the Mexican Constitution of 1824 protected their freedom.

In July 1835, Austin was released from prison. Later that year, Santa Anna sent troops to Texas. This was another cause of the Texas Revolution. Fighting broke out on October 2, 1835, in the town of Gonzales. Mexican soldiers had orders to remove a cannon from the town. The townspeople had other ideas. Someone drew a picture of a cannon on a huge white flag with the words *COME AND TAKE IT*. A short battle took place. In the battle, settlers and a group of Texas soldiers defeated the Mexican soldiers. The next week, a small group of Texas soldiers took Goliad. They believed the Mexican fort there threatened settlers.

The battles at Gonzales and Goliad were small victories, but they boosted the settlers' morale. They had the courage and experience to defeat Santa Anna's army. They were ready for revolution. The map shows some of the early battles in the war for Texas Independence. As one settler put it:

"We have either to fight for our homes or fly and leave them."

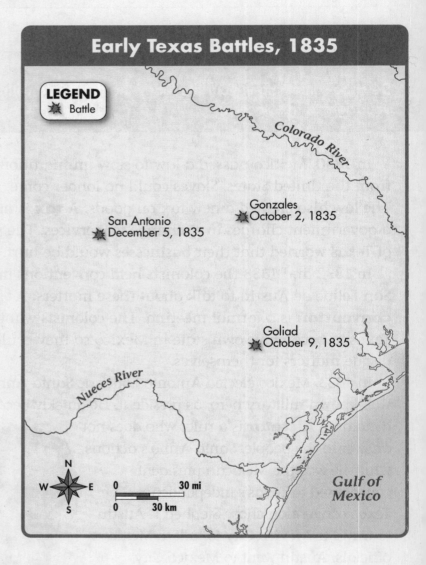

Early Texas Battles, 1835

LEGEND
✷ Battle

Colorado River

San Antonio
December 5, 1835

Gonzales
October 2, 1835

Goliad
October 9, 1835

Nueces River

Gulf of Mexico

N
W E
S

0   30 mi
0   30 km

2. ◎ **Draw Conclusions Identify** the battles of Goliad and Gonzales on the map and circle them. **Explain** why these two victories were important to the fight for independence.

....

....

March on San Antonio

The people of Texas flocked to Gonzales. They chose Stephen F. Austin as their general. "On to San Antonio!" they shouted. Mexican General Martin Perfecto de Cos and more than 1,000 soldiers had control of San Antonio.

About 300 men started the march to San Antonio. They made up the Texas "Army of the People." Many more armed men joined the fighters as they headed west. Juan N. Seguín was one of the men who joined the effort and made a significant contribution to Texas's Independence. Seguín, a young and wealthy Tejano rancher and leader, arrived with 37 Tejanos. Years later, he said,

"I embraced the cause of Texas at the sound of the first cannon." —Juan Seguín

Residents of San Antonio on the Main Plaza before the attack

Another clash between Mexicans and Texians came when Austin sent James Bowie and James Fannin ahead with 90 soldiers to scout the area. General Cos sent 275 soldiers to attack them. Texian James Bowie made a significant contribution by leading the scouts and commanding the soldiers who defeated superior Mexican forces in battle.

Winter was coming. Most of the Texas troops wanted to find shelter. However, Ben Milam thought it was time to attack. "Who will go with old Ben Milam into San Antonio?" he yelled. Three hundred men volunteered. On December 5, 1835, Milam and Francis Johnson led an attack that lasted five days. Milam was killed. On December 9, 1835, General Cos surrendered.

The people of Texas now controlled San Antonio and all of Texas. Many men in the army went home. They didn't know that their victory had made Santa Anna furious. Santa Anna quickly gathered a large army in Mexico and headed for Texas.

3. ◉ **Summarize** **Sum up** the contributions of Texian James Bowie and Tejano Juan N. Seguín to the fight against General Cos.

James Bowie: ....

Juan N. Seguín: ....

A New Government

While the army was busy at San Antonio, Texas leaders met in San Felipe to discuss what to do next. This meeting was called the Consultation.

Those who supported Stephen F. Austin wanted to stay loyal to Mexico and the Constitution of 1824. Others wanted to declare independence. In the end, the men agreed to create a short-term government for Texas.

The delegates chose Henry Smith to be the governor. A **delegate** is someone who represents other people. The Texas delegates elected Sam Houston to command the army. They agreed to meet again in March of 1836 to plan their fight against Santa Anna.

From the start, the Texas government had problems. Many people still wanted to be part of Mexico. Also, Texas had no money to pay soldiers. Stephen F. Austin and others asked the United States for money and help.

General Santa Anna and the Mexican army reached San Antonio at the end of February 1836. Santa Anna intended to take the Alamo. You will read more about the important battle at the Alamo in Lesson 2.

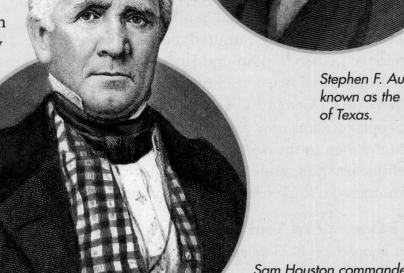

Henry Smith was the first American governor of Texas.

Stephen F. Austin is known as the Father of Texas.

Sam Houston commanded the Texas army.

The Texas Declaration of Independence

Texas leaders gathered on March 1 at the town of Washington-on-the-Brazos. This meeting is known as the Convention of 1836, and it was a major event in the Texas Revolution.

The delegates wanted to create a new country, the Republic of Texas. In a **republic** the citizens choose leaders to represent them. Some of the leaders were men who had served in the U.S. Congress. Others were Tejanos, like José Antonio Navarro. All of the delegates were leaders who were important to the founding of Texas as a republic.

George C. Childress led the committee that wrote the Texas Declaration of Independence. The importance of the Texas Declaration of Independence is that it clearly stated what the people of Texas wanted from Mexico and why. The purpose of the document was to state the complaints about Mexican rule. All of these complaints were some of the causes of the Texas Revolution. They did not have freedom of religion or the right to a trial by jury. They also could not **petition,** or make requests of the leaders or government. This declaration was one of Texian George Childress's significant contributions.

This is a modern courtroom. Today, Texans have the right to a trial by jury.

On March 2, 1836, the delegates voted in favor of the declaration. There were three Tejanos who signed the declaration with the other delegates: José Antonio Navarro, José Francisco Ruiz, and Lorenzo de Zavala. Today, Texans celebrate the second of March as Texas Independence Day. The origin of this state celebration is that it began as a way to remember the day when the Declaration of Texas Independence was signed.

4. **Analyze** major causes of the Texas Revolution. **Identify** and underline three rights that the people of Texas did not have under Mexican rule. How did not having these rights lead to the Texas Revolution?

....

....

....

A New Constitution

Next, the delegates needed to create a constitution. The purpose of the Texas Constitution was to explain how the government would work.

It took the delegates two weeks to complete the document. This written constitution was one of the successes of the Republic of Texas. The constitution was important because the laws were written down for everyone to be able to read. The Texas Constitution created three branches of government: the courts, the Congress, and the president.

The Texas Constitution included a Bill of Rights just like the U.S. Constitution. It stated that all people had specific rights. These included freedom of religion and speech. Immigrants were again encouraged to move to Texas.

However, the new constitution did not treat everyone equally. American Indians were not granted citizenship. Slaves were not granted freedom. And free African Americans needed permission to stay. Greenbury Logan protested. Logan was a blacksmith and a free black soldier who had been injured in the fight against Mexico.

The constitution took away "every privilege dear to a freeman . . . no vote or say in any way." —Greenbury Logan

Logan participated in the democratic process by writing a petition. He did get 23 signatures for the petition, but the constitution was not changed.

5. Summarize how Greenbury Logan contributed in the development of Texas during and after the war for Texas independence.

....

....

....

....

....

....

....

....

Greenbury Logan wrote a petition that 23 people signed.

Texas still had to fight for its independence. On March 4, the convention again made Sam Houston commander in chief of all armed soldiers in Texas. He immediately headed south. Leading the army was one way that Sam Houston was important to the founding of Texas as a republic. The convention then set up a short-term government. The delegates elected David G. Burnet to be president of Texas. He was a lawyer and a landowner. For vice president, the delegates chose Lorenzo de Zavala. Zavala, an important and learned Mexican statesman, had helped in drafting the new constitution. The two men were sworn in on March 17, 1836. Texas now had a new government. Could Sam Houston's army defend it?

Lorenzo de Zavala helped draft the Texas Constitution.

TEKS 3.A, 15.A, 17.D

6. **Draw Conclusions** **Explain** the importance of the Texas Constitution of 1836.

....

....

....

7. **Identify** the important historical figure who modeled active participation in the democratic process. Circle the name of the person who helped write Texas's constitution. Then write about how this shaped the future of Texas.

my Story Ideas

Sam Houston   Lorenzo de Zavala   David G. Burnet

This affected the future by ....

....

8. **Analyze** the major events of the Texas Revolution. Suppose you were a delegate at the Convention of 1836. On a separate sheet of paper, write a letter to a friend **explaining** the importance of the Texas Declaration of Independence.

Sequence

Sequence is the order of events. It tells how things happened in time. Understanding a sequence of events helps you to understand how things took place in history. Dates, including days, months, and years, may indicate a sequence of events. Clue words that show a sequence include *first, second, third, then, after, next, finally, past, future, now,* and *later*.

Read and **analyze** the information below about José Antonio Navarro.

José Antonio Navarro

José Antonio Navarro was a leader in the Texas Revolution. Born in San Antonio in 1795, he grew up to be a wealthy Tejano rancher, merchant, and lawyer. He married Margarita de la Garza in 1825, and the couple had seven children.

In the 1820s, Navarro became friends with Stephen F. Austin and supported the colonization of Texas. As a statesman, Navarro served in the legislature of the Mexican state of Coahuila and Texas, and later in the Mexican Congress in Mexico City. In 1835, he supported Texas statehood. The following year, he supported Texas independence. In 1836, Navarro signed the Texas Declaration of Independence. Navarro was one of three Tejanos to do so. Later, he was elected to the Texas Congress. Navarro spent his life making difficult choices. He worked to bring justice to all Texans.

José Antonio Navarro

> José Antonio Navarro was born in San Antonio in 1795.

⬇

> He served as a statesman in Mexico.

⬇

> In 1836, he signed the Texas Declaration of Independence.

I will know how to analyze information by sequencing.

 TEKS

ELA 11.C Describe explicit and implicit relationships among ideas in texts organized by sequence.

SS 3.B Summarize the significant contributions of individuals such as Juan N. Seguín.

SS 3.C Identify leaders important to the founding of Texas as a republic and state including José Antonio Navarro.

SS 21.B Analyze information by sequencing.

 **Try it!**

Read and **analyze** the passage about Juan N. Seguín. Circle the words or dates in the passage that help you recognize the sequence. Then fill in the sequence of events in the chart below.

Juan Seguín was born in San Antonio in 1806. He started his long life of service early. In 1828 when he was 22 years old, he was elected to San Antonio's town council. For the next several years Seguín continued to serve the people of Texas under the Mexican government. This ended in 1835 when Seguín became a captain, leading other Tejanos in the fight for independence. Seguín's unit fought at the Battle of San Jacinto in 1836.

After the war ended, Seguín went back to serving Texas as a government leader. Only now he was serving the Republic of Texas and he was a senator. Juan N. Seguín was the only Tejano to serve in the Senate of the Republic of Texas.

Juan Seguín

Juan Seguín

[ ]

↓

[ ]

↓

[ ]

 SAVVAS realize Go online to access your interactive digital lesson.

189

The Battle of the Alamo

The fighters from Texas lost the Battle of the Alamo. Instead of giving up, they fought harder for their independence.

1. ⊙ **Cause and Effect Identify** details about a cause of the Battle of the Alamo.

....

....

....

James Bowie led the Texas volunteers but fell ill before the battle.

General Santa Anna was very angry when Mexican General Cos was defeated in December 1835. Santa Anna gathered his troops and headed north. On February 23, 1836, Santa Anna and about 1,800 Mexican soldiers marched into San Antonio.

Soldiers Gather

When Santa Anna's army arrived, there were only about 150 Texians and Tejanos at the Alamo. The defenders of the Alamo had more than a dozen cannons, but they did not have enough powder to keep firing them for long. Santa Anna decided to lay siege to the Alamo. A **siege** is the surrounding of a place by enemy forces trying to capture it.

Santa Anna flew a blood-red flag from the bell tower of a nearby church. The fighters at the Alamo could see it. The message was plain: surrender or die. Santa Anna also sent a messenger to the Alamo demanding that the men surrender. The Texians and Tejanos replied with the boom of a cannon!

Heroes of the Battle

The fighters at the Alamo could have escaped. The Mexican siege had not yet cut them off completely. But Texians William B. Travis and James Bowie agreed they would hold the Alamo. They were significant in contributing to the war for Texas independence. The two men commanded together until Bowie became too sick to continue.

UNLOCK THE BIG ? I will know the causes and major events in the Battle of the Alamo.

Vocabulary

siege

non-combatant

preserve

Think of a time when things did not work out the way you expected. Did you give up or try harder? Explain what you did and why.

At dawn on February 24, the Mexicans attacked. Cannon balls struck the walls, knocking holes in them. Travis sent a plea for help to the people of Texas and all Americans in the world:

> *". . . I call on you in the name of Liberty, of patriotism and everything dear to the American character, to come to our aid. . . ."*
> —William B. Travis, 1836

There were others who contributed to the effort at the Alamo. Texian David (Davy) Crockett of Tennessee had once served in the U.S. Congress. Crockett was an important leader who fought hard and encouraged the soldiers. Carlos Espalier was a 17-year-old Tejano who was being trained by Bowie. He, too, decided to stay and fight. Espalier contributed to Texas's independence by fighting at the Alamo. All of the men who fought and died at the Alamo helped Texas gain independence.

TEKS
3.A, 3.B, 16.A, 17.A, 17.B

2. **Summarize** the contributions of Texians William B. Travis and David Crockett by underlining each man's contribution in the captions.

Lieutenant Colonel William Travis, a 26-year-old lawyer, commanded the Texians at the Alamo with James Bowie.

David (Davy) Crockett, a frontiersman and former U.S. congressman, led a group of fighters known as the Tennessee Mounted Volunteers who helped fight for freedom.

The Battle Goes On

A few dozen men responded to Travis's call, fighting their way into the Alamo. The Texas force grew to about 185 soldiers. The last man to make it through the gates was James Bonham, an officer. He had been sent to get help for the Alamo. Bonham brought with him a letter that said help was on the way. Sadly, that help didn't come in time.

An old Texas legend says that Colonel Travis drew a line in the sand with his sword. He told the men they could cross the line and fight or they could escape. As the story goes, all but two men "stepped over." One, Bowie, was too sick to move, so he asked to be carried over. The other was Moses Rose who was being paid to fight.

The Fall of the Alamo

The battle raged for days. Santa Anna chose 1,400 trained Mexican soldiers for a final fight. On March 6, before dawn, a bugle sounded the first notes of "El Degüello." The war music told Santa Anna's army to show the enemy no mercy.

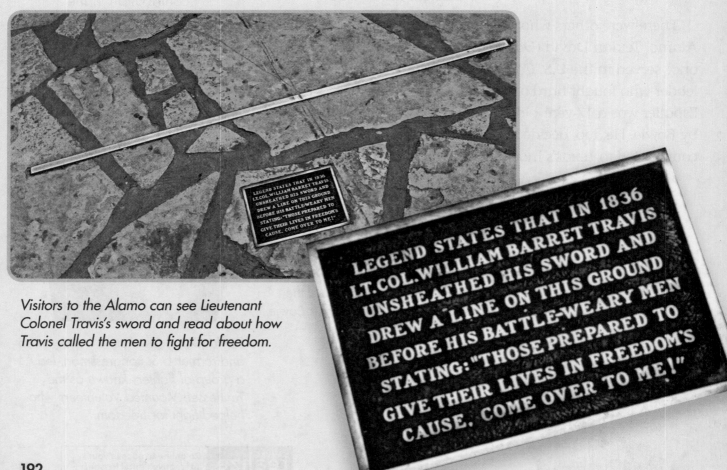

Visitors to the Alamo can see Lieutenant Colonel Travis's sword and read about how Travis called the men to fight for freedom.

LEGEND STATES THAT IN 1836 LT.COL.WILLIAM BARRET TRAVIS UNSHEATHED HIS SWORD AND DREW A LINE ON THIS GROUND BEFORE HIS BATTLE-WEARY MEN STATING: "THOSE PREPARED TO GIVE THEIR LIVES IN FREEDOM'S CAUSE. COME OVER TO ME!"

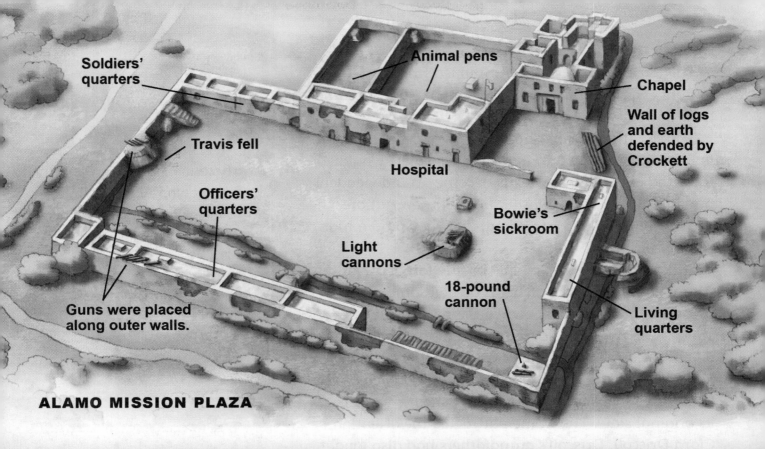

ALAMO MISSION PLAZA

Labels on image: Soldiers' quarters · Animal pens · Chapel · Travis fell · Wall of logs and earth defended by Crockett · Hospital · Officers' quarters · Bowie's sickroom · Light cannons · Guns were placed along outer walls. · 18-pound cannon · Living quarters

The Texians and Tejanos were awakened by the noise and leapt to their posts. Mexican soldiers climbed the walls and entered the plaza. The soldiers from Texas shot back and gave everything they had. People say that Travis's last words were *"¡No rendirse, muchachos!"* ("Don't surrender, boys!")

In less than two hours, every Texian and Tejano soldier lay dead. Mexico had won, but the price was very high. About 600 Mexican soldiers were killed or wounded at the Alamo.

A small group of women, children, and slaves survived the fight at the Alamo. Santa Anna let them go, giving each woman two dollars in silver and a blanket. Eight-year-old Enrique Esparza lost his father in the attack. Years later, he told newspapers what he had seen during the fight. Another survivor was Susanna Dickinson. Dickinson's husband was killed. She and her young daughter, Angelina, traveled to Gonzales where Sam Houston was. Dickinson told him about the tragic fall of the Alamo. Dickinson and Esparza were **non-combatants,** or people who were there, but did not fight in the war. As non-combatants, Dickinson and Esparza contributed to Texas's struggle for independence by telling others about what they had seen.

3. **Summarize** the contributions of non-combatants Susanna Dickinson and Enrique Esparza. Write what they did. Then tell why you think this was important to the Texas Revolution.

....
....
....
....
....
....
....
....

Remember the Alamo!

The terrible battle at the Alamo led Houston's troops to fight even harder. "Remember the Alamo!" became their battle cry.

The sacrifice at the Alamo still gives people hope today. The brave Texian and Tejano soldiers who died there did not live to see Texas become an independent nation. They weren't fighting for their new nation. They were fighting for freedom, and they paid a high price, their lives.

Still, as time passed, people mostly forgot about the Alamo itself. The state of Texas owned some of the property, but a business owned the rest. In the late 1800s, Adina de Zavala, the granddaughter of Lorenzo de Zavala, and others joined the Daughters of the Republic of Texas. This group of patriotic women worked to preserve the Alamo. To **preserve** means to keep in its original state. The women attracted the attention of Clara Driscoll. Driscoll's grandfathers had also fought in the Texas Revolution. Clara Driscoll used her fortune to help buy the remaining property that had once been the Alamo mission. Through their civic affairs, or activities, these two women helped to protect the Alamo, an important part of history, for Texas citizens.

4. **Analyze** the major events of the Battle of the Alamo. Why do you think the cry "Remember the Alamo!" still holds meaning today?

....

....

....

....

....

The Alamo is a historic landmark.

Today, you can visit the Alamo in downtown San Antonio. The area has been restored and is now a historic landmark. The landmark has a very special meaning as a place where we remember the people who fought and died for freedom in Texas. The Alamo holds exhibits that retell the story of the Texas Revolution. More than two and a half million people visit each year. This landmark is also important to Texans because it is the site of a key battle in the struggle for independence.

Clara Driscoll and Adina de Zavala

5. Explain the meaning of the Alamo. Why is it important to honor people who fought in the Alamo?

....

....

....

Got it?

TEKS 17.A, 17.B

6. ⊙ **Sequence** Number these events in the **sequence** in which they occurred.

.... William B. Travis wrote a letter pleading for help.

.... Santa Anna flew a blood-red flag.

.... James Bonham entered the Alamo.

7. ? **Explain** how individuals can participate voluntarily in civic affairs at the state or local level.

my Story Ideas

....

....

8. Identify important individuals who participated voluntarily in civic affairs at state and local levels. Who were two women who helped to create the historic landmark at the Alamo?

....

Interpret Timelines

History is full of sequences of events. How can you keep track of the most important ones? One way is to use a timeline. A **timeline** is a kind of chart that organizes important information such as events and dates in the order they happened. A timeline can help you interpret events and understand how one event leads to another.

Usually, timelines are divided into equal time periods, just as a ruler is divided into equal units of measurement. Timelines can show events over one week or many weeks, months, a year, ten years, and so on.

The units of measure will help you visually see how much time has passed. For example, the timeline below is divided into days. The space between each day is the same. This helps you to better understand the sequence of events. The first three events on the timeline happened close together. Then several days passed before the next major event.

Timelines can be vertical or horizontal. Vertical timelines are read from top to bottom. The earliest event is at the top. Look at the timeline below. It is a horizontal timeline. In a horizontal timeline, the earliest event is on the left. The most recent event is on the right. As you read the events from left to right, you will understand how events progressed during that period of time.

The Battle of the Alamo, 1836

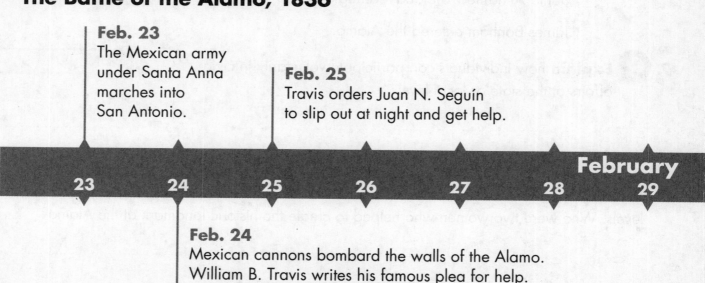

Feb. 23
The Mexican army under Santa Anna marches into San Antonio.

Feb. 25
Travis orders Juan N. Seguín to slip out at night and get help.

February
23 24 25 26 27 28 29

Feb. 24
Mexican cannons bombard the walls of the Alamo.
William B. Travis writes his famous plea for help.
James Bowie becomes ill and can't lead.

TEKS

ELA 13.B Explain factual information presented graphically.

SS 3.A Analyze the major events of the Texas Revolution, including the Battle of the Alamo.

SS 21.C Organize and interpret information in visuals, including timelines.

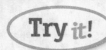

The timeline shows important events in the Battle of the Alamo. The events are placed in the order they happened.

1. How much time is covered by this timeline?

   ....

2. **Identify** the earliest event.

   ....

   ....

3. **Identify** the latest event.

   ....

4. **Interpret** the information on the timeline. How long did the men wait for help after Seguín left?

   ....

5. On a separate sheet of paper, make a timeline to **organize** and show six important events in your life in the order that they happened.

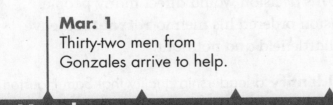

Mar. 6
Mexican forces take the Alamo and kill all soldiers defending it.

Mar. 1
Thirty-two men from Gonzales arrive to help.

March
1   2   3   4   5   6   7

Mar. 3
James Bonham returns to the Alamo with news: James Fannin cannot bring his troops.

SAVVAS realize Go online to access your interactive digital lesson.

197

Victory at San Jacinto

Mexican soldiers wore uniforms like these. Most of the Texas soldiers had no uniforms.

Word reached Sam Houston on March 11, 1836 that the Alamo had fallen. Houston had just arrived in Gonzales where he found nearly 400 men who had come on their own hoping to help Travis at the Alamo. Houston sent scouts west for news.

A **scout** is a person who gathers clues about an enemy or location. The scouts included brave Erastus "Deaf" Smith, who had already been wounded in battle. Smith returned with the non-combatants who survived the Alamo, including Susanna Dickinson and her daughter.

The Runaway Scrape

Santa Anna's troops were sweeping through Texas, burning settlements as they went. They were nearly at Gonzales. Houston's army was not ready to fight. Should Houston order his men to fight anyway? Houston was a leader who knew that his decision would affect many people. Houston ordered his men to **retreat**, or leave the battlefield and not fight.

1. **Identify** a leadership quality that Sam Houston showed when he decided not to fight at Gonzales.

....

....

....

The Runaway Scrape

Vocabulary

scout   treaty

retreat   monument

scrape

All people, not just soldiers, had to leave. Houston sent riders to warn everyone that Mexican troops were coming. Fear swept Texas. People fled east, hoping to get to the safety of the United States. Unfortunately, many people died along the way. People left quickly and did not pack for the long trip. They did not have enough blankets, warm clothes, or food.

This great flight of the people from danger is known as the Runaway Scrape. A **scrape** is a tricky situation or a problem. This was a major event of the Texas Revolution. Here is what one teenager wrote about the journey:

> "O! the cruel runaway scrape—how much distress, suffering and loss it caused!"

TEKS
3.A, 3.B, 6.A, 16.A, 18.B

2.  **Cause and Effect**
Identify two missing causes.

Analyzing the Runaway Scrape

Cause

Mexican army burns settlements to crush the revolution.

Cause

....
....
....

Cause

....
....

Effect

People flee east without preparing for the journey.

SAVVAS realize Go online to access your interactive digital lesson.

199

The Fighting Continues

Even though settlers were fleeing east in March 1836, the fighting continued. Sam Houston ordered Colonel James Fannin to blow up the fort at Goliad and leave. Instead of obeying, Fannin sent some of his troops to help the fleeing settlers. Fannin and his men fought and lost to soldiers commanded by Mexican General Don José Urrea.

Fannin surrendered to Urrea. Fannin did not know that Santa Anna had ordered his army to shoot all Texas prisoners. On March 26, some of the prisoners escaped. They were helped by Francita Alavez, who is called the "Angel of Goliad." Unfortunately, most of the Texas prisoners did not survive.

On March 27, Fannin and hundreds of his men were marched onto the prairie near the fort. Urrea did not want to obey Santa Anna's command to kill the prisoners. But Urrea was not at Goliad that day. The Mexican soldiers fired on Fannin and his men.

The mass killing of hundreds of unarmed men shocked the people of Texas and the world. Santa Anna's terrible cruelty roused them to fight. People in the United States gave the people of Texas their support. And they gained another awful battle cry: "Remember Goliad!"

The memorial at Goliad

3. **⊙ Cause and Effect** **Analyze** the causes of the Texas Revolution. How did the events at Goliad help the people of Texas get support from the United States?

....

....

....

....

....

....

Preparing for Battle

Texas had already lost many men in the fight for independence. Texas could not win if it lost many more. Sam Houston's soldiers were mostly settlers whose homes had been burned. He knew they couldn't face Santa Anna's well-trained troops on open ground.

For two weeks in April 1836, Houston drilled his army. They must learn to work together. "Deaf" Smith taught some of the men to be scouts. An African American freedman, Hendrick Arnold, served as a spy for Smith. Arnold pretended to be a runaway slave and slipped into the Mexican army camps. The information he brought back helped Houston prepare.

Help came in unexpected ways, too. The citizens of Cincinnati, Ohio, sent two cannons. The people of Texas were grateful and called them the Twin Sisters.

Houston was waiting for the right time to attack. The scouts reported that Santa Anna's army was camped near Harrisburg on the San Jacinto River. The Texas army was ready. It was time to fight. The map shows where they fought in 1836.

4. **Analyze** the major battles of the Texas Revolution shown on this map. Why is there no green line shown from the battles at San Patricio, Refugio, and Goliad?

....

....

....

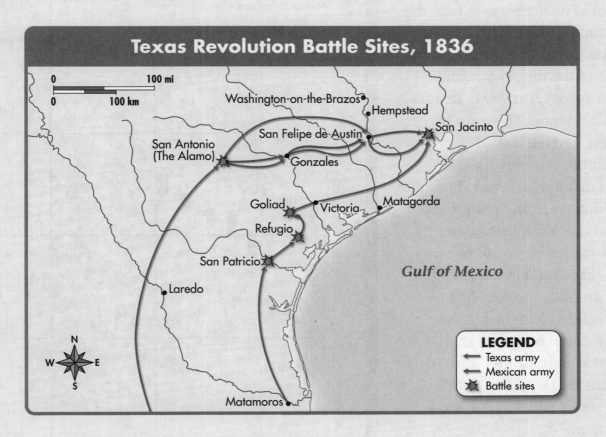

Texas Revolution Battle Sites, 1836

Washington-on-the-Brazos
Hempstead
San Jacinto
San Felipe de Austin
San Antonio (The Alamo)
Gonzales
Goliad
Victoria
Matagorda
Refugio
San Patricio
Laredo
Gulf of Mexico
Matamoros

0   100 mi
0   100 km

N W E S

LEGEND
← Texas army
← Mexican army
✸ Battle sites

The Battle of San Jacinto

On April 20, Houston's army took up their positions. With their backs to the San Jacinto River and Buffalo Bayou, they pitched camp among the live oak trees.

Santa Anna soon found them. He thought he had them trapped. A short fight took place between a small group of Mexican and soldiers from Texas. When the Twin Sisters cannons boomed, both sides stopped.

By now, Santa Anna's army had grown to about 1,200 soldiers. The soldiers from Texas had just over 900 soldiers. Santa Anna had the advantage in numbers. Santa Anna rested his men and prepared for battle. He was sure that he could beat them again. But the Texas forces did not wait for Santa Anna to attack them.

As the Mexicans dozed, the Texas forces crossed the open prairie between them in full daylight. It was the afternoon of April 21. They took the Mexican army completely by surprise.

"Remember the Alamo!" cried the Texas forces. "Remember Goliad!" The map shows how the landscape helped them make a surprise attack in full daylight.

One of the men commanding part of Texas's army was Texian Sidney Sherman. Sherman was a soldier and businessman. His contribution was that he commanded soldiers and brought 52 volunteers from Kentucky to fight in the Texas Revolution. The battle lasted just 18 minutes. Texas had won. More than 600 Mexican soldiers died. Nine Texas soldiers lost their lives. Sam Houston had been shot in the ankle. Santa Anna and Cos fled. The Battle of San Jacinto was a major event in the Texas Revolution.

5. **Interpret** the map by using the geographic tool of the legend. **Explain** how the map and legend help you to **analyze** how the Texas forces were able to sneak up on the Mexicans in daylight during the Battle of San Jacinto.

....

....

....

....

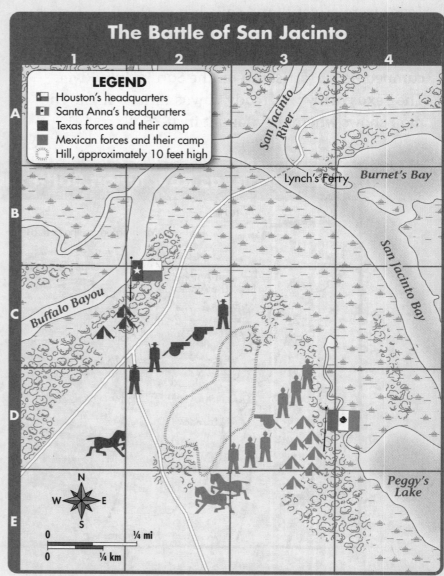

The Battle of San Jacinto

LEGEND
- Houston's headquarters
- Santa Anna's headquarters
- Texas forces and their camp
- Mexican forces and their camp
- Hill, approximately 10 feet high

San Jacinto River

Lynch's Ferry   Burnet's Bay

San Jacinto Bay

Buffalo Bayou

Peggy's Lake

N W E S

0   ¼ mi
0   ¼ km

The capture of Santa Anna

The Treaty of Velasco

The day after the battle, Houston sent soldiers to search for Santa Anna. They caught a Mexican soldier wearing common clothing. As they brought him back to camp, other Mexican prisoners shouted, *"El Presidente!"* Houston knew it must be Santa Anna.

Houston stopped his men from hurting Santa Anna. But he insisted the Mexican president end the fighting. Santa Anna agreed to order all Mexican troops to leave Texas. He sent word to his second-in-command, General Vicente Filisola, telling him to move all of the Mexican troops out of San Antonio. Filisola contributed to Texas's independence by leading the Mexican army in battle as the second-in-command. His other significant contribution was in leading the Mexican army out of San Antonio. The people of Texas had won their independence.

Even though Filisola and the Mexican forces were allowed to leave, Santa Anna could not leave. Santa Anna was forced to stay in Texas to talk with the new president of the republic, David G. Burnet. Sam Houston left for New Orleans to have his ankle treated.

6. **Identify** Santa Anna in this painting. Write how you know which one he is.

....

....

....

....

....

....

....

....

President Burnet met with Santa Anna at Velasco. On May 14, 1836, the two men signed the Treaty of Velasco. A **treaty** is a formal agreement between two countries. This treaty put an end to war between Mexico and the Republic of Texas. All Mexican forces would move south of the Rio Grande. American prisoners would be released.

A second, secret treaty was also signed. Santa Anna promised to work to get his government to agree to the independence of Texas. Still, it was several months before Santa Anna was allowed to return to Mexico.

Other Leaders of the Revolution

Many other people made significant contributions to the Texas Revolution. Tejanos Plácido Benavides and Juan Antonio Padilla were two officials who helped Texas gain its independence. Plácido Benavides who was also a rancher fought bravely in many of the early battles against Santa Anna's forces. However, because of his loyalty to Mexico, Benavides did not support Texas independence. Remember that in the early battles, the people of Texas wanted to be an independent state of Mexico.

Juan Antonio Padilla was a friend of Stephen F. Austin. Padilla supported and fought in the Texas Revolution.

José Francisco Ruiz, a Tejano, contributed to the Texas Revolution by serving as a delegate at the Convention of 1836. He was one of only two native Tejanos who signed the Texas Declaration of Independence. The other native Tejano who signed this important document was his nephew, José Antonio Navarro.

Juan N. Seguín was a rancher before the war. Seguín contributed by serving as a captain in the Texas Revolution and leading a Tejano unit at the Battle of San Jacinto. Seguín was later elected to the Texas Senate.

General Vicente Filisola

7. Write a caption to **summarize** the contribution of General Vicente Filisola in the Texas Revolution.

....

....

....

....

....

The San Jacinto Monument

Today, the San Jacinto battleground is just a short ride from downtown Houston. Texans have preserved 1,200 acres there as a state historic site. Each year, people gather to watch a reenactment of the Battle of San Jacinto. The battleground also has a monument that was built in 1939. A **monument** is a structure built to show respect for a past event. At 570 feet high, the San Jacinto Monument is the tallest war monument in the world. The meaning of this landmark is that it stands as a reminder of the victory at the Battle of San Jacinto, the final battle of the Texas Revolution.

The San Jacinto Monument

Got it?

TEKS 3.A, 16.A

8. **Sequence Identify** one major event that occurred *before* Sam Houston ordered James Fannin to leave Goliad. **Identify** another major event that occurred *after* Goliad.

....

....

9. **Explain** the meaning of the landmark known as the San Jacinto Monument.

my Story Ideas

....

....

....

10. **Analyze** the Runaway Scrape. What happened during this major event of the Texas Revolution?

....

....

....

SAVVAS realize. Go online to access your interactive digital lesson.

205

The Republic of Texas

Envision It!

The new Republic of Texas printed its own money.

The Texas Revolution was over. What were its effects? Texas was free! It was now independent of Mexico. Texas citizens had fought for and created a new republic. Now they had to take steps to set up a government.

Texas Rangers

The New Republic

The Constitution of 1836 outlined how the government would work. The government was one organization of the Republic of Texas. Voters chose Sam Houston to be their first president. They elected Mirabeau B. Lamar (MIR uh boh bee luh MAR) as vice president. Lamar had political experience and had fought at the Battle of San Jacinto.

They also voted on people to send to the Congress of the Republic of Texas. The constitution also provided for courts. Judges would decide whether the laws were fair and how to apply them. To pay for the work of the government, Texas taxed citizens.

Revolution and the Republic of Texas

Oct. 2
Mexican troops fail to take cannons from Gonzales.

Mar. 2
The Texas Declaration of Independence is adopted.

Mar. 11
The Runaway Scrape begins.

1835 | **1836**

Oct | Nov | Dec | Jan | Feb | Mar

Nov.
The Consultation of 1835 takes place.

Mar. 6
The Alamo falls.

Mar. 27
Prisoners are executed at Goliad.

Design and draw your own dollar bill. Include pictures that show something about everyday life in Texas.

Vocabulary

term

economic

debt

The new government set up a special force called the Texas Rangers. This organization of the Republic of Texas was created to protect the frontier. The men supplied their own horses and equipment to defend the settlers from attacks.

Immigrants also flocked to the Republic of Texas. The republic became a success as the population grew by about 7,000 people each year in the 1840s. Within a short time, there were private and religious schools, academies, and colleges in Texas.

The Lone Star Flag

The new nation needed a new flag. Some say that Joanna Troutman from Georgia made the first Lone Star flag. The blue star in her flag reminded the people of Texas about their struggle for independence. But in 1836, the Republic of Texas chose a different flag. Three years later, in 1839, the Republic changed its flag. Today's state flag is the same as the 1839 flag.

TEKS

3.A, 3.C, 3.D, 7.A, 17.D

1. **Describe** the organization known as the Texas Rangers.

....

....

....

....

....

Apr. 21
Texas wins the
Battle of San Jacinto.

Sept.
Voters elect Sam Houston
first president of Texas.

| Apr | May | June | July | Aug | Sept |

May 14
The two treaties of
Velasco are signed.

Presidents of the Republic of Texas

David G. Burnet

Served as a temporary president of the new republic from March 17 to October 22, 1836.

Sam Houston

Served in the U.S. Congress. He later became governor of Tennessee. He was elected president of the Republic of Texas in 1836 and in 1841.

Mirabeau B. Lamar

Is known as the Father of Texas Education. He supported schools during his presidency, which lasted from 1838 to 1841.

Anson Jones

Served as the president of the Republic of Texas from 1844 to 1846. He was the last president of the Republic of Texas.

A Successful Government

After the election, the new leaders helped make the new government a success. They named Columbia as the capital of Texas. In December, the capital moved to Houston, which was a small town named for Sam Houston. The town grew quickly after becoming the capital. Within four months, 1,500 people lived in Houston.

After his term in office, Sam Houston stepped down as president. The constitution said that a president could not hold the same office two terms in a row. A **term** is the time a person serves in office after each election. Obeying the democratic process, Houston served instead as a Texas congressman.

In 1838, Mirabeau B. Lamar became president of the republic. He believed Texas should expand to the west. Government leaders decided to move the capital to the western frontier along the Colorado River. The new capital city was named Austin to honor Stephen F. Austin.

In 1841, Houston ran for president a second time and was elected. Following Houston's second term, Anson Jones was elected president of the republic. Jones served until Texas became a state. David Burnet, Sam Houston, Mirabeau Lamar, and Anson Jones were all important to the successful founding of Texas as a republic.

2. In the images above, **identify** and circle the name of the president who served two terms, but not in a row. How did this leader model active participation in the democratic process?

....

....

....

....

....

....

....

Challenges to the Republic

Independence brought new responsibilities to the people of Texas. The new republic faced many problems. Some of the problems facing the Republic of Texas were economic. When something is **economic** it relates to money and paying bills. Texas had borrowed money to pay for the war. Now Texas had economic problems with debt. A **debt** is money owed to others. President Houston planned ways to repay the debt.

The new government also sought to keep the people safe. Mexico might attack again. Settlers moving into western Texas fought frequently with American Indians over the claim to the land.

Along with these problems loomed a serious question. Should Texas remain a separate nation? Or should Texas become a state in the United States?

Texas Faces Problems
Economic
....
....
Relations with American Indians
....
....
....
....

3. ◉ **Main Idea and Details** **Describe** the problems of the Republic of Texas by completing the chart.

Got it?

TEKS 3.C

4. ◉ **Sequence** Number the following events in the **sequence** in which they took place.

.... Mirabeau B. Lamar is elected president.

.... The capital is moved to Houston.

.... The capital is moved to Austin.

5. ❓ **Identify** leaders important to the founding of Texas as a republic. Write the name of the man who is known as the Father of Texas Education. How does the work he did affect Texans today?

my Story Ideas

....

....

6. You work at a Texas newspaper in the 1830s. On a separate sheet of paper, write a short article to **explain** how human activity created the capital city in Austin.

Lesson 1 TEKS 3.B, 3.C, 3.D, 15.A, 16.D

Conflict Leads to Revolution

1. Read the question carefully. Determine the best answer to the question from the four answer choices provided. Circle the best answer.

   Which statement describes one of the successes of the Republic of Texas?

   A It created a written constitution.

   B It gave all people the same freedoms.

   C It stopped immigrants from coming to Texas.

   D It made slavery illegal for immigrants.

2. **Describe** the origins of the state celebration known as Texas Independence Day.

   ....

   ....

   ....

3. **Summarize** the significant contribution of Texian George Childress.

   ....

   ....

   ....

4. **Identify** leaders important to the founding of Texas as a republic. Match the person with his description.

José Antonio Navarro	Commanded the Texas army
Sam Houston	Led Tejanos to fight for Texas
Juan N. Seguín	A Tejano who signed the Texas Declaration of Independence

5. **Identify** the purposes of the following documents:

   Texas Declaration of Independence

   ....

   ....

   Texas Constitution of 1836

   ....

   ....

Lesson 2 TEKS 3.A, 3.B

The Battle of the Alamo

6. ◉ **Sequence** Number the following events in the sequence in which they took place.

   _____ James Bonham returned to the Alamo.

   _____ Santa Anna laid siege to the Alamo.

   _____ William Travis wrote a plea for help.

7. Summarize the contribution of Tejano Carlos Espalier to the war for Texas independence.

....

....

....

8. Explain one major effect of the Battle of the Alamo on the people of Texas.

....

....

....

Lesson 3 TEKS 3.A, 3.B, 16.A

Victory at San Jacinto

9. Analyze the major events of the Texas Revolution, including the Runaway Scrape. Fill in the blanks to complete the sentences.

a. During the Runaway Scrape, people fled from their homes to escape

....

b. .... ordered everyone to leave.

10. Summarize the contribution of Tejano Plácido Benavides in the war for Texas independence.

....

....

....

11. Identify and circle the letter of the entry that best completes the timeline.

March 10
Runaway Scrape begins

March 27 _____

March   April   May

April 21
Victory at San Jacinto

A Susanna Dickinson meets General Houston.

B General Filisola moves his troops to San Antonio.

C Colonel Fannin and his men are shot at Goliad.

12. Explain the meaning of the San Jacinto Monument.

....

....

....

13. Write the name of each person in the sentence that **summarizes** his contributions to Texas's independence.

> Juan Antonio Padilla   José Francisco Ruiz
>
> Sidney Sherman

a. Stephen Austin's friend,

, was

a Tejano who supported and fought in the Texas Revolution.

b. .... was a commander who brought volunteers from Kentucky to fight in the Texas Revolution.

c. One of the two native Tejanos who signed the Texas Declaration of Independence was

....

Lesson 4   TEKS 3.A, 3.C

The Republic of Texas

14. Analyze and write about the effects of the Texas Revolution.

....

....

....

....

15. The following leaders were important to the founding of Texas. **Describe** what Anson Jones and Mirabeau Lamar had in common.

....

....

16. ◎ **Sequence** Number the towns below in the sequence in which they were made capitals of the Republic of Texas.

_____ Austin

_____ Columbia

_____ Houston

17. ❓ **How does the past shape our present and future?**   TEKS 3.A, 16.A

Look at the landmark below and answer the question.

Explain the meaning of the Alamo to Texans today.

....

....

....

....

Go online to write and illustrate your own **myStory Book** using the **myStory Ideas** from this chapter.

 THE BIG ?

How does the past shape our present and future?

TEKS
ELA 15

So many brave, intelligent, and inspiring people took part in the Texas Revolution that books and movies are still written about them today. Their lives, the goals they aimed for, and the choices they made to meet them changed Texas forever.

Think about the ways people shape our present and future today. How can one person's actions change other people's lives? Identify at least three examples of actions people can take today that can help make a better future for Texas.

....

....

....

Now draw a picture that shows how your community would be in the future, if people took that action today.

SAVVAS realize Go online to access your interactive digital lesson.

213

The Road to Statehood

 my Story Spark

When does change become necessary?

Identify a time when you felt change was necessary in a group you belonged to. **Analyze** the reasons why the change was needed. **Describe** how the change happened or how you would like it to happen.

....

....

....

....

Texas Essential Knowledge and Skills

1.C Describe the regions in which American Indians lived and identify American Indian groups remaining in Texas such as the Ysleta Del Sur Pueblo, Alabama-Coushatta, and Kickapoo.

3.C Identify leaders important to the founding of Texas as a republic and state, including José Antonio Navarro, Sam Houston, Mirabeau Lamar, and Anson Jones.

3.D Describe the successes, problems, and organizations of the Republic of Texas such as the establishment of a constitution, economic struggles, relations with American Indians, and the Texas Rangers.

3.E Explain the events that led to the annexation of Texas to the United States, including the impact of the U.S.-Mexican War.

7.A Describe a variety of regions in Texas and the United States such as political, population, and economic regions that result from patterns of human activity.

8.A Identify and explain clusters and patterns of settlement in Texas at different time periods such as prior to the Texas Revolution, after the building of the railroads, and following World War II.

8.B Describe and explain the location and distribution of various towns and cities in Texas, past and present.

8.C Explain the geographic factors such as landforms and climate that influence patterns of settlement and the distribution of population in Texas, past and present.

10.B Explain the economic activities early immigrants to Texas used to meet their needs and wants.

12.A Explain how people in different regions of Texas earn their living, past and present, through a subsistence economy and providing goods and services.

12.B Explain how geographic factors such as climate, transportation, and natural resources have influenced the location of economic activities in Texas.

12.C Analyze the effects of exploration, immigration, migration, and limited resources on the economic development and growth of Texas.

15.A Identify the purposes and explain the importance of the Texas Declaration of Independence, the Texas Constitution, and other documents such as the Meusebach-Comanche Treaty.

17.D Identify the importance of historical figures and important individuals who modeled active participation in the democratic process such as Sam Houston, Barbara Jordan, Lorenzo de Zavala, Ann Richards, Sam Rayburn, Henry B. González, James A. Baker III, Wallace Jefferson, and other local individuals.

19.A Identify the similarities and differences among various racial, ethnic, and religious groups in Texas.

19.B Identify customs, celebrations, and traditions of various cultural, regional, and local groups in Texas such as Cinco de Mayo, Oktoberfest, the Strawberry Festival, and Fiesta San Antonio.

21.B Analyze information by sequencing, categorizing, identifying cause-and-effect relationships, comparing, contrasting, finding the main idea, summarizing, making generalizations and predictions, and drawing inferences and conclusions.

23.B Use a decision-making process to identify a situation that requires a decision, gather information, identify options, predict consequences, and take action to implement a decision.

New Braunfels
A Community Built by Immigrants

my Story Video

"This place is so cool!" says Zen. "It's like visiting a small town in Germany!" Welcome to the Sophienburg Museum in New Braunfels, Texas. This local site is dedicated to preserving the long German heritage found in the state. "When I think of Texas, I think of our Mexican roots, not European influences," Zen says. "I wonder why there is such a strong European influence, too."

To learn more, Zen meets up with Keva, a local historian at the museum. *"Willkommen,"* says Keva. "That's German for 'welcome.'" Keva has worked at the museum for many years and is very proud to share her German heritage with visitors.

"I know that Texas was originally part of Mexico, but why does it also have traces of German influence?" asks Zen. "Texas has gone through some big changes over the years," says Keva. When Texas was a republic, its leaders wanted to attract people to the area. They decided to sell public land to Americans and Europeans.

Zen is visiting the Sophienburg Museum in New Braunfels, Texas.

215

Zen learns about some of the artifacts the German immigrants brought with them.

The first windmills in Texas were built by Dutch and German immigrants.

"That's when Prince Carl of Solms-Braunfels, of Germany, came to Texas," explains Keva. "In 1845, he purchased more than 1,000 acres of land and established the town of New Braunfels."

"Why Texas?" asks Zen. "Isn't that a pretty far move?" Keva replies, "It was quite the journey, but during that time things were uneasy in Germany." Prince Carl was looking for a place that had lots of opportunity. It turns out that Texas wasn't only big, but the land had rich waterways and lush vegetation, too.

"So what did German immigrants do when they got here?" asks Zen. "They used the river as a source of power to create mills," says Keva. "They used the mills to process grains. As the town continued to grow, so did the need for additional services and businesses. People opened stores and craft shops that made things such as farm tools, leather goods, furniture, and clothing."

They also faced some challenges. They had to learn a new language and new trades. Some also had to learn how to farm in a different environment.

Keva shows Zen a map of the area the Germans settled.

German immigrants brought their customs and traditions with them. This display at the museum shows traditional German breads.

Zen learns that German immigrants worked hard, but they also found time for games.

The immigrants also brought their customs and traditions to Texas. "Even though they started a new life, most immigrants stayed true to their roots," says Keva. "German language, traditions, literature, food, and even music made their way to the town of New Braunfels." "I get it now," says Zen. "The Germans may have moved, but they were proud of their heritage." he adds. "Right," explains Keva. "Just like Mexican influences can be seen throughout other parts of Texas, the German immigrants had a remarkable effect on the city of New Braunfels."

As Zen walks through the rest of the Sophienburg Museum, he realizes all the changes the state, the town, and its people must have gone through. In order to take advantage of new opportunities, the Germans needed to move to a foreign land and begin a new life. "Today I've learned that change can be a good thing," says Zen. "And it can also provide new opportunities."

Think About It How do you think German and other immigrants helped transform Texas? As you read the chapter ahead, think about why change may become necessary for a people, a state, or a country. Then think about the positive and negative consequences of the change.

SAVVAS realize. Go online to access your interactive digital lesson.

217

The Rise of the Lone Star State

This was the flag of the Republic of Texas. If Texas became a state, it would need a state flag.

Sam Houston was the president of the Republic of Texas from 1836 to 1838 and 1841 to 1844.

"Texas must be defended and liberty maintained." Those were Sam Houston's words in 1836. Texans had fought for liberty and won. Was it time for another change? Should Texas remain a republic? Or should it join the powerful nation to the north and east, the United States?

The Last Days of the Republic

Sam Houston had led Texans in the fight for independence. And twice he was elected president of the republic. His loyalty and love for Texas were not questioned. But Sam Houston did not think Texas should remain a republic. He was in favor of **annexation.** In other words, he wanted Texas to be added to the United States.

Houston tried to convince the people of Texas to agree with him. He told them that the Republic of Texas had problems it could not overcome as an independent country. First, it needed the protection of the powerful United States. Another problem was Texas's large debts. It needed the financial support the United States could offer. And it needed services a large nation could provide.

1. **Identify** how Sam Houston served the Republic of Texas. **Identify** and underline in the text the problems Houston thought Texas could not overcome as an independent country.

....

....

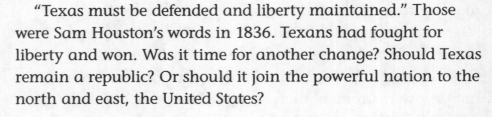

Design a state flag for Texas. Draw it in the box.

UNLOCK THE BIG ?

I will know that people in both Texas and the United States had differing opinions about whether Texas should be independent or part of the United States.

Vocabulary

annexation   legislature

resolution

Sam Houston was a popular president, but not everyone agreed with him. The people had been under the control of Mexico for many years. Some did not want to lose that independence by becoming part of the United States.

TEKS

1.C, 3.C, 3.D, 3.E, 7.A, 8.A, 8.B, 8.C, 10.B, 12.A, 12.B, 12.C, 15.A, 17.D, 19.A, 19.B

Within the United States there was disagreement too. Some U.S. leaders wanted Texas as a state. Others did not. Texas's debt was one issue. But the big problem was slavery. Texas laws allowed slavery. Other states in the South also allowed slavery. But many Americans opposed it. They did not want to admit another slave state to the United States.

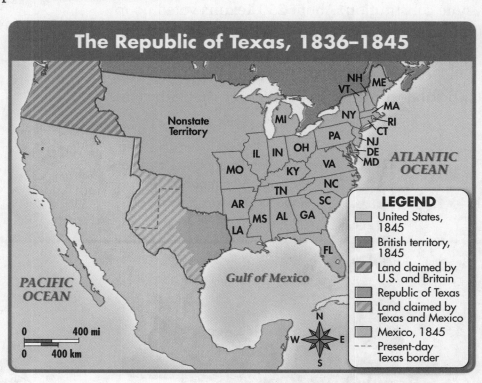

The Republic of Texas, 1836–1845

Nonstate Territory

ATLANTIC OCEAN

PACIFIC OCEAN

Gulf of Mexico

LEGEND
- United States, 1845
- British territory, 1845
- Land claimed by U.S. and Britain
- Republic of Texas
- Land claimed by Texas and Mexico
- Mexico, 1845
- - - Present-day Texas border

0   400 mi
0   400 km

2. **Identify** and outline on the map lands claimed by both Texas and Mexico. **Explain** what problems might be caused by these claims.

....

....

Texas Joins the United States

Several events led to the annexation of Texas to the United States. In 1844 the United States elected James K. Polk as president. He wanted Texas to become a state. Polk asked Congress to pass a **resolution**, or decision, for Texas to become a state. Congress passed the resolution on February 28, 1845. It said that Texas could keep land it owned but had to turn over its forts to the U.S. government.

The next step was for Texas to agree to the terms of the resolution. Anson Jones was the president of the Republic of Texas at the time. The Texas congress voted unanimously for annexation on June 16, 1845. The state constitutional convention approved it on July 4. All but one voted yes.

On October 13, the people of Texas also voted. Over 4,000 voted to approve annexation and the state constitution. About 250 Texans voted no to annexation. About 300 voted no to the constitution. The U.S. Congress approved the Texas Constitution. On December 29, 1845, President Polk signed the official documents. Texas became the 28th state.

3. **Sequence** the events that led to Texas becoming a state.

....

....

....

....

....

President Anson Jones lowered the flag of the republic. "The Republic of Texas is no more," he said.

The Constitution of 1845

The constitution would have many purposes. Writing the state constitution was an important job. Some of the state leaders worked to write the laws for how the new state would be run. One writer was José Antonio Navarro. He was the only Tejano who took part in the process.

José Antonio Navarro

They took ideas from the constitutions of the Republic of Texas, the state of Louisiana, and the United States. Two months later, they had completed a new plan for governing Texas.

The constitution had rules for who could hold office in the state government. It set taxes and provided for public schools. Most important, it said how the government would be set up. A **legislature** would meet every two years. This is the group of elected people who make new laws. Texas would also have a governor. Voters would elect a new governor every two years. The first governor of Texas was James Pinckney Henderson.

The constitution also had rules about who could vote. African Americans, women, and American Indians did not have the right to vote. They also were not allowed to hold public office. Only men over the age of 21 who were Anglo, or European, and Tejano, or Mexican Texans, could vote and hold office.

4. ◉ **Compare and Contrast Identify** who could and could not vote according to the new Texas state constitution. Add a check mark for each group in the correct column.

Group	Could Vote and Hold Office	Could Not Vote or Hold Office
Anglo Men		
African Americans		
Women		
Tejano Men		
American Indians		

Texas Grows

Texas had land to be settled. When Texas became a state, it had kept control of public land. The state was given the right to sell or give away the land for settlement. So the state welcomed new Texans. People arrived from Mexico and the southern United States. They also came from Germany, Poland, and other countries of Europe.

Just who had the right to the land was not a simple matter, however. Sometimes these "public" lands had been used by American Indians for centuries. In one case, for example, Texas had granted a large area of land to a group of Germans. They wanted to attract 1,000 families from Germany and other European countries. It turned out, however, that the land was the hunting grounds of the Comanche people. The Comanche leader Buffalo Hump expressed his people's distress: "I object to any more settlements," he said. "I want this country to hunt in."

By 1845, Baron John O. Meusebach was the head of the German settlement. Meusebach worked to find a solution so that the lands could be settled. On May 9, 1847, the Meusebach-Comanche Treaty was signed. Its purpose was to settle the dispute between the new immigrants and the Comanche. This important treaty made more than 3 million acres of land available for settlement.

Texas grew as immigrants settled new towns.

Present-day image of Fredericksburg founded by John O. Meusebach.

5. **Identify** the purpose of the Meusebach-Comanche Treaty and underline it in the text.

The Call of the Land

Immigrants came to Texas for many reasons. Some wanted to escape problems in their home countries. But all came for the new opportunities. Texas developed and grew as they established towns and farms on the millions of acres of land Texas had to offer. These new towns were distributed throughout Texas. The largest number of people moved west from the southern United States. Many also moved north from Mexico.

The rich natural resources of Texas were great for farming. This also attracted many immigrants. In Germany, people learned about Texas from books like the ones Prince Carl of Solms-Braunfels read, which described a land and waterways filled with resources. Especially after the Meusebach-Comanche Treaty, many German families came to Texas. About 20,000 Germans settled in Texas by 1860. Immigrants usually clustered together in different parts of Texas. Located in the central part of the state, Germans built Fredericksburg, New Braunfels, and other towns.

Many immigrants came from Poland and Czechoslovakia, too. Czechoslovakia is now divided into the Czech Republic and Slovakia. They settled in central and southeast Texas. The town of Panna Maria, founded in 1854, is the nation's oldest permanent Polish settlement.

6. Evaluate the reasons why immigrants moved to Texas. Underline the sentences in the text.

7. Identify the areas in which large populations of immigrants settled.

....

....

Interior of a store in Panna Maria in the early 1900s

The New Texans

In the years after statehood, the population of Texas grew quickly. In 1847 there were about 140,000 people living in the state. Just 13 years later, the population was more than 600,000!

New Texans engaged in a variety of economic activities to meet their needs and wants, and earn a living. Many lived a subsistence economy. They relied on the food they grew and the animals they raised for their families' basic needs. Many were farmers. Some were ranchers. No matter what immigrants had done in their old countries, now they had one job. They had to find ways to supply their families with their basic needs. For most, this meant growing food. It was a hard job, but the rich land of Texas made this possible.

Even today, Texans celebrate holidays from their past. Cinco de Mayo honors the heritage of Mexico.

As the number of Texans grew, new towns, distributed throughout Texas, were being formed. Immigrants also enlarged old towns such as San Antonio. In the towns, they opened stores such as hardware stores that supplied tools needed on the farm. They also opened hotels. Some supplied services such as mills to process grains from the farms.

Several racial and ethnic groups lived in Texas. These immigrants came to build new lives, but they brought much from their old lives. In the new German towns in the Hill Country, for example, settlers spoke German and celebrated Oktoberfest. They read German books. They ate German food. In southwestern Texas, immigrants from Mexico settled in towns like El Paso and Eagle Pass. There, people continued to speak and write Spanish and celebrate holidays such as *Cinco de Mayo*. Different groups celebrated their own holidays and had special customs.

8. Explain the distribution of towns in Texas.

....

....

....

9. Identify and underline in the text the types of economic activities early Texans engaged in to meet their needs and earn their living. **Explain** what types of goods and services they provided.

....

....

....

Together, all of the immigrants helped to create a new Texas. They brought new ideas that helped the state grow and prosper, different ideas about how to farm or how to run a business.

They brought their cultures, too. Today you can see signs of those cultures throughout the state. A building in the Hill Country may look very different from one in southwestern Texas, for example. You can still find food, music, and customs from the past. All of this makes Texas what it is today.

Oktoberfest, a German custom, is still celebrated today.

 **Got it?**

TEKS 10.B, 12.C, 15.A

10. **Make Predictions Explain** the importance of the Meusebach-Comanche Treaty and its effect on the amount of land for settlement. Suppose you were a Texan in 1847. **Predict** what would happen to immigration.

....

....

11. Immigrants to Texas in the 1850s faced big changes. **Analyze** some of the changes you might face if you immigrated to another country today.

 my Story Ideas

....

....

....

12. If you wanted to attract German people to come to Texas after 1845, what would you say? On a separate sheet of paper, write an advertisement to place in a German newspaper.

Make Decisions

Some decisions are easy to make. Which shirt shall I wear today? Should I have sausage on my pizza or not? Other decisions are far more complicated. They can affect our lives in important ways.

Suppose you lived in Louisiana in 1849. Texas is part of the United States, the Mexican War is over, and the United States is larger than it has ever been. Your parents are thinking about moving west. This is a big decision! It would change everyone's life. How do your parents make that decision?

Look at the chart below.

Questions to Ask Yourself When Making Decisions

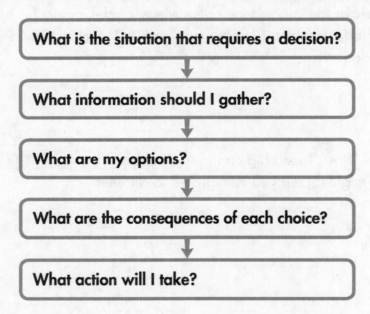

> What is the situation that requires a decision?
>
> What information should I gather?
>
> What are my options?
>
> What are the consequences of each choice?
>
> What action will I take?

You might ask your parents why they want to move. They want new opportunities, they reply. But they have to decide where to go.

What information do they need? Your parents would need to figure out just how they would move the family. They'd also need to think about how much the move would cost. And what time of year would be best? You can't take everything with you. Your parents have to decide what things stay and what they can carry.

Learning Objective

I will know how to make decisions.

 TEKS

SS 23.B Use a decision-making process to identify a situation that requires a decision, gather information, identify options, predict consequences, and take action to implement a decision.

You might ask them what the choices are. You could go to Texas, where there is a lot of land. Or the family could move out to California, where the Gold Rush is going on. Or you could decide to stay in Louisiana. There are lots of choices.

Next, they think about the consequences, or the results, of each choice. Your parents talk to you and your brothers and sisters. Finally, they tell you they have made a choice: TEXAS! The next step would be to implement their decision.

 **Try it!**

Reread the section titled **The Last Days of the Republic** on pages 218–219. Then, answer each question using the steps you learned for making decisions.

1. **Identify** the decision Sam Houston had to make. What were his options?

   ....

   ....

   ....

2. Read the section titled **Texas Joins the United States** on page 220. What decision did President Polk make? **Explain** the action he took.

   ....

   ....

   ....

3. **Apply** Identify a situation and a decision you have made. On another sheet of paper, make a diagram, like the one on page 226, to outline the way you made your decision. **Explain** the final action you took.

SAVVAS realize Go online to access your interactive digital lesson.

227

The Mexican War

Envision It!

Conflict between Mexico and Texas did not end when Texas became a state.

Disagreement Over Boundaries

Texas's relationship with Mexico was unsettled. It would take two years to resolve the conflict.

In the mid-1800s, U.S. citizens wanted their country to **expand**, or spread out. They believed it was their right. Many people were moving west. The United States had expanded west when Texas became a state. But what were the boundaries of the state? The United States and Mexico disputed, or disagreed, about this.

Mexico said the land in its northern frontier belonged to Mexico. The United States wanted that land. Much of it made up what is now the state of Texas. The president of the United States, James K. Polk, offered to buy it. Mexico refused.

1. **Analyze** the map. **Identify** the land Mexico and the United States disputed. Mark an X on that land.

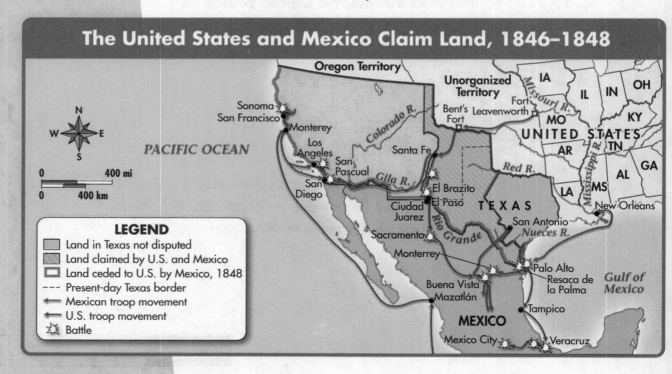

The United States and Mexico Claim Land, 1846–1848

Oregon Territory

Unorganized Territory

Sonoma
San Francisco
Monterey
Los Angeles
San Diego

PACIFIC OCEAN

Colorado R.

Bent's Fort

Fort Leavenworth

Missouri R.

IA

IL   IN   OH

MO   KY

UNITED STATES

AR   TN

Santa Fe

San Pascual

Gila R.

El Brazito
El Paso
Ciudad Juarez

Red R.

TEXAS

San Antonio
Nueces R.

Mississippi R.

LA   MS   AL   GA

New Orleans

Sacramento

Rio Grande

Monterrey

Buena Vista
Mazatlán

Palo Alto
Resaca de la Palma

Gulf of Mexico

Tampico

MEXICO

Mexico City   Veracruz

0   400 mi
0   400 km

LEGEND
- Land in Texas not disputed
- Land claimed by U.S. and Mexico
- Land ceded to U.S. by Mexico, 1848
- - - Present-day Texas border
- ← Mexican troop movement
- ← U.S. troop movement
- ✸ Battle

UNLOCK THE BIG ?

I will know that the United States and Mexico went to war to settle boundary disputes.

Vocabulary

expand
boundary
skirmish

Fighting is one result of conflict. What are some other ways that conflict might be resolved?

The United States and Mexico also had another major disagreement. Mexico insisted the Nueces River was the **boundary**, or line, between the two countries. The United States said the Rio Grande was the boundary.

When Mexico refused to talk about the dispute, President Polk took action. In January 1846 he ordered General Zachary Taylor to march an army toward the Rio Grande. Mexican soldiers crossed the river into the disputed territory on April 25 and attacked a small U.S. Army unit. There was a **skirmish**, or small battle. Mexican soldiers won.

Soon President Polk asked Congress to declare war on Mexico. Mexico had shed "American blood upon American soil," he said. On May 8, 1846, Mexican soldiers fought U.S. soldiers in a major attack. In this fight, the Battle of Palo Alto, the United States won. It was the first real battle in a new war.

TEKS
3.D, 3.E

2. ⊙ **Cause and Effect** Complete this cause-and-effect chart about conflict between the United States and Mexico.

Cause	Effect
After the annexation of Texas to the United States there were disputes with Mexico over boundaries. Mexican soldiers attacked a small U.S. army unit.	

War With Mexico

The United States declared war on Mexico on May 13, 1846. In this country the conflict is called the Mexican War. President Polk had one main goal. He wanted to take control of all the land Mexico claimed north of the Rio Grande and all the way west to the Pacific!

Some Americans did not like to have the country go to war. But many Texans wanted to end Mexico's claims. They wanted the disputed land to be part of the United States.

The Texas Rangers fought in the war, too. This group of volunteers had helped defend Texas since 1835 in the days of the Republic. They were especially good scouts, getting information to the army. In fact, they were known as General Taylor's "eyes and ears."

The fighting went on, with victories on both sides. Finally, in August 1847, U.S. General Winfield Scott marched an army toward Mexico City. They captured the city in mid-September. The war was over.

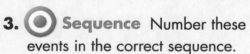

The Texas Rangers played a part in the U.S. victories in Mexico.

3. ◎ **Sequence** Number these events in the correct sequence.

_____ Treaty of Guadalupe Hidalgo

_____ U.S. declaration of war

_____ Battle of Palo Alto

_____ U.S. victory in Mexico City

For two days in September 1847, U.S. soldiers battled Mexican forces in the Mexican capital.

The Treaty of Guadalupe Hidalgo

On February 2, 1848, leaders from Mexico and the United States signed a treaty to end the war. The Treaty of Guadalupe Hidalgo was named for the village where it was signed.

There were several impacts of the war. The Rio Grande became the southern border of Texas. Mexico gave more than 500,000 square miles of land to the United States. In exchange, the United States paid Mexico $15 million.

Also, Tejanos gained important rights. They were granted U.S. citizenship. The treaty promised to protect property rights of Tejanos. A new age had come in the relations between Mexico and the United States.

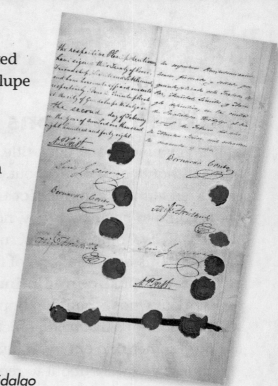

4. **Identify** and underline in the text what the United States gained as part of the Treaty of Guadalupe Hidalgo.

The Treaty of Guadalupe Hidalgo

Got it?

🔹 TEKS 3.E

5. ⊙ **Make Predictions** Write a newspaper headline that could have appeared after the victory in Mexico City. **Predict** what you think will happen next.

....

....

6. ❓ Suppose you were a Tejano in 1848. You lived in an area newly part of Texas. **Analyze** how you would have felt about the Treaty of Guadalupe Hidalgo. Write a letter to a cousin living in Mexico City.　　my Story Ideas

....

....

....

7. **Explain** the events that led to the annexation to the United States, including the impact of the Mexican War.

....

....

Make Predictions

When you look at a book title, you often have an idea of what that book will be about. That's because you are a smart reader! You can **predict** that *The Journey of a Young Boy* is going to be about a boy, not a dog. What about *A Wrinkle in Time*? Since time doesn't really have wrinkles, do you think this book is a kind of fantasy?

When you make a **prediction**, you make an educated guess about what is going to happen or what something will be about. It's like being a detective. You are using clues to figure something out by analyzing the information.

Suppose you were about to read Chapter 6. What clues would tell you what the chapter will be about? What does *the road to statehood* mean? A road is something you travel. You can infer that the chapter will be about events that happen on the way to statehood.

Then look at the lesson titles. What word tells you Lesson 1 will be about something positive? Hint: This is the story of a rise, not a fall. What about Lesson 2? You know from the title that there was a war. Look at the headings in the lesson. What can you learn from them? What does the first heading say about reasons for the conflict?

You can use a graphic organizer to keep track of clues and predictions as you read. Look at the map on page 228. Now, reread the text on page 231. Make a prediction about how the United States would use the land it acquired from Mexico.

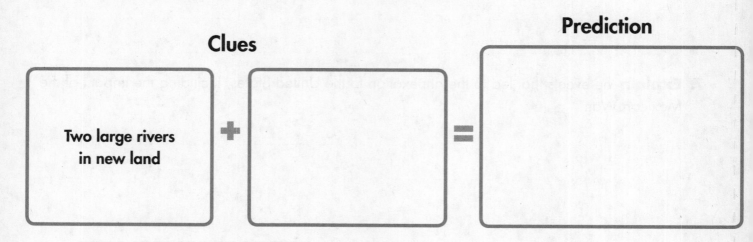

Clues

Prediction

Two large rivers
in new land

+

=

Try it!

1. Skim through the lesson titles in Chapter 7. **Analyze** the information to make predictions on what the chapter is about.

   ....

   ....

   ....

2. In Chapter 7, **identify** what the headings in Lesson 1 tell.

   ....

   ....

   ....

3. In Chapter 7, **identify** the headings, images, and image captions in Lesson 2. Pay close attention to the timeline on page 255. What do they tell?

   ....

   ....

   ....

   ....

4. **Apply** Think about a change that has happened in your life. Then imagine you are going to write a story about it. **Identify** the title of your story and four headings that will help a reader predict what happens.

   ....

   ....

   ....

   ....

SAVVAS realize Go online to access your interactive digital lesson.

233

Lesson 1 ⬗ TEKS 3.E, 8.A, 8.B, 10.B, 12.A, 15.A, 19.A, 19.B, 21.B

The Rise of the Lone Star State

1. ◎ **Make Predictions** Write a new title for Lesson 1. Readers should be able to **predict** what the lesson will be about.

....

....

....

....

2. Read the question carefully. Determine the best answer to the question from the four answer choices provided. Circle the best answer.

   Which statement is correct about Texas statehood?

   A All Texans were in favor of statehood.

   B Sam Houston supported statehood.

   C All Texans were against statehood.

   D Everyone in the United States wanted Texas as a state.

3. **Identify** the purposes of the Texas constitution.

....

....

....

....

....

4. ◎ **Compare and Contrast** What were the similarities and differences among the new settlers of Texas? Fill in the chart to identify similarities and differences.

Similarities	Differences

5. **Explain** what economic activities early immigrants to Texas used to meet their needs and wants?

....

....

....

....

....

6. Answer these questions to **explain** the importance of the Meusebach-Comanche Treaty.

a. How did Texas want to use its public land?

....

....

b. Why did the Comanche object?

....

....

c. What was the result of the treaty?

....

....

....

7. Where did the various ethnic groups settle? After each town, write the origin of the people who settled it.

a. Fredericksburg ....

b. Panna Maria ....

c. El Paso ....

8. **Identify** a custom that each ethnic group celebrates.

a. Mexican ....

b. German ....

9. Read this letter an immigrant to Texas might have written. **Explain** how this immigrant lived on a subsistence economy.

"Dear Brother, We had a good harvest this year. I grew enough vegetables and raised enough cattle to feed the family for the winter."

....

....

....

10. **Identify** clusters of immigrant settlements located in Texas in the 1850s and 1860s? **Identify** and **explain** each location. On a separate sheet of paper **explain** the patterns of settlement of these immigrant groups.

German Immigrants
....
....
....
....
....
Polish and Czechoslovakian Immigrants
....
....
....
....

Lesson 2 ⬩ TEKS 3.D, 3.E

The Mexican War

11. Identify the importance of the Nueces River and the Rio Grande.

....

....

....

....

12. Explain why the United States wanted Mexico's northern frontier.

....

....

....

13. Describe the Texas Rangers and why they were important in the Mexican War.

....

....

....

....

....

14. How did the Treaty of Guadalupe Hidalgo effect Tejanos?

....

....

....

....

15. ⬥ **When does change become necessary?** ⬩ TEKS 3.E

Read the following quotation.

Mexico has shed "American blood upon American soil."

a. Who said this and when?

....

....

....

b. How did the speaker use this idea to bring about change?

....

....

....

....

....

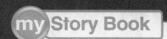my Story Book

Go online to write and illustrate your own **myStory Book** using the **myStory Ideas** from this chapter.

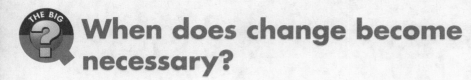

When does change become necessary?

TEKS

SS 3.E, 21.E
ELA 15

Think about what it was like to live in Texas after it became a state. List some of the changes you would have experienced.

....

....

....

....

....

....

Draw an image to show Texas before statehood and after the Mexican War.

New Challenges for Texas

 my Story Spark

What is worth fighting for?

Think about a time when you stood up for something you felt was important. **Explain** why this made a difference to you and to others.

....

....

....

....

....

....

....

....

★ Texas Essential Knowledge and Skills

4.A Describe the impact of the Civil War and Reconstruction on Texas.

4.D Examine the effects upon American Indian life resulting from changes in Texas, including the Red River War, building of U.S. forts and railroads, and loss of buffalo.

6.B Translate geographic data, population distribution, and natural resources into a variety of formats.

10.A Explain the economic activities various early American Indian groups in Texas and North America used to meet their needs and wants such as farming, trading, and hunting.

12.C Analyze the effects of exploration, immigration, migration, and limited resources on the economic development and growth of Texas.

16.A Explain the meaning of various patriotic symbols and landmarks of Texas, including the six flags that flew over Texas, the San Jacinto Monument, the Alamo, and various missions.

16.D Describe the origins and significance of state celebrations such as Texas Independence Day and Juneteenth.

19.C Summarize the contributions of people of various racial, ethnic, and religious groups in the development of Texas such as Lydia Mendoza, Chelo Silva, and Julius Lorenzo Cobb Bledsoe.

23.A Use a problem-solving process to identify a problem, gather information, list and consider options, consider advantages and disadvantages, choose and implement a solution, and evaluate the effectiveness of the solution.

Juneteenth
A Celebration of Freedom

my Story Video

"I remember that drummer! He was really good!" exclaims Giovanni as he looks through some photos of his family at last year's Juneteenth celebration. Giovanni's extended family goes every year on June 19 to celebrate the abolition of slavery. "I think my favorite part of that day was the barbecue. I ate so much, my stomach was hurting after that!" Giovanni groans. And while the celebration is a huge event in Houston, with parades and bands and barbecues, Giovanni understands that the day is more than just a party. It's a celebration of freedom.

Texas, as well as the rest of the states in the South, was built largely with slave labor. By 1860, three out of every ten Texans were enslaved African Americans. Many worked on the cotton plantations and farms located in the fertile river valleys of Texas. People who were enslaved had no rights. Landowners bought them and sold them and forced them to work.

Giovanni learned about the Civil War in school, and he knows that slavery was one of the biggest issues that divided the nation. "Was Texas part of the Civil War?" he asks his mom. "It was," she replies.

Giovanni is learning about Juneteenth, a celebration that commemorates the abolition of slavery in Texas.

239

The Lincoln Memorial in Washington, D.C., honors this president who led the nation during the Civil War.

Today, segregation is illegal. Here, Giovanni enjoys playing in the park with children of different backgrounds.

Giovanni's mom explains that during the Civil War, Texas sided with the Confederacy, or the states that were in favor of slavery. To protect the right of Southern states to have slavery, they seceded from the nation. That means that they separated from the rest of the United States.

But the Confederacy was ultimately defeated and, in May of 1865, the war ended. It took a while for word to spread to Texas. "Do you know what day Texas heard about the end of the Civil War?" Giovanni's mom asks him. "I don't know," he replies. "June 19," she says. "Hey, that's Juneteenth!" Giovanni replies. "Yes, that's because it was on that day in 1865 that Union Army Major General Gordon Granger rode through Galveston to announce the war was over and slaves were free." On June 19, 1866, African Americans in Texas celebrated their first year of freedom. They gave thanks, listened to speeches, sang, and enjoyed picnics. This tradition continues today. "Oh! I always wondered why the big party was in June!" Giovanni exclaims.

The emancipation, or freeing, of slaves did not bring immediate relief to many African Americans. While they gained the right to an education and African American men were allowed to vote, they still struggled. Many Texans were opposed to the new rights given to African Americans, and years of segregation and discrimination gripped the state.

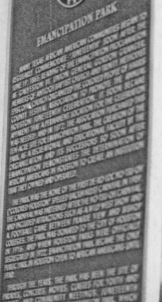

This plaque at Emancipation Park, in Houston, tells about the significance of Juneteenth for African Americans in Texas.

Giovanni and his mom take a stroll in Emancipation Park, where Juneteenth festivities take place every year.

Emancipation Park was founded in 1872 by former slaves. The park was acquired by the city of Houston in 1918.

Later in the day, Giovanni and his mom visit Emancipation Park in Houston. "This is where we came for last year's celebration," Giovanni says. His mom tells him that freed slaves bought this land in order to celebrate Emancipation Day. "Many of the African Americans lived nearby, in an area known as Freedman Town," his mom explains. "During segregation, they came to Emancipation Park because it was one of the few city parks open to African Americans."

"I remember Grandpa telling me he went to a school that only had African American children in it. Was that part of segregation?" Giovanni asks his mom. "Yes," she replies. Giovanni's mom also explains that his grandfather had to use separate bathrooms and water fountains that were only for African Americans, and he couldn't eat in some restaurants. "During this time, it was very difficult for Grandpa and many African Americans," she says.

"Well," says Giovanni. "I'm glad things are different now. I have a lot of friends of diverse cultures, and we all get along. I guess that's why we have such a big party on Juneteenth, not only to remember the past but also to celebrate the freedoms that we have now!"

Think About It Based on the story, how are things different for Giovanni than they were for his grandfather when he was growing up? As you read this chapter, think about the events that occur and how they affect the freedom of the people involved and the freedom of people in the future.

Texas and the Civil War

Envision It!

The Confederate soldier, on the right, and the Union soldier, on the left, fought on opposite sides in the Civil War.

Texas became the 28th state in the United States in 1845. But 16 years later, Texans would decide to leave. What happened? Like people in other southern states, many white Texans had different beliefs from people living in the northern United States. The most important difference was about slavery.

Slavery in Texas

African Americans had come to Texas with the first settlers, but they did not come freely. Planters from the South brought them as slaves. As slaves, African Americans worked for people who bought and sold them like property.

A small number of free African Americans had settled in Texas before it became a state. But most African Americans in Texas were slaves. Their labor helped build the state.

Most African American slaves worked on plantations. A **plantation** is a large farm that produces crops to sell. Enslaved men, women, and children labored long hours in the fields. Others worked in the house and at trades such as carpentry or blacksmithing. Whatever type of work they did, they were not paid and they had no say over their lives.

From "sun to sun" (sunrise to sunset), slaves planted and picked crops.

242

Vocabulary

plantation	secede
abolitionist	cavalry
tariff	blockade
nullify	

Compare the two pictures and explain what they tell you about the people who fought in the Civil War.

By 1860, three out of every ten Texans were enslaved African Americans. There were more than 182,000 African American slaves in the state. The chart shows how the population distribution changed between 1836 and 1860. The population distribution tells about the different groups of people living in an area. In this case, the percentage of enslaved people increased greatly. One reason for this change was the growth of the cotton industry.

In the 1850s the demand for cotton was growing. Much of it was exported to countries in Europe and to textile mills in the North. For Texas landowners this was good news. As cotton passed through the Texas ports, Texas planters earned more and more money. As a result, they needed more workers to grow and pick cotton. Those workers were African American slaves.

Only one in four Texas families "owned" slaves. But many people in the state believed slavery was important to the economy.

1. **Translate** the population distribution into a line graph. Use the information in the chart to create a line graph showing the increase in slavery.

TEKS
4.A, 6.B

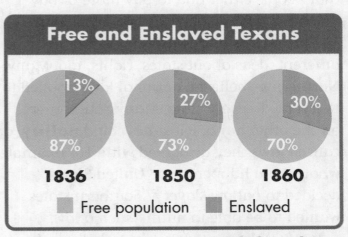

Free and Enslaved Texans

13% / 87% — 1836
27% / 73% — 1850
30% / 70% — 1860

Free population   Enslaved

Source: U.S. Census Bureau

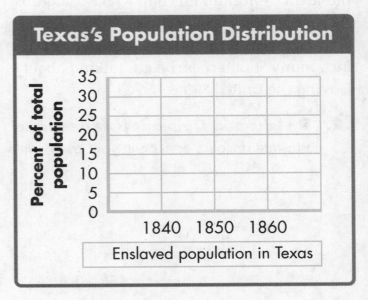

Texas's Population Distribution

Percent of total population: 35 30 25 20 15 10 5 0

1840 1850 1860

Enslaved population in Texas

SAVVAS realize™ Go online to access your interactive digital lesson.

243

North and South Disagree

The issue of slavery had divided the United States from its beginnings. By the mid-1800s, many Anglo Americans in the South believed in slavery. They said their agriculture depended on slave labor. But a growing number of Northerners opposed slavery. They believed all people should be free. People who wanted to end slavery were known as **abolitionists.** Some Texans were abolitionists, too.

Tariffs were another issue. A **tariff** is a tax paid on goods that come from another country. The North had many factories, and tariffs helped them sell goods. Their goods were less expensive than imported goods that were taxed. Since the South had few factories, tariffs did not help their economy. Instead, tariffs meant that people either had to pay more or buy northern goods. They felt that was unfair.

Northerners and Southerners had different ideas about states' rights, too. Many Northerners believed national laws applied to everyone, to every state. Many Southerners, on the other hand, felt states could **nullify,** or cancel, laws they disagreed with. For example, what would happen if the United States decided to outlaw slavery? Southern states wanted to be able to nullify such a law.

In 1860 the United States elected a new president, Abraham Lincoln, who was against the spread of slavery. Many people in the South strongly disagreed with Lincoln. In fact, many Southerners began talking about leaving the United States.

2. **Fact and Opinion** Write a sentence to restate Lincoln's opinion in your own words.

....

....

....

Abraham Lincoln was against the spread of slavery.

"As I would not be a slave, so I would not be a master."

Map legend:

LEGEND
- Union states
- Confederate states
- Union-held territories

0 — 500 mi
0 — 500 km

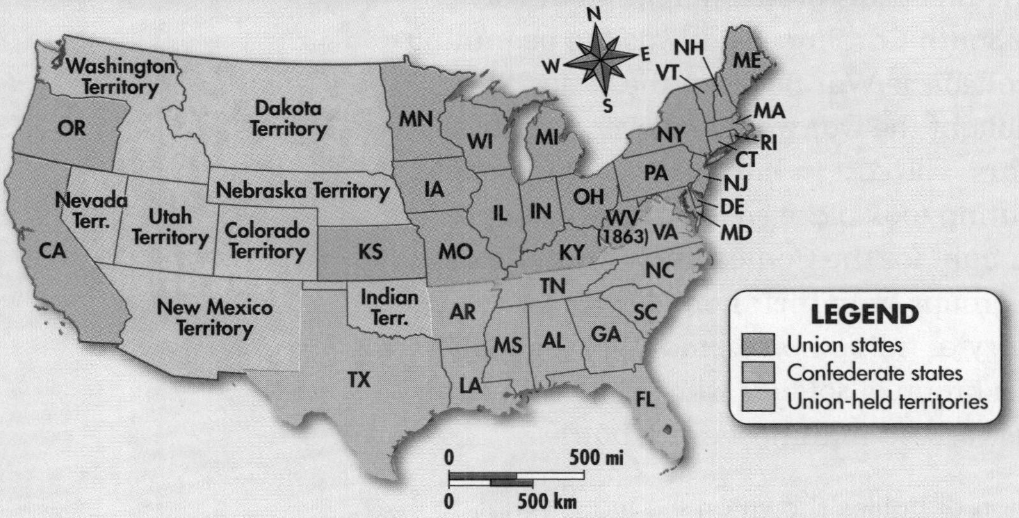

3. Analyze the map and outline the Confederacy. Which has more land, the Union states or the Confederate states?

Texas Secedes

In December 1860, just a few months before Lincoln took office as president, South Carolina seceded from the United States. To **secede** is to officially leave or separate from a group. One by one, other southern states followed South Carolina.

In January 1861, Texas called for a convention to decide if they would also secede. A majority of the 174 delegates were slave owners. At the convention, delegates protested "the insults, threats, and aggressions" of the North. In the end, more than 46,000 Texans voted for secession. Still, almost 15,000 Texans voted against it. Sam Houston was one of the Texans who opposed secession. On March 5, 1861, Texas officially seceded from the United States of America.

Eleven southern states, including Texas, formed a new government. They called it the Confederate States of America, or the Confederacy. The Confederacy named Jefferson Davis of Mississippi as president.

President Lincoln did not accept the states seceding. He said they were still part of the United States. Lincoln promised to do everything he could to keep the country together. This side was called the Union. The map shows how the country was divided. The chart shows the difference in the populations of the Union and Confederate states.

Union and Confederate Populations in 1861

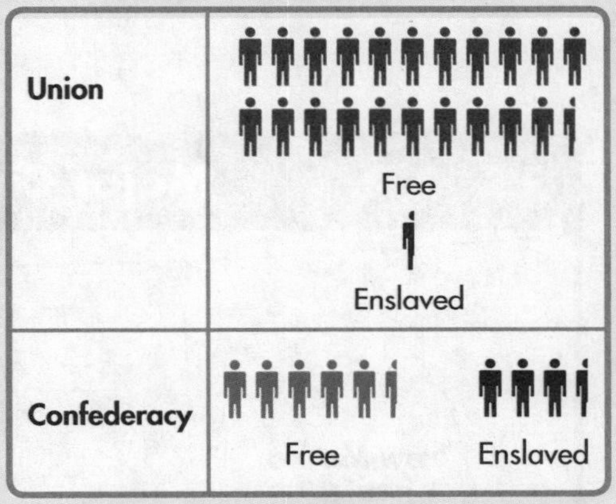

Each picture of a person = 1 million people

4. Analyze and interpret the population chart. What does the graph show about the distribution of the population in the Confederacy?

Texas Goes to War

On April 12, 1861, the first shots of war were fired at Fort Sumter, a Union fort in South Carolina. That was the beginning of the Civil War, also called the War Between the States. Although both sides thought the war would be over quickly, it lasted for four bitter years. The cost in human lives was terrible.

Almost all of the fighting took place east of the Mississippi. About 90,000 Texans fought for the Confederacy. Many Texas soldiers joined units or groups from their hometowns. Since Texans had a long history of riding horses, many Texas soldiers joined the **cavalry,** or a group of soldiers who fight battles on horseback. Texas soldiers served in almost every battle.

5. Analyze the location of battles shown on the map. What do they have in common?

....

....

Major Civil War Battles in Texas

New Mexico Territory

•Amarillo

Indian Territory

Arkansas

Tennessee

•Lubbock

Mississippi

Dallas•

Tyler •

•El Paso

Texas

Louisiana

N
W   E
S

Rio Grande

Austin •

Sabine Pass
(September 8, 1863)

Houston •

San Antonio •

Galveston
(January 1, 1863)

MEXICO

Corpus Christi•

Gulf of Mexico

LEGEND
▨ Confederate states
☐ Land not yet divided into states
✳ Battle
⛴ Union blockade

Laredo
(March 19, 1864)

Palmito Ranch
(May 12–13, 1865)

0   100 mi
0   100 km

246

The war had a direct impact on Texas's port cities. During the war, southern states wanted to ship cotton out of Texas ports. They also wanted to import supplies and arms into the ports. But Union ships set up blockades along the Texas coast, as they had at other southern ports. A **blockade** is an effort to stop ships from going in or out of a port. Many Texas cotton growers got around this by shipping cotton to the Rio Grande Valley and then out through Mexico.

As the war went on, Texas soldiers faced Union troops in several battles along the coast. In October 1862, Union troops captured Galveston, the state's largest port. By January, though, Confederate soldiers had taken it back. In September 1863, Texas soldiers met Union forces at Sabine Pass. The Union forces pulled back after the attack. Later, Union forces lost the Battle of Laredo. Colonel Santos Benavides led the Confederate soldiers at Laredo. He was the highest ranking Mexican American who served the Confederacy.

6. **Describe** the impact of the Civil War on Texas port cities.

Reenacting a Civil War battle in Bellmead, Texas

The Promise of Freedom

The war continued on. In 1863, President Abraham Lincoln issued the Emancipation Proclamation. This document declared "that all persons held as slaves" in the Confederacy were free. Emancipation is the act of freeing someone. When a president makes a proclamation, it is an order. Of course, the Confederacy was not acting as part of the union, so slavery was still the law in the South. Slavery was not outlawed in the United States completely until after the war ended. But the stage was set for slavery to end in the United States once and for all.

On the Home Front

The Civil War impacted Texas in many ways, both on the battlefield and at home. By the end of 1863 most free Texas men had left home for the war. So, many women ran their households alone. They took care of farms, ranches, and businesses until their husbands returned. Children helped, too.

Women also were active in the war. Some sewed uniforms for soldiers. Others ran or worked in hospitals for the wounded.

Everyone had to live with shortages caused by the blockade. From food to clothes to medicines, Texas families could not get many goods they counted on. People did what they could to deal with the shortages. For example, people spun their own fabric and made their own clothing. And when they needed paper to write something down, they used wallpaper.

And for everyone left at home, one of the greatest hardships was worry about the men who were fighting. One Texas woman wrote,

"Sorrow is added to sorrow. War makes its widows by the thousands."

7. Describe the impact of the Civil War on Texans. How did the war affect women in Texas?

....

....

....

The War Ends

By 1865, the Confederate army was worn out, and the Confederate economy was broken. The loss of life was overwhelming. Almost 500,000 Confederate soldiers were dead or wounded.

After many hard battles, the Union finally won. In April 1865, Confederate General Robert E. Lee surrendered to Union General Ulysses S. Grant in the village of Appomattox Court House near Richmond, Virginia. But other Confederate forces fought on. On May 13, 1865, Texas troops defeated Union soldiers at the Battle of Palmito Ranch, near Brownsville. It was the very last battle of the Civil War.

The Union victory in war kept the country from breaking apart forever. The Civil War also ended slavery in the United States. In 1865, the Thirteenth Amendment made slavery illegal in all states. The Civil War was over, but it would take the country many years to heal.

General Lee, on the left, and General Grant, on the right, sign the terms of surrender at Appomattox.

Got it?

◆ TEKS 4.A

8. ◉ **Cause and Effect Explain** how slavery was linked to growing cotton in Texas.

....

....

....

9. ❓ **Identify** three issues that people in the North and South viewed differently. Choose one issue and explain how it led to war.

my Story Ideas

....

....

....

....

10. Describe the Union blockades that were near Texas. Then tell how they affected Texans.

....

....

....

Fact and Opinion

> **1.** Texas seceded from the United States in 1861.
>
> **2.** "I think Texas should join the Confederacy. I want to support our state's rights."

What is the difference between these two statements? The first is a fact. A **fact** is a statement that you can check. You can prove that it is true. The second statement is an opinion. An **opinion** tells someone's personal feelings. You cannot prove an opinion as true or false.

You read and hear both facts and opinions every day. It is important to know the difference between them. Why? When you are studying the history of Texas, for example, you need to know whether something is true or not. You need to be able to sort out facts from opinions.

As you have read, Sam Houston opposed secession. In 1860, he said:

> *"To secede from the Union and set up another government would cause war. If you go to war with the United States, you will never conquer her, as she has the money and the men."*
>
> —*Sam Houston*

Sam Houston was describing the United States as a "she." The Civil War would not begin for more than a year. But it was Houston's opinion that secession would lead to war. It was his opinion that the Southern states could not win. Eventually his statements would come true: Secession led to war, and the South lost. But these were Houston's opinions. In 1860, you could not prove them true or false.

Sam Houston

Learning Objective

I will know how to distinguish fact from opinion.

TEKS

ELA 11.B Distinguish fact from opinion in a text and explain how to verify what is a fact.
SS 4.A Describe the impact of the Civil War on Texas.

Try it!

1. Americans disagreed about slavery. Reread the section "North and South Disagree" on page 244. **Identify** two different opinions about slavery.

   ....

   ....

   ....

2. What opinion did Abraham Lincoln state about slavery?

   ....

   ....

   ....

3. Reread the section "Texas Secedes" on page 245. **Identify** two facts about secession.

   ....

   ....

   ....

   ....

4. **Explain** how to verify what is a fact. Look at the facts you identified in question 3. Tell how you know these are facts.

   ....

   ....

   ....

   ....

Reconstruction

The picture shows a school for freed African American children after the Civil War.

After the Civil War, a lot of work needed to be done in the South. Many soldiers had died. Cities, forts, farms, and homes had been destroyed. The South also needed to build a new society and economy that did not have enslaved workers. This time of rebuilding and change was called **Reconstruction**.

Freedom and Change

Two years before the war ended, President Abraham Lincoln had issued the Emancipation Proclamation, which freed all enslaved people in the Confederacy. After the war, the Thirteenth Amendment outlawed slavery throughout the United States.

On June 19, 1865, General Gordon Granger arrived in Galveston with an important message: All enslaved Texans were free under United States law. Granger rode through Texas bringing everyone the news. One year later, June 19, 1866 African Americans celebrated the anniversary of this great news. This holiday is known as **Juneteenth**, and it is a state celebration of the day slaves in Texas learned that they were free.

Texans still celebrate Juneteenth.

1. Describe the origin of the state celebration known as Juneteenth.

....

....

....

....

UNLOCK THE BIG ?

I will know what challenges Texans faced during Reconstruction and how they met those challenges.

Vocabulary

Reconstruction   sharecropper
Juneteenth   segregation

What other opportunities do you think African Americans had after the Civil War?

Rebuilding Texas

Reconstruction was a difficult time. Across the South, everyone had to learn to solve problems in new ways. Few Civil War battles were fought in Texas, so the state had little property damage. Still the state's economy had suffered. Texans had to rebuild businesses. And both landowners and newly freed African Americans had to learn new ways of life.

Ending slavery changed the South politically, socially, and economically. To help with these changes, the federal government created the Freedmen's Bureau. The Freedmen's Bureau helped African Americans in many different ways. The Bureau gave them food and clothes. It helped them find work and places to live. It helped both African Americans and white landowners adjust to the new economy.

TEKS
4.A, 16.A, 16.D, 19.C

The Freedmen's Bureau helped create schools for African Americans.

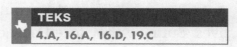

2. **Explain** why the government created the Freedmen's Bureau.

....

....

....

The Freedmen's Bureau also helped African Americans with education. Under slavery, most African Americans were not allowed to go to school. So the bureau started more than 1,000 schools and colleges in the South. In Texas the bureau opened about 150 schools for African American adults and children. Reconstruction impacted Texas in many ways. For example, it was during this time that African Americans began to go to school.

For African Americans who had been slaves, these were exciting but sometimes confusing times. Former slave owners told them that they were now free. African Americans could come and go as they pleased. According to the law, they could control their lives. But now they faced new challenges. Where could they find jobs? What land could they farm?

Many African Americans became sharecroppers. A **sharecropper** is a farmer who pays part of what he or she grows to a landowner. Here is how it worked. A landowner rented land to a farmer. The landowner also loaned the farmer tools and seeds. The farmer paid the landowner with a share of the crops. If crops were bad, sharecroppers could end up in debt.

3. The man on the left is a landowner. The man on the right is a sharecropper. **Infer** and write what each person might say about his experiences.

Sharecropper

Landowner

254

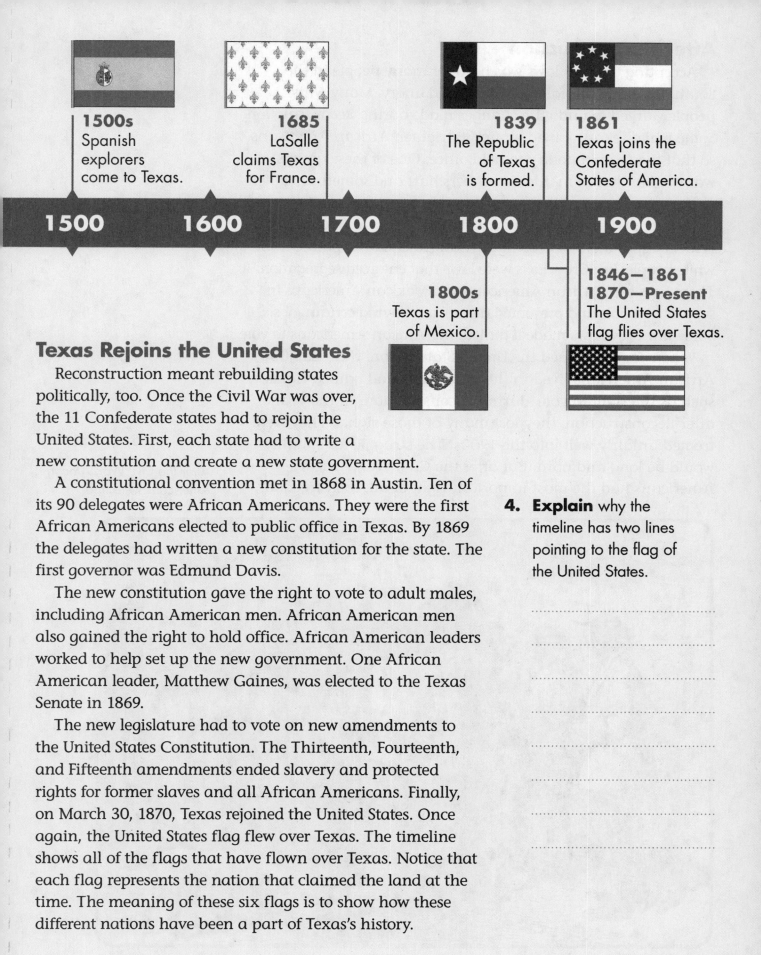

1500s
Spanish explorers come to Texas.

1685
LaSalle claims Texas for France.

1839
The Republic of Texas is formed.

1861
Texas joins the Confederate States of America.

1500   1600   1700   1800   1900

1800s
Texas is part of Mexico.

1846–1861
1870–Present
The United States flag flies over Texas.

Texas Rejoins the United States

Reconstruction meant rebuilding states politically, too. Once the Civil War was over, the 11 Confederate states had to rejoin the United States. First, each state had to write a new constitution and create a new state government.

A constitutional convention met in 1868 in Austin. Ten of its 90 delegates were African Americans. They were the first African Americans elected to public office in Texas. By 1869 the delegates had written a new constitution for the state. The first governor was Edmund Davis.

The new constitution gave the right to vote to adult males, including African American men. African American men also gained the right to hold office. African American leaders worked to help set up the new government. One African American leader, Matthew Gaines, was elected to the Texas Senate in 1869.

The new legislature had to vote on new amendments to the United States Constitution. The Thirteenth, Fourteenth, and Fifteenth amendments ended slavery and protected rights for former slaves and all African Americans. Finally, on March 30, 1870, Texas rejoined the United States. Once again, the United States flag flew over Texas. The timeline shows all of the flags that have flown over Texas. Notice that each flag represents the nation that claimed the land at the time. The meaning of these six flags is to show how these different nations have been a part of Texas's history.

4. Explain why the timeline has two lines pointing to the flag of the United States.

....

....

....

....

....

....

After Reconstruction

Accepting the new laws was hard for many people in the South. By the 1870s, talk grew loud and angry. Many white people wanted to undo the changes made during Reconstruction. Some white Texans joined groups to frighten African Americans so that they would not try to hold office. One of these groups was the Ku Klux Klan. Klan members hurt and sometimes killed African Americans. They wanted to stop them from voting.

Southern states set up a system of segregation. **Segregation** is racial separation, or keeping African Americans separate from white people. Jim Crow laws were laws that enforced segregation. These laws kept African Americans and Mexican Americans in separate schools and prevented them from having certain jobs. Some Jim Crow laws made it difficult for African Americans to vote.

When Texas rejoined the United States, more than 250,000 African Americans lived in the state. They had gained rights, such as the right to vote, during Reconstruction. In the years after Reconstruction, they lost many of those rights. They were treated unfairly well into the 1900s. The struggle for equality would be long and hard. But after the Civil War, African Americans had the most important right of all, their freedom.

After the Civil War, African Americans were free.

5. **Cause and Effect** Complete the cause-and-effect chart. **Identify** and write an effect in the box.

Cause		Effect
Some people did not want African Americans to have rights.	→	....

Got it?

TEKS 16.A, 16.D

6. **Fact and Opinion** **Label** each statement F for Fact or O for Opinion.

I am glad to have land to farm, but sharecropping is hard. ....

Juneteenth is a happy day. ....

Juneteenth is still celebrated today. ....

Sharecropping is a system of farming. ....

7. **Describe** the significance of the state celebration known as Juneteenth. Why is it important to celebrate this event?

my Story Ideas

....

....

....

8. Write to **explain** the meaning of the six flags that flew over Texas.

....

....

....

SAVVAS realize Go online to access your interactive digital lesson.

The Indian Wars

Envision It!

The Comanche are one group of American Indians who lived in Texas.

As Texas grew, so did conflict on the frontier. For thousands of years, American Indians had lived and hunted on land that was now part of Texas. Since the mid-1800s, Anglo American settlers had also claimed that same land as their own. After the Civil War, the situation worsened.

Conflict on the Frontier

The nation was expanding. As the United States built railroads across the country, more people migrated west. This brought more Anglo Americans to Texas. One effect of this migration was economic development and growth of Texas. The railroads and the migration of people also affected American Indian life in Texas. Now there were more Anglo Americans fighting for the land. During the Civil War, the conflict and the violence grew more intense.

For the Comanche people, it was an honor to fight in battles to defend their people. So Comanche warriors, along with warriors from other groups, raided frontier settlements. They destroyed farms and homes. Many people on both sides lost their lives.

Spaniards brought horses to America in the 1500s. Horses changed the lives of American Indians such as the Comanche.

Write how the lives of American Indians might change during a war.

UNLOCK THE BIG ?

I will know that Texas settlers and American Indians fought for control of the land and that the American Indians were moved to reservations.

Vocabulary

fort
Buffalo Soldiers
Indian Territory

When the Civil War ended, the United States soldiers who had been posted on the frontier went home. During the Civil War, Texans were focused on battles in the east. Many frontier forts closed. A **fort** is a strongly constructed building used to house soldiers and weapons. As the conflict between settlers and American Indians on the frontier increased, settlers asked the United States government for help. Eventually the government sent soldiers to the old forts and built new ones. These forts and soldiers affected American Indian life. There were more battles. And eventually, the soldiers forced American Indians off of the land and onto reservations, forever changing the way of life of the American Indians.

Among the troops were several units of **Buffalo Soldiers**, or African American soldiers who fought against the Plains Indians. They were sent to Texas and the Southwest to fight in the Indian Wars. Called the Buffalo Soldiers, these men were known for their courage and skill.

TEKS
4.D, 10.A, 12.C, 19.C

Buffalo Soldiers

1. **Examine** the effects of the building of U.S. forts in Texas upon American Indian life. Underline the effects described in the text.

End of the Buffalo Days

In October 1867 the United States government tried to solve the conflict with the Treaty of Medicine Lodge Creek. Under the treaty, the Comanche and Kiowa people had to move to a large reservation in the **Indian Territory.** This land had been set aside for American Indians in 1830. (Today this is the state of Oklahoma.) In exchange, the United States government promised food and clothing, as well as supplies to begin farming.

Most, but not all, of the American Indian chiefs signed the treaty. One of the chiefs who did not sign was the Kiowa leader Satanta. "I love to roam the prairies," he said. "There I feel free and happy." The Kiowa and others continued to lead raids on the settlers.

Being moved to reservations was not the only change facing the Plains people. Another important change was the fact that the buffalo herds were disappearing. Plains Indians used all parts of the buffalo for food, clothing, tools, and shelter. The buffalo were important to their way of life. They respected the buffalo even as they hunted them.

For hundreds of years, Plains Indians also had been trading buffalo as a way to meet their needs and wants. The American Indians traded buffalo skins in exchange for supplies from frontier merchants. Over time, some Anglo hunters also came to the Plains to kill buffalo. In the 1870s, the buffalo trade increased greatly. Now, many more Anglo buffalo hunters appeared on the Plains. These hunters wanted to make money so they killed thousands of buffalo. They sold the skins but left the bodies to rot.

The United States Army killed buffalo as a way of defeating the Plains Indians. Without the buffalo, the Plains Indians could not survive. By the late 1800s, the huge herds of buffalo were gone. The loss of the buffalo was a major change in Texas. The loss of the buffalo greatly affected American Indians because it destroyed their way of life.

Railroad companies offered travelers a chance to hunt for buffalo as a form of sport.

2. Compare and Contrast
After each group, **explain** their reason for killing buffalo.

Reason for Killing Buffalo
Plains Indians:
Anglo hunters:
United States Army:

The Second Battle of Adobe Walls

The Plains Indians faced more problems in the 1870s. In the Treaty of Medicine Lodge Creek, the United States government had promised supplies that did not come. This meant the American Indians did not have food. The treaty also promised to keep white settlers and hunters out of Indian lands. But the buffalo hunters came anyway. In fact, the Anglo buffalo hunters even set up a trading post at an old fort called Adobe Walls.

On June 27, 1874, the conflict between the Plains Indians and the buffalo hunters got worse. Early that morning a large group of Plains Indians attacked a small group of buffalo hunters at Adobe Walls.

Quanah, a Comanche chief, led the Cheyenne, Comanche, and Kiowa in the attack. Angry over the slaughter of buffalo, the Plains Indians charged on horseback. Since the Anglo buffalo hunters were armed with powerful guns, they were able to hold off the Plains warriors. Only a few hunters were killed, but many Plains Indians were injured or died in the attack. The battle is known as the Second Battle of Adobe Walls because the American Indians and United States soldiers had fought a battle there a few years earlier. The map shows where the Second Battle of Adobe Walls took place. The Second Battle of Adobe Walls did not settle the conflict. In fact, it would lead to the Red River War of 1874–75.

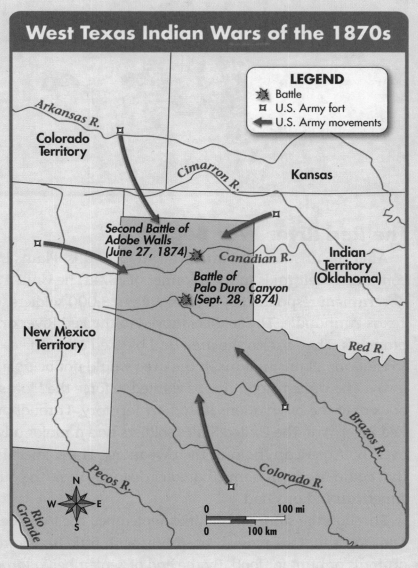

West Texas Indian Wars of the 1870s

LEGEND
- Battle
- U.S. Army fort
- U.S. Army movements

Arkansas R.

Colorado Territory

Cimarron R.

Kansas

Second Battle of Adobe Walls (June 27, 1874)

Canadian R.

Indian Territory (Oklahoma)

Battle of Palo Duro Canyon (Sept. 28, 1874)

New Mexico Territory

Red R.

Brazos R.

Pecos R.

Colorado R.

Rio Grande

N W E S

0   100 mi
0   100 km

3. **Make Predictions** Circle the two battles shown on the map. Underline the dates. What can you **predict** about the conflict between the Plains Indians and the Anglo Americans?

....

....

....

This painting shows United States soldiers who were fighting American Indians on the Great Plains.

The Red River War Begins

After the unsuccessful attack at Adobe Walls, Plains Indians continued their raids in the summer of 1874. The United States government responded by sending about 3,000 soldiers to the Texas Panhandle. The soldiers moved to the Red River and its branches. They circled the area and blocked all of the escape routes so that any Plains Indians in the area would not be able to get away. The United States troops wanted to force the Plains Indians back onto the reservations in Indian Territory. Throughout the Red River War, the United States soldiers had a major advantage over the American Indians: their weapons. The soldiers had guns that could fire from a much greater distance than the guns the American Indians had.

Through the summer and into September, the two sides fought. The Plains Indians moved constantly, with little time to rest their animals or hunt for food. By the end of September, a large army of United States soldiers had gathered on Catfish Creek in north Texas.

4. **Examine** the effects of the Red River War on American Indian life. Write to describe how American Indians were affected during the war.

....

....

....

The Battle of Palo Duro Canyon

The United States soldiers were under the command of Colonel Ranald S. Mackenzie. Early on the morning of September 28, 1874, Mackenzie and his soldiers trapped a large group of Plains Indians in Palo Duro Canyon. Comanche, Cheyenne, and Kiowa families were camped in the canyon. They had with them more than 1,400 horses and mules, as well as their tepees and belongings.

Most of the Plains Indians escaped on foot. But they had to leave everything behind. The soldiers set fire to the Plains Indians' belongings. And they destroyed most of the animals. Without their animals or their belongings, including food, the people returned to Indian Territory in defeat. They left behind the open plains that had been central to their lives.

The winter that followed was a wet one. In fact, the Plains Indians called the war the Wrinkled Hand Chase. The weather was so bad that their hands were wrinkled from the cold and damp. Finally, by June, the war was over.

Today, historical markers remind people of the importance of the Battle of Palo Duro Canyon.

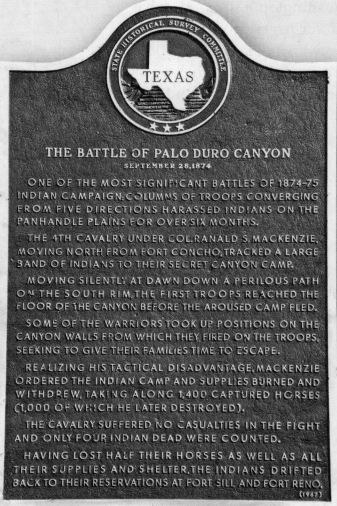

5. **Create** a historical marker for the Battle of Palo Duro Canyon.

Plains Indians Leave Texas

The end came in June 1875. Just one group of warriors remained on the Plains. These warriors were a band of Comanche, led by Chief Quanah. On June 2, Chief Quanah surrendered to Colonel Mackenzie. The war had ended.

The Red River War brought great changes to the Plains Indians. The buffalo on which they depended were gone. And the people had been forced to leave the Plains for the reservations of Indian Territory. The old ways of life were gone.

Chief Quanah's mother was Cynthia Ann Parker, a white woman who had been taken by the Comanche as a young girl. Chief Quanah was later known as Quanah Parker because he took his mother's name out of respect for her. Quanah Parker led his people while living on the reservation as well. He went to Washington, D.C., and spoke out for American Indians. He rented tribal lands to cattle ranchers and used the money for American Indian families living on the reservation. Quanah Parker also encouraged Plains Indians to set up schools for their children.

As the Plains Indians left their homeland, the region was opened to white settlement. Soon, it would be the home of cattle and sheep ranchers and other settlers.

6. **Describe** what you think Chief Quanah might have said about the Red River War.

Chief Quanah played an important role in the Red River War.

....

....

....

7. ⊙ **Cause and Effect Examine** how changes in Texas affected American Indian life. Write an effect for each of the changes listed.

Change in Texas	Effect on American Indians
The building of United States railroads bring more settlers	
Loss of the buffalo	

Got it?

TEKS 4.D, 10.A

8. ⊙ **Fact and Opinion Identify** one fact about the Buffalo Soldiers. Then **identify** one opinion. Tell whose opinion it is.

Fact: ....

....

Opinion: ....

....

9. ❓ You and your family are part of Chief Quanah's Comanche followers. Write to **describe** how you feel about the loss of the buffalo.

my Story Ideas

....

....

....

10. Explain the economic activities that American Indians used to meet their needs and wants. Write about how the buffalo helped American Indians economically.

....

....

....

Resolve Conflict

What do you think of when you see the word *conflict?* A **conflict** can be a disagreement with your best friend when each of you wants to do something different. Or it can be a disagreement as huge and life-changing as who had the right to inhabit the Texas plains in the 1800s.

Resolving conflicts takes time and patience, and it doesn't always happen peacefully. But taking these steps can help.

1. Identify the conflict. Who is involved? What is the disagreement?

2. Gather information about how to resolve the conflict. How does each side feel about the conflict?

3. List and consider options. Identify different possible solutions to resolve the conflict. What things can each side give up?

4. Consider the advantages and disadvantages of each solution.

5. Choose and implement a solution.

6. Evaluate the effectiveness of the solution. How does each side feel about the solution?

	Position A gets what it needs	Position A doesn't get what it needs
Position B gets what it needs	win-win	win-lose
Position B doesn't get what it needs	lose-win	lose-lose

When resolving a conflict, both sides should be prepared to give up some of the things they want. In most conflicts, neither side gets all of what they want. Sometimes one side gets all that it wants, but the other side gets nothing. This is called a win-lose or lose-win solution.

Sometimes both sides can find a way to solve the conflict in a way that is good for everyone. This is called a win-win solution. It does not mean that both sides got everything they wanted. It means that both sides benefited from the solution.

Sometimes the end result is so harmful to both sides that it is really a lose-lose solution. In this case, the conflict did not end with a good result for anyone.

In the Red River War, was there a win-win solution? No. The United States government won, and the Plains Indians lost.

TEKS

SS 4.D Examine the effects upon American Indian life resulting from changes in Texas, including the Red River War.

SS 23.A Use a problem-solving process to identify a problem, gather information, list and consider options, consider advantages and disadvantages, choose and implement a solution, and evaluate the effectiveness of the solution.

Try it!

1. Reread the section "North and South Disagree" on page 244. **Identify** the conflict. Who was involved in the conflict?

....

....

2. **Explain** how you think the two sides felt about the Red River War conflict.

....

....

....

....

....

....

3. **Apply** Think about a conflict between two groups in your school or community. Use the steps on page 266 to think about ways to resolve it. **Identify** the conflict. Then **identify** and write two different possible solutions to resolve the conflict.

Conflict: ....

....

....

Possible solutions: ....

....

....

....

Texas and the Civil War

1. ◉ **Fact and Opinion Explain** Sam Houston's opinion about Texas seceding.

....

....

....

2. Use the chart to answer the question.

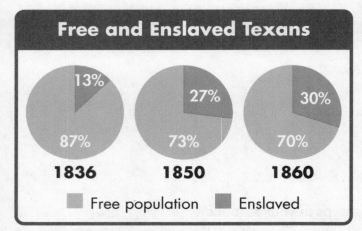

Free and Enslaved Texans

13%
87%
1836

27%
73%
1850

30%
70%
1860

■ Free population   ■ Enslaved

Source: U.S. Census Bureau

How does the chart help to **explain** why many Texans wanted to secede?

....

....

....

....

....

3. **Identify** the best ending to the sentence from the four answer choices provided. Circle the best answer.

An abolitionist is someone who wanted to _____

A outlaw slavery in the Confederate states only.

B end slavery in all of the states.

C allow states to decide about slavery.

D allow immigrants to bring their slaves.

4. How did Northerners and Southerners disagree about slavery? **Explain** how this affected Texas.

....

....

....

....

....

5. **Describe** the impact of the Civil War on Texas. Give three examples of ways that the war affected the lives of Texans.

....

....

....

....

....

....

Reconstruction

6. Read the question carefully. Determine the best answer to the question from the four answer choices provided. Circle the best answer.

   Which statement describes the origin of state celebration of Juneteenth?

   F the first time an African American voted in Texas

   G the one-year anniversary of the last Civil War battle in Texas

   H the day the law was signed that granted African Americans their freedom

   J the one-year anniversary of the day African Americans in Texas learned they were free

7. **Identify** an advantage and disadvantage of sharecropping.

   Advantage: ....

   ....

   ....

   Disadvantage: ....

   ....

   ....

8. **Describe** the impact of Reconstruction on Texas.

   ....

   ....

9. Match the name or group in Column A with the description in Column B.

Column A	Column B
Edmund Davis	A group opposed to the rights of African Americans
Ku Klux Klan	A group created to help African Americans during Reconstruction
Matthew Gaines	The first governor of Texas during Reconstruction
Freedmen's Bureau	An African American senator from Texas

10. **Sequence Explain** the meaning of the six flags that flew over Texas by numbering them in order from 1 to 7. One flag will have two numbers.

....

....

....

....

....

....

Lesson 3 ➤ TEKS 4.D, 12.C, 19.C

The Indian Wars

11. Which sentence **summarizes** the contribution of the Buffalo Soldiers?

   A They served as soldiers in Texas.

   B They made sure that no buffalo remained in Texas.

   C They hunted buffalo to provide food for Indians in Texas.

   D They built the first forts in Texas.

12. **Examine** the effects of the Red River War. Write two effects of the Red River War on American Indian life.

....

....

....

....

....

13. **Analyze** the effects of migration on the economic development and growth of Texas. How did people migrating west affect the economic development of Texas?

....

....

....

....

14. ❓ **What is worth fighting for?** ➤ TEKS 4.D

Examine the effects upon American Indian life resulting from changes in Texas.

What were some of the changes in Texas that led to the Indian Wars?

....

....

....

....

....

....

....

....

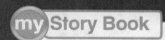 **my Story Book**

 THE BIG

What is worth fighting for?

TEKS
SS 4.A, 4.D
ELA 15

Both the Civil War and the Red River War brought big changes to Texas. In each conflict, people on both sides had to decide what is worth fighting for. In both conflicts, some people were fighting to preserve their way of life.

Think about what is important to you about your way of life.
Describe some of the most important things about your way of life.

....

....

....

....

Draw a picture of one of the things you listed.

A Growing State

my Story Spark

THE BIG ?

How does economic growth provide opportunity?

Identify your favorite local store and the items you buy there. **Explain** how you, your family, and the people in your community depend on the store and the items it sells.

....

....

....

Texas Essential Knowledge and Skills

4.B Explain the growth, development, and impact of the cattle industry, including contributions made by Charles Goodnight, Richard King, and Lizzie Johnson.

4.C Identify the impact of railroads on life in Texas, including changes to cities and major industries.

4.D Examine the effects upon American Indian life resulting from changes in Texas, including the Red River War, building of U.S. forts and railroads, and loss of buffalo.

5.A Identify the impact of various issues and events on life in Texas such as urbanization, increased use of oil and gas, the Great Depression, the Dust Bowl, and World War II.

5.B Explain the development and impact of the oil and gas industry upon industrialization and urbanization in Texas, including important places and people such as Spindletop and Pattillo Higgins.

8.A Identify and explain clusters and patterns of settlement in Texas at different time periods such as prior to the Texas Revolution, after the building of the railroads, and following World War II.

9.A Describe ways people have adapted to and modified their environment in Texas, past and present, such as timber clearing, agricultural production, wetlands drainage, energy production, and construction of dams.

9.B Identify reasons why people have adapted to and modified their environment in Texas, past and present, such as the use of natural resources to meet basic needs, facilitate transportation, and enhance recreational activities.

11.A Describe the development of the free enterprise system in Texas.

11.B Describe how the free enterprise system works, including supply and demand.

11.C Give examples of the benefits of the free enterprise system.

12.A Explain how people in different regions of Texas earn their living, past and present, through a subsistence economy and providing goods and services.

12.B Explain how geographic factors such as climate, transportation, and natural resources have influenced the location of economic activities in Texas.

12.D Describe the impact of mass production, specialization, and division of labor on the economic growth of Texas.

12.E Explain how developments in transportation and communication have influenced economic activities in Texas.

13.A Identify ways in which technological changes in areas such as transportation and communication have resulted in increased interdependence among Texas, the United States, and the world.

13.B Identify oil and gas, agricultural, and technological products of Texas that are purchased to meet needs in the United States and around the world.

19.C Summarize the contributions of people of various racial, ethnic, and religious groups in the development of Texas such as Lydia Mendoza, Chelo Silva, and Julius Lorenzo Cobb Bledsoe.

20.A Identify famous inventors and scientists such as Gail Borden, Joseph Glidden, Michael DeBakey, and Millie Hughes-Fulford and their contributions.

20.B Describe how scientific discoveries and innovations such as in aerospace, agriculture, energy, and technology have benefited individuals, businesses, and society in Texas.

21.B Analyze information by sequencing, categorizing, identifying cause-and-effect relationships, comparing, contrasting, finding the main idea, summarizing, making generalizations and predictions, and drawing inferences and conclusions.

21.C Organize and interpret information in outlines, reports, databases, and visuals, including graphs, charts, timelines, and maps.

Also, **6.A, 6.B, 7.A, 8.B, 9.C, 12.C, 18.B**

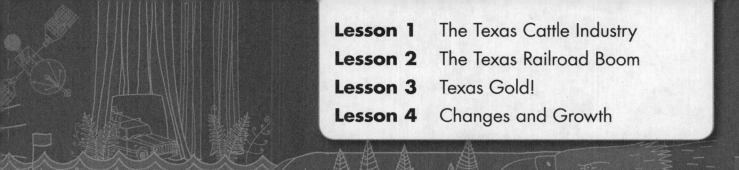

The Cattle Ranching Industry
Longhorns Change Texas

my **Story Video**

"Wow, real longhorns!" exclaims Zeb. Zeb is learning about the cattle industry in Texas. He recently visited the Chisholm Trail Heritage Museum in Cuero, but today he is getting some hands-on experience at a living history ranch outside of Houston. Cookie is Zeb's guide and the executive chef and chuck wagon cook at the ranch.

"Longhorns are a mix of the different cattle the Spanish and American settlers brought into Texas. They're tough as nails," Cookie explains. "Why are they so important in Texas?" "Well, the longhorns had a lot to do with building Texas's economy," Cookie shares. An economy is the exchange of goods and services for money. When people make money by selling things or by working, that's part of the economy.

When the Civil War ended, Texas ranchers saw both trouble and opportunity. "You see," explains Cookie, "a longhorn was worth just between two to four dollars in Texas. But in the eastern United States, people wanted to eat beef, and a longhorn was worth as much as forty dollars." "But Texas is a long way from the eastern United States," replies Zeb. "You're right, but have you ever heard of a cattle drive?" "Of course!" Zeb replies.

Zeb is learning about the golden days of Texas cattle drives.

273

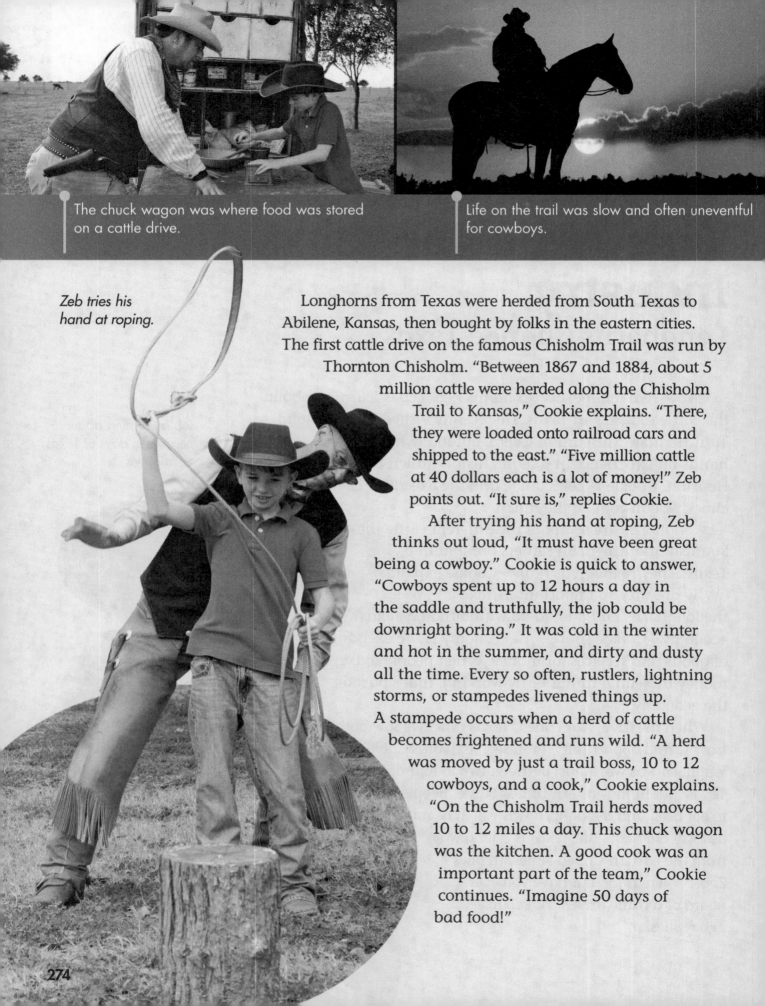

The chuck wagon was where food was stored on a cattle drive.

Life on the trail was slow and often uneventful for cowboys.

Zeb tries his hand at roping.

Longhorns from Texas were herded from South Texas to Abilene, Kansas, then bought by folks in the eastern cities. The first cattle drive on the famous Chisholm Trail was run by Thornton Chisholm. "Between 1867 and 1884, about 5 million cattle were herded along the Chisholm Trail to Kansas," Cookie explains. "There, they were loaded onto railroad cars and shipped to the east." "Five million cattle at 40 dollars each is a lot of money!" Zeb points out. "It sure is," replies Cookie.

After trying his hand at roping, Zeb thinks out loud, "It must have been great being a cowboy." Cookie is quick to answer, "Cowboys spent up to 12 hours a day in the saddle and truthfully, the job could be downright boring." It was cold in the winter and hot in the summer, and dirty and dusty all the time. Every so often, rustlers, lightning storms, or stampedes livened things up. A stampede occurs when a herd of cattle becomes frightened and runs wild. "A herd was moved by just a trail boss, 10 to 12 cowboys, and a cook," Cookie explains. "On the Chisholm Trail herds moved 10 to 12 miles a day. This chuck wagon was the kitchen. A good cook was an important part of the team," Cookie continues. "Imagine 50 days of bad food!"

In 1995, the longhorn became the official state large mammal of Texas.

Barbed wire allowed ranchers to separate their cattle from other cattle as well as keep them safe.

Early on, cattle roamed on public land or the open range. To keep the cattle from getting mixed up, cowboys branded their cattle with branding irons. At roundup time, the cowboys herded the cattle to one place and separated them by brands. This worked well for a long time, until barbed wire was invented. "I saw a barbed wire display at the Chisholm Trail Heritage Museum, too," says Zeb. "There were all different kinds." Barbed wire is a twisted wire with very sharp points, and it was used by ranchers to fence in the livestock.

"Ranchers began buying land and fencing it in, and it became harder to move cattle because of the fences," explains Cookie. After railroads expanded in Texas, there was no longer a need to drive herds out of state. Ranchers now just drove cattle to the railroad station in the nearest town. "Barbed wire and railroads marked the end of the cattle drives," Cookie says. "That's kind of sad," replies Zeb. "That's progress, Zeb."

Cookie explains that things have changed a lot since the days of free-range ranching. Modern ranchers hire "helicopter cowboys" and raise sheep, goats, and even ostriches and zebras along with cattle. Still, Texas raises more cattle than any other state in the country. "So cattle raising is still an important part of the Texas economy," Zeb says. "You got that right, cowboy!" declares Cookie.

Think About It How did the growth of the cattle industry provide economic opportunity for Texans? As you read, think about how ranching and other industries impact the people of our state.

The Texas Cattle Industry

Envision It!

Cowboys like this played a big role in Texas history.

Cattle have a long history in our state. Spanish explorers and missionaries began to bring cattle to Texas in the 1600s.

When Anglo Americans settled in Texas after 1820, they also brought cattle. The Spanish and Anglo American cattle mixed and became a new breed. This new breed, along with the contributions of some enterprising Texans, would spur the growth and development of the cattle industry in Texas. Ranching would soon become an important Texas industry.

A New Breed

The two types of cattle mixed and produced something new, the Texas longhorn. It is easy to see how longhorn cattle got their name. The tips of their long curved horns are usually six feet apart. On some longhorns, though, the horns measure eight feet across!

Longhorn cattle are known for their strength. They have long legs and can roam for miles without water. These hardy cattle are not afraid of a fight either. Here's how Texas writer J. Frank Dobie described them:

"They could horn off the fiercest wolf, smell out the most cunning panther . . . (they) did not hesitate to engage with grizzly bears."

—J. Frank Dobie

The longhorn, a Texas symbol, is the official state large mammal.

UNLOCK
THE BIG
?

I will know that cattle ranching provided economic opportunities to Texans.

Vocabulary

open range   roundup

brand   stampede

line riders   barbed wire

What do you know about cowboys? List some of the jobs that a cowboy might do.

The Open Range

The grassy plains of Texas were called the **open range.** Texas cattle once roamed this grassland freely. Before the 1880s, there were no fences to limit their movement. Ranchers owned some of the rangeland, and the state owned some of it. By 1865, Texas had become home to between 3 and 4 million longhorns.

TEKS
4.B, 9.A, 9.B, 12.A, 12.B, 12.C, 19.C, 20.A

1. **Draw Inferences** **Explain** why you think the longhorn became a symbol of Texas.

....

....

....

In 1927, a herd of official state longhorns was formed to preserve the breed.

Ranches and Roundups

The cattle industry developed and grew rapidly in Texas after the Civil War. Many new settlers brought their cattle with them. Others caught wild longhorns and formed herds. Texas ranchers began to mix other types of cattle with longhorns.

Richard King was one of the new settlers who helped with the development and growth of this industry. Born in New York, King bought his first land in Texas in 1853. Over the years, he added more land, horses, and cattle. King showed that ranching could be a major industry. Today, the King Ranch, which is over 800,000 acres in size, is still in the cattle business.

Lizzie Johnson was another well-known Texas rancher who contributed to the growth and development of the cattle industry. A good businesswoman, Johnson began buying land in the 1870s. She was also the first woman in Texas to drive her cattle up the Chisholm Trail to Kansas with her own herd of cattle.

In Texas, ranchers could buy land from private owners or from the state. Ranchers could also let their cattle run on state land for free. That wasn't as easy as it sounds. Different herds of cattle often mixed together on state land. It was hard to tell which cattle belonged to which ranch. So ranchers began to brand their cattle. A **brand** is a design burned into the hide of a cow.

Richard King

Lizzie Johnson

2. Locate each brand on the map. **Identify** what it stands for using the legend. Then, suppose you have a ranch in Texas. In the box, write the name of your ranch, and design a brand for it.

Legend

ᴡ King Ranch
ᴄ Long S Ranch
ᴀ JA Ranch
XII XIT Ranch

A Cowhand's Work

Cowhands, or cowboys, branded and tended the cattle. Some cowhands called **line riders** rode along the borders of a ranch to watch the cattle. In Texas, many cowhands were African American, Hispanic, or American Indian.

Spring and fall were busy times on Texas ranches. That's when ranchers held a **roundup.** Cowboys from different ranches rounded up all the cattle they could find. They drove them into one area. There, everyone worked to separate the cattle by brands. At the roundup, cowhands also branded new calves.

Charles Goodnight

Charles Goodnight was one of Texas's best-known cattle ranchers and was important to the development and growth of the cattle industry in Texas. Goodnight established a large and productive ranch in the Texas Panhandle. He also worked to establish the Texas State Bison herd. In the 1850s, he followed his own herd over long distances. In this way, he got to know Texas well. Later, he used this knowledge as an army scout.

Goodnight drove his cattle to faraway markets where beef prices were higher. To get there, he blazed new trails. One was the Goodnight-Loving Trail from central Texas to Wyoming. It became one of the most heavily used cattle trails of all.

Charles Goodnight

3. **Explain** the contribution of each person to the growth of the cattle industry in Texas.

Richard King ....

....

....

Lizzie Johnson ....

....

....

Charles Goodnight ....

....

Cattle Drives on Texas Trails

After the Civil War, Texas ranchers faced a problem. Cattle in Texas were worth only $3 or $4 each. The same animal in a northern city might be worth $30 or $40. The ranchers needed a way to get their cattle to the north. Texas had few railroads at this time. So ranchers organized cattle drives. They hired cowhands to drive their cattle north to the railroads.

Driving cattle was hard work. Cowhands rode all day in all kinds of weather. They slept outside at night. Sometimes they had to fight off cattle thieves or stop stampedes. Cattle **stampede**, or run around wildly, when they become frightened.

A drive could cover hundreds of miles. Cattle drives began all over Texas and ended in railroad towns such as Abilene, Kansas. There, buyers bought the cattle and shipped them north by railroad.

Between the late 1860s and the 1880s, 5 to 10 million cattle were ridden out of Texas. This massive movement of cattle helped revive Texas's economy after the Civil War.

Texas Cattle Trails

LEGEND
— Main cattle trails from Texas, 1860–1880s

4. Where did the Western Trail end? **Identify** and circle the name of the town on the map. About how long was the Shawnee Trail?

....

Spanish Words on the Trail

Mexican vaqueros had been driving cattle for centuries. Texans learned about trail drives from them. Ranchers and cowboys used Spanish words that they learned from the vaqueros. Some Spanish words, such as *rodeo* and *corral*, stayed the same. Others changed slightly. The Spanish word *rancho*, for example, became *ranch*. *La reata* (lah ray AH tah), a rope used to catch cattle, became *lariat* (LEHR ee ut).

Fencing the Open Range

In 1874, a new invention changed the landscape of Texas. Joseph Farwell Glidden figured out a way to make **barbed wire.** This twisted wire had sharp points, or barbs, along it. Strung between wooden posts, barbed wire fenced cattle in or out.

Farmers in Texas were interested in keeping cattle out of their crops. Ranchers with prize cattle also liked the new fencing. It kept their cattle from mixing with common cattle.

Cattlemen without ranches didn't like barbed wire. Some fences blocked the open range. Other fences cut off water holes and streams where cattle drank. To get water to their cattle, some ranchers had to build windmills. The windmills pumped water from underground into tanks.

The Closing of the Range

The widespread use of barbed wire and windmills changed Texas ranching. By 1890, the open range was all closed off. So were the old cattle trails north. Ranching was still big business, but the days of long cattle drives were over.

This song shows how one cowhand felt about the closing of the open range:

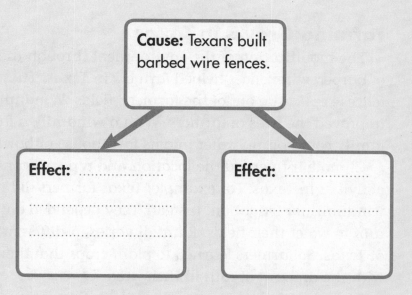

Cause: Texans built barbed wire fences.

Effect: ....

Effect: ....

5. Cause and Effect
Identify and underline a famous Texas inventor in the text. Complete the chart with two effects of his invention.

Barbed wire on the Texas range

Old Texas
(The Cowman's Lament)

I'm going to leave old Texas now;
They have no use for the Longhorn cow.

They plowed and fenced my cattle range,
And the people here all seem so strange.

I'll take my horse and I'll take my rope,
And I'll hit the trail upon a lope.

I'll bid adiós to the Alamo,
And set my face toward Mexico.

Farming Grows in Texas

The modification of the environment through the use of barbed wire fences helped farmers in Texas. These fences kept cattle out of the farmers' fields. Windmills also improved the lives of farmers. With a windmill, a farm family could pump water into its farmhouse or barn.

Climate influenced the location and type of economic activities in Texas. For example, Texas farmers did not use windmills for irrigation. Instead, they depended on the rain to water their fields. Rainfall varies in different parts of Texas. So farmers learned to plant crops that grew well with the amount of rain in their area.

After the Civil War, some Texas farmers continued to earn their living providing goods such as cotton. Large landowners now rented small fields to tenant farmers. Many tenant farmers were African Americans. Most tenants grew about 20 acres of cotton. Two thirds of each crop usually went to the landowner to pay for seeds, tools, supplies, and the rent of the land.

Many Texas farmers owned their land. Small farms ranged in size from 120 to 160 acres. These Texas farmers planted a little cotton or sugar cane as cash crops. Cash crops are sold for money. Small farmers also raised vegetables, fruit, hogs, and chickens for their own use.

6. Identify and underline in the text how farmers modified the environment in Texas.

Farmers used windmills to pump water into the farmhouse or barn.

The number of farms in Texas rose rapidly in the late 1800s. Texas had about 61,000 farms in 1870. The number rose to 174,000 in 1880. By 1900, there were 350,000 farms.

Railroads were one reason for the rapid rise. With railroads, farmers had a fast way to send crops to markets. So they could now grow more cash crops, especially grain. Railroads also brought tools and supplies to farmers. By 1900, farming had become a bigger industry than ranching.

Cotton plant

Got it?

TEKS 4.B, 12.B

7. **Generalize Describe** one example of how Texas's climate influenced the location and type of economic activities in Texas.

....

....

....

8. **Explain** how the cattle industry impacted Texas's economy.   my Story Ideas

....

....

....

9. During the 1880s, you decide to move to Texas and start a farm. **Explain** how geographic factors such as climate, transportation, and natural resources help you decide where to start your farm.

....

....

....

....

Draw Inferences

An **inference** is something you figure out based on clues and information that you already know. Drawing inferences is a way to better understand what you read.

Authors don't state everything when they write. Sometimes meanings and connections are not completely clear. Drawing an inference is a way to fill in some information.

To draw an inference, begin by analyzing the clues in the text. Make sure you understand them. Then think about any related information you already know, information from your own life or from what you have read recently. Combine the text clues with what you already know to draw an inference.

Read the lines from a cowboy song, "The Old Chisholm Trail." Then read the information below to see how to draw an inference.

> Oh come along, boys, and listen to my tale,
> I'll tell you all my troubles on the ol' Chisholm trail.
>
> (chorus)
>
> Come a-ti yi youpy youpy yea youpy yea
> Come a-ti yi youpy youpy yea
>
> On a ten dollar horse and a forty dollar saddle,
> I was ridin', and a punchin' Texas cattle.
>
> We left ol' Texas October twenty-third
> Drivin' up the trail with the U-2 herd.
>
> I'm up in the morning before daylight,
> And before I sleep the moon shines bright.

Clues: The cattle are called the U-2 herd.

What I already know: Ranchers branded their cattle to identify them.

Inference: The cattle were from the U-2 ranch and had the U-2 brand.

Learning Objective

I will know how to draw inferences.

 TEKS

ELA 10 Make inferences about the author's purpose in cultural, historical, and contemporary contexts and provide evidence from the text to support their understanding.

ELA 11 Make inferences about expository text and provide evidence from text to support their understanding.

SS 11.B Describe how the free enterprise system works, including supply and demand.

SS 21.B Analyze information by drawing inferences.

 Try it!

1. **Draw an inference** by analyzing the last two lines of the song.

   Clues: Cowboys get up before dawn and sleep when the moon shines.

   What I already know: From sunup to night takes about 14 hours.

   Inference: ....

2. Reread these sentences from page 280. **Draw an inference** about why the price of cattle was much lower in Texas than in the north.

   > *After the Civil War, Texas ranchers faced a problem. Cattle in Texas were worth only $3 or $4 each. The same animal in a northern city might be worth $30 or $40. The ranchers needed a way to get their cattle to the north.*

   Clues: ....

   ....

   What I already know: ....

   ....

   Inference: ....

   ....

3. Go back to an earlier chapter. Find a passage in which you drew and inference. **Explain** why your inference was helpful.

   ....

   ....

4. **Create** an inference outline like the ones above. Use the passage you found for question 3 and show how you drew the inference.

   ....

The Texas Railroad Boom

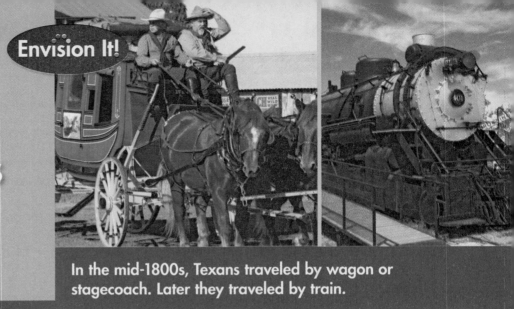

Envision It!

In the mid-1800s, Texans traveled by wagon or stagecoach. Later they traveled by train.

Before railroads, agricultural products traveled from the farm to ports by steamship. Richard King came to Texas as a steamboat captain. However, rivers were only passable for short distances and roads could only be used during dry weather. This is why railroads improved the lives of farmers in Texas. Railroads also changed the lives of many other Texans.

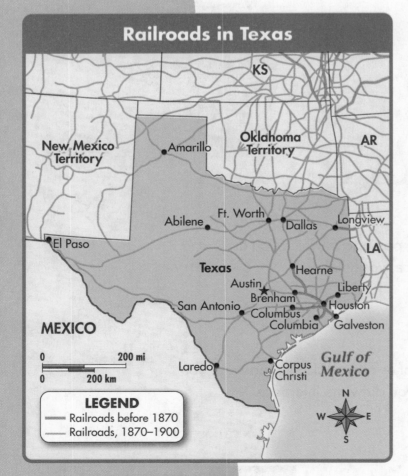

Railroads in Texas

KS

New Mexico Territory

Amarillo

Oklahoma Territory

AR

Abilene   Ft. Worth

El Paso

Dallas   Longview

LA

Texas

Hearne

Austin   Liberty

Brenham

San Antonio   Houston

Columbus

Columbia   Galveston

MEXICO

0   200 mi

0   200 km

Laredo   Corpus Christi   Gulf of Mexico

N W E S

LEGEND
—— Railroads before 1870
—— Railroads, 1870–1900

Trains Reach Texas

Texas had only 400 miles of railroad track in 1860. Then a railroad boom hit Texas. A **boom** is a time of rapid growth. By 1890, Texas had more than 8,000 miles of track. The boom began at the port cities along the Gulf Coast. Then it spread northward.

1. **Sequence Identify** where the Texas railroad boom began on the map. To which cities did the railroad boom later spread?

....

....

....

UNLOCK THE BIG ?

I will know that the growth of railroads brought economic opportunities to Texas.

How might a train trip be different from a stagecoach trip? List some ways above.

These developments in transportation influenced economic activities in Texas. The impact of the railroad boom in Texas was huge. Cities and towns sprang up along the new railroad lines. Businesses could now ship and receive goods quickly. Texans could visit other parts of their state and the nation more easily. Some railroads were linked to other lines in the United States and to lines in Mexico. This let Texans trade with other states and with Mexico.

Railroads did not help everyone. American Indian life was negatively affected by these changes in Texas. Tracks were laid across American Indian lands. The environment also suffered. Railroad companies slaughtered buffalo on and off American Indian lands. This loss of buffalo affected American Indians, who relied on buffalo for food and clothing.

TEKS
4.C, 4.D, 6.B, 7.A, 8.A, 8.B, 9.A, 9.B, 9.C, 11.A, 11.B, 11.C, 12.A, 12.B, 12.C, 12.E, 13.A, 13.B

Many of the workers who built Texas railroads were Chinese.

2. **Examine** the effects of the railroad on American Indian life in Texas.

....

....

....

Newcomers Arrive by Train

The railroads brought new settlers to Texas. People from other states moved to Texas by train. Others came from foreign countries by ship, then used trains to travel to their new homes in Texas. One group of newcomers were the Chinese.

Thousands of Chinese workers came to Texas to build the railroads. These workers laid track under difficult conditions. Most earned $20 a month plus food and shelter. Some saved their money and returned to China. Others stayed after the railroads were built and found new jobs.

Boom Times

During the railroad boom, from about 1870 to 1900, the population of Texas more than doubled. It grew from 800,000 to more than 2 million people. These newcomers brought their ideas, culture, religions, and music and art with them. The **locomotive,** or train steam engine, was also an engine of change. The impact of the railroads on life in Texas and the changes to major industries ran deep.

Railroad companies put up advertisements that promoted Texas in other states. Special "homeseeker trains" let people explore Texas. New settlers could ride these trains for low rates.

Railroad companies also impacted the farming industry. The railroads earned money by shipping out farm crops and bringing in farm supplies throughout Texas and to other parts of the country. So they encouraged farmers to try new and better ways to raise crops. If farmers were successful, the railroads would be, too.

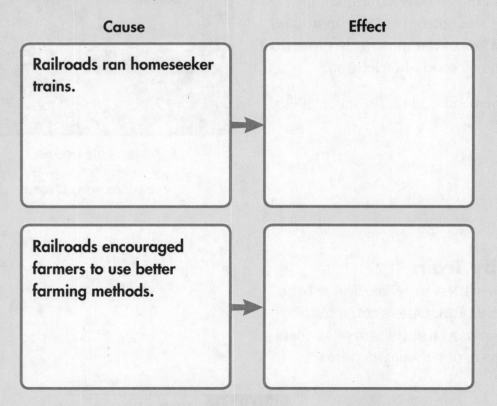

Cause

Railroads ran homeseeker trains.

Railroads encouraged farmers to use better farming methods.

Effect

3. ◉ **Cause and Effect** Complete the chart. **Explain** how each cause impacted life in Texas.

Locomotives were powered by steam. The railroads needed water to make steam, so they built wells throughout Texas. As the railroad lines stretched farther into the frontier, they continued to dig wells. The railroads then sold land around the wells to settlers. New towns were distributed along Texas railroad lines and near wells.

Growing Industries in Texas

The railroad boom led to a boom in many Texas businesses. By the 1870s, for example, railroads had reached the pine forests of East Texas. Lumber companies now had a fast way to ship the trees they cut. The lumber was loaded onto railroad cars. The trains quickly carried it to distant buyers. As a result, the lumber industry grew rapidly.

Shipping was a major industry along the Gulf Coast. Galveston was a busy port city. Ships from all over the world unloaded goods there. Railroads moved these goods to other parts of Texas and the United States. Railroads also brought goods to the port to be shipped by sea. In 1860, a railroad was built to link Galveston to Houston. This link was important because it enabled Houston to grow.

Railroads Change Ranching

Texas's first industry, ranching, was changing, too. By 1890, the days of the trail drive were over. The railroads had reached cattle country. Cowhands only had to herd the cattle to nearby shipping points. There, the cattle were loaded onto cattle cars. The towns around the shipping points grew. Then, as today, the industries of Texas were changing.

Railroads made it easier for Texas ranchers to sell the cattle to other parts of the state and country.

4. **Identify** the impact of railroads on life in Texas including the ranching industry.

....

....

....

People nicknamed Fort Worth "Cowtown."

Growing Cities

Railroads had a big impact on the growth of Texas cities. Clusters of settlements grew around the railroad junctions. A **junction** is where two or more rail lines meet. This pattern of settlement continued into the early 1900s as most major Texas cities were railroad junctions. These meeting points attracted business and industry. They also attracted workers looking for jobs.

Fort Worth, for example, was a junction. It had more than 20,000 people in 1900. Fort Worth became home to stockyards and meatpacking plants. The railroads that met there brought in cattle and shipped out beef products. People called the city "Cowtown," a nickname it still has today.

The city of Marshall was another junction. There, the railroads built large repair shops. Skilled workers serviced and repaired locomotives. In the Panhandle, the railroad companies repaired equipment at Childress. Walter Chrysler worked as a manager there. Later he moved to Michigan and formed his own automobile company, the Chrysler Corporation.

5. **Interpret** the graph, **identify** and circle the city that grew the most between 1870 and 1900. **Explain** where clusters of settlements grew in Texas in the 1900s.

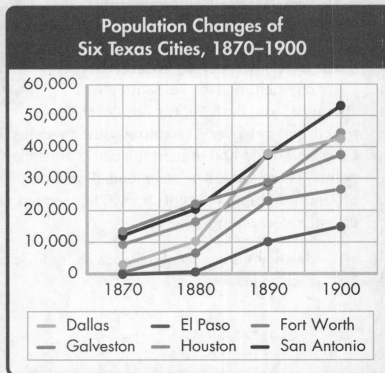

Population Changes of Six Texas Cities, 1870–1900

— Dallas — El Paso — Fort Worth
— Galveston — Houston — San Antonio

Source: Texas State Historical Association, Texas Almanac

In East Texas, the city of Tyler was in a rich cotton-growing region. After the Civil War, its cotton industry was in ruins. Early railroads bypassed the city, making matters worse. Then, in 1874, town citizens persuaded a railroad to build a line to Tyler. The railroad created jobs. It also helped farmers ship their cotton. In ten years, the population of Tyler had tripled.

How important were railroads to the growth and life of Texas cities and towns? Take the example of Clarendon. In 1897, the people of that town moved their houses five miles. That way, they would be close to the depot, or train station, of a busy rail line.

After 1900, Texas began to build electric railways within cities. The largest was in the Dallas area. There, the Texas Electric Railway had 226 miles of track. Electric railways were a fast way to travel in and around cities.

Electric railway cars totaled nearly 500 miles in Texas. About 70 percent of these were in the Dallas-Fort Worth area.

A Texas Record

By 1910, Texas had set a record: It had more miles of railroad track than any other state. The state also had more railroad employees than any other state. Texas still holds these records today!

6. **◉ Draw Inferences Identify** the impact of the railroads and the electric railway on life in Texas cities.

....

....

....

The Growth of Free Enterprise

Businesses in Texas grew rapidly as the need for goods and services grew. These businesses developed under the free enterprise system. **Free enterprise** is an economic system in which people are free to buy and sell goods and services with little control by the government. The benefit of free enterprise is that it helps both producers and consumers. A **producer** is a person or company that makes or sells goods or offers a service. A **consumer** is a person or company that buys or uses goods and services.

Cotton planters wait for cotton buyers in Palestine, Texas, in 1890.

For example, under free enterprise, farmers have the freedom to grow cotton, corn, or some other crop. Whatever the farmer chooses, he or she has the right to grow as much or as little of the crop as possible. The farmer is free to sell, or not sell, the crop to a buyer.

Why would a farmer not want to sell a crop? Under free enterprise, producers hope to make a profit. A profit is money left over after paying the costs of producing something. A cotton farmer, for example, has many costs: seeds, machinery, land, and so on. To be profitable, farmers try to find the best time to sell, the time when they can get the most money for their crop.

A cotton buyer has the right to buy any cotton that is for sale. Some cotton might not look or feel right. The consumer is free to keep shopping till he or she finds the right cotton at the right price.

Supply and Demand

Free enterprise is based on supply and demand. **Supply** is the number of items that producers offer for sale at a certain price. **Demand** is the number of items that consumers, or buyers, are willing to buy at a certain price.

Think again about the Texas cotton farmer. Suppose that it was a bad year for growing cotton. Disease killed some of the crop. The supply of cotton would be low. In this case, the price of cotton would rise. Buyers would have to pay more to get some of the limited supply.

7. **Describe** how free enterprise developed in Texas.

....

....

....

....

....

....

Another year, the cotton crop might be very good. There would be plenty of cotton available for sale. If demand stays the same as the year before, there would be more supply than demand. Then the price of cotton would fall. Cotton producers would lower their prices to attract buyers.

An Efficient System

Free enterprise is efficient. Supply and demand lets prices rise and fall to the right level. Free enterprise also leads to new technology. That's because producers want to produce goods more efficiently. And consumers benefit from the increased supply.

8. ◉ **Summarize** **Describe** how supply and demand works in the free enterprise system.

....

....

TEKS 4.C, 8.A, 12.E

9. ◉ **Draw Inferences** Suppose you lived in a Texas town without a railroad during the railroad boom. As the years passed, businesses closed and people moved away from town. **Explain** why this may have happened.

....

....

10. ❓ **Identify** some of the economic opportunities in towns such as Galveston, Dallas, and Fort Worth in the 1900s. **Explain** how this helped the towns grow.

my Story Ideas

....

....

11. **Explain** how developments in transportation influenced economic activities in Texas.

....

....

....

....

Interpret Graphs

Information about economic growth and change usually involves lots of data, or numbers and information. Two ways to organize data visually are line graphs and bar graphs.

A **line graph** organizes data in a way that allows you to interpret change over time. Look at the line graph titled "Texas Railroad Mileage,

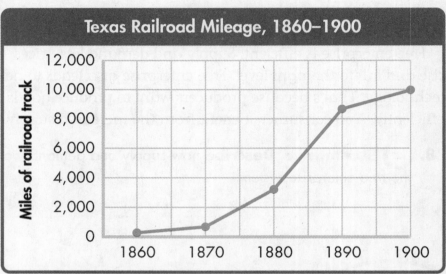

Texas Railroad Mileage, 1860–1900

Source: U.S. Census Bureau

1860–1900." The horizontal axis shows decades, or periods of 10 years. The vertical axis shows the number of miles of railroad track in Texas. The line in the middle of the graph connects the data points on the graph. This line shows how the total mileage changed over 40 years, or 4 decades. The line graph represents data about the period from 1860 to 1900.

Like a line graph, a **bar graph** is a way to organize information visually. Bar graphs are better at comparing and contrasting information than showing data over time.

A bar graph uses bars to compare information. In the bar graph titled "Total Rail Mileage of Selected States, 1900," you can compare the rail mileage of selected states in the same year, 1900. The graph compares each state's total miles of railroad track.

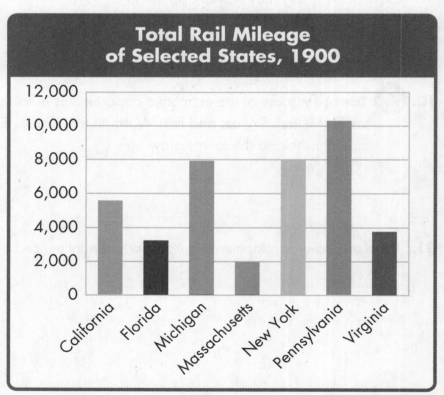

Total Rail Mileage of Selected States, 1900

Source: U.S. Census Bureau

Learning Objective

I will know how to interpret information from line and bar graphs.

TEKS

ELA 13.B Explain factual information presented graphically (e.g., graphs).
SS 4.C Identify the impact of railroads on life in Texas, including changes to cities and major industries.
SS 21.C Organize and interpret information in visuals, including graphs.

To interpret a line graph, first read the title of the graph. It tells you what type of data the graph displays. Next, read the labels for each axis. Then, look at the line that connects the data points on the graph. Does it go up or down?

To interpret a bar graph, first read the title of the graph. Next, read the labels for the vertical axis. Then, look at the labels for each bar on the graph. Compare the information by comparing the heights of the bars.

Examine and **interpret** the line graph on page 294 and answer the following two questions:

1. About how many miles of railroad track did Texas have in 1870?

....

2. During which decade did rail mileage go up fastest in Texas?

....

Examine and **interpret** the bar graph on page 294 and answer the following two questions:

3. About how many miles of railroad track did California have in 1900? What about Florida?

....

....

4. Use your math skills and map scale to **estimate** how many more miles of track New York had than Massachusetts in 1900.

....

5. **Compare** the data in the two graphs. Which state had about the same amount of railroad track as Texas in 1900?

....

SAVVAS **realize** Go online to access your interactive digital lesson.

295

Texas Gold!

This image shows oil derricks in Texas around 1900.

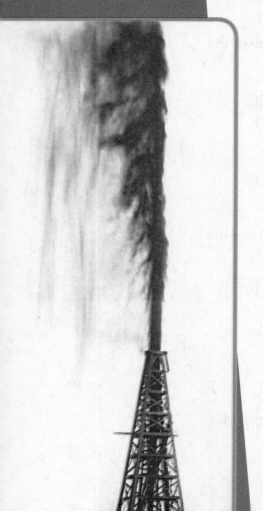

The Lucas Gusher at Spindletop, January 1901

The railroad boom helped Texas grow. By 1900, Texas cities and industries were growing fast. Texas's biggest boom, however, was still to come.

Black Gold at Spindletop

The presence of natural oil, or **petroleum,** in Texas had been known for hundreds of years before Europeans arrived in the area. When Spanish conquistadores came to the area, they used the natural tar that forms when crude oil seeps to the surface to cover holes or cracks in their ships.

The first oil wells were drilled in Nacogdoches County. They produced only small amounts of oil. At that time, demand for oil was low, and so was the price. So the oil field was not developed.

Pattillo Higgins, who lived in Beaumont, owned a brick making company. He wanted an even-burning fuel source for making bricks. Spindletop Hill was a salt dome south of Beaumont. Higgins believed that oil and gas could be found beneath salt domes. So he bought about half of Spindletop.

Higgins began drilling for oil in 1893 in hopes of finding a fuel source for making bricks. He was unsuccessful. So the oil field was not developed. In 1899, Pattillo Higgins hired Captain Anthony F. Lucas to help with finding oil at Spindletop. Their discovery at Spindletop helped drive industrialization and urbanization in Texas.

1. **Identify** in the text how the oil industry developed in Texas. Who helped develop the industry?

Write or draw two uses of oil that you know of.

UNLOCK THE BIG ?

I will know how the growing oil and gas industries provided economic opportunities to Texas.

Vocabulary

petroleum

oil refinery

January 10, 1901, was a day to remember. Lucas had drilled down 1,139 feet. Suddenly, with a sound like a cannon, mud shot out of the well. Next came a cloud of gas. Finally oil, also called black gold, gushed out. The powerful gusher, or flow of oil, blasted high into the air.

TEKS

5.A, 5.B, 6.A, 6.B, 12.A, 13.B, 20.B

Texas Oil Fields

Lucas and Higgins's discovery at Spindletop was Texas's first major oil well. Their discovery would soon spur urbanization in Texas. In 1902, Spindletop alone produced more than 17 million barrels, or 94 percent of the state's total. Over the next three years, other major oil fields were developed in the area around Spindletop. They included Sour Lake, Batson, and Humble.

Between 1902 and 1910, drillers found oil in North Central Texas, with spots at Brownwood, Petrolia, and Wichita Falls. In the years that followed, many more wells were drilled. The oil business was booming!

2. **Interpret** the map. **Identify** and circle the earliest oil field shown on the map. **Identify** and draw a box around the latest oil fields shown on the map.

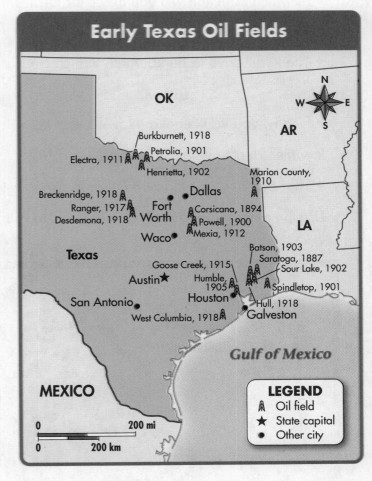

Early Texas Oil Fields

OK

AR

Burkburnett, 1918
Petrolia, 1901
Electra, 1911
Henrietta, 1902
Marion County, 1910
Breckenridge, 1918
Ranger, 1917   Fort   Dallas
Desdemona, 1918 Worth   Corsicana, 1894
                         Powell, 1900
        Waco   Mexia, 1912
Texas   Batson, 1903
            Goose Creek, 1915   Saratoga, 1887
Austin ★   Humble,   Sour Lake, 1902
            1905   Spindletop, 1901
San Antonio Houston Hull, 1918
West Columbia, 1918 Galveston

Gulf of Mexico

MEXICO

0   200 mi
0   200 km

LEGEND
⚒ Oil field
★ State capital
● Other city

SAVVAS realize™   Go online to access your interactive digital lesson.

297

An Oil Boom in Texas

The Lucas Gusher was big news. Thousands of people rushed to the region around Spindletop. Beaumont had been a town of 9,000 people. In just a few months, the population grew to 50,000.

Most newcomers were in the oil business. Some bought land and drilled for oil. Others sold drilling equipment. Workers also moved to Beaumont to get jobs. Beaumont became a center of industrialization in Texas. The newcomers ran drills or built pipelines to move the oil to refineries. An **oil refinery** is a factory that cleans and processes oil into products such as gasoline or kerosene. Many refineries were built along the Gulf Coast. From its ports there, Texas shipped oil to countries all over the world.

By 1918, oil was flowing in Electra, Burkburnett, and other Texas cities. The development of the oil industry meant more jobs and money for Texans. By 1928, Texas was the nation's leading oil producer.

3. It is 1918. Suppose you are a reporter in Wichita Falls, writing an article about the oil boom in Texas. You visit three oil fields in the company's new "horseless carriage," an automobile.

• In which direction will you travel for Electra from Wichita Falls?

....

• Then you drive to Burkburnett. Which river is it near?

....

• Finally, you visit Petrolia. How far is it from Burkburnett?

In which direction will you drive? ....

• That evening, you learn the photographer is lost in Oklahoma.

Use the map grid system to **identify** where Petrolia is. ....

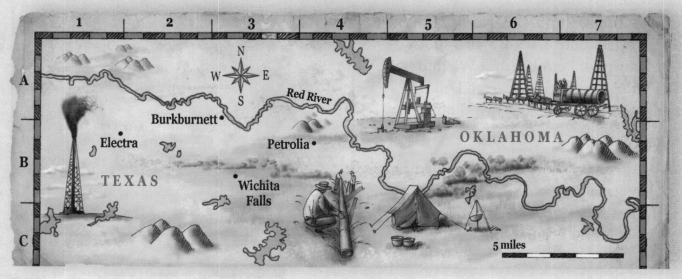

4. **Describe** how the car was an innovation that benefited individuals in Texas.

....

....

New Uses for Oil

During the Texas boom, oil was plentiful and cheap. So people found new uses for oil. Railroads and ships began to use oil instead of coal.

The discovery of oil benefited many individuals in Texas. In the early 1900s, many Americans began to drive cars. Every year, more and more cars were seen on Texas roads. Cars ran on gasoline, an oil product. As the number of cars rose, so did demand for oil. The new cars also needed paved roads. Petroleum was used to make the pavement.

Oil changed life on the farm, too. Farmers had always used horses and mules to pull equipment. Now, they began to use tractors. The tractors ran on gasoline. With gasoline-powered equipment, farmers could plant and harvest more land. So farms got larger.

After the oil boom, Texas became more industrialized. The number of factories increased because cheap oil was used to power the machinery in factories. This spurred urbanization in Texas. Many Texans from small farms sold their land and went to work in the new factories in towns and cities.

As the years passed, people found many more uses for oil. Paint, for example, is made from oil. So are many lotions and medicines. Even the lip balm you use for chapped lips is an oil product. Plastic is one of the most common items made from oil. From clothes to cars to containers, plastic is used to make countless products.

The use of cars grew quickly in Texas in the 1920s.

Gas-powered equipment made farms more productive.

5. ◉ **Draw Conclusions** **Describe** how scientific discoveries and innovations in energy have benefited Texas.

....

....

....

....

The Gas Industry in Texas

During the Texas oil boom, well drillers found more than oil. They also discovered natural gas. Oil and gas deposits are often in the same area. Over time, natural gas became a major industry in Texas.

Like oil, natural gas formed millions of years ago. As plants and animals died, their remains were covered with sand and mud. Over time, the sand and mud turned into rock, trapping the remains. Eventually, heat and pressure changed the remains into gas. To reach this gas, well drillers cut through the rock above it.

The first gas well in Texas was drilled in 1907. This well was part of the Petrolia oil field near Wichita Falls. A businessman named Edwy Brown contributed to the urbanization of Texas. He began piping gas to nearby towns and cities. By 1913, his company, Lone Star Gas, was supplying this clean-burning fuel to Dallas and Fort Worth.

More towns became urban centers. As in Dallas and Fort Worth, gas was piped to towns and cities near gas deposits. At first, gas was mainly used to heat furnaces and water heaters. But by the late 1880s, manufacturers started selling stoves fueled by gas. Eventually gas became a major source of power for industries. Natural gas came to be used to produce products such as steel, glass, paper, clothing, brick, and electricity. These are used in the United States and around the world.

Modern gas wells, like these, are a common sight in Texas.

Natural Gas Pipelines

Supplying gas to consumers was no easy task. Gas companies had to build pipelines. These underground pipes stretched from the gas wells to homes and factories. Some were hundreds of miles long. Building and caring for the pipelines became a major industry.

Most gas pipelines led to cities, not the countryside. The new clean fuel was a benefit of city life. Factories and businesses opened in places where they could get natural gas. That helped cities grow. Today, Texas has more natural gas pipelines than any other state.

6. **Identify** and underline in the text how the natural gas industry developed in Texas. Where was the first natural gas well drilled in Texas?

....

A Big Discovery

In 1925, a major natural gas field was discovered in the Texas Panhandle near Amarillo. One well there produced more than 100 million cubic feet of gas a day! People rushed to the region to find jobs and opportunities. A new town, Borger, sprang up. Thousands of people rushed to the new boomtown. The population of Amarillo soon tripled. The Panhandle gas field supplied jobs and wealth for a long time. Over 75 years, it produced 8 trillion cubic feet of gas.

Today, Texas produces more natural gas than any other state. Our state produces nearly 30 percent of our country's natural gas. Texas also has 30 percent of the natural gas still underground in the United States.

 **Got it?**

TEKS 5.A, 5.B, 13.B

7. ◉ **Summarize** **Explain** how Pattillo Higgins, Anthony F. Lucas, and Edwy Brown impacted urbanization in Texas.

....

....

8. ❓ **Identify** the impact that the oil boom had on life in Texas. List three ways.

my Story Ideas

1. ....

....

2. ....

....

3. ....

....

9. **Identify** and write three products made from oil that are purchased to meet people's needs in the United States and around the world.

....

SAVVAS realize Go online to access your interactive digital lesson.

301

Changes and Growth

New developments in communication, such as the telephone, influenced economic activities in Texas.

Electric trolleys in Dallas in 1905

Inventions Bring Change

The oil boom brought big changes to Texas in the early 1900s. Many Texans lived an **urban** life, a life in a city. People who lived in cities such as Dallas saw life change rapidly. **Inventions**, or newly created products, brought about the changes. Cities had electric lines first. So people there had electric lights. That allowed them to work longer hours. The first telephone lines were in cities. That speeded up communication in business and everyday life. City people could use a phone instead of writing letters or sending telegrams. Cities also built electric streetcars called trolleys. That helped people get around quickly.

In some parts of the state, however, the changes came slowly. Many Texans lived a **rural** life, a life in the countryside. For them, life went on much as it had before. Rural Texans used mules to pull their plows. They traveled in horse-drawn buggies. They used firewood to heat and cook. Their rural homes had no electricity or indoor plumbing.

1. **Identify** and circle the part of the photo that shows how the trolley got electricity.

2. **Explain** how developments in communication influenced economic activities in Texas.

....

....

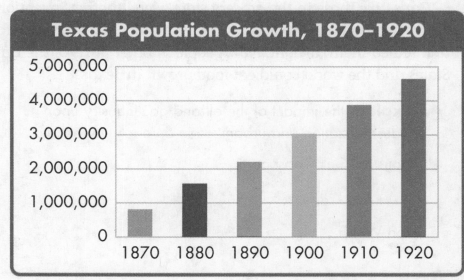

Describe how the telephone may have changed Texans' lives.

I will know that inventions and the growth of industries provided economic opportunities to Texans.

Vocabulary

urban

invention

rural

industry

manufacture

assembly line

Cars also changed the way people lived. By 1910, cars were a common sight on Texas roads. The use of cars grew so quickly that by the 1920s cities began to install traffic signs and write laws controlling speed.

TEKS

5.A, 5.B, 6.B, 7.A, 12.A, 12.C, 12.D, 12.E, 20.B

New People and New Opportunities

Many people moved to Texas. Look at the bar graph. It shows that Texas's population grew by more than 1.5 million people between 1900 and 1920.

Many new Texans came from other states. Others immigrated from Mexico and other nearby countries. Some came from faraway nations in Europe, Asia, and Africa. The artist Elizabet Ney came to Texas from Germany, a country in Europe. Ney carved the sculptures of Sam Houston and Stephen F. Austin that stand in our state capitol.

3. **Identify** and underline in the text three reasons why people moved to Texas cities in the early 1900s.

What brought the newcomers to Texas cities? The cities offered theaters, concerts, and cultural opportunities. There were good schools and hospitals. Most important, however, were the economic opportunities. People usually moved to Texas cities to find well-paying jobs. The effects of immigration were to put more people to work in the new industries growing in Texas.

Texas Population Growth, 1870–1920

Year	Population
1870	~800,000
1880	~1,600,000
1890	~2,200,000
1900	~3,000,000
1910	~3,900,000
1920	~4,600,000

Source: U.S. Census Bureau

SAVVAS realize™ Go online to access your interactive digital lesson.

303

Growing Industries

Jobs were available in Texas industries. An **industry** is a group of businesses that makes a type of product or provides a type of service. Thanks to the railroads and the discovery of oil, many Texas industries grew fast.

The oil industry was booming. Many people moved to Houston to work in oil refineries. Others worked in the Gulf Coast port cities, shipping oil overseas. Later, the natural gas industry created many jobs. Workers were needed to build gas pipelines to Texas cities.

Meatpacking was another growing industry in Texas. Fort Worth was a center of the cattle trade. The cattle industry impacted the meatpacking industry. As more cattle were raised to sell, it led to a need for more meatpacking plants. Large meatpacking plants there hired many workers. The workers slaughtered cattle and prepared meat for shipment to markets.

Many Texans found jobs in manufacturing. To **manufacture** is to make or process goods, especially by machine in large quantities. By 1910, Texas had a number of cotton mills.

Logging companies and sawmills were active in East Texas. Sawmill towns sprang up there to house workers. Lufkin became a center of the growing lumber industry. Businesses in Lufkin made and sold supplies to companies and workers who were cutting down the big pine forests of East Texas.

Textile mills manufactured cotton cloth.

New Inventions Help Industry

Cans, like those in the grocery store, were another invention. They kept food from spoiling. Canneries filled the cans with food and sealed them airtight. Now people in other parts of the United States and the world could eat food grown in Texas.

4. **Explain** the impact of the oil and gas industry upon industrialization and urbanization on each city below.

Houston, Gulf Coast ports ....

....

Fort Worth ....

....

Assembly Lines and Mass Production

Henry Ford began to make automobiles in Detroit, Michigan, in 1903. At first, Ford's workers could only make a few cars a day. Then Ford put in a moving assembly line. An **assembly line** moves a product past workers who stay in place. Each worker specializes in one small task. Breaking down a big job into small parts like this is called the division of labor. Ford's factory could make a car every 90 minutes. This is called mass production.

In 1913, Henry Ford brought his new technology to Texas. He opened a car factory in Deep Ellum, near Dallas. The impact of mass production and specialization on the economic growth of Texas was huge. Mass production, specialization, and the division of labor let factories produce more goods and produce them cheaply. This meant that more people could buy more cheaply and that factories would need more workers to produce these goods.

With division of labor, each worker along the assembly line did one small part of a big job.

Got it?

TEKS 12.D, 12.E, 20.B

5. ◉ **Make Inferences** **Describe** the impact of mass production, specialization, and the division of labor on the economic growth of Texas.

....

....

6.  It is 1910. Your family has just moved to a Texas city. Write a letter **describing** the economic and other opportunities in the city.

my Story Ideas

7. **Describe** how each scientific discovery or innovation in technology benefited Texas.

telephone ....

....

trolley ....

assembly line ....

....

Lesson 1 TEKS 4.B, 20.A

The Texas Cattle Industry

1. **Explain** the contribution of each person to the development of the Texas cattle industry.

   Charles Goodnight ....

   ....

   ....

   Richard King ....

   ....

   ....

   Lizzie Johnson ....

   ....

   ....

2. Read the question carefully. Determine the best answer to the question from the four answer choices provided. Circle the best answer.

   How did cattle trails help make ranching an important industry in Texas?

   A The trails led to rich grassland and water holes.

   B The trails helped ranchers keep their herds separate.

   C The trails let ranchers sell cattle for a higher price.

   D The trails opened up new areas for ranching.

3. Complete the chart below. **Identify** Joseph Glidden's contribution to the development of Texas in the cause box. Then **describe** one effect.

   > **Cause:**
   >
   >

   ↓

   > **Effect:**
   > Farmers protected their crops from roaming cattle.

   ↓

   > **Effect:**
   >
   >

Lesson 2 TEKS 8.A, 9.C, 11.C, 13.A

The Texas Railroad Boom

4. **Identify** patterns of settlement in Texas after the building of the railroads.

   ....

   ....

5. Compare the positive and negative consequences of modification of the environment by railroad companies.

....

....

....

....

....

6. Describe choice and opportunity in the free enterprise system.

Choice: ....

....

....

....

Opportunity: ....

....

....

7. Explain how the railroad helped to increase Texas's economic activities with other states and countries.

....

....

....

....

Texas Gold!

8. Identify and **explain** the impact of the development of the oil and gas industry on industrialization and urbanization on life in Texas. Give one example.

....

....

....

....

....

....

9. Explain how Pattillo Higgins impacted industrialization and urbanization in Texas.

....

....

....

....

10. Describe how the discovery of oil in Texas benefited individuals.

....

....

....

11. In addition to oil, **identify** a Texas product that is purchased to meet energy needs in the United States and the world.

....

12. **Identify** three people important to the development of the oil and gas industry in Texas, and **explain** how they impacted urbanization and industrialization in Texas.

....

....

....

....

....

....

....

....

Lesson 4   TEKS 12.D, 20.B

Changes and Growth

13. **Identify** Texas agricultural products that could be sold throughout the United States and the world because of the invention of the modern can.

....

....

....

14. **Define** each term. Then **describe** its impact on the economic growth of Texas.

Division of labor: ....

....

....

....

Mass production: ....

....

....

....

15. **How does economic growth provide opportunity?** TEKS 12.D

Most years, Texas is the number one job creator in the country. Texas creates more jobs than any other state.

a. **Explain** why economic growth creates new jobs.

....

....

b. How do new jobs provide opportunity?

....

....

....

Go online to write and illustrate your own **myStory Book** using the **myStory Ideas** from this chapter.

How does economic growth provide opportunity?

TEKS

SS 4.B, 4.C, 5.A, 5.B
ELA 15

The history of Texas is a story of economic growth. Ranching, the railroad boom, and the oil boom all created opportunity in Texas. So did the growth of Texas cities and factories. Today Texas is still enjoying economic growth. New industries provide opportunities to our people.

Think about the industries that provide opportunities to Texans today. List your examples and **explain** why you chose them.

....

....

....

....

Draw an image that shows one of your examples. Show where you might find economic opportunity someday.

Hard Times at Home and Abroad

 my Story Spark

How do people respond to good times and bad?

In the chart, read the things that happen when times are good. Then fill in what it would be like if the good things weren't happening anymore.

Good Times	Bad Times
Music and art classes at school	
Plenty of jobs	

★ Texas Essential Knowledge and Skills

5.A Identify the impact of various issues and events on life in Texas.

5.C Identify the accomplishments of notable individuals.

8.A Identify and explain clusters and patterns of settlement in Texas at different time periods.

11.B Describe how the free enterprise system works, including supply and demand.

11.C Give examples of the benefits of the free enterprise system such as choice and opportunity.

12.B Explain how geographic factors such as climate, transportation, and natural resources have influenced the location of economic activities in Texas.

12.F Explain the impact of American ideas about progress and equality of opportunity on the economic development and growth of Texas.

13.A Identify ways in which technological changes in areas such as transportation and communication have resulted in increased interdependence among Texas, the United States, and the world.

13.B Identify oil and gas, agricultural, and technological products of Texas that are purchased to meet needs in the United States and around the world.

17.A Identify important individuals who have participated voluntarily in civic affairs at state and local levels.

17.B Explain how individuals can participate voluntarily in civic affairs at state and local levels through activities.

17.D Identify the importance of historical figures and important individuals who modeled active participation in the democratic process.

18.A Identify leaders in state, local, and national governments.

19.C Summarize the contributions of people of various racial, ethnic, and religious groups in the development of Texas.

21.A Differentiate between, locate, and use valid primary and secondary sources such as oral, print, and visual material to acquire information about the United States and Texas.

21.B Analyze information by summarizing.

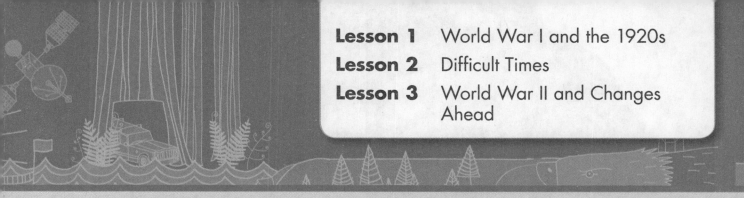
Latinos and Latinas During World War II
Fighting for Our Country

José learns about the U.S. Latino and Latina World War II Oral History Project.

my Story Video

"I can't wait to get to Austin!" José calls out eagerly, as he peers out the car window. "I wonder if we'll get to see pictures of World War II veterans. My friend Jorge's great-grandfather was a soldier in World War II, but he doesn't have any pictures." José is about to meet Dr. Maggie Rivas-Rodriguez, a journalism professor at the University of Texas, Austin.

Dr. Rivas-Rodriguez has an extensive collection of recordings and narratives, or written accounts, of World War II Latino veterans. She has been collecting them since 1999, when she started the United States Latino and Latina World War II Oral History Project.

"Hello, Dr. Rivas-Rodriguez. Thanks for meeting me today," José says shyly. "Welcome," says Dr. Rivas-Rodriguez as she shakes José's hand. José doesn't waste any time getting down to business. Before they've sat down, he asks his first question. "How many veterans of World War II were Latino?" he asks. "Well, we aren't certain, but somewhere around 450,000 Latinos and Latinas served in the United States military during World War II," she answers. "Wow! That's a lot of people!" he says. "It sure is," answers the professor.

A veteran holds his right hand over his heart.

Dr. Rivas-Rodriguez tells José that many Latinos and Latinas contributed to the war effort, both at the front and at home.

Sergeant José M. Lopez receives his Medal of Honor.

World War II was a war between many different countries, and it affected more people around the world than any other war. More men from Texas joined the armed forces than from any other state. Many men also trained for the war in Texas before they were deployed, or sent out to battlefields in Europe, Africa, and Asia.

When most people hear about World War II veterans, they usually think of the soldiers who fought on the front lines, or fighter pilots, or submarine captains. "But," Dr. Rivas-Rodriguez reminds us, "we have to remember the folks at home, too." "How did the war change things here at home?" asks José. "Well, back in the 1940s, people at home helped the war effort in many different ways. The war changed a lot of people's lives. Wives, mothers, and daughters went to work in factories to make the machines and supplies needed for the war. Others volunteered outside the home in jobs that supported the soldiers who were defending the country. Farmers and farm laborers took jobs in towns," explains Dr. Rivas-Rodriguez.

The professor tells José that people from all over Texas and throughout the United States came together to help the war effort. People at home planted vegetable gardens, and children collected metals and other materials that could be used to make weapons and supplies. "We recycle today, too!" José interjects. As José scans the professor's vast collection of artifacts, he asks, "Who was one of the more famous Latino veterans of World War II?"

This image of José M. Lopez is on display at the World War II Memorial in the Texas State Capitol.

This World War II aircraft is on display in Burnet, Texas.

"A man with the same first name as you received the Medal of Honor," she tells José. "José M. Lopez won the Medal of Honor for his bravery during the Battle of the Bulge in Europe. Another Latino who won the Medal of Honor was Cleto L. Rodriguez. He was recognized for his brave fighting in the South Pacific. Of course, thousands of military men and women performed other important jobs that were not on the front lines," she adds. Many of their stories can be found in Dr. Rivas-Rodriguez's archives, and the stories do a good job of describing how the war changed lives. "It's pretty amazing what these folks did for our country," she tells José. "There is a lot here to take in."

As José continues to sift through the pictures, the stories, and the videos, he wonders out loud, "What was it like to fly overseas and fight in a strange land at such a young age? Some of the soldiers weren't that much older than me!" "That's right, José. And we have captured hundreds of stories of men and women in all facets of the war," Dr. Rivas-Rodriguez explains. "A lot of them talk about how life was different for them after the war."

Watching José continue to look through the archives, Dr. Rivas-Rodriguez senses that he could stay here for a long time. "I could look at these files for hours," he tells her. "Let's grab lunch and I can tell you some of my favorite stories," she says. "OK, but afterwards, can we come back?" he asks. Dr. Rivas-Rodriguez replies, "For as long as you want, José. There is a lot of history here, and I'm so glad that you enjoy it!"

Think About It Based on the story, do you think people can solve problems that they did not create? As you read, think about how Texans responded to bad times by working to solve problems.

World War I and the 1920s

Envision It!

Before 1920, women were denied the right to vote. Posters pointed out how unfair this was.

Far across the ocean, in 1914, war broke out in Europe. Britain, France, Italy, and Russia formed an alliance. An **alliance** is a formal agreement of friendship between countries. These four countries were known as the Allied Powers. Germany, Austria-Hungary, and the Ottoman Empire, or Turkey, formed the Central Powers.

Major Allied and Central Powers, 1917

GERMANY

GREAT BRITAIN

FRANCE

UNITED STATES

RUSSIA

ITALY

AUSTRIA-HUNGARY

TURKEY

PACIFIC OCEAN

ATLANTIC OCEAN

INDIAN OCEAN

N W E S

0 4,000 mi
0 4,000 km

LEGEND
Major Allied Powers in 1917
Major Central Powers in 1917

World War I

President Woodrow Wilson asked the people of the United States not to take sides in the war. Then in 1915, a German submarine sank a British passenger ship, the *Lusitania*. More than 1,100 people died, including 128 Americans. Though angry, the United States still did not declare war. German naval attacks on merchant and other ships increased. In April 1917, the United States joined the Allied Powers to fight Germany and the Central Powers.

1. **Identify** and write the names of the continents on which the major Allied and Central Powers were located.

UNLOCK
THE BIG
?

I will know how events in the first two decades of the 1900s affected life in Texas.

Vocabulary

alliance   suffrage

conserve   jazz

bond   prejudice

interest

Design and draw a poster that you think would have helped women win the right to vote.

Texans Go to War

TEKS
5.A, 5.C, 11.C, 12.F, 13.B, 17.A, 17.B, 18.A

World War I had a big impact on life in Texas and the nation. Millions of Americans joined the armed services to fight the Central Powers. More than 20,000 of them were women who went to Europe to serve as nurses. Nearly 200,000 Texans also joined up. Among them were 450 women nurses.

The new soldiers needed training. The United States set up camps where they could learn new skills and work as a team. In Texas, the largest included Camp MacArthur at Waco, Camp Logan at Houston, Camp Travis at San Antonio, and Camp Bowie at Fort Worth. Training for officers took place at Leon Springs.

Airplanes came into common use during World War I. Many new pilots trained in San Antonio. At Kelly Field, more than 1,500 men learned to fly. Thousands more learned how to be airplane mechanics. Pilots also trained at the nearby Stinson School of Flying. Marjorie Stinson, a licensed pilot, had founded the school. She, her sister Katherine, and her brothers all helped run it.

Men reporting for service at Camp Travis. They leave the base building in their new military uniforms.

2. ◎ **Summarize Identify** how World War I impacted life in Texas.

....

....

SAVVAS
realize™   Go online to access your interactive digital lesson.

315

Texas During World War I

World War I also had an impact on life at home in Texas. More food for soldiers and supplies for the armed forces were needed to win. But as farmers became soldiers and left their fields, food shortages occurred. The Texas farmers who stayed behind worked hard to grow more food crops and meet the demand. The United States government then purchased these agricultural products from Texas and other states.

Texan agricultural products were purchased by the United States government to meet the nation's wartime needs.

People throughout the country and in Texas volunteered to help the war. Millions conserved food. To **conserve** means to limit the use of something in order to protect from waste or overuse. People followed a plan set out by the United States Food Administration. They volunteered to cut down on sugar and meat every day. Many Texas families grew their own vegetables. That way more canned foods could be sent to soldiers.

People also took jobs that helped the war. Texas's refineries produced oil products that were bought by the United States government for the war. Raising livestock and packing meat was also important. Women went to work in factories, taking jobs that soldiers left behind. Some worked for volunteer groups such as the Red Cross.

Many people helped the government raise money for the war by buying liberty bonds. A **bond** is a document received in exchange for money. People return the bond at a certain date and get back their money with interest. **Interest** is money earned at a regular rate for the use of money lent.

The war ended in 1918. The Allied Powers had won, but the cost was great. More than 5,000 Texans died while serving in the armed forces.

3. **Explain** how individuals voluntarily took part in winning the war.

....

....

Women's Rights Issues

Even as women supported the war, many continued to fight for their own rights. For many years, women had called for suffrage. **Suffrage** is the right to vote. In the early 1900s, women were not allowed to vote in national or in Texas elections.

To gain their rights, Texas women became voluntarily active in civic affairs at state and local levels. Jessie Daniel Ames grew up in Texas. She founded the Texas League of Women Voters in 1919. She brought African American and white women together to work for suffrage. Mary Eleanor Brackenridge supported many women's rights issues, including suffrage. She was the first woman in Bexar County to register to vote when Texas made it legal in 1918. But women still could not vote in national elections.

Also in 1918, Texas elected its first woman to statewide office. Annie Webb Blanton was a college teacher and an author who believed in equal rights for women. She became Texas's first female state superintendent of public instruction.

In 1920, the United States finally ratified, or gave consent to, the Nineteenth Amendment of the United States Constitution. This law granted women citizens across the country the right to vote in all elections.

Texas women fought hard and won limited local voting rights, two years before full voting rights were approved for all women in the United States.

4. **Identify** important individuals in the suffragist movement who have participated voluntarily in civic affairs at state and local levels.

....

....

....

....

The Roaring Twenties

It was an era of progress. Life changed quickly for Texas and the United States during the 1920s. The experience of war and the issue of women's equality had an impact on people's lives in Texas and the nation. It changed people's views. Society was becoming more modern.

Businesses developed and grew. Today, we call this period the Roaring Twenties. Between 1920 and 1929, the free enterprise system helped industries and cities grow rapidly. Factories that had made products for World War I turned to making things people would buy. To keep up with the demand, they hired more workers.

More people had more jobs and money than ever before. Many people bought their own homes. Progress also meant having the latest inventions. Radios, telephones, and refrigerators were popular.

New technology made the automobile more affordable. People began to use more oil and gas than ever before. In Texas, the oil industry boomed. Using Texas oil, gasoline companies built more oil refineries. By 1928, Texans owned more than a million cars and trucks. Cities and states built better roads for vehicles. The paved highways encouraged people to travel more. New businesses developed to meet the needs of drivers. Gas stations and motorist hotels, or motels, became more common.

Texaco Motor Oil, founded in 1902, is today one of the largest oil companies in the world.

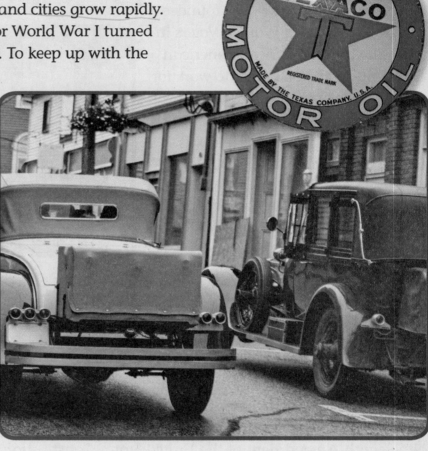

Americans drove more cars in the 1920s.

5. **Identify** the impact on life in Texas of increased use of oil and gas during the 1920s.

....

....

....

The Jazz Age

During the 1920s, American cities grew at a fast pace. Farmers left their land and took factory jobs. The price for farm products had dropped. Many farmers could no longer earn a living on the land. They moved to cities to look for jobs.

The cities moved to a fresh new beat, jazz! **Jazz** is a type of music started in African American communities. Its exciting, strong rhythms gave the 1920s another nickname: the Jazz Age.

People looked for new things to do and new ways to have fun. The "ragtime" music of Texas-born musician Scott Joplin was popular. In Deep Ellum, a Dallas neighborhood, people went to nightclubs to dance and listen to live music. Deep Ellum was a center for jazz and blues music. The blues gave voice through song to the experiences of African Americans in the South. Texas blues singer, Blind Lemon Jefferson, recorded more than 100 songs.

Radio and movies played a role in entertainment, too. Many families in Texas and other states gathered around the radio after dusk. They heard news reports, radio plays, comedy shows, and musical programs. At the "picture show," people watched black and white silent movies. Not until the late 1920s did the first major "talkie," or a movie with sound, come out. It was called *The Jazz Singer*.

6. ◉ **Summarize** **Explain** why cities grew in the 1920s. Use details from the text to support your answer.

....

....

....

Dance crazes swept the nation in the 1920s.

SAVVAS realize. Go online to access your interactive digital lesson.

319

Troubling Times

Despite the good times of the 1920s, there were plenty of hard times as well. African Americans throughout the United States faced very unfair treatment. Many southern blacks traveled to cities in the North hoping to find equal opportunity for work. They found factory jobs but poor working conditions. They faced racism and intolerance.

At the same time, the Ku Klux Klan, or the KKK, grew stronger in Texas. They wanted to deny African Americans their rights. The beliefs of the KKK were based on prejudice and hatred. **Prejudice** is a strong opinion formed without facts. However, many Americans, both white and black, opposed the KKK. Politicians like Miriam "Ma" Ferguson and other Texans helped to defeat KKK members trying to win elections. Miriam Ferguson became the first Texas woman elected governor in 1924. She ran for office and won after her husband, who had also been governor, was forced out of office. When Ma Ferguson took office as governor, the KKK weakened, losing members and power.

In some places, African Americans were kept separate from whites.

In other places, such as this lumber company in Camden, Texas, African Americans worked alongside white people.

7. Explain why many African Americans and whites, including Ma Ferguson, opposed the KKK.

....

....

....

....

....

....

....

Miriam "Ma" Ferguson, the first woman governor of Texas, fought against prejudice.

Got it?

TEKS 11.C, 12.F, 13.B

8. ◉ **Summarize Identify** how Texan agricultural products met the needs of Americans during World War I.

....

....

9. ❓ Write a short dialogue that **describes** two people who have moved my Story Ideas
to a large city seeking equal opportunity in the 1920s and what they face.

....

....

10. Use evidence from the text to **give examples** about how people benefited from the free enterprise system during the Roaring Twenties.

....

....

....

Summarize

When you **summarize** in reading, you analyze and then retell the main points of a passage or chapter. Summarizing helps you check your understanding of what you've read. A summary is short. It is no more than a few sentences.

To summarize, find the main idea of the passage you are reading. Then, find important details about the main idea. Finally, put the main idea and details in your own words.

Bessie Coleman, Pilot (1892–1926)

Bessie Coleman, or Queen Bess, as people called her, was a stunt flier and the world's first licensed African American pilot. She was born in Atlanta, Texas, in 1892, as one of 13 children. As a child, she picked cotton and helped her mother wash people's laundry for money, but she dreamed of learning to fly. Coleman graduated from high school but couldn't afford to complete more than one semester of college.

Bessie Coleman

Coleman moved to Chicago and worked for a few years. She continued to think about flying. The flying schools she contacted refused to teach her, because she was an African American and a woman. Instead of giving up, Coleman sailed to France. She studied for 10 months at an aviation school there and earned her license. Returning to the United States in 1921, Coleman took part in air shows. Her daredevil stunts made her one of America's most popular fliers. She gave lectures encouraging young African American men and women to become pilots.

TEKS

ELA 11.A Summarize the main idea and supporting
details in text in ways that maintain meaning.
SS 5.C Identify the accomplishments of notable
individuals such as Bessie Coleman.
SS 21.B Analyze information by summarizing.

1. **Analyze** the passage about Bessie Coleman on the previous page.

2. **Summarize** the main idea.

   ....

   ....

   ....

3. Use the passage to **identify** the accomplishments of Bessie Coleman.

   ....

   ....

   ....

   ....

4. **Summarize** why Bessie Coleman is a notable individual of the
   twentieth century in Texas.

   ....

   ....

   ....

   ....

   ....

   ....

   ....

SAVVAS
realize. **Go online to access your
interactive digital lesson.**   323

Difficult Times

Envision It!

Throughout its history, Texas has faced long spells of weather so dry and dusty that day looks like night.

During the Roaring Twenties, businesses boomed. People wanted to earn money from thriving American companies. So they bought stocks. A **stock** is a share of ownership in a company. People can buy and sell shares in the stock market. When companies make a profit, the price of their stocks go up. A **profit** is money left over after the costs of running a business are paid for. When companies lose money, the price of their stocks goes down.

The Stock Market Crashes

To get in on soaring profits, many people in the late 1920s spent their savings on stock. Others borrowed money to buy it. They took out loans against their homes and other possessions. Then companies began to fail. Stock prices began to fall.

In October 1929, the stock market crashed. People rushed to sell their now-worthless stocks. When they couldn't, they found they owed more money than they had. People lost their savings. They could not pay back loans. Banks that had loaned money closed. More people lost their savings. So many people lost money that companies found it difficult to sell their products. They stopped hiring and began to lay off workers. Many companies closed.

Newspapers around the country reported on the 1929 stock market crash.

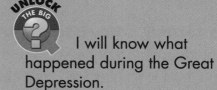
Identify a problem that you think long spells of dry weather might cause.

Vocabulary

stock   unemployed
profit   drought
depression   discrimination
charity

Trouble in Texas

At first, many Texans refused to believe that the troubles with the stock market would cause a depression in Texas. A **depression** is a time when business slows and prices fall. But the Great Depression, as it became known, hurt people across the nation, including in Texas, and in countries around the world.

Many Texans and people in other states lost their jobs. Then they found it difficult to buy what they needed to live. People lost their homes. Many went hungry. Some traveled from place to place looking for work or begging for food. Charities tried to help. A **charity** is an organization that helps people in need.

TEKS
5.A, 11.B, 12.B, 12.F, 17.D, 18.A

Children at a Texas temporary workers' camp

1. ◉ **Summarize Identify** the impact of ~~like in G.D.~~ the stock market crash on life in Texas.

....

....

....

....

....

....

The Great Depression and the Dust Bowl

The depression got even worse. In the early 1930s, so many people had lost their jobs that charities helping them ran out of money. Government and community leaders in Texas stepped in. Some towns sponsored gardening programs. They gave people seed and land to grow vegetables for food. Austin, Dallas, Fort Worth, and Houston held plays and musicals to raise money for soup kitchens and bread lines to help feed the hungry.

Many people who lost their jobs and homes moved in with relatives. Others had nowhere to live. They began to cluster outside of large cities. Using scraps of wood, cardboard, and sheet metal, they built shanties, or shacks. Hundreds of thousands of unemployed and homeless American families lived in these shantytowns. To be **unemployed** is to have no job. The shantytowns became known as Hoovervilles. They were named after United States President Herbert Hoover.

During the Roaring Twenties, farmers in Texas and across the Great Plains had plowed up millions of acres of grasslands for crops. So much wheat was grown that prices fell. Wheat farmers could barely earn a living. Prices fell even more after the stock market crashed. Texas farmers lost money growing wheat and cotton.

Then, in the mid-1930s, things got even worse. Texas and much of the Great Plains region experienced a terrible drought. A **drought** is a period of time with little rain. Without steady rain, crops didn't grow.

A shantytown in Texas

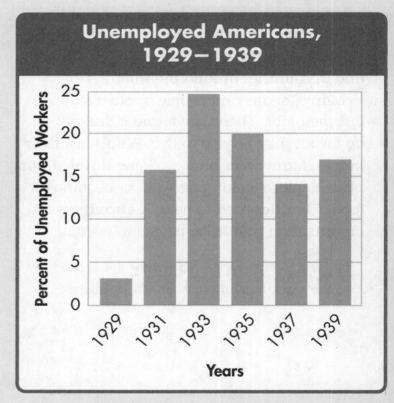

Source: U.S. Bureau of the Census, Historical Statistics of the United States, Colonial Times to 1957

2. **Analyze** the bar graph. Circle the year that had the highest rate of unemployment. Then underline the year that had the lowest rate of unemployment.

Many farmers had not taken steps to conserve or enrich the soil. Topsoil quickly dried out and lay exposed beneath the sun. Then came the winds. Blowing nonstop across the dry farmlands, the winds swept the dusty topsoil into the sky. Great windstorms swirled dust high into the air. They darkened the sky for days and sometimes reached all the way to the East Coast. Much of the Great Plains region became known as the Dust Bowl.

– Dust bowl

Dust storms scoured the land clean of topsoil in some places. It piled dust onto fields in others. Crops were ruined and couldn't grow. People shoveled dust from their yards the way snow is shoveled. One dust storm in Amarillo lasted for more than three days.

Because they couldn't grow anything, many farmers left their land to look for other work. Some moved to California to work on farms there. Whole families packed up and migrated, looking for a new start.

3. **Identify** how the Great Depression and the Dust Bowl impacted life in Texas.

....

....

....

The Dust Bowl impacted many Texans in the 1930s.

The New Deal

Americans elected Franklin D. Roosevelt to be president of the United States in 1932. Roosevelt believed that the government should help its people. He proposed and signed laws to create jobs, relieve poverty, and improve the economy. This program was called the New Deal.

One New Deal program, the Civilian Conservation Corps (CCC), put 3 million young men to work. They worked in the nation's forests and wild lands, digging ditches or building paths, roads, and state parks. Another program, the Works Progress Administration (WPA), hired more than 8 million workers. They built dams, bridges, roads, parks, and airports. Some WPA artists painted murals on the walls of public buildings. The jobs the New Deal workers did improved local communities.

The president ordered that, under the WPA, working Americans were to be given equal opportunity. This meant that no one would be turned away based on race or religion. The WPA hired thousands of African Americans who helped build and repair hospitals, homes, and schools. They also served as teachers and doctors. Still, African Americans in the WPA faced discrimination. **Discrimination** is the unequal treatment of people. African American workers often received less pay than white workers and were made to take the least desirable positions.

Civilian Conservation Corps Parks in Texas

Palo Duro Canyon
Bonham
Daingerfield
Caddo Lake
Big Spring
Abilene
Cleburne
Tyler
Meridian
Lake Brownwood
Fort Parker
Mission Tejas
Balmorhea
Mother Neff
Huntsville
Davis Mountains
Indian Lodge
Inks Lake
Longhorn Cavern
Blanco
Bastrop
Buescher
Garner
Lockhart
Palmetto
Goliad
Lake Corpus Christi
Goose Island
Gulf of Mexico

LEGEND
● CCC state park

4. ◉ **Summarize** **Analyze** the map. Circle the CCC state park nearest where you live. Then **summarize** how the CCC helped in the economic development and growth of Texas.

Texans played important roles in the New Deal. John Nance Garner of Uvalde, Texas, served as vice president under Franklin D. Roosevelt. United States Congressman Sam Rayburn of Bonham, Texas, helped pass many New Deal laws. One law he promoted helped bring electricity to rural farms. A young man named Lyndon B. Johnson ran a New Deal program that helped young people find jobs in Texas. Many years later, he became president of the United States.

Not everyone in Texas agreed with President Roosevelt's New Deal. Some people worried that it gave too much power to the federal government. Others felt that the government should not interfere too much in the free enterprise system. Nonetheless, jobs created by government programs lifted spirits of many workers. Earning money meant families could buy food and pay for services.

Texan Lyndon Johnson shakes hands with President Roosevelt. Governor James Allred of Texas is also present.

Got it?

TEKS 12.F, 17.D

5. ◉ **Summarize** Write an explanation about the impact of President Roosevelt's ideas about equal opportunity and how these affected hiring at the WPA.

....

....

....

6. ❓ Suppose you work for the CCC. **Analyze** how the CCC helped during bad times. Then write an advertisement to get young people to work outdoors in the country's forests and wild lands.

my Story Ideas

....

7. Identify and **summarize** how Sam Rayburn is an important individual who modeled active participation in the democratic process.

....

....

Analyze Images

Images are everywhere and are primary sources, so it's important to understand them. There is a saying: "A picture is worth a thousand words." This means that images tell us something in a way that writing does not.

Analyzing an image means looking at it in a new way. Instead of looking at the picture as a whole, try looking first at the people, then the objects, and finally the activities that are going on in the picture.

Observe the image below. You can acquire information about the United States and Texas from it. The painting shows a Dust Bowl farm engulfed in sand dunes. The caption tells you the name of the painting and who painted it. Captions add information about the image. They can give you a better understanding of the story the artist wanted to tell through his or her work.

Drouth Stricken Area, 1934 by Texan artist Alexandre Hogue

TEKS

ELA 13.B Explain factual information presented graphically.

ELA 14 Use comprehension skills to analyze how words, images, graphics, and sounds work together in various forms to impact meaning.

SS 5.A Identify the impact of various issues and events on life in Texas such as the Dust Bowl.

SS 21.A Differentiate between, locate, and use valid primary and secondary sources such as oral, print, and visual material to acquire information about the United States and Texas.

Analyze the image on page 330. Then use it to answer the questions.

1. **Describe** the creatures and objects in the painting. Then **explain** why you think the artist painted them instead of people.

....

....

....

....

2. What information about the United States and Texas can you infer from the painting?

....

....

3. **Describe** how you think the artist feels about the drought.

....

....

....

4. **Apply** **Explain** how a painting or another kind of image can be used to acquire information about the United States and Texas.

....

....

....

....

World War II and Changes Ahead

After World War II, new neighborhoods outside of cities were created for soldiers and their families.

"above and beyond the call of duty"

DORIE MILLER
Received the Navy Cross
at Pearl Harbor, May 27, 1942

Doris "Dorie" Miller

People had hoped that World War I would be "the war to end all wars." But the years following the war, though peaceful, were troubled. Then in 1939, Germany attacked Poland. Once again, countries in Europe took sides. Britain, France, and the Soviet Union joined together as the Allies. They fought the Axis Powers—Germany, Italy, and Japan. World War II had begun.

World War II

At first, the United States tried to remain neutral. **Neutral** means not supporting one side or the other. Then the Japanese launched a surprise attack on Pearl Harbor, Hawaii. On the morning of December 7, 1941, Japanese planes bombed American ships anchored in the harbor. Doris Miller, a Texas sailor aboard the USS *West Virginia*, saw it all. He defended his ship by shooting at the Japanese planes and received the Navy Cross for his bravery under fire.

The United States declared war on Japan and Germany. They joined the Allies. Americans, including many Texans, rushed to defend their country. In fact, Texas sent a larger proportion of its population to serve during the war than any other state, about 750,000 people, including 12,000 women.

A number of divisions, or army groups, trained in Texas. The men of the Thirty-sixth Division proudly wore a patch with a "T" on an arrowhead. They were called the "Texas Division." They were among the first Americans to go overseas.

Design, label, and explain a new kind of neighborhood for people to live in today.

UNLOCK THE BIG ?

I will know how World War II affected Texas and the United States.

Vocabulary

neutral

communism

suburb

civil rights

Texans fought bravely in Africa, Asia, and Europe. Thirty-three Texans won the Medal of Honor. This is the highest military honor. It is given for acts of valor above and beyond the call of duty. In fact, the most decorated American in the war was Lieutenant Audie Murphy of Farmersville, Texas. Murphy joined the army as a private. He was 18. He personally stopped an attack by enemy tanks and received 33 awards, citations, and decorations. Later, he became a successful actor and songwriter.

General Dwight D. Eisenhower commanded United States forces in Europe. He led the troops in important battles and invasions and accepted the surrender of the Germans in 1945. Born in Denison, Texas, Eisenhower later became the 34th president of the United States.

TEKS
5.A, 5.C, 8.A, 11.B, 11.C, 12.F, 13.A, 13.B, 17.B, 17.D, 18.A, 19.C

1. ◉ **Summarize Identify** and then briefly **explain** the impact that the bombing of Pearl Harbor had on life in Texas.

....

....

....

....

Lieutenant Audie Murphy

More Texans in the War

About 500,000 Latinos fought bravely in WWII; many of them were from Texas. Cleto Rodriguez of San Antonio was one of five Mexican Americans to win the Medal of Honor. He saw action in the South Pacific where he helped to defeat the Japanese. In 1975, an elementary school was named in his honor.

Texan women played a vital role in the war. About 1,000 women served as pilots during the war. Most of them were trained in Texas. Oveta Culp Hobby of Houston helped to plan and run the Women's Army Auxiliary Corps (WAAC) for the United States. The WAAC provided female volunteers a way to serve during the war. Under Hobby's direction, hundreds of thousands of women did a wide range of useful army jobs, from parachute folding to secretarial work.

Industry and War

Texas industries boomed during the war. Front and center was the oil industry. Battleships, planes, tanks, and jeeps all ran on gasoline. Texas oil and gas companies supplied about half of all the fuel needed for the war. Rubber, made from petroleum and other materials, also came from Texas factories. The United States government purchased these products from Texas.

Old businesses retooled to supply war materials. Materials were needed to make uniforms and tents. For example, Texas businessman Stanley Marcus found ways to help conserve textiles. Marcus had developed his family's company, Neiman Marcus, into a luxury clothing store. In 1941, he joined the War Production Board. He helped convince Americans to make do with the clothing they had.

2. **Identify** and underline two accomplishments of Stanley Marcus.

AMERICANOS TODOS
★
LUCHAMOS POR LA VICTORIA

★ AMERICANS ALL
LET'S FIGHT FOR VICTORY

Mexican Americans fought bravely in WW II.

Other Texas industries also helped the war effort. Texas farmers grew huge amounts of crops to feed the Allies. To meet the demand for steel, mills in Houston and Daingerfield produced thousands of tons. Factories in Houston, Galveston, and Corpus Christi built ships. Airplanes were built near Dallas and Fort Worth.

As the demand for war materials increased, so did the demand for workers. Women took the jobs of men who had gone to war. Half a million rural Texans moved to Texas cities to work in wartime factories. So did people from around the country and from Mexico. Cities grew rapidly. The number of wage earners in Texas more than doubled from 1939 to 1945.

In 1945, the Axis Powers surrendered. The Allies had won. Millions of people, including about 22,000 Texans, had died in the fighting and from other causes. Those who came home found a different place. The Great Depression was over. Texas industry was on the move.

3. Suppose you were an airplane factory worker from rural Texas during World War II. **Describe** how the economic laws of supply and demand allowed you this work opportunity.

....

....

....

....

....

During World War II, many women helped the war effort.

Texas Culture and Art

As times changed rapidly in the 1900s, some Texans saw a need to preserve the past. Objects and inventions that had once seemed modern were being quickly replaced with newer things. So Texans built museums to preserve our rich history. The oldest state museum is the Panhandle-Plains Historical Museum. It holds a real windmill, a chuck wagon, arrowheads, and more. Many other museums were built when Texas celebrated its 100 years of independence in 1936. One of these, the San Jacinto Monument and Museum, honors the heroes of the Battle of San Jacinto. The museum tells the history of Texas and the region over thousands of years.

Texas musicians of the early twentieth century also left their mark on Texas history. Julius Lorenzo Cobb Bledsoe of Waco sang opera and musicals, composed music, and acted in film. An African American, he was famous in Europe as well as the United States. Tejana singer Chelo Silva of Brownsville became an international star with her hits on the radio. Lydia Mendoza of Houston was called "the Lark of the Border." She recorded an estimated 50 albums during her long career as a *conjunto* singer. The *conjunto* style combines traditional Mexican music and German polkas. For her contribution to Mexican American music, Lydia Mendoza received many awards, including the National Medal of Arts in 1999.

Texas's rich history is preserved at the Panhandle-Plains Historical Museum in Amarillo, Texas.

4. 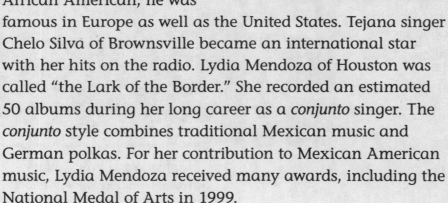 **Summarize** Restate the contributions of Julius Lorenzo Cobb Bledsoe and Chelo Silva in the development of Texas.

....

....

....

336

A Changing Country

Following World War II, new troubles arose. The United States and the Soviet Union entered a conflict called the Cold War. It was fought in smaller conflicts like the Korean and Vietnam Wars. The two countries also fought with ideas, words, and money. As a democracy, the United States opposed communism, the political system of the Soviets. **Communism** is a system in which the government owns all the property in a country. Under the free enterprise system in the United States, private individuals own most of the property.

In spite of the Cold War, the United States experienced economic prosperity. Many Texans had more money than ever before. They bought things such as cars and homes.

Cars and new highways had an impact on life in Texas. In the 1950s, the United States government began building the Interstate Highway system. It connected the large cities of the country. The new roads linked Americans in new ways. They added to the interdependence of states and regions. The new roads made trade and travel between states easier.

new roads and highway

New roads in Texas also meant that people could live farther from their jobs than they had before. Many people began moving to the suburbs. A **suburb** is a community next to or near a city. In the 1950s, the building of expressways for automobiles helped suburbs to develop and grow all around cities, such as Houston. This was a new pattern of settlement. People could buy less expensive houses in the suburbs. Families clustered there.

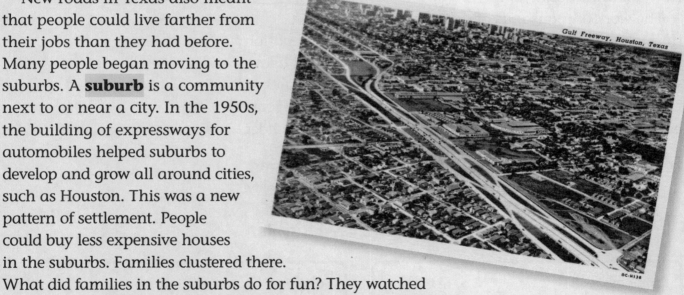

A new interstate highway helped Houston's suburbs to grow in the 1950s.

What did families in the suburbs do for fun? They watched the newest invention, television! Grocery stores soon began selling another new idea, special frozen meals called TV dinners.

5. **Identify** and **explain** where and why suburbs developed in Texas after World War II.

....

....

The Civil Rights Movement

While many Americans prospered in the 1950s and 1960s, others continued to face serious problems. Many African Americans and Mexican Americans did not have the same rights as Anglo Americans. Denied equal opportunity, they earned less money for the same jobs. They were treated unfairly at schools and work. African Americans could not go into some restaurants and movie theaters or ride in the front seats of buses. Some Mexican American children had to go to separate schools in Texas. This unfair separation, based on race, is called segregation.

— segregation

African Americans and Mexican Americans struggled to end segregation and discrimination in all their forms. Dr. Martin Luther King, Jr., led a national movement to give all individuals equal rights. People marched to show their support. In Texas, the League of United Latin American Citizens (LULAC) fought in the courts for the desegregation of Mexican schools and other civil rights for Mexican Americans. **Civil rights** are the rights of people to enjoy freedom and equality.

The work of thousands of activists helped people throughout Texas gain their civil rights. Today, segregation is illegal. In 1964, the United States Congress created a law sponsored by President Lyndon B. Johnson. The Civil Rights Act made fair treatment the law of the land. People could no longer be treated differently, based on their race, religion, or gender.

6. ◎ Summarize Complete the chart by **summarizing** how Texans and other Americans worked to end inequality.

A Need for Civil Rights

Problem	Solution
Many African Americans and Mexican Americans did not have the same rights and opportunities as Anglo Americans.	

In 1967, Texans elected Barbara Jordan to the Texas Senate. She was the first black state senator since 1883. She helped African Americans register to vote in the 1960s. The civil rights activist and lawyer from Houston went on to become president of the Texas Senate. Later she became the first African American woman from a southern state to serve in the United States Congress. In 1994, she received the Presidential Medal of Freedom.

Many changes have taken place since the 1960s. But more work remains to secure fair treatment and equal rights and opportunity for everyone.

Barbara Jordan

 **Got it?**

🔹 TEKS 5.A, 17.B, 17.D

7. ◉ **Summarize Identify** the impact on life in Texas of major events faced by Texas and the United States following the attack on Pearl Harbor.

....

....

....

8. ❓ Suppose you are a student in Texas during World War II. Write a letter to a relative in another state. **Describe** how your life has changed in good ways and bad.

my Story Ideas

....

....

....

....

9. Summarize the ways in which Barbara Jordan participated in the democratic process.

....

....

....

Lesson 1 ← TEKS 5.A, 5.C, 11.C, 12.F, 13.B, 17.A, 18.A

World War I and the 1920s

1. **Identify** at least two ways in which life in Texas was impacted by World War I.

   ....

   ....

   ....

2. **Identify** the notable individual with his or her accomplishment of the twentieth century in Texas.

Mary Eleanor Brackenridge	Fought for women's suffrage
Miriam Ferguson	Ragtime musician
Scott Joplin	Governor of Texas

3. **Explain** the impact of American ideas about progress on the economic development and growth of Texas during the Roaring Twenties.

   ....

   ....

   ....

   ....

   ....

   ....

   ....

4. Fill in the blanks to **identify** the benefits of the free enterprise system in Texas during the 1920s. The demand for cars and trucks helped the Texas .... industry boom. To meet the needs of drivers, new kinds of .... were started, such as gas stations and motels.

5. **Summarize Describe** the experience of many African Americans who moved to cities during the 1920s.

   ....

   ....

   ....

Lesson 2 ← TEKS 5.A, 11.B, 12.B, 12.F, 17.D, 18.A

Difficult Times

6. Read the question carefully. Determine the best answer to the question from the four answer choices provided. Circle the best answer.

   What program created jobs and improved the economy in the 1930s?

   A the New Deal

   B the Dust Bowl

   C the Stock Market Crash

   D the Great Depression

7. **Explain** why people bought stock in American companies during the Roaring Twenties.

....

....

....

8. **Describe** how the principles of supply and demand affected Texas farmers during the Roaring Twenties.

....

....

....

....

....

9. Read the question carefully. Determine the best answer to the question from the four answer choices provided. Circle the best answer.

Who was Lyndon B. Johnson?

F a worker in the Works Progress Administration

G a banker who lost money in the stock market crash

H a Texan who opposed Roosevelt's New Deal

J a Texan who ran a New Deal program and later became president of the United States

10. **Explain** how geographic factors have influenced the location of economic agricultural activities in Texas during the 1930s.

....

....

....

....

....

Lesson 3   TEKS 5.A, 5.C, 8.A, 19.C

World War II and Changes Ahead

11. **Identify** an accomplishment of notable twentieth century Texas individuals Audie Murphy and Cleto Rodriguez.

....

....

....

....

....

12. Give an example of economic opportunities available to Texans after World War II.

....

....

....

....

13. Identify and **explain** the clusters and patterns of settlement in Texas following World War II.

....

....

....

....

....

....

....

....

....

....

....

....

14. ◎ **Summarize Identify** the contributions of Lydia Mendoza to Texas.

....

....

....

....

....

....

15. ❓ **How do people respond to good times and bad?** 🔹 **TEKS 5.A**

Analyze the picture of the factory workers below and answer the question.

How did American women respond to the challenges that came when the United States entered World War II?

....

....

....

....

....

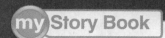 my Story Book

Go online to write and illustrate your own **myStory Book** using the **myStory Ideas** from this chapter.

 THE BIG

How do people respond to good times and bad?

 TEKS
ELA 15

Texas transformed in the early 1900s. There were good times and bad times. New inventions and improved products helped make life easier. But an economic boom in the 1920s ended with a serious depression. The Dust Bowl ruined farmers. Texans fought in two world wars.

Think about life today. How do people respond to good times and bad times? How do you respond to good times and bad times?

Describe how you might respond to good times, such as buying or receiving something that you had hoped for.

....

....

Draw how you might respond to hard times, such as having to leave your home.

SAVVAS realize™ | Go online to access your interactive digital lesson.

343

Texas Today

my Story Spark

THE BIG ?

What goals should we set for our state?

Analyze what you like most about living in Texas today. **Identify** what Texans might need or want in the next hundred years. **Describe** how Texas might be made even better for the future.

....

....

....

....

Texas Essential Knowledge and Skills

6.B Translate geographic data, population distribution, and natural resources into a variety of formats.

7.A Describe a variety of regions in Texas and the United States such as political, population, and economic regions that result from patterns of human activity.

8.A Identify and explain clusters and patterns of settlement in Texas at different time periods such as prior to the Texas Revolution, after the building of the railroads, and following World War II.

8.B Describe and explain the location and distribution of various towns and cities in Texas, past and present.

9.A Describe ways people have adapted to and modified their environment in Texas, past and present, such as timber clearing, agricultural production, wetlands drainage, energy production, and construction of dams.

9.B Identify reasons why people have adapted to and modified their environment in Texas, past and present, such as the use of natural resources to meet basic needs, facilitate transportation, and enhance recreational activities.

9.C Compare the positive and negative consequences of human modification of the environment in Texas, past and present, both governmental and private, such as economic development and the impact on habitats and wildlife as well as air and water quality.

11.C Give examples of the benefits of the free enterprise system such as choice and opportunity.

12.A Explain how people in different regions of Texas earn their living, past and present, through a subsistence economy and providing goods and services.

12.B Explain how geographic factors such as climate, transportation, and natural resources have influenced the location of economic activities in Texas.

12.C Analyze the effects of exploration, immigration, migration, and limited resources on the economic development and growth of Texas.

12.E Explain how developments in transportation and communication have influenced economic activities in Texas.

13.A Identify ways in which technological changes in areas such as transportation and communication have resulted in increased interdependence among Texas, the United States, and the world.

13.B Identify oil and gas, agricultural, and technological products of Texas that are purchased to meet needs in the United States and around the world.

13.C Explain how Texans meet some of their needs through the purchase of products from the United States and the rest of the world.

16.D Describe the origins and significance of state celebrations such as Texas Independence Day and Juneteenth.

19.A Identify the similarities and differences among various racial, ethnic, and religious groups in Texas.

19.B Identify customs, celebrations, and traditions of various cultural, regional, and local groups in Texas such as Cinco de Mayo, Oktoberfest, the Strawberry Festival, and Fiesta San Antonio.

20.A Identify famous inventors and scientists such as Gail Borden, Joseph Glidden, Michael DeBakey, and Millie Hughes-Fulford and their contributions.

20.B Describe how scientific discoveries and innovations such as in aerospace, agriculture, energy, and technology have benefited individuals, businesses, and society in Texas.

20.C Predict how future scientific discoveries and technological innovations might affect life in Texas.

21.B Analyze information by sequencing, categorizing, identifying cause-and-effect relationships, comparing, contrasting, finding the main idea, summarizing, making generalizations and predictions, and drawing inferences and conclusions.

21.C Organize and interpret information in outlines, reports, databases, and visuals, including graphs, charts, timelines, and maps.

21.D Identify different points of view about an issue, topic, historical event, or current event.

The Johnson Space Center

Learning About the Space Program

my Story Video

If you visit Houston, you can't miss the Johnson Space Center. Parked right in front of it is a replica of the space shuttle, towering 54 feet high above the ground. "I can't believe how big it is!" exclaims 10-year-old Gianna. "I guess you need a pretty big engine to get something like that into space."

Gianna is visiting Space Center Houston, the official visitors' center for the Johnson Space Center. She knows there's a lot of history at this complex. She also knows that the aerospace industry is very important to the economy of Texas. This industry, which builds and operates spacecraft, brings many jobs to Texas. But right now all she's interested in is how astronauts live in space. "How do they sleep if they're floating around?" she asks her guide, Jack. At the Living in Space Module, she gets her answer. Jack tells Gianna that astronauts in the International Space Station actually zip themselves into sleeping bags that are attached to the station, so they don't float around. "It's probably pretty peaceful up there at night," Gianna decides.

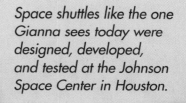

Space shuttles like the one Gianna sees today were designed, developed, and tested at the Johnson Space Center in Houston.

To find out more about the International Space Station, she heads to a gallery that tells her all about it. She finds out that the first crew to stay in the International Space Station arrived in November 2000. Astronauts from all over the world have worked at the floating lab, which is about the size of a football field. Gianna learns that many astronauts train right here, in Houston, for their International Space Station missions. "In fact," Jack tells her, "Mission Control, the room where engineers and scientists on Earth monitor the International Space Station, is here at Johnson Space Center."

Jack takes Gianna to another Mission Control room. It was here that people on Earth first heard from a man on the moon. On July 20, 1969, astronauts Neil A. Armstrong and Edwin "Buzz" Aldrin, Jr. landed on the moon. Armstrong radioed back to Earth to tell everyone they had landed, and dozens of people here at Johnson Space Center cheered their success.

Like Gianna, you can visit the Johnson Space Center and view rockets, spacecraft, Mission Control, and satellites that have been in space.

Back at Space Center Houston, Gianna is getting a taste of what it feels like in space. "I'm a little scared!" she exclaims. At this exhibit, a mock spacecraft gives riders the sense that they are blasting off into space. "That was awesome!" Gianna says. "I wish I could do that every day!" Jack explains that astronauts train for months before they blast off into space. The National Aeronautics and Space Administration, or NASA, has a training facility here where astronauts practice everything from how to eat dinner to how to fix billion-dollar satellites in zero gravity.

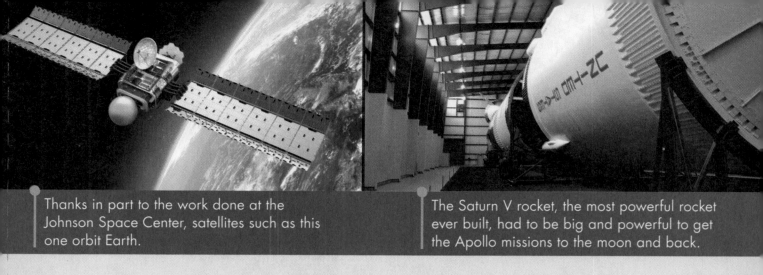

Thanks in part to the work done at the Johnson Space Center, satellites such as this one orbit Earth.

The Saturn V rocket, the most powerful rocket ever built, had to be big and powerful to get the Apollo missions to the moon and back.

With her feet back on the ground, Gianna visits her favorite place on her trip today, Building 9. Here, she gets to look down as engineers and scientists work on developing new technologies for space. She remembers that her friend's mom is an aeronautical engineer and wonders if she ever gets to work in this amazing place. She sees robots and space vehicles, even new spacesuits. "I would love to wear one of those in space someday," she tells Jack.

Before she leaves, Gianna and Jack walk through Rocket Park. Gianna marvels at the Saturn V rocket, the most powerful rocket ever built. "This rocket, which is over 36 stories tall, is responsible for transporting the American astronauts to the moon during the Apollo missions," Jack tells her. Gianna can't believe that all this amazing technology is right in her hometown. She's hooked on the idea of exploring space. She tells Jack, "Someday I'll be back, only I won't be a visitor. I'll be an employee."

Think About It How important is Texas's role in our country's space program? As you read the chapter, think about how Texas and Texans are making innovative discoveries and working toward new goals all the time.

Rocket Park at Johnson Space Center

The Economy of Texas

NASA's Lyndon B. Johnson Space Center in Houston is an important location for the United States space program.

Texas refineries process 27 percent of our nation's oil.

Today, Texas has a strong economy. Economic regions have developed as a result of these patterns of human activity. These include cities such as Austin and Dallas, which have become economic centers of high technology. An economic region has also developed around the oil and gas industry in the Great Plains and Central Plains.

The Petrochemical Industry in Texas

Our state is the leading producer of oil in the United States. Texas also produces nearly 30 percent of the natural gas in the country. Both oil and gas are limited resources that have been good to the economic development of Texas. Today, Texas oil and gas are purchased to meet the needs of Texas, the United States, and the world.

Texas had so much oil and gas, oil companies built refineries in Texas. Businesses also built factories that use gas and oil to make plastics, fertilizer, chemicals, and fabrics. These products and many others, as well as gas and oil, are used by people around the world. They fuel cars, heat homes, and provide products that people need. These industries, refineries, and factories form the **petrochemical industry**.

Many Texans found good-paying jobs such as project or structural engineers. This helped Texas's economy to grow.

1. **Identify** and underline in the text oil and gas products of Texas that are purchased to meet needs in Texas, the United States, and around the world. On a separate piece of paper, **analyze** the effects of these limited resources on the economic development of Texas.

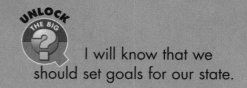
Vocabulary

petrochemical industry
philanthropist
recession
aerospace

technology
software
interdependent
pesticide

How do you think Texas benefits from the United States' space program?

The oil boom of the 1970s also attracted new people to Texas. Some came from northern states, where steel mills and auto plants were closing down. Others came from countries such as South Korea, Pakistan, India, El Salvador, and Guatemala. The face of Texas was changing!

Oil and gas has helped education in Texas. Some oil and gas wells are on state-owned land. Money from these wells goes into a special fund. Every year, it helps pay for schools and universities. Also, some Texas oil millionaires became philanthropists. **Philanthropists** give away money to help other people. In Texas, philanthropists gave money to build hospitals, museums, and universities.

Challenges and Changes

During the 1980s, the United States suffered a recession. A **recession** is a period of reduced economic activity. Demand and prices for Texas oil and gas fell. Many workers in the Texas petrochemical industry lost their jobs.

By the 1990s, the United States economy was growing again. Texas's petrochemical industry was an important part of Texas's economy. Even so, leaders in Texas had set a new goal for the state. They decided to attract new industries to the state.

TEKS

7.A, 8.A, 9.A, 9.B, 9.C, 11.C, 12.A, 12.B, 12.C, 12.E, 13.A, 13.B, 13.C, 20.A, 20.B, 20.C, 21.C

2. In the text, **analyze** and then **identify** the effect of dependence on limited resources on the economic development of Texas in the 1980s.

School children such as these in Corpus Christi benefit from the oil and gas industry in Texas.

The workers at Mission Control in Houston's Johnson Space Center made the first moon walk possible.

Space and Technology

July 20, 1969, was a day to remember. The tiny spacecraft *Eagle* was approaching the moon. Years of scientific innovation had made the trip possible. Astronaut Neil Armstrong was on board. When the *Eagle* touched down, Armstrong announced, "Houston, Tranquility Base here. The *Eagle* has landed."

Today, Mission Control is part of the Johnson Space Center. It is in Houston. Named in honor of President Lyndon B. Johnson, it is the center of operations for our country's activities on the International Space Station. Scientific discoveries and innovations in the aerospace industry have benefited Texas by bringing many jobs to the state.

The Johnson Space Center is part of the National Aeronautics and Space Administration, or NASA. This group runs the United States space program and trains astronauts.

The Aerospace Industry

The Johnson Space Center is part of Texas's **aerospace** industry. This industry builds and operates aircraft, spacecraft, and satellites. It's an important part of Texas's economy. Aerospace employs scientists, engineers, and other specialists.

One of those specialists was Texas biologist Dr. Millie Hughes-Fulford. In 1991, she flew for nine days in a NASA craft called *Spacelab*. During that time, she completed 18 important scientific experiments. Her scientific contributions to the aerospace industry have helped astronauts stay in space longer.

Dr. Millie Hughes-Fulford's work for NASA helped to allow future astronauts stay in space longer.

3. **Identify** and write the contribution that the scientist Dr. Millie Hughes-Fulford made.

....

....

High Technology

Scientific discoveries in technology have benefited Texas, too. The microchip, created a huge industry. Smaller than a fingernail, a microchip is the "brain" of a computer. Computers soon got smaller, more powerful, and less expensive. Individuals and businesses all over the world began to use computers.

The rise of computers made the high technology, or high-tech, industry possible. **Technology** is the use of scientific knowledge, skills, and tools to help people meet their needs. Since the 1980s, many companies in Texas have specialized in high technology.

Today, many high-tech companies have offices in Austin and Dallas. Some specialize in building computers. Others make **software,** or special programs that tell computers what to do. These companies provide many jobs. They have also helped cities grow. Computers and software from Texas are sold all over the world.

These technological developments in communication have resulted in a faster way to work, the growth of businesses, and increased profit. They have also benefited individuals and businesses in Texas by letting them keep in touch with businesses and people in other parts of Texas, the United States, and the world. As a result, the world is more **interdependent.** That means that people and businesses in Texas and all over the world depend on each other to get their jobs done.

4. **Identify** and **explain** how technological changes in communications have influenced economic activities and increased interdependence among Texas, the United States, and the world.

....

....

....

....

....

1969
The U.S. military establishes an early version of the Internet. The Internet we know began in 1983.

1957
Sputnik, the first human-made satellite, was launched by Russia.

5. Below, **identify** a technological product that has influenced economic activities in Texas and is used to meet needs in the U.S. and around the world.

1975
The first personal computers began to appear in the mid-1970s.

1959
The first integrated circuits, or microchips, were made.

1951
The U.S. government uses UNIVAC, an early computer that weighed 16,000 pounds.

Other Changing Industries in Texas

In 1945, Texas had about 385,000 farms. In 2010, there were 240,000 farms. That's because today's farms are larger than ever. The average farm in Texas is 527 acres, and many are much larger.

New inventions, scientific discoveries, and technologies helped farms grow. For example, farmers bought larger and better machinery to plant and harvest more land. Universities taught scientific farming methods. Farmers began to use pesticides. **Pesticides** are chemicals that kill the pests that damage crops. These changes made agriculture more productive than ever.

Texas farmers normally raise more cotton than do farmers in any other state.

More productive farms meant many new jobs in Texas. These jobs, such as food processing, depended on a strong agricultural industry.

The manufacturing industry in Texas is also changing. Texas factories have long made automobiles and oil-field equipment. They've processed food and milled lumber. Today, however, Texas manufactures many new products. These products result from recent advances in science and engineering. Texas now manufactures computer equipment, satellites, and aircraft. High-tech manufacturing provides many opportunities in Texas.

In all regions of Texas there are people who earn their living through providing services. Hospitals, schools, and repair shops are examples of service industries. Many Texans work in the service industry. Today nearly one out of five Texans work in service industry jobs.

6. **Explain** how people in different regions of Texas earn their living through providing services.

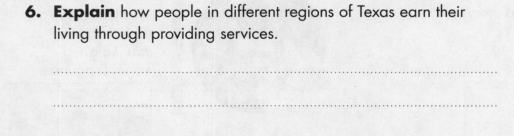

Scientific Discoveries and Innovations

New scientific discoveries and technological innovations have helped Texas's economy grow. An innovation is a new invention or way of doing something. Inventions in machinery helped Texas agriculture. Innovations such as the assembly line and the division of labor made factories in Texas more productive. Many of these innovations that began in Texas have benefited individuals, businesses, and society.

You have read about the microchip. Jack Kilby, a scientist at Texas Instruments, made the first microchip in 1958. Kilby's invention has had a lasting impact on society. Today, microchips control cell phones, computers, TVs, automobiles, and more. This one invention has created many new industries and job opportunities.

Jack Kilby won a Nobel prize for his work.

In the field of medicine, there have also been scientific discoveries and technological innovations that have benefited Texans. Dr. Michael DeBakey is a famous Texas inventor and scientist who made important contributions. He was a world-famous heart surgeon and later became the president of the Baylor College of Medicine in Houston. Dr. DeBakey helped build the first artificial heart. He also invented ways to operate on unhealthy hearts. DeBakey's innovations benefited people in Texas and around the world. His work helps people live longer.

7. Describe how scientific innovations have benefited society in Texas.

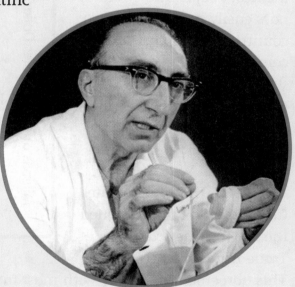

Dr. Michael DeBakey's inventions save lives.

....

....

....

8. ◎ **Make Predictions Describe** scientific discoveries and technological innovations that might be invented in your lifetime. **Predict** how these might affect life in Texas.

....

....

A Global Economy

Texas is part of a global economy. The global economy is all the economic activity that occurs among various countries around the world. Texas companies, for example, sell goods in other parts of the United States, Europe, Asia, Africa, and South America. Texans are able to meet their needs because they purchase products from the United States and from around the world. For example, a company that makes bicycles in Canada may buy parts to build the bicycle that are made in the United States. After the bicycle is built, the company may sell the bicycle to stores in Texas, which in turn sells the bicycles to Texans. The world's economy is interdependent.

Texas's trade with Mexico is part of the global economy. Texas has a 1,241-mile border with Mexico. People and goods pass easily between the two countries. American car companies, for example, ship car and truck parts to Mexico. The cars and trucks are assembled in Mexico, in factories along its border with Texas.

In 1993, the United States, Canada, and Mexico signed the North American Free Trade Agreement (NAFTA).

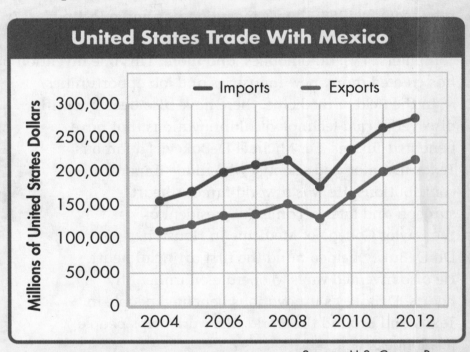

Source: U.S. Census Bureau

This agreement did away with most tariffs. Tariffs are taxes charged on goods imported from other countries. Free trade helped Texas businesses. They were able to export more goods to Canada and especially Mexico.

9. **Cause and Effect** **Explain** how technological changes resulted in increased interdependence among Texas, the United States, and the world.

....

....

....

Industrial Growth and the Environment

The energy industry has modified the environment through energy production. The positive impact of this is jobs. However, there are also negative impacts to the environment. For example, in 2010, an oil rig in the Gulf of Mexico exploded. Nearly 5 million barrels of oil spilled into the water. The pollution missed most of Texas, but nearby states were not so lucky.

As our state grows, we must be especially thoughtful about protecting the environment. Many of Texas's petrochemical plants are on or near the Gulf Coast. Pollution from them damages the habitats of birds and fish. Some Texas species are in danger of dying out. Pollution also dirties our air and water. That has an impact on our health.

Texans want a strong economy. That means industries need to grow. But Texans also want a safe and clean environment. To meet these economic and environmental goals, industries and citizens must work together.

This oil rig is in the Gulf of Mexico.

TEKS 8.A, 12.E, 13.A, 20.A

10. ◉ **Summarize** **Identify** two famous scientists and **describe** their scientific contributions, discoveries, and innovations.

....

....

....

11. ❓ **Describe** technological changes in areas such as communication and transportation. Tell how these have resulted in increased interdependence among Texas, the United States, and the world.

my Story Ideas

....

....

12. In 1945, 2.2 million Texans lived in rural areas. **Explain** how you think the patterns of settlement have changed since then. Why?

....

....

SAVVAS realize Go online to access your interactive digital lesson.

355

Identify Points of View

Everyone has a point of view. A **point of view** is what a person believes about something. A person's point of view affects what he or she says and does.

Suppose your school decided all fourth-grade students have to study a foreign language. Some students might be against the plan. They might say learning another language would add more schoolwork and homework. From their point of view, studying a language is a bad idea.

Other students might be for the plan. They might say in today's world, a second language is very useful. From their point of view, studying a foreign language is a good idea.

In the last lesson, you read about the petrochemical industry. The statements below show how points of view on this industry can differ.

We need to build a new oil refinery. Gasoline is the lifeblood of our nation. Right now, we're running on empty. It will also create jobs in our community.

We should not build another refinery. Refineries pollute our air and water. They also pollute the habitat of shore birds and ocean life.

Learning Objective

I will know how to identify different points of view.

TEKS

SS 21.D Identify different points of view about an issue, topic, historical event, or current event.

Try it!

To identify point of view, follow these steps:

- First, identify the subject, or topic. For example, the subject in the statements on the previous page is about the petrochemical industry.

- Next, ask yourself what the person is saying about the subject. Find words and phrases that tell you the person's point of view.

- Finally, ask yourself who would say this. What is the person's point of view?

1. What subject is being discussed in the two statements on page 356?

....

2. **Identify** a phrase from each statement that tells you the point of view.

Statement 1: ....

Statement 2: ....

3. Who might have each opinion?

Statement 1: ....

Statement 2: ....

4. **Apply** Think about the environment you live in. Then think about all you have learned about the petrochemical industry. **Analyze** the positive and negative consequences of building an oil refinery on the environment, natural habitats, and the air and water quality. Then, in the space below, write your point of view about building a refinery. Explain your point of view.

....

....

....

....

SAVVAS realize. Go online to access your interactive digital lesson.

357

Texas Cultural Expressions

Envision It!

My favorite food is tacos.

My favorite dish is scallion pancakes with shrimp.

These children are talking about their favorite foods.

A group plays Capoeira, a Brazilian martial art, at the Texas Folklife Festival in San Antonio.

A Diverse State

People from all over the world have brought their cultures to Texas. At the Texas Folklife Festival, you can sample their food, music, dancing, art, and storytelling.

A culture is the way of life of a group of people. Language, music, food, and holidays are all part of culture. So are religious beliefs and other beliefs, too. Every cultural group has its own **heritage**, or shared history.

Ethnic groups have similarities and differences. All ethnic groups have important celebrations and customs, but they may be different. A **custom** is a way a group of people do something. You are a member of a cultural group. And your cultural group has customs and traditions. The way your family cooks and eats food or celebrates events, for example, are customs.

1. **Compare and Contrast Describe** some customs of your family or ethnic group. **Compare** them to other customs you know.

....

....

....

....

Draw a picture of your favorite food. Write what it is and what country it came from.

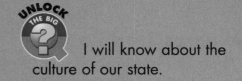

Vocabulary

heritage   bat mitzvah
custom   bar mitzvah
quinceañera

Customs and Traditions

Texas has many different ethnic groups with different cultures. Some of these include American Indian and Tejano cultures. Others are from people who have settled here from around the world. In recent decades, people have come from Asia, South America, Central America, and other parts of the world. They bring their culture, which includes their customs, celebrations, and traditions, with them. For example, it is a custom for people of Mexican culture in Texas to celebrate *El Día de Los Muertos*, or Day of the Dead, to remember their loved ones.

Among many Spanish speakers, it is a tradition to celebrate a birthday with a treat-filled *piñata*. Children swing a stick and try to break it and collect the treats. A **quinceañera** is another tradition. It celebrates a girl's transition from childhood to adult status. It often begins with a religious ceremony and ends with a party.

About 35,000 Vietnamese Americans live in Houston. To share their culture, arts, and traditions with other Texans, they host a Vietnamese Festival. This celebration is usually held in a different city in Texas each year.

Another celebration in Texas is Chinese New Year. Every winter, in Houston, there's a parade of dragons on giant floats to help celebrate the occasion.

More than 100,000 Filipinos live in Texas today. Traditional dances are part of Filipino culture. These dances mark important events, such as birth or marriage.

TEKS
6.B, 12.A, 16.D, 19.A, 19.B

A *piñata*

2. **Identify** similarities and differences among various ethnic groups in Texas.

....

....

....

....

Religious Traditions

There are similarities and differences among various religious groups in Texas. Jewish people, for example, have a custom for their children. A girl becomes a **bat mitzvah** when she turns 12 or 13 and a boy becomes a **bar mitzvah** when he reaches the age of 13. In this ceremony, they accept religious responsibilities.

The ninth month of the Islamic calendar is Ramadan. Muslims celebrate the month by thinking about their faith. For the whole month, they don't eat or drink between sunrise and sunset.

Traditional festivals often mark the seasons. In December, Christians celebrate Christmas and the birth of Jesus. Giving gifts to family and friends is a Christmas tradition.

Kwanzaa is another winter celebration. Based on African harvest festivals, it lasts several days. Some African Americans celebrate Kwanzaa. It is a way to honor their African heritage.

Traditional Texas Holidays

Some holidays mark historical events. For Texans, it's a tradition to celebrate these state celebrations.

Texans celebrate Texas Independence Day on March 2. Its origin goes back to March 2, 1836, and has important significance to Texans. On that day, Texas leaders signed the Texas Declaration of Independence.

Texas Independence Day is a time to remember the past. It is a day to celebrate freedom. Many towns and cities hold festivals. Sometimes there are barbecues or chili cook-offs, and there is always lots of fun.

A Texas Independence Day celebration

3. **Identify** similarities and differences among various religious groups in Texas. Give examples.

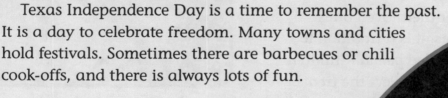

After declaring their independence, Texans had to fight for it. Their final victory came at the Battle of San Jacinto on April 21, 1836. Today, San Antonio celebrates this day with the Fiesta San Antonio. People from all over come to San Antonio to be part of this local custom.

Cinco de Mayo is Spanish for "the fifth of May." It is another holiday with historical origins. In 1861, a large French army tried to take over Mexico. However, on May 5, 1862, the Mexicans defeated the French.

On *Cinco de Mayo*, people remember this event. In Texas, communities hold special events that highlight Mexican heritage. Mariachi bands play. Dancers in traditional costumes perform folk dances, or *baile folklórico*. Mexican food is a big part of the celebrations. People also honor Mexican and Mexican American leaders and heroes.

People of all racial and ethnic groups in Texas have important holidays, traditions, and customs. Juneteenth, for example, began as an African American holiday. Today, Juneteenth is a state celebration with huge significance. Its origin goes back to the mid-1800s. On June 19, 1865, Union General Gordon Granger made an important announcement: All slaves in Texas and other states had to be freed immediately.

African Americans celebrate Juneteenth on June 19.

The freed slaves in Texas called the day "Juneteenth," or Freedom Day. In the years that followed, they celebrated every June 19. Today, African Americans all over the country celebrate Juneteenth. Although racial and ethnic groups in Texas celebrate holidays of different origins, all the celebrations are festive occasions that include Texans of all racial and ethnic groups.

4. 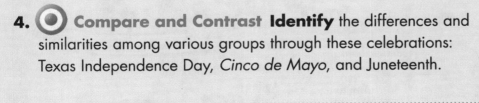 **Compare and Contrast Identify** the differences and similarities among various groups through these celebrations: Texas Independence Day, *Cinco de Mayo*, and Juneteenth.

....

....

....

....

Other Texas Festivals

Another local custom in Texas is the Strawberry Festival in Poteet. Poteet is a small city in Atascosa County, outside San Antonio. More than sixty years ago, local farmers held a strawberry festival. They invited people to come taste and buy their strawberries. Every year, the festival got bigger. About 100,000 people now visit the festival every year.

Texas also has many traditional cultural celebrations. Texas has a rich German heritage. During the 1840s, many immigrants from Germany came to Texas. Most settled in New Braunfels, Fredericksburg, and nearby communities. It is a tradition for people in the region to celebrate their heritage every October. This regional celebration in Texas is called Oktoberfest.

Another regional festival in Texas is the Austin Energy Regional Science Festival. At this science fair, students from central Texas present innovative science projects.

The Texas Book Festival is a newer tradition. Laura Bush established it in 1995, and the first festival was held in 1996. Visitors get to see and buy the latest books. Texas writers read and talk about their work. The festival raises money for libraries, too.

Laura Bush established the Texas Book Festival in 1995.

5. **◎ Make Inferences**
Locate the Chisholm Trail Roundup festival on the map. What do you think you might see if you went to it?

....

....

....

Texas Festivals

XIT Rodeo

Dalhart

Texas Cowboy Reunion

Stamford

Ft. Worth

Chisholm Trail Roundup

East Texas Jamboree

Gilmer

Texas Book Festival

Cantaloupe Festival

Pecos

Fredericksburg

Austin

Texas Renaissance Festival

Plantersville

San Antonio

Luling

Oktoberfest

Poteet

Watermelon Thump

Fiesta San Antonio

Strawberry Festival

Texas Citrus Fiesta Parade

Mission

Sports in Texas

Do you play sports in school? What about after school? Sports are an important part of Texas culture.

Some Texans made huge accomplishments as professional athletes. Their career is sports. Some of them are world famous. Texas athletes, past and present, have received many awards in competitions.

Nolan Ryan was one of the best pitchers in baseball. Born in Refugio, Texas, he played baseball for 27 years, a record. He also holds the record for the most strikeouts ever thrown. Today Nolan Ryan is a member of the Baseball Hall of Fame.

Mildred "Babe" Didrikson Zaharias was an all-around athlete. She was born in Port Arthur and grew up in Beaumont. At the 1932 Olympics, she won two gold medals and one silver medal in track and field. Later she focused on golf. In all, she won 82 golf tournaments.

Carl Lewis was one of our country's greatest Olympic athletes. At the University of Houston, he was the top-ranked track and field athlete in the country. Lewis went on to win ten Olympic medals, nine gold and one silver, in track and field events.

Lee Trevino grew up in Dallas. He won the United States Open golf tournament twice and the Professional Golf Association (PGA) title two times.

Sheryl Swoopes is a great basketball player. Born in Brownfield, Texas, she led Texas Tech University to the 1993 national women's basketball title. She has also won three Olympic gold medals.

6. Identify the accomplishments of Carl Lewis.

....

....

Nolan Ryan

Babe Didrikson Zaharias

Carl Lewis

Lee Trevino

Sheryl Swoopes

The Arts in Texas

The arts in Texas are alive and well. You can see that from the Texas Medal of Arts Awards. Every two years, the Texas Cultural Trust Council chooses the winners. The awards celebrate the creativity of Texans. Singer Willie Nelson, actor Tommy Lee Jones, and writer Sandra Cisneros have won the award. So have the Houston Ballet, jazz musician Ornette Coleman, and artist Robert Rauschenberg. These artists and many others contribute to culture in Texas.

Creative Texans often receive awards from outside Texas, too. For example, Texas playwright Horton Foote received a National Medal of Arts award. His plays, such as *The Trip to Bountiful,* tell of small-town Texas life.

Texas Museums

Museums are places that help us appreciate art and culture. Texas has great museums. The Dallas Museum of Art is one of the country's best. You can also see some of the world's greatest paintings at the Museum of Fine Arts in Houston. There are hundreds of other museums in Texas. Together, they show how important art and culture are in our state.

At the Bullock Museum of Texas History, you might see American Indian pots and blankets, branding irons, and saddles.

The Bullock Museum of Texas History stands near the capitol in Austin. Its purpose is to tell the whole story of Texas. And the museum is big enough to do it! Each of the three floors has a theme: Land, Identity, and Opportunity. The artifacts and exhibits bring these themes to life. A walk through the museum is a tour of our state's history and culture.

7. **Draw Inferences** What types of exhibits might you see on the Opportunity floor of the Bullock Museum?

....

....

Texas Films

Movies are an important part of culture today. Many movies have been filmed in Texas. For example, parts of *Cast Away, Apollo 13,* and *Spy Kids*, were all shot in Texas.

Building a film industry was a goal of Texas leaders. In 1971 Governor Preston Smith created the Texas Film Commission to help encourage the film industry to develop more films in Texas. In 1987 it was made part of the Texas Economic Development Commission. In 2007 and 2009 laws were passed to help filmmakers. One law provides grants and tax breaks to make movies in Texas.

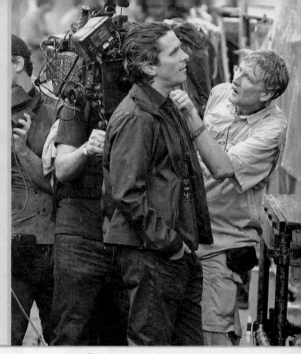

With the help of the Texas Film Commission, many movies are made in Texas.

TEKS 16.D, 19.B

8. ● **Draw Conclusions Identify** how people in Texas feel about culture and the arts.

....

9. **?** What goal did Texas set for the film industry? **Describe** how state leaders tried to reach this goal.

my Story Ideas

....

10. Fill in the chart. **Describe** the origins and significance of each celebration in Texas.

Celebration	Date	Origin	Significance
Texas Independence Day			
Juneteenth			
Cinco de Mayo			

Draw Conclusions

When we **draw conclusions**, we think about facts and details and then decide something about them. You use what you know and what you have learned to draw conclusions. Drawing conclusions helps you understand your reading.

We draw conclusions all the time in everyday life. Suppose, for example, that your family is driving through a part of Texas you've never seen before. It's a beautiful March day. In one town, you see a big crowd of people. They've gathered in front of the courthouse. What's going on?

To draw a conclusion:

First, **gather** and **analyze information**.
You look closer at the crowd and gather information. You see some people dressed in clothes from the early 1800s. Some children are waving Texas flags. A man on a small stage is giving a speech. It's about freedom. After the speech, the crowd sings "Texas, Our Texas."

Next, **look for connections between the pieces of information**.
What connects all the details you've noticed? The flags and the song suggest the event is about Texas. From the costumes, it might have something to do with history. Finally, the speech suggests the event is celebrating freedom.

Finally, **draw a conclusion**.
You conclude that the people are celebrating Texas Independence Day. That conclusion makes sense with all the facts and details you've noticed.

Facts and Details	**Conclusion**
Texas flags and song; historical costumes; speech about celebrating freedom	Texas Independence Day

Learning Objective

I will know how to analyze information by drawing conclusions.

TEKS

ELA 10 Draw conclusions about the author's purpose in cultural, historical, and contemporary contexts and provide evidence from the text to support their understanding.

ELA 11 Draw conclusions about expository text and provide evidence from text to support their understanding.

SS 20.B Describe how scientific discoveries and innovations have benefited individuals, businesses, and society in Texas.

SS 21.B Analyze information by drawing conclusions.

Try it!

1. **Identify** and underline important facts and details about the economy of Texas in the following paragraph.

> The Texas economy grew 3.2% in 2012. The United States economy grew 2.2% that year. Texas created more new jobs in 2012 than any other state. The unemployment rate, or the percentage of people out of work, is lower in Texas than in the nation as a whole.

2. **Analyze** the information in the paragraph. What comparisons are made?

....

....

3. **Draw a conclusion** from the paragraph.

....

....

4. Read the following paragraph. **Draw a conclusion** about the economy of Texas today.

> Advances in computer technology made space travel possible. The petrochemical industry relies on computers when searching for oil. To deliver services quickly, the service industry relies on computers, too. Computer technology is a huge industry.

Conclusion: ....

....

5. Go to an earlier portion of the book and find a specific event. **Identify** the important facts and details. Note the connection between the facts. Then **draw a conclusion** and write it below.

....

....

Life in Texas Today

Envision It!

Life and work in Texas will be very different in the future.

Urban Growth in Texas

Texas is changing rapidly. In 2000, Texas had a population of 20,851,820. By 2013, the state had more than 26 million. In the United States, only California has more people than Texas.

Urbanization has changed Texas. **Urbanization** is the process by which towns and cities are formed and grow as more and more people begin living and working in central areas. Today, about 85 percent of Texans live in urban areas. Almost all Texas's growth has occurred in these population regions. The most growth is in the so-called Texas Triangle. That's the region bounded by Dallas-Fort Worth, Houston, and San Antonio. Cities along the border, like El Paso, are also growing fast.

Population distribution in Texas has not been uniform. Today, fewer people live in rural areas. That's because fewer people are needed to work on farms. So Texans have been moving to urban areas to find work.

1. **Analyze** the bar graph. Which ten-year period might see the smallest increase in Texas's population?

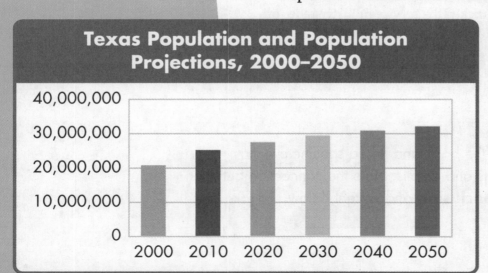

Texas Population and Population Projections, 2000–2050

Source: U.S. Census Bureau, Texas State Data Center

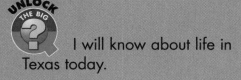
Vocabulary

urbanization

urban sprawl

automation

List the top three jobs that you might want to do in the future.

Challenges of Urbanization

The rapid growth of Texas cities has created challenges such as slow-moving traffic. Light rail is one solution. These trains usually use electricity as an energy source. Houston has a light rail system called METRORail. Dallas also has a light rail called DART. Good transportation options have also influenced the location of economic activities in Texas.

Another challenge is urban sprawl. **Urban sprawl** is the rapid growth of areas just outside a city. Housing developments, malls, and office parks are all part of urban sprawl. People in these areas travel long distances to get to jobs or services in the city center.

As these population regions grow, they need more water. Finding new sources of water is a goal of many Texas cities. San Antonio, for example, is trying a new water source, the Gulf of Mexico. Saltwater is pumped into a plant where the salt is removed. It is then pumped to nearby areas.

2. **Calculate** by what percentage the population distribution in Texas changed between 1950 and 2005. **Explain** what has caused this change.

TEKS
6.B, 7.A, 8.B, 9.A, 9.B, 9.C, 12.B, 12.E

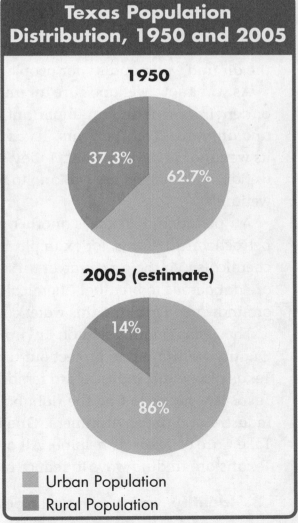

Texas Population Distribution, 1950 and 2005

1950

37.3% 62.7%

2005 (estimate)

14% 86%

Urban Population
Rural Population

Source: U.S. Census Bureau

Scientists in Texas work to restore lost wetlands.

Working for Our Future

Modifications to the environment by private industry and a growing population have had positive consequences. Building roads and homes in what were once natural areas provides businesses and people with water and homes. However, these modifications to the environment can also have negative consequences. The natural habitat of plants and animals and the air and water quality for people can be harmed.

As you know, wetlands are an important part of our environment and an important habitat for plants and animals. Over the years, Texas lost much of its wetlands to development. Today, Texas protects its wetlands. Engineers are working to rebuild damaged wetlands.

Air pollution in Texas is another problem. Texas's petrochemical plants, for example, release many chemicals into the air. Some of these chemicals are dangerous to breathe. Chemicals also get into groundwater. Drinking this water can cause disease.

The Texas Commission on Environmental Quality works hard to protect our air and water. But Texas also wants industries to remain profitable. Texas is working to find the right balance between industry and the environment. One new program, Take Care of Texas, is helping. All over the state, Texans are finding ways to reduce air and water pollution.

Take Care of Texas helps Texans learn about how they can conserve water and energy and keep our air and water clean.

TakeCareOfTexas.org

3. **Identify** two environmental problems in Texas.

....

370

Educating for the Future

Jobs in Texas and the rest of the world are changing. More industries are using high technology. Automation has done away with many of the low-skill jobs once done by people. **Automation** is the use of computers and machines to do jobs in a factory or workplace. The workplaces of today and tomorrow need workers with special skills.

Jobs in the future will require workers to have good training and education. As of 2010, 25.9 percent of Texans 25 or older have at least a Bachelor's degree. Our state is working to increase the number of Texans completing college or training for special jobs. Meeting these goals will help keep our economy strong.

Today, workers need special skills to work in many industries.

TEKS 7.A, 12.B, 12.E

4. ⊙ **Draw Conclusions Describe** population regions in Texas that have resulted from patterns of human activity.

....

....

5. ❓ You have been asked to participate in a group planning for Texas's future. **Explain** to the group how transportation might influence the location of economic activities in Texas. What goals would you set for the state?

my Story Ideas

....

....

....

6. **Identify** education goals you should set for yourself. Why are they important?

....

....

....

Lesson 1 **TEKS 7.A, 9.C, 11.C, 13.C, 20.B**

The Economy of Texas

1. **Explain** how interdependence has allowed Texans to better meet their needs.

....

....

....

2. Read the question carefully. Determine the best answer to the question from the four answer choices provided. Circle the best answer.

   Which statement correctly compares the positive and negative consequences of modification of the environment in the present?

   A The economy grows, but many people become sick.

   B The economy grows, but people lose their jobs.

   C New jobs are created, but the environment is sometimes harmed.

   D New industries are created, but old industries begin to fail.

3. **Describe** economic regions in Texas that result from patterns of human activity.

....

....

....

4. ⊙ **Draw Conclusions Analyze** how future developments in technology might benefit society and individuals. Complete the chart.

Facts and Details

- Technology has made space travel possible.
- Computer technology has created new businesses.
- Technology has allowed artists to create new works.

Conclusion

5. **Describe** how scientific discoveries and technological innovations in the following industries have benefited businesses, individuals, and society in Texas.

Aerospace: ....

....

....

Agriculture: ....

....

....

....

6. **Explain** how Texans meet some of their needs through the purchase of products from the United States and around the world.

....

....

....

....

....

7. **Identify** two famous inventors from Texas.

....

Lesson 2 🔹 TEKS 16.D, 19.A, 19.B

Texas Cultural Expressions

8. **Identify** cultural, regional, and local celebrations in Texas.

....

....

....

....

9. **Identify** one custom and one tradition for each group in Texas.

cultural groups ....

....

....

regional groups ....

....

local groups ....

....

10. **Identify** two Texas athletes who have helped make Texas a special place.

....

....

....

....

11. **Identify** the similarities and differences among various racial groups in Texas.

....

....

....

....

Lesson 3 TEKS 12.B, 21.B

Life in Texas Today

12. **Cause and Effect** In the chart, read the effect and **identify** the cause.

Cause

↓

Effect
The percentage of Texas's population living in rural areas has been falling.

13. **Identify** one solution for each of the problems of urbanization listed below.

A rapid growth of traffic in and around Texas cities

....

....

B the need for more water for a growing population

....

....

14. **What goals should we set for our state?** TEKS 9.B

Texans enjoy recreational activities along the Gulf Coast. **Identify** reasons why it is important for Texans to protect the Gulf Coast and other natural areas of Texas.

a. Why is it important to have plenty of places for Texans to rest, relax, and have fun?

....

....

....

b. How can we make sure that places such as the Gulf Coast are clean and safe for Texans in the future?

....

....

....

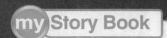
Go online to write and illustrate your own **myStory Book** using the **myStory Ideas** from this chapter.

 # What goals should we set for our state?

 TEKS
SS 20.C
ELA 15

As you have read in this chapter, Texas today is a lively place. We have successful industries, an exciting culture, and fast-growing cities.

Texas is constantly changing. And it will continue to change in the years ahead. To help our state change in the right ways, the people of Texas need to set goals.

Identify an important change you think could occur in Texas by the year 2050. Write down things you and other Texans can do to make this change happen. Draw a picture showing Texas in 2050.

....

....

....

....

SAVVAS **realize.** Go online to access your interactive digital lesson.

375

Texas Government

my Story Spark

THE BIG ?

What should be the goals of government?

Identify the things the government does. **Analyze** how the actions of government affect the people of Texas. **Describe** what you would make a goal of government if you were governor of Texas.

....

....

....

....

⭐ Texas Essential Knowledge and Skills

5.C Identify the accomplishments of notable individuals such as John Tower, Scott Joplin, Audie Murphy, Cleto Rodríguez, Stanley Marcus, Bessie Coleman, Raul A. Gonzalez Jr., and other local notable individuals.

7.A Describe a variety of regions in Texas and the United States such as political, population, and economic regions that result from patterns of human activity.

15.A Identify the purposes and explain the importance of the Texas Declaration of Independence, the Texas Constitution, and other documents such as the Meusebach-Comanche Treaty.

15.B Identify and explain the basic functions of the three branches of government according to the Texas Constitution.

15.C Identify the intent, meaning, and importance of the Declaration of Independence, the U.S. Constitution, and the Bill of Rights.

17.A Identify important individuals who have participated voluntarily in civic affairs at state and local levels such as Adina de Zavala and Clara Driscoll.

17.B Explain how individuals can participate voluntarily in civic affairs at state and local levels through activities such as holding public officials to their word, writing letters, and participating in historic preservation and service projects.

17.C Explain the duty of the individual in state and local elections such as being informed and voting.

17.D Identify the importance of historical figures and important individuals who modeled active participation in the democratic process such as Sam Houston, Barbara Jordan, Lorenzo de Zavala, Ann Richards, Sam Rayburn, Henry B. González, James A. Baker III, Wallace Jefferson, and other local individuals.

17.E Explain how to contact elected and appointed leaders in state and local governments.

18.A Identify leaders in state, local, and national governments, including the governor, local members of the Texas Legislature, the local mayor, U.S. senators, local U.S. representatives, and Texans who have been president of the United States.

18.B Identify leadership qualities of state and local leaders, past and present.

21.B Analyze information by sequencing, categorizing, identifying cause-and-effect relationships, comparing, contrasting, finding the main idea, summarizing, making generalizations and predictions, and drawing inferences and conclusions.

23.A Use a problem-solving process to identify a problem, gather information, list and consider options, consider advantages and disadvantages, choose and implement a solution, and evaluate the effectiveness of the solution.

A Visit to the Capital
The Texas Capitol

my Story Video

As Lauren walks down the tree-lined Great Walk on the grounds of the Texas State Capitol in Austin, she marvels at the monuments that border the walkway. "Mom, this was installed in 1891. That's a long time ago! Can you believe it's still here?" she asks.

Lauren is taking a tour of the capitol to get a closer look at the government in her home state of Texas. "Legislative, judicial, and executive, those are the three branches of state government," Lauren proudly proclaims. As she and her mom take in the grounds, they think about the goals of government. The Capitol contains the offices of the Texas Legislature, which makes the laws for our state, and the office of the governor. "What do you think they do here every day?" Lauren's mom asks her. "Well, they must do a lot, because this place is pretty big," she kids. "I think the Texans who work in these buildings make a lot of decisions for the people of our state," she says more seriously.

Lauren makes a good point. The Texas government is based on its Constitution, and the state representatives and senators who work in these buildings do their best to uphold the Texas Constitution.

Lauren is visiting the Texas State Capitol in Austin. The Capitol and its 22 acres of grounds are the center of government for the state of Texas.

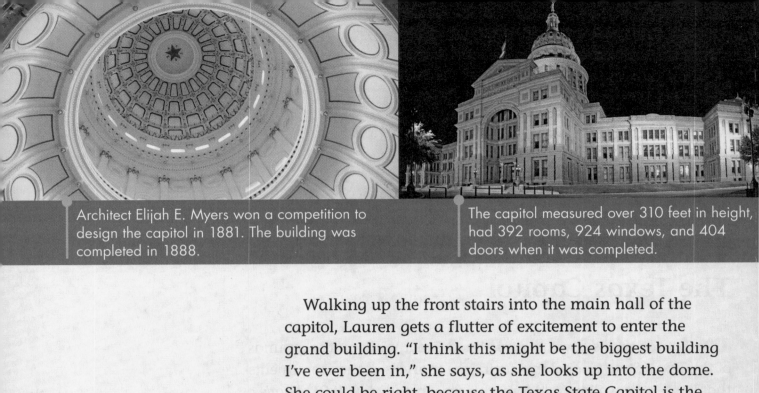

Architect Elijah E. Myers won a competition to design the capitol in 1881. The building was completed in 1888.

The capitol measured over 310 feet in height, had 392 rooms, 924 windows, and 404 doors when it was completed.

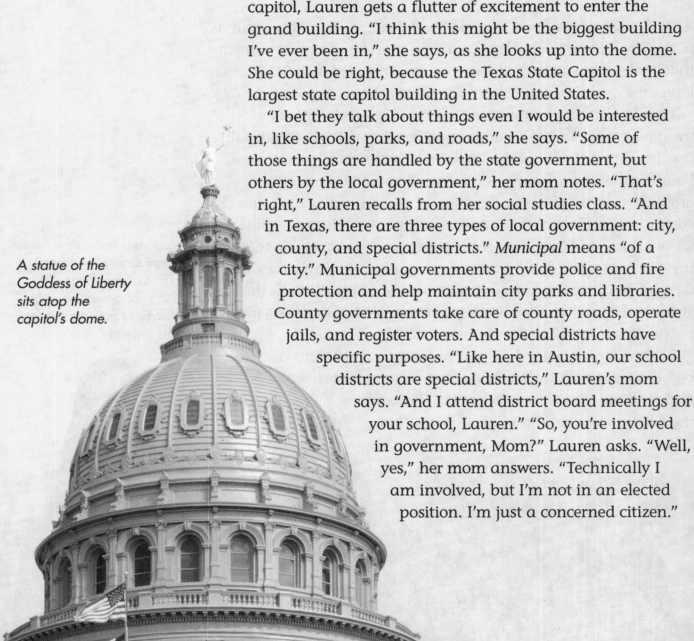

A statue of the Goddess of Liberty sits atop the capitol's dome.

Walking up the front stairs into the main hall of the capitol, Lauren gets a flutter of excitement to enter the grand building. "I think this might be the biggest building I've ever been in," she says, as she looks up into the dome. She could be right, because the Texas State Capitol is the largest state capitol building in the United States.

"I bet they talk about things even I would be interested in, like schools, parks, and roads," she says. "Some of those things are handled by the state government, but others by the local government," her mom notes. "That's right," Lauren recalls from her social studies class. "And in Texas, there are three types of local government: city, county, and special districts." *Municipal* means "of a city." Municipal governments provide police and fire protection and help maintain city parks and libraries. County governments take care of county roads, operate jails, and register voters. And special districts have specific purposes. "Like here in Austin, our school districts are special districts," Lauren's mom says. "And I attend district board meetings for your school, Lauren." "So, you're involved in government, Mom?" Lauren asks. "Well, yes," her mom answers. "Technically I am involved, but I'm not in an elected position. I'm just a concerned citizen."

The Senate chamber has an impressive collection of historical Texas paintings.

The skyscrapers and waterfront in downtown Austin surround the Texas State Capitol.

Citizens of cities and towns play a role in government, too. Citizens must follow rules and obey the laws. It's the privilege and duty of all citizens 18 and over to vote to choose their leaders for local, state, and national offices. Good citizens are active in their communities and volunteer time to help others, or they help clean up areas that need it.

Peering into some of the legislative chambers and meeting rooms, Lauren begins to imagine all the conversations and decisions that take place here. "Hmm," she wonders out loud. "It would be pretty neat to be a fly on the wall in there." "Well, maybe you can actually be elected to serve here someday," her mom comments. Lauren can hardly contain her big smile at the thought. "Or maybe in Washington, D.C.," she says. "There have been four United States presidents from Texas!" she exclaims.

When Lauren and her mom conclude their tour, Lauren can't get the thought of government out of her head. As she bounds down the stairs of the impressive capitol, she says to herself, "What could I start doing now to be an active citizen?"

This sculpture of James E. "Pete" Laney is in one of the hallways of the Capitol. He was a member of the Texas House of Representatives and Speaker of the House.

Think About It What do you think should be the goals of government? As you read the chapter, think about what goals your state and local government should have. What goals should you have as a citizen?

Governing Texas

Rules help us play games together. They also help people in communities to get along with and respect one another.

Dwight D. Eisenhower

Lyndon B. Johnson

George H. W. Bush

George W. Bush

Who decides what the rules are in government? Who makes sure the rules, or laws, are kept? Leaders in government have these responsibilities and others.

Leaders in Government

Many government leaders are elected, or chosen by voters. Others are appointed, or given jobs by the elected leaders. For example, in Texas, voters elect the governor, who then appoints the secretary of state.

Since Texas is part of the United States, Texans participate in national politics. Texas sends senators and representatives to Washington, D.C., to help run the country. National leaders serve Texans as well as other Americans.

Four Texans have been presidents of the United States. Dwight D. Eisenhower was born in Denison, Texas. He became president in 1953. Lyndon B. Johnson was born near Stonewall, Texas. He was elected vice president and became president after President John F. Kennedy was killed in 1963. Johnson was then elected president in 1964.

George H. W. Bush was born in Massachusetts, but he moved to Texas. Like Eisenhower, he served in World War II. He became president in 1989. His son, George W. Bush, was born in Connecticut but grew up in Midland, Texas. He was governor of Texas before becoming president in 2001.

1. **Identify** and name two Texans who have been president of the United States.

_____

Write what might happen if games had no rules.

UNLOCK THE BIG ?

I will know the responsibilities of each branch of the state government of Texas.

Vocabulary

citizen

municipal

county

executive branch

veto

legislative branch

judicial branch

constitutional republic

The Texas Constitution

The government of Texas is based on a constitution. The purpose of the Texas Constitution is to provide a plan for governing Texas and to protect the rights of Texas citizens. A **citizen** is a member of a nation, state, county, or town.

You probably know some of your rights. You have the right to freedom of speech and religion. A person charged with a crime has the right to a fair trial. When you turn 18, you will have the right to vote. These and other rights are protected by both the state of Texas and the United States.

The Texas Constitution also contains a plan for the state government. This plan divides the government into three parts, or branches. They are the legislative branch, the executive branch, and the judicial branch. The three branches work together to run the state. Power is divided among the three branches so that no one branch can become too powerful.

2. **Identify** the purposes of the Texas Constitution. Why is it important to have a state constitution?

....

....

....

....

....

> TEKS
> 7.A, 15.A, 15.B, 15.C, 17.B, 17.C, 17.D, 18.A, 18.B

3. **Identify** and underline the sentences in the text that explain the plan for state government in the Texas Constitution.

This is the first page of the Texas Constitution, adopted in 1876.

SAVVAS realize
Go online to access your interactive digital lesson.

381

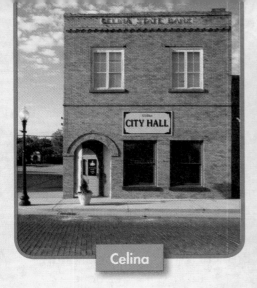
Celina

Dallas

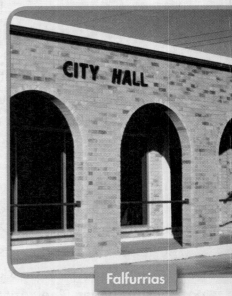
Falfurrias

Local Government in Texas

In addition to national and state governments, your community has a local government. In Texas, there are three types of local government: city, county, and special districts.

City government is often called municipal government. **Municipal** means "of a city." A municipal government serves people who live in cities and towns. It provides important services, such as police and fire protection. It also takes care of city parks and libraries. For example, if your library needs more books or the local park needs new equipment, the municipal government would take care of these things.

There are three forms of municipal government in Texas. One form is headed by an elected mayor. Another form of municipal government is headed by a city manager. In both forms, there is a city council. Members of the city council are elected. Council members make laws and help run the local government. The different departments, such as police, fire, or parks, report to the mayor or city manager of the city or town where they work. A third type of municipal government is the commission form. In this form, voters elect a small group of people responsible for taxation and other general functions of the city.

A city's government meets in a city hall. City halls can be large or small, or somewhere in between. They can also be old or new.

4. ◉ **Draw Conclusions Explain** why you think city halls in different cities or towns are so different.

....

....

Recall that there are a variety of regions in Texas that result from human activity. You have read about economic regions on page 348, and population regions on page 368. A political region is an area that is governed as a unit. The main political region in Texas is the **county**. Most counties are larger than cities. There are 254 counties.

County government is another type of local government. The city or town chosen to be the center of a county's government is called the county seat. County governments keep records of births, deaths, and marriages. They register voters. They also operate jails and take care of some of the county's roads.

A county's government is led by five elected officials: four county commissioners and one county judge. A commissioner is in charge of a government department. The judge is the leader and works with the four commissioners. This group is known as the county commissioners court. Counties also have elected sheriffs who make sure that people obey county and state laws.

A special district is a third type of local government. Special districts are run by elected officials. A special district has a certain purpose. Some special districts manage water resources. Other special districts provide fire protection in rural areas.

School districts are special districts. A school district oversees all the schools in its area. To lead the school district, citizens in the district elect school board members, or trustees. The school board decides how schools in the district will be run. Anyone who lives in the school district can attend most meetings of the school board.

5. **Analyze** the economic, population, and political regions you have read about in chapters 10 and 11. **Describe** at least three of these regions in Texas that result from patterns of human activity.

....

....

....

....

....

....

6. ◉ **Categorize** **Describe** each type of local government in the chart below.

City Government	County Government	Special Districts

City and county governments and special districts are political regions. Political regions result from patterns of human activity in the state. The United States also has political regions.

State Government

The center of state government for Texas is the city of Austin. Many government offices are located in Austin. The city is also home to the governor's mansion and the capitol. The capitol, which was completed in 1888, is the largest state capitol in the United States.

The capitol in Austin

As you read, the Texas Constitution divides the state government into three branches. It also establishes the power of the three branches. The state constitution requires that the three branches work separately. This helps balance power so no one branch can take control.

The Three Branches of Government

The basic function of the **executive branch** is to enforce the law. A governor is elected by the people of Texas to head the executive branch. A governor can suggest new laws for the legislature to consider, but the governor does not create laws. Governors provide leadership and appoint many state officials.

When a law is sent from the legislature to the governor, the governor can sign it if he or she thinks the law is good. If not, the governor can **veto,** or refuse to sign, a law. The law then goes back to the legislature. A vetoed law can still be passed if two thirds of the legislators vote for it.

The executive branch has more than 150 agencies. An agency is a group that is responsible for making sure certain laws are followed. For example, the Texas Education Agency oversees all schools in Texas.

7. Explain the job of the executive branch.

....

The basic function of the **legislative branch** is to make the laws for Texas. This branch has two parts, the Senate and the House of Representatives. The Senate has 31 members. The House of Representatives has 150 members. The state is divided into political districts. Voters in each district elect their own senators and representatives.

The people of Texas also elect a lieutenant governor, who heads the Senate. The person who heads the House of Representatives is known as the speaker of the house. He or she is an elected representative who is chosen by other members of the House. In 2009 Joe Strauss became the speaker of the house.

The **judicial branch** is made up of courts and judges. Its basic function is to make sure state laws are applied fairly and correctly. In Texas, there are more than 2,500 courts and 3,468 judges. Many of these serve local areas. District courts are where some jury trials take place.

The Texas Supreme Court and the Court of Criminal Appeals are the state's highest courts. The Supreme Court has nine members who are elected by the people of Texas. This court is the top court for civil matters.

Wallace B. Jefferson

The members of the Supreme Court are called justices. Wallace B. Jefferson worked as a lawyer and judge, and then made history in 2004 when he became the first African American Chief Justice of the Texas Supreme Court. Jefferson was an active participant of the democratic process from 2004 to 2013.

The Court of Criminal Appeals also has nine elected members. It hears criminal cases. Anyone found guilty of a crime in a lower court has the right to appeal, or ask for another trial. These appeals go to the Court of Criminal Appeals.

State senators meet in this room, inside the capitol in Austin, to discuss and create laws that affect the state.

8. ⊙ **Compare and Contrast**

Identify what the Texas Supreme Court and Court of Criminal Appeals have in common by circling the text.

Explain how they are different.

Texas Supreme Court:

....

Court of Criminal Appeals:

....

How a Bill Becomes a Law

A bill is a suggested law. Members of the Texas House of Representatives or the Senate write a bill. They then consider whether it would make a good law. When the members of the House of Representatives and the Senate approve the bill, it is sent to the governor. If the governor signs the bill, it becomes law. If the governor vetoes the bill, it returns to the legislature for a vote. If two thirds of the legislature votes for the vetoed bill, it becomes a law.

Our National Government

Our national government began with the Declaration of Independence in 1776. Its intent and purpose was to explain why the American colonies were breaking away from Great Britain. Then, two more important documents were written. The intents and purposes of these were to create a plan for government and to outline the rights and responsibilities of citizens. The United States Constitution was the new plan for governing the country. Many Americans were not confident it would protect their rights. So new laws called the Bill of Rights were added. The Bill of Rights outlines the rights of citizens. These documents meant that the citizens would always have their rights protected under the law.

A political region is an area that is governed as a unit. The main political region of the United States is the state. The government of the state of Texas has many similarities to the United States government. For example, the Texas Constitution reflects many of the ideas of the United States Constitution. The federal Constitution is also divided into three branches.

The voters of each state elect senators and representatives to represent them in the capital in Washington, D.C. Each state elects two senators to send to Washington. The number of representatives depends on a state's population. Texas is divided into 36 congressional districts and so has 36 representatives. The citizens in each district vote for their own representative.

9. **Identify** and underline in the text the three documents of the U.S. government and their purposes. What is the importance of these documents?

....

....

....

The governor, a legislator, or a citizen has an idea for a new law. The bill is introduced.

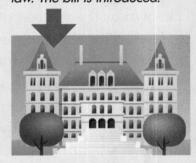

Legislators in both houses discuss and then vote on the bill. If both houses approve the bill, it goes to the governor.

If the governor approves the bill, it becomes law. If the governor vetoes the bill, it goes back to the legislature.

If two thirds of each house of the legislature approves the bill after a veto, it becomes law.

The United States is a constitutional republic. A **constitutional republic** is a form of government in which representatives get their authority from the people, serve for an established amount of time, and have sworn to uphold the United States Constitution. The Constitution limits the power of the government, leaving many important decisions to state and local governments.

Everyone who serves in the national government is sworn to uphold the Constitution. That means it is their job to make sure the freedoms and rights guaranteed in the Constitution are protected, the laws are followed, and the government continues to serve the people.

The United States Constitution defines the power and responsibilities of each branch of government. It also defines how long someone serves in office before another election is held. Representatives are elected for two-year terms. Senators are elected for six-year terms.

United States Constitution

Got it?

TEKS 7.A, 15.B, 15.C

10. ● **Summarize** **Identify** and **explain** the basic functions of the three branches of government according to the Texas Constitution.

....

....

11. ? **Identify** the intent, or goal, of each of these documents:

my Story Ideas

Declaration of Independence: ....

....

United States Constitution: ....

Bill of Rights: ....

12. **Describe** the following political region in Texas.

County: ....

....

Categorize

To **categorize** means to organize things, ideas, or people based on related characteristics. A category is the group you put things in when you organize them. Everything in a category is related in some way. However, many things fit in more than one category. For example, an airplane and a train both go in the category of transportation, but the airplane could also go into the category of things that fly.

Because things in a category are similar, categorizing can help us understand them. It can also help us understand what we read and sort information when we are doing research.

To categorize anything, you can follow these steps:

1. Identify what it is you want to categorize.
2. Look for similarities among the things you want to categorize.
3. Decide on the categories that are most useful for organizing the things you are categorizing.
4. Create a chart, as visual material, to analyze your information.

In Lesson 1, you read about different local, state, and federal governments. The chart below categorizes the powers of our state and federal governments. What other category might be added to the chart "Powers and Responsibilities of Government"?

Powers and Responsibilities of Government

Federal Government	State Government
• Print money • Regulate trade within the country and internationally • Make treaties and conduct foreign policy • Declare war • Provide an army and navy • Establish post offices • Make laws necessary to carry out these powers	• Issue licenses • Regulate trade within the state • Conduct elections • Establish local governments • Ratify amendments to the Constitution • Take measures for public health and safety • May exert powers the Constitution does not prohibit the states from using or delegate to the national government

TEKS

ELA 24.C Take simple notes and sort evidence into provided categories or an organizer.

SS 15.B Identify the basic functions of the three branches of government according to the Texas Constitution.

SS 21.B Analyze information by categorizing.

In Lesson 1, you read about local, state, and national government. There are many ways you could categorize this information. Here are a few ideas for you to try.

1. What are the three different types of local government?

....

2. List at least two things you could include in the Municipal Government category.

....

....

3. What are the three branches of government for both state and national government?

....

....

4. **Apply Look** back at pages 384–385. Create a chart like the one below to **analyze** the information on these pages. It can help you **categorize** information about the different branches of government.

Executive Branch		Judicial Branch
....	Makes the laws	....
....		....
	Divided into two parts	....
Signs or vetoes laws		....

Active Citizenship in Texas

Students can improve their community by helping people who live there. These students are planting trees.

You read in Lesson 1 about the different levels of government. You also read about some of the jobs in government. Now, you will read about what part individual citizens play in communities and government. When we speak of United States citizens, we are speaking of people who were either born in the country or who have earned the right to be citizens of the country.

A Citizen's Role

Citizens are protected by the laws of the country. However, it is also their duty to obey the laws. A **duty** is something that you must do. Young citizens have a duty to go to school. All citizens have a duty to respect the rights of others.

In the United States, citizens have many freedoms and rights. Rights we have include freedom of speech, freedom of religion, and the right to vote for the leaders who represent us. Some of these rights are limited. For example, to vote, you must be at least 18 years old.

Another right is to have a fair trial. Citizens are sometimes asked to serve on a jury. A **jury** is a group of people who listen to evidence and decide the outcome of a trial. Juries make sure laws are carried out fairly. Serving on a jury is a duty.

1. **Identify** and underline three different duties described in the text.

Going to school is a duty for students. Studying is a responsibility.

What could you do to help someone in your community?
Explain your idea and write it above.

UNLOCK
THE BIG
?

I will know how citizens can work together to improve their community and affect how their government is run.

Vocabulary

duty	volunteer
jury	political party
responsibility	petition

Voting is not just a right. It is also a **responsibility**, or something that a person should do. It is also the duty of individual citizens to vote and to be informed about issues and people when voting. Helping solve problems where you live is another responsibility.

Good citizens often **volunteer**, or give their time, to help wherever they are needed. For example, people often volunteer to help at senior centers or schools. They might also volunteer for clean-up projects.

TEKS

5.C, 7.A, 15.A, 17.A, 17.B, 17.C, 17.D, 17.E, 18.A, 18.B, 21.B

A Citizen's Rights	Responsibilities and Duties
freedom of speech	volunteering

2. ⊙ **Categorize**
Think of some missing rights, responsibilities, and duties. **Categorize** them in the chart.

Local Leaders

Local individuals are also important to the democratic process. While everyone wants leaders who are honest and well informed, there are other important qualities local leaders should have. Depending on the jobs they are doing, they need to know local laws. They also need to understand the local economy. It is important that they know local people and issues.

For leaders of special districts, knowing about the function of their district is important. For example, someone who is a leader in a school district should care about education and know how the schools work.

Almost everyone who runs for office is identified with a specific political party. A **political party** is an organized group of people who share similar ideas about how to run the government. There are many political parties, but most people belong to the Republican Party or Democratic Party.

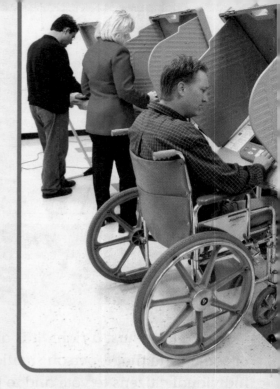

Before people go to vote, they should find out as much as they can about people running for office.

It is an honor to serve in local government. Many people have had to work hard to hold office. Houston resident Hattie Mae White became the first African American to be elected to office in Texas in 1958. She was elected to the school board.

When Birdie Harwood was elected mayor of Marble Falls, Texas, in 1917, she was the first female mayor in the United States. You will read about some other firsts later in this lesson.

Different leaders have different backgrounds and different issues that are important to them. For example, Robert Cluck, the mayor of Arlington, Texas, is a doctor. The issue that is most important to him is clean air.

Though leaders often disagree, most of them want to do a good job for the people who elected them. Of course, it is the responsibility of the people being represented to make sure their leaders are doing what they promised.

3. Using the Internet, newspapers, or other resources, **identify** a local member of the Texas Legislature and one other local leader currently in office such as the mayor or county commissioner. Write the office each one holds and their leadership qualities and responsibilities.

....

....

State Leaders

There have been many important individuals who have participated voluntarily in civic affairs at state and local levels in Texas. To run for any office, a person must be a United States citizen. There are also age restrictions for different offices. For example, a person must be 30 years old to become governor.

Most Texas governors have been men. However, two women served as governor. Miriam "Ma" Ferguson was the first woman to be elected governor. She served from 1925 to 1927 and again from 1933 to 1935.

Ann Richards is another important individual who actively participated in the democratic process. She was the second woman to serve as Texas governor. She held several offices during her political career. She was elected county commissioner in 1976. In 1982, she became state treasurer. She served as governor of Texas from 1991 to 1995.

Raul A. Gonzalez, Jr. got involved in politics while in college. Like many politicians, he served at the local level before moving to the state level. He served at both the local and state levels as a lawyer. In 1978, he became a judge. Then, in 1984, he became the first Hispanic American to serve on the Texas Supreme Court.

Many local and state leaders enjoy working in their hometowns or want to stay in Texas. However, local leaders may move to state leadership roles. State leaders may move up to national leadership roles. For example, George W. Bush was governor of Texas before he became president of the United States.

4. **Identify** and underline in the text individuals who have modeled active participation in the democratic process.

5. Using the Internet, newspapers, or other resources, research and **identify** the names of at least two state leaders currently in office. For example, you might look up the governor, your state representative, or a justice on the state Supreme Court. Also, **identify** the office each one holds.

Governor Miriam Ma Ferguson

Governor Ann Richards

Justice Raul A. Gonzalez, Jr.

How to Contact Your Local and State Leaders

Citizens can take part in government by voting for leaders who will represent them. When you are 18, you will be able to vote. However, even now, you can contact your elected and appointed state and local leaders. You can ask questions, offer opinions, tell them how you would like them to vote on a bill, or share information with them. Or you can let public officials know you expect them to keep their word. To learn more about your state government, you can visit these sites on the Internet:

http://www.senate.state.tx.us/kids/	http://governor.state.tx.us/
http://www.house.state.tx.us/	http://www.courts.state.tx.us/

Here is where you can contact your state leaders.

Governor	**Speaker of the House**
P.O. Box 12428	Room CAP 2W.13, Capitol
Austin, Texas 78711	P.O. Box 2910
1 (512) 463-2000	Austin, Texas 78768
	1 (512) 463-1000
Lieutenant Governor	**Supreme Court Justice**
Capitol Station	201 W. 14th
P.O. Box 12068	Austin, Texas 78701
Austin, Texas 78711	1 (512) 463-1312
1 (512) 463-0001	

To contact local leaders, the Internet can help. For example, a search for "mayor of Dallas Texas" turns up http://www .dallascityhall.com/government/mayor/. Or search for your county courthouse. For example, a search for "Anderson County Texas courthouse" brings up http://www.co.anderson.tx.us/. On both of these sites, you can find your leaders' contact information.

6. **Identify** in the text why you might want to contact state or local leaders. **Explain** how you might contact your local mayor or a local appointed leader.

....

....

Making a Difference in Texas

The first line of the United States Constitution begins, "We the People ..." Citizens created the United States and its Constitution, and citizens continue to make the country work.

You don't have to be 18 or a politician to make a difference. Individuals of all ages can participate voluntarily in civic affairs at state and local levels. You've already read about writing to leaders, but here are some other things you can do:

- Help in local, state, or national election campaigns. Find out who is running for the different offices. Talk to people who understand the issues. Find news articles that are for and against the people running.

- Start a politics club. Discuss with friends things that affect you. Collect articles about the issues. When you are a little older, you could become part of a program such as Texas Youth and Government, which helps teens learn about government and even prepare to be leaders. Once you're in high school, you could become part of the Texas United States Senate Youth Program.

- Pass out information about issues. If something is important, make sure other people know about it. For example, you might pass along information on the dangers of smoking or eating too much sugar.

- Start a petition. A **petition** is an official request to the government signed by many citizens. Seeing that many people care about an issue can often get leaders to look at the issue.

There is a lot that citizens can do without becoming elected officials. There are many volunteer opportunities available in almost every community. Picking up litter in a park or volunteering at a school makes life nicer for those you help. Getting involved in state and local issues makes life better for everyone.

These students are participating in the civic affairs of their state by writing to their senator about a cause they believe in.

7. **Explain** how individuals volunteer in civic affairs at state and local levels.

....

....

....

....

....

....

....

Representing Texas in Washington, D.C.

Many historical individuals have actively participated in the democratic process for Texas and for the country in Washington, D.C. Texas has two senators in the nation's capital. There are also 36 Texans in the United States House of Representatives. Here are a few noteworthy Texans who have represented Texas in Washington, D.C.

Henry B. González

Henry B. González was the first Hispanic American from Texas to be elected to the United States House of Representatives. A Democrat, he had served as a San Antonio councilman and a state senator. He was elected in 1961 and served for 37 years.

Republican John Tower had a long career of service to Texas and the United States. He served in the United States Senate from 1961 to 1985. He was also the first Republican senator from Texas since 1870.

John Tower

Barbara Jordan worked hard to advance the cause of African Americans. In 1973 she became the first African American woman from the south to be elected to the United States House of Representatives. Jordan was a Democrat from Houston. She served three terms and then returned to Texas to teach at the University of Texas in Austin.

From 1993 to 2013, Republican Kay Bailey Hutchison served in the United States Senate. She was the first woman to represent Texas in the Senate. Hutchison had held jobs in business and state government before being elected senator.

Barbara Jordan

Like Barbara Jordan, Sheila Jackson Lee is a Democrat from Houston. She has served in the United States House of Representatives since 1995. Before that, she served on the Houston City Council and as an associate municipal court judge.

Kay Granger was the first Republican woman to represent Texas in the United States House of Representatives. She began serving in 1997, and her current term runs until 2015.

8. Using the Internet, newspapers, or other resources, **identify** and write the names of both Texas United States senators and your United States representative in the national government.

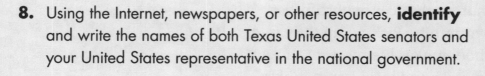

Kay Granger

In addition, people have actively participated in the democratic process by going to Washington to help keep our national government working. Republican James A. Baker III, from Houston, is one example. He held several important positions for Presidents Gerald Ford, Ronald Reagan, and George H. W. Bush. Baker served as under secretary of commerce, White House chief of staff, secretary of the treasury, and secretary of state. In 1991, Baker was awarded the Presidential Medal of Freedom.

James A. Baker III

9. **Identify** and underline in the text the ways in which James A. Baker III modeled active participation in the democratic process.

TEKS 5.C, 17.C, 17.D

10. ⦿ **Main Idea and Details** **Identify** the importance of the individuals in the chart.

Kay Bailey Hutchison	
Henry B. González	
John Tower	
Barbara Jordan	

11. In the United States, people are encouraged to talk to their representatives. **Explain** what this tells you about our government.

my Story Ideas

....

....

12. **Explain** why it is the duty of individuals to vote and to be informed about state and local elections.

....

....

Solve Problems

People and communities face problems every day. To solve a problem, people need to follow these five steps:

- Identify the problem.
- Gather information about ways to solve the problem.
- List and consider your options.
- Consider the advantages and disadvantages of each of the different possible solutions.
- Implement a solution.
- Evaluate the effectiveness of the solution.

A community recently decided that students were eating too many unhealthy snacks. They could buy soda and candy right at school. Parents, teachers, and community leaders discussed the problem. They gathered information. They learned snacks high in fat and sugar had bad effects on students' health. In addition, people learned that eating a lot of sugar hurt students' performance in school. It made it harder for students to pay attention and to learn.

Schools in the community got rid of the vending machines that let students buy soda and candy. Some schools began to look at how they could make lunches healthier, too. If getting rid of sugar helped students learn better and stay healthier, what else could be done with nutrition?

Learning Objective

I will know how to solve problems.

TEKS

SS 23.A Use a problem-solving process to identify a problem, gather information, list and consider options, consider advantages and disadvantages, choose and implement a solution, and evaluate the effectiveness of the solution.

Try it!

1. **Identify** another solution that parents could have come up with if the schools had not banned sweets at school.

   ....

   ....

   ....

2. **Explain** what the school and the parents could do to help students get involved in the effort to get rid of unhealthy snacks.

   ....

   ....

   ....

   ....

3. **Apply** Use the problem solving steps you learned about to **identify** a problem, gather information, identify possible solutions, and evaluate your solution.

   Problem:

   ....

   ....

   ....

   Possible solution and evaluation:

   ....

   ....

   ....

   ....

SAVVAS realize Go online to access your interactive digital lesson.

399

Lesson 1   TEKS 7.A, 15.B, 15.C, 17.D

Governing Texas

1. **Identify** two ways government leaders are selected.

   ....

2. **Identify** the United States president from Texas who was the son of another United States president.

   ....

3. **Identify** at least two rights guaranteed by the Texas Constitution.

   ....

   ....

4. **Identify** the meaning of *municipal*.

   ....

5. Read the question carefully. Determine the best answer to the question from the four answer choices provided. Circle the best answer.

   What type of local government takes care of things like schools and water management?

   A state government

   B special districts

   C county government

   D rural government

6. **Identify** the meaning of the following documents.

   Declaration of Independence:

   ....

   ....

   United States Constitution:

   ....

   ....

   ....

   Bill of Rights:

   ....

   ....

   ....

7. **Explain** the basic functions of the three branches of government according to the Texas Constitution.

   ....

   ....

   ....

   ....

   ....

   ....

8. **Describe** the main political region of the United States.

....

....

9. **Identify** the importance of Wallace B. Jefferson. How did he model active participation in the democratic process?

....

....

....

....

10. **Identify** what a bill is.

....

11. **Explain** what it means when we say that the United States is a constitutional republic.

....

....

....

Lesson 2 TEKS 5.C, 17.C, 17.D, 17.E, 18.A

Active Citizenship in Texas

12. **Identify** two responsibilities or duties that citizens of the United States have.

....

13. ⊙ **Draw Conclusions Explain** why learning about issues and people running for office is an important part of a voter's responsibility.

....

....

....

....

14. ⊙ **Categorize** The positions listed below are local, state, and national offices. To **categorize** these offices, place an *L* for local, *S* for state, or *N* for national next to each title or position.

_____ mayor

_____ United States Senator

_____ governor

15. **Identify** the importance of Ann Richards. How did she model active participation in the democratic process?

....

....

....

16. Identify the accomplishments of Raul A. Gonzalez, Jr.

....

....

....

17. Identify the search terms you could use to find the following information.

a. The name of the mayor of Galveston

....

....

b. The address of city hall for Fort Worth

....

....

c. The commissioners for your county

....

....

18. Explain what a petition is.

....

....

....

19. Explain why it is important to be involved in the political process.

....

....

....

....

20. Identify the importance of Barbara Jordan. How did she model active participation in the democratic process?

....

....

....

....

21. Identify the Texan who worked in Washington, D.C., with both Ronald Reagan and George H. W. Bush.

....

22. ❓ **What should be the goals of government?** 🔽 **TEKS 21.B**

Our leaders make laws that we are expected to obey. **Describe** the goal of each of the following types of laws.

a. traffic laws

....

....

b. health laws

....

....

c. clean air laws

....

....

Go online to write and illustrate your own **myStory Book** using the **myStory Ideas** from this chapter.

What should be the goals of government?

TEKS
SS 17.B
ELA 15

You have read about local, state, and national government. You have also read about the services provided by different levels of government. In addition, you have read that citizens can take part in making communities work.

Think about something in your community that you would like to see improved. **Explain** how you could participate in your community to make these improvements happen.

....

....

....

....

Now draw a picture showing ways you could work for these same improvements at the state level.

The Declaration of Independence

The first part of the Declaration of Independence is called the Preamble. A preamble is an introduction, or the part that comes before the main message. The Preamble states why the Declaration was written.

The second paragraph lists the basic rights that all people should have. The founders called these **unalienable** rights, meaning that these rights cannot be taken or given away. If a government cannot protect these rights, the people must change the government or create a new one.

1. According to the Declaration, what are three "unalienable rights?" **Identify** and circle these words in the text. Then write the meaning of the Declaration.

....

....

....

....

The third paragraph introduces the List of Grievances. Each part of this list begins with the words, "He has...." These words refer to King George III's actions in the colonies. To prove that the king had abused his power over the colonies, this list of 27 complaints described how the British government and the king had treated the colonists.

In Congress, July 4, 1776
The Unanimous Declaration of the Thirteen United States of America

When in the Course of human events it becomes necessary for one people to dissolve the political bands which have connected them with another, and to assume among the powers of the earth, the separate and equal station to which the Laws of nature and of nature's God entitle them, a decent respect to the opinions of mankind requires that they should declare the causes which impel them to the separation.

We hold these truths to be self-evident, that all men are created equal, that they are endowed by their Creator with certain unalienable Rights, that among these are Life, Liberty and the Pursuit of Happiness. That to secure these rights, Governments are instituted among Men, deriving their just powers from the consent of the governed; That whenever any Form of Government becomes destructive of these ends it is the Right of the People to alter or to abolish it, and to institute new Government, laying its foundation on such principles and organizing its powers in such form, as to them shall seem most likely to effect their Safety and Happiness. Prudence, indeed, will dictate that Governments long established should not be changed for light and transient causes; and accordingly all experience hath shown, that mankind are more disposed to suffer, while evils are sufferable, than to right themselves by abolishing the forms to which they are accustomed. But when a long train of abuses and usurpations, pursuing invariably the same Object evinces a design to reduce them under absolute Despotism, it is their right, it is their duty, to throw off such Government, and to provide new Guards for their future security.

Such has been the patient sufferance of these Colonies; and such is now the necessity which constrains them to alter their former Systems of Government. The history of the present King of Great Britain is a history of repeated injuries and usurpations, all having in direct object the establishment of an absolute Tyranny over these States. To prove this, let Facts be submitted to a candid world.

He has refused his Assent to Laws, the most wholesome and necessary for the public good.

He has forbidden his Governors to pass Laws of immediate and pressing importance, unless suspended in their operation till his

Assent should be obtained; and when so suspended, he has utterly neglected to attend to them.

He has refused to pass other Laws for the accommodation of large districts of people, unless those people would relinquish the right of Representation in the Legislature, a right inestimable to them and formidable to tyrants only.

He has called together legislative bodies at places unusual, uncomfortable, and distant from the depository of their Public Records, for the sole purpose of fatiguing them into compliance with his measures.

He has dissolved Representative Houses repeatedly, for opposing with manly firmness his invasions on the rights of the people.

He has refused for a long time, after such dissolutions, to cause others to be elected; whereby the Legislative powers, incapable of Annihilation, have returned to the People at large for their exercise; the State remaining in the mean time exposed to all the dangers of invasions from without, and convulsions within.

He has endeavored to prevent the population of these States; for that purpose obstructing the Laws for Naturalization of Foreigners; refusing to pass others to encourage their migration hither, and raising the conditions of new Appropriations of Lands.

He has obstructed the Administration of Justice, by refusing his Assent to Laws for establishing Judiciary powers.

He has made Judges dependent on his Will alone for the tenure of their offices, and the amount and payment of their salaries.

He has erected a multitude of New Offices, and sent hither swarms of Officers to harass our people and eat out their substance.

He has kept among us in time of peace, Standing Armies, without the Consent of our legislatures.

He has affected to render the Military independent of, and superior to, the Civil Power.

He has combined with others to subject us to a jurisdiction foreign to our constitutions, and unacknowledged by our laws; giving his Assent to their Acts of pretended Legislation:

For quartering large bodies of armed troops among us;

For protecting them, by a mock Trial, from punishment for any Murders which they should commit on the Inhabitants of these States;

In the List of Grievances the colonists complain that they have no say in choosing the laws that govern them. They say that King George III is not concerned about their safety and happiness. They list the times when the king denied them the right to representation. The colonists also state that the king has interfered with judges, with the court system, and with foreigners who want to become citizens.

2. There are many words in the Declaration that may be unfamiliar to you. **Identify** and circle three words you do not know. Look the words up in the dictionary. Write one word and its meaning on the lines below.

....

....

....

....

....

....

....

....

This page continues the colonists' long List of Grievances.

3. In your own words, briefly **summarize** three grievances.

....

....

....

....

4. Match each word from the Declaration with its meaning. Use a dictionary if you need help with a word.

abolishing	tried to achieve
plundered	changing
suspending	doing away with
altering	stopping for a time
endeavored	robbed

Statement of Independence
After listing their many grievances, the signers begin their statement of independence. Because the king has refused to correct the problems, he is an unfair ruler. Therefore, he is not fit to rule the free people of America.

For cutting off our Trade with all parts of the world;

For imposing Taxes on us without our Consent;

For depriving us, in many cases, of the benefits of Trial by Jury;

For transporting us beyond Seas to be tried for pretended offenses;

For abolishing the free System of English Laws in a neighboring Province, establishing therein an Arbitrary government, and enlarging its Boundaries so as to render it at once an example and fit instrument for introducing the same absolute rule into these Colonies;

For taking away our Charters, abolishing our most valuable Laws, and altering fundamentally the Forms of our Governments;

For suspending our own Legislatures, and declaring themselves invested with Power to legislate for us in all cases whatsoever.

He has abdicated Government here, by declaring us out of his Protection, and waging War against us.

He has plundered our seas, ravaged our Coasts, burned our towns, and destroyed the lives of our people.

He is at this time transporting large Armies of foreign mercenaries to complete the works of death, desolation and tyranny, already begun with circumstances of Cruelty and perfidy scarcely paralleled in the most barbarous ages, and totally unworthy the Head of a civilized nation.

He has constrained our fellow Citizens taken Captive on the high Seas to bear Arms against their Country, to become the executioners of their friends and Brethren, or to fall themselves by their Hands.

He has excited domestic insurrections amongst us, and has endeavored to bring on the inhabitants of our frontiers the merciless Indian Savages whose known rule of warfare, is an undistinguished destruction of all ages, sexes, and conditions.

In every stage of these Oppressions We have Petitioned for Redress in the most humble terms. Our repeated Petitions have been answered only by repeated injury. A Prince, whose character is thus marked by every act which may define a Tyrant, is unfit to be the ruler of a free People.

Nor have We been wanting in attentions to our British brethren. We have warned them from time to time of attempts by their legislature to extend an unwarrantable jurisdiction over us. We have reminded them of the circumstances of our emigration and settlement here. We have appealed to their native justice and magnanimity, and we have conjured them by the ties of our common kindred to disavow these usurpations, which, would inevitably interrupt our connections and correspondence. They too have been deaf to the voice of justice and of consanguinity. We must, therefore, acquiesce in the necessity, which denounces our Separation, and hold them, as we hold the rest of mankind, Enemies in War, in Peace Friends.

We, therefore, the Representatives of the United States of America, in General Congress, Assembled, appealing to the Supreme Judge of the world for the rectitude of our intentions, do, in the Name, and by the Authority of the good People of these Colonies, solemnly publish and declare, That these United Colonies are, and of right ought to be Free and Independent States; that they are Absolved from all Allegiance to the British Crown, and that all political connection between them and the State of Great Britain, is and ought to be totally dissolved, and that as Free and Independent States, they have full Power to levy War, conclude Peace, contract Alliances, establish Commerce, and to do all other Acts and Things which Independent States may of right do. And for the support of this Declaration, with a firm reliance on the protection of Divine Providence, we mutually pledge to each other our Lives, our Fortunes, and our sacred Honor.

New Hampshire:
Josiah Bartlett
William Whipple
Matthew Thornton

Massachusetts Bay:
John Hancock
Samuel Adams
John Adams
Robert Treat Paine
Elbridge Gerry

Rhode Island:
Stephan Hopkins
William Ellery

Connecticut:
Roger Sherman
Samuel Huntington
William Williams
  Oliver Wolcott

New York:
William Floyd
Philip Livingston
Francis Lewis
Lewis Morris

New Jersey:
Richard Stockton
John Witherspoon
Francis Hopkinson
John Hart
Abraham Clark

Delaware:
Caesar Rodney
George Read
Thomas M'Kean

Maryland:
Samuel Chase
William Paca
Thomas Stone
Charles Carroll of
  Carrollton

Virginia:
George Wythe
Richard Henry Lee
Thomas Jefferson
Benjamin Harrison
Thomas Nelson, Jr.
Francis Lightfoot Lee
Carter Braxton

Pennsylvania:
Robert Morris
Benjamin Rush
Benjamin Franklin
John Morton
George Clymer
James Smith
George Taylor
James Wilson
George Ross

North Carolina:
William Hooper
Joseph Hewes
John Penn

South Carolina:
Edward Rutledge
Thomas Heyward, Jr.
Thomas Lynch, Jr.
Arthur Middleton

Georgia:
Button Gwinnett
Lyman Hall
George Walton

In this paragraph, the signers point out that they have asked the British people for help many times. The colonists hoped the British would listen to them because they have so much in common. The British people, however, paid no attention to their demand for justice. This is another reason for why the colonies must break away from Great Britain.

In the last paragraph, the members of the Continental Congress declare that the thirteen colonies are no longer colonies. They are now a free nation with no ties to Great Britain. The United States now has all the powers of other independent countries.

5. Identify three powers that the signers claim the new nation now has.

....

....

....

....

....

6. The signers promised to support the Declaration of Independence and each other with their lives, their fortunes, and their honor. On a separate sheet of paper, tell what you think this means. Then **explain** why it was a brave thing to do.

United States Constitution

This **Preamble** gives the reasons for writing and having a Constitution. The Constitution will form a stronger and more united nation. It will lead to peace, justice, and liberty and will defend American citizens. Finally, it will improve the lives of people.

Section 1. Congress

The legislative branch of government makes the country's laws. Called the Congress, it has two parts, or houses: the House of Representatives and the Senate.

Section 2. The House of Representatives

Members of the House of Representatives are elected every two years. Representatives must be 25 years old and United States citizens. They must also live in the states that elect them.

The number of Representatives for each state is based on the population, or number of people who live there.

1. Explain why some states have more representatives in Congress than other states.

....

....

....

....

Over the years, the Constitution has been altered, or changed. These altered parts are shown here in gray type.

PREAMBLE

We the People of the United States, in Order to form a more perfect Union, establish Justice, insure domestic Tranquility, provide for the common defense, promote the general Welfare, and secure the Blessings of Liberty to ourselves and our Posterity, do ordain and establish this Constitution for the United States of America.

ARTICLE I

Section 1.

All legislative Powers herein granted shall be vested in a Congress of the United States, which shall consist of a Senate and House of Representatives.

Section 2.

1. The House of Representatives shall be composed of Members chosen every second Year by the People of the several States, and the Electors in each State shall have the Qualifications requisite for Electors of the most numerous Branch of the State Legislature.

2. No Person shall be a Representative who shall not have attained to the age of twenty-five Years, and been seven Years a Citizen of the United States, and who shall not, when elected, be an Inhabitant of that State in which he shall be chosen.

3. Representatives and direct Taxes shall be apportioned among the several States which may be included within this Union, according to their respective Numbers, which shall be determined by adding to the whole Number of free Persons, including those bound to Service for a Term of Years and excluding Indians not taxed, three fifths of all other Persons. The actual Enumeration shall be made within three Years after the first Meeting of the Congress of the United States, and within every subsequent Term of ten Years, in such Manner as they shall by Law direct. The Number of Representatives shall not exceed one for every thirty Thousand, but each State shall have at Least one Representative; and, until such enumeration shall be made, the State of New Hampshire shall be entitled to choose three, Massachusetts eight, Rhode Island and Providence Plantations one, Connecticut five, New York six, New Jersey four, Pennsylvania eight, Delaware one, Maryland six, Virginia ten, North Carolina five, South Carolina five, and Georgia three.

4. When vacancies happen in the Representation from any State, the Executive Authority thereof shall issue Writs of Election to fill such Vacancies.

5. The House of Representatives shall choose their Speaker and other Officers; and shall have the sole Power of Impeachment.

Section 3.

1. The Senate of the United States shall be composed of two Senators from each State chosen by the Legislature thereof for six Years; and each Senator shall have one Vote.

2. Immediately after they shall be assembled in Consequences of the first Election, they shall be divided, as equally as may be, into three Classes. The Seats of the Senators of the first Class shall be vacated at the Expiration of the second Year; of the second Class, at the Expiration of the fourth Year; and of the third Class, at the Expiration of the sixth Year; so that one-third may be chosen every second Year; and if Vacancies happen by Resignation, or otherwise, during the Recess of the Legislature of any State, the Executive thereof may make temporary Appointments until the next Meeting of the Legislature, which shall then fill such Vacancies.

3. No Person shall be a Senator who shall not have attained to the Age of thirty Years, and been nine Years a Citizen of the United States, and who shall not, when elected, be an Inhabitant of that State for which he shall be chosen.

4. The Vice President of the United States shall be President of the Senate but shall have no Vote, unless they be equally divided.

5. The Senate shall choose their other Officers, and also a President pro tempore, in the Absence of the Vice President, or when he shall exercise the Office of President of the United States.

6. The Senate shall have the sole Power to try all Impeachments. When sitting for that Purpose, they shall be on Oath or Affirmation. When the President of the United States is tried, the Chief Justice shall preside: And no Person shall be convicted without the Concurrence of two thirds of the Members present.

7. Judgment in Cases of Impeachment shall not extend further than to removal from Office, and disqualification to hold and enjoy any Office of honor, Trust, or Profit under the United States: but the Party convicted shall nevertheless be liable and subject to Indictment, Trial, Judgment and Punishment, according to Law.

A state governor calls a special election to fill an empty seat in the House of Representatives.

Members of the House of Representatives choose their own leaders. They also have the power to impeach, or accuse, government officials of crimes.

Section 3. Senate

Each state has two Senators. A Senator serves a six-year term.

At first, each state legislature elected its two Senators. The Seventeenth Amendment changed that. Today the voters of each state elect their Senators.

Senators must be 30 years old and United States citizens. They must also live in the states they represent.

2. How is the length of a Senator's term different from a Representative's term?

....

....

The Vice President is the officer in charge of the Senate but only votes to break a tie. When the Vice President is absent, a temporary leader (President Pro Tempore) leads the Senate.

The Senate holds impeachment trials. When the President is impeached, the Chief Justice of the Supreme Court is the judge. A two-thirds vote is needed to convict. Once convicted, an official can be removed from office. Other courts of law can impose other punishments.

SECTION 4. Elections and Meetings of Congress

The state legislatures determine the times, places, and method of holding elections for senators and representatives.

SECTION 5. Rules for Congress

The Senate and House of Representatives judge the fairness of the elections and the qualifications of its own members. At least half of the members must be present to do business. Each house may determine the rules of its proceedings and punish its member for disorderly behavior. Each house of Congress shall keep a record of its proceedings, and from time to time publish the record.

3. Explain why it is important for Congress to publish a record of what they do.

....

....

....

....

....

SECTION 6. Rights and Restrictions of Members of Congress

The senators and representatives shall receive payment for their services to be paid out of the Treasury of the United States. Members of Congress cannot be arrested during their attendance at the session of Congress, except for a very serious crime, and they cannot be arrested for anything they say in Congress. No person can have a government job while serving as a member of Congress.

Section 4.

1. The Times, Places and Manner of holding Elections for Senators and Representatives, shall be prescribed in each State by the Legislature thereof; but the Congress may at any time by law make or alter such Regulations, except as to the Places of choosing Senators.
2. The Congress shall assemble at least once in every Year, and such Meeting shall be on the first Monday in December, unless they shall by Law appoint a different Day.

Section 5.

1. Each House shall be the Judge of the Elections, Returns and Qualifications of its own Members, and a Majority of each shall constitute a Quorum to do Business; but a smaller Number may adjourn from day to day, and may be authorized to compel the Attendance of absent Members, in such Manner, and under such Penalties, as each House may provide.
2. Each House may determine the Rules of its Proceedings, punish its Members for disorderly Behavior, and, with the Concurrence of two thirds, expel a Member.
3. Each House shall keep a Journal of its Proceedings, and from time to time publish the same, excepting such Parts as may in their Judgment require Secrecy; and the Yeas and Nays of the Members of either House on any question shall, at the Desire of one fifth of those Present, be entered on the Journal.
4. Neither House, during the Session of Congress, shall, without the Consent of the other, adjourn for more than three days, nor to any other Place than that in which the two Houses shall be sitting.

Section 6.

1. The Senators and Representatives shall receive a Compensation for their Services, to be ascertained by Law, and paid out of the Treasury of the United States. They shall in all Cases, except Treason, Felony, and Breach of the Peace, be privileged from Arrest during their Attendance at the Session of their respective Houses, and in going to and returning from the same; and for any Speech or Debate in either House, they shall not be questioned in any other Place.
2. No Senator or Representative shall, during the Time for which he was elected, be appointed to any civil Office under the Authority of the United States, which shall have been created, or the Emoluments whereof shall have been increased during such time; and no Person holding any Office under the United States, shall be a Member of either House during his Continuance in Office.

Section 7.

1. All Bills for raising Revenue shall originate in the House of Representatives; but the Senate may propose or concur with amendments as on other Bills.

2. Every Bill which shall have passed the House of Representatives and the Senate, shall, before it become a law, be presented to the President of the United States: If he approve, he shall sign it, but if not he shall return it, with his Objections to that House in which it shall have originated, who shall enter the Objections at large on their Journal, and proceed to reconsider it. If after such Reconsideration two thirds of the House shall agree to pass the Bill, it shall be sent, together with the Objections, to the other House, by which it shall likewise be reconsidered, and if approved by two thirds of that House, it shall become a Law. But in all such Cases the Votes of both Houses shall be determined by Yeas and Nays, and the Names of the Persons voting for and against the Bill shall be entered on the Journal of each House respectively. If any Bill shall not be returned by the President within ten Days (Sunday excepted) after it shall have been presented to him, the Same shall be a law, in like Manner as if he had signed it, unless the Congress by their Adjournment, prevent its Return, in which Case it shall not be a Law.

3. Every Order, Resolution, or Vote to which the Concurrence of the Senate and House of Representatives may be necessary (except on a question of adjournment) shall be presented to the President of the United States; and before the Same shall take Effect, shall be approved by him, or, being disapproved by him, shall be repassed by two thirds of the Senate and House of Representatives, according to the Rules and Limitations prescribed in the Case of a Bill.

Section 8.

The Congress shall have Power

1. To lay and collect Taxes, Duties, Imposts and Excises to pay the Debts and provide for the common Defense and general Welfare of the United States; but all Duties, Imposts and Excises, shall be uniform throughout the United States;

2. To borrow Money on the credit of the United States;

3. To regulate Commerce with foreign Nations, and among the several States, and with the Indian Tribes;

4. To establish an uniform Rule of Naturalization, and uniform Laws on the subject of Bankruptcies throughout the United States;

SECTION 7. How Laws are Made

All bills for raising money shall begin in the House of Representatives. The Senate may suggest or agree with amendments to these tax bills, as with other bills.

Every bill which has passed the House of Representatives and the Senate must be presented to the President of the United States before it becomes a law. If the President approves of the bill, the President shall sign it. If the President does not approve, then the bill may be vetoed. The President then sends it back to the house in which it began, with an explanation of the objections. That house writes the objections on their record, and begins to reconsider it. If two-thirds of each house agrees to pass the bill, it shall become a law. If any bill is neither signed nor vetoed by the President within ten days, (except for Sundays) after it has been sent to the President, the bill shall be a law. If Congress adjourns before ten days have passed, the bill does not become a law.

SECTION 8. Powers of Congress

Among the powers of Congress listed in Section 8 are:

- establish and collect taxes on imported and exported goods and on goods sold within the country. Congress also shall pay the debts and provide for the defense and general welfare of the United States. All federal taxes shall be the same throughout the United States.

- borrow money on the credit of the United States;

- make laws about trade with other countries, among the states, and with the American Indian tribes;

- establish one procedure by which a person from another country can become a legal citizen of the United States;

- protect the works of scientists, artists, authors, and inventors;

- create federal courts lower than the Supreme Court;

- declare war;
- establish and support an army and navy;
- organize and train a National Guard and call them up in times of emergency;
- govern the capital and military sites of the United States; and
- make all laws necessary to carry out the powers of Congress.

4. The last clause of Section 8 is called "the elastic clause" because it stretches the power of Congress. **Explain** why you think it was added to the Constitution.

....

....

....

....

....

....

....

5. To coin Money, regulate the Value thereof, and of foreign Coin, and fix the Standard of Weights and Measures;

6. To provide for the Punishment of counterfeiting the Securities and current Coin of the United States;

7. To establish Post Offices and post Roads;

8. To promote the Progress of Science and useful Arts, by securing, for limited Times to Authors and Inventors the exclusive Right to their respective Writings and Discoveries;

9. To constitute Tribunals inferior to the supreme Court;

10. To define and punish Piracies and Felonies committed on the high Seas, and Offences against the Law of nations;

11. To declare War, grant Letters of Marque and Reprisal, and make Rules concerning Captures on Land and Water;

12. To raise and support Armies; but no Appropriation of Money to that Use shall be for a longer Term than two Years;

13. To provide and maintain a Navy;

14. To make Rules for the Government and Regulation of the land and naval Forces;

15. To provide for calling forth the Militia to execute the Laws of the Union, suppress Insurrections and repel Invasions;

16. To provide for organizing, arming, and disciplining the Militia, and for governing such Part of them as may be employed in the Service of the United States, reserving to the States respectively the Appointment of the Officers, and the Authority of training the Militia according to the discipline prescribed by Congress;

17. To exercise exclusive Legislation in all Cases whatsoever, over such District (not exceeding ten Miles square) as may, by Cession of Particular States, and the Acceptance of Congress, become the Seat of the Government of the United States, and to exercise like Authority over all Places purchased by the Consent of the Legislature of the State in which the Same shall be, for the Erection of Forts, Magazines, Arsenals, Dockyards and other needful Buildings;—And

18. To make all Laws which shall be necessary and proper for carrying into Execution the foregoing Powers and all other Powers vested by this Constitution in the Government of the United States, or in any Department or Officer thereof.

Section 9.

1. The Migration or Importation of such Persons as any of the States now existing shall think proper to admit, shall not be prohibited by the Congress prior to the Year one thousand eight hundred and eight, but a Tax or duty may be imposed on such Importation, not exceeding ten dollars for each Person.

2. The Privilege of the Writ of Habeas Corpus shall not be suspended, unless when in Cases of Rebellion or Invasion the public safety may require it.

3. No Bill of Attainder or ex post facto Law shall be passed.

4. No Capitation, or other direct, Tax shall be laid, unless in Proportion to the Census of Enumeration herein before directed to be taken.

5. No Tax or Duty shall be laid on Articles exported from any State.

6. No Preference shall be given by any Regulation of Commerce or Revenue to the Ports of one State over those of another: nor shall Vessels bound to, or from, one State, be obliged to enter, clear or pay Duties in another.

7. No Money shall be drawn from the Treasury, but in Consequence of Appropriations made by Law; and a regular Statement and Account of the Receipts and Expenditures of all public Money shall be published from time to time.

8. No Title of Nobility shall be granted by the United States: And no Person holding any Office of Profit or Trust under them, shall, without the Consent of the Congress, accept of any present, Emolument, Office, or Title, of any kind whatever, from any King, Prince, or foreign State.

Section 10.

1. No State shall enter into any Treaty, Alliance, or Confederation; grant Letters of Marque and Reprisal; coin Money; emit Bills of Credit; make any Thing but gold and silver Coin a Tender in Payment of Debts; pass any Bill of Attainder, ex post facto Law, or Law impairing the Obligation of Contracts, or grant any Title of Nobility.

2. No State shall, without the Consent of the Congress, lay any Imposts or Duties on Imports or Exports, except what may be absolutely necessary for executing its inspection Laws; and the net Produce of all Duties and Imposts, laid by any State on Imports or Exports, shall be for the Use of the Treasury of the United States; and all such Laws shall be subject to the Revision and Control of the Congress.

SECTION 9: Powers Denied to Congress

Congress cannot

- stop slaves from being brought into the United States until 1808;

- arrest and jail people without charging them with a crime, except during an emergency;

- punish a person without a trial; punish a person for something that was not a crime when he or she did it;

- pass a direct tax, such as an income tax, unless it is in proportion to the population;

- tax goods sent out of a state;

- give the seaports of one state an advantage over another state's ports; let one state tax the ships of another state;

- spend money without passing a law to make it legal; spend money without keeping good records;

- give titles, such as king and queen, to anyone; allow federal workers to accept gifts or titles from foreign governments.

5. Explain why you think the writers included the last clause of Section 9.

....

....

....

....

....

....

Section 10: Powers Denied to the States

After listing what Congress is not allowed to do, the Constitution tells what powers are denied to the states.

State governments do not have the power to

- make treaties with foreign countries; print money; do anything that Section 9 of the Constitution says the federal government cannot;
- tax goods sent into or out of a state unless Congress agrees;
- keep armed forces or go to war; make agreements with other states or foreign governments unless Congress agrees.

6. Identify a problem that might arise if one state went to war with a foreign country.

....

....

....

....

....

Article 2 describes the executive branch.

Section 1. Office of President and Vice President

The President has power to execute, or carry out, the laws of the United States. Electors from each state choose the President. Today, these electors are called the Electoral College and are chosen by the voters.

Before 1804, the person with the most electoral votes became President. The person with the next-highest number became Vice President. The Twelfth Amendment changed this way of electing presidents.

3. No State shall, without the Consent of Congress, lay any Duty of Tonnage, keep Troops, or Ships of War in time of Peace, enter into any Agreement or Compact with another State, or with a foreign Power, or engage in War, unless actually invaded, or in such imminent Danger as will not admit of delay.

ARTICLE II
The Executive Branch

Section 1.

1. The executive Power shall be vested in a President of the United States of America. He shall hold his Office during the Term of four Years, and, together with the Vice President, chosen for the same Term, be elected as follows:

2. Each State shall appoint, in such Manner as the Legislature thereof may direct, a Number of Electors, equal to the whole Number of Senators and Representatives to which the State may be entitled in the Congress: but no Senator or Representative, or Person holding an Office of Trust or Profit, under the United States, shall be appointed an Elector.

3. The Electors shall meet in their respective States, and vote by Ballot for two Persons, of whom one at least shall not be an Inhabitant of the same State with themselves. And they shall make a List of all the Persons voted for, and of the Number of Votes for each; which List they shall sign and certify, and transmit sealed to the Seat of the Government of the United States, directed to the President of the Senate. The President of the Senate shall, in the Presence of the Senate and House of Representatives, open all the Certificates, and the Votes shall then be counted. The Person having the greatest Number of Votes shall be the President, if such Number be a majority of the whole Number of Electors appointed; and if there be more than one who have such Majority, and have an equal Number of Votes, then, the House of Representatives shall immediately choose by Ballot one of them for President; and if no Person have a Majority, then from the five highest on the List the said House shall in like Manner choose the President. But in choosing the President, the Votes shall be taken by States, the Representatives from each State having one Vote; a quorum for this Purpose shall consist of a Member or Members from two thirds of the States, and a Majority of all the States shall be necessary to a Choice. In every Case, after

the Choice of the President, the Person having the greatest Number of Votes of the Electors shall be the Vice President. But if there should remain two or more who have equal Votes, the Senate shall choose from them by Ballot the Vice President.

4. The Congress may determine the Time of choosing the Electors, and the Day on which they shall give their Votes; which Day shall be the same throughout the United States.

5. No Person except a natural born Citizen, or a Citizen of the United States, at the time of the Adoption of this Constitution, shall be eligible to the Office of President; neither shall any person be eligible to that Office who shall not have attained to the Age of thirty-five Years, and been fourteen Years a Resident within the United States.

6. In Case of the Removal of the President from Office, or of his Death, Resignation, or Inability to discharge the Powers and Duties of the said Office, the Same shall devolve on the Vice President, and the Congress may by Law provide for the Case of Removal, Death, Resignation or Inability, both of the President and Vice President, declaring what Officer shall then act as President, and such Officer shall act accordingly, until the Disability be removed, or a President shall be elected.

7. The President shall, at stated Times, receive for his Services, a Compensation, which shall neither be increased nor diminished during the Period for which he shall have been elected, and he shall not receive within that Period any other Emolument from the United States, or any of them.

8. Before he enter on the Execution of his Office, he shall take the following Oath or Affirmation: "I do solemnly swear (or affirm) that I will faithfully execute the Office of President of the United States, and will to the best of my Ability, preserve, protect and defend the Constitution of the United States."

Section 2.

1. The President shall be Commander in Chief of the Army and Navy of the United States, and of the Militia of the several States, when called into the actual Service of the United States; he may require the Opinion, in writing, of the principal Officer in each of the executive Departments, upon any Subject relating to the Duties of their respective Offices, and he shall have Power to Grant Reprieves and Pardons for Offences against the United States, except in Cases of Impeachment.

Congress decides when electors are chosen and when they vote for President. Americans now vote for the electors on Election Day, the Tuesday after the first Monday in November.

To become President, a person must be born in the United States and be a citizen. Presidents also have to be at least 35 years old and have lived in the United States for at least 14 years.

If a President dies or leaves office for any reason, the Vice President becomes President. If there is no Vice-President, Congress decides on the next President. (In 1967, the Twenty-fifth Amendment changed how these offices are filled.)

7. **Explain** why it is important to agree on how to replace the President or Vice President if one should suddenly die or leave office.

....

....

....

....

The President's salary cannot be raised or lowered while he is in office. The President cannot accept other money or gifts while in office.

Before taking office, the President must swear to preserve, protect, and defend the Constitution.

SECTION 2. Powers of the President
The President is in charge of the armed forces and National Guard. The President can ask for the advice and opinions of those in charge of government departments. (Today we call these advisers the President's Cabinet.) The President can pardon, or free, people convicted of federal crimes.

The President can make treaties, but two-thirds of the Senate must approve them. The President, with Senate approval, can name Supreme Court judges, ambassadors, and other important officials.

8. Explain why it is good for the Senate to have to approve treaties that the president makes.

....

....

....

SECTION 3. Duties of the President
From time to time, the President must talk to Congress about the condition of the nation. (Today we call this speech the State of the Union address. It is given once a year in late January.) In an emergency, the President can call on Congress to meet. The President also meets with foreign leaders, makes sure the nation's laws are carried out, and signs the orders of military officers.

SECTION 4. Removal From Office
The President, Vice-President, and other high officials can be impeached. If proved guilty, they are removed from office.

2. He shall have Power, by and with the Advice and Consent of the Senate, to make Treaties, provided two thirds of the Senators present concur; and he shall nominate, and by and with the Advice and Consent of the Senate, shall appoint Ambassadors, other public Ministers and Consuls, Judges of the supreme Court, and all other Officers of the United States, whose Appointments are not herein otherwise provided for, and which shall be established by Law: but the Congress may by Law vest the Appointment of such inferior Officers, as they think proper, in the President alone, in the Courts of Law, or in the Heads of Departments.

3. The President shall have Power to fill up all Vacancies that may happen during the Recess of the Senate, by granting Commissions which shall expire at the End of their next Session.

Section 3.

He shall from time to time give to the Congress Information of the State of the Union, and recommend to their Consideration such Measures as he shall judge necessary and expedient; he may, on extraordinary Occasions, convene both Houses, or either of them, and in Case of Disagreement between them, with Respect to the Time of Adjournment, he may adjourn them to such Time as he shall think proper; he shall receive Ambassadors and other public Ministers; he shall take Care that the Laws be faithfully executed, and shall Commission all the Officers of the United States.

Section 4.

The President, Vice President and all Civil Officers of the United States, shall be removed from Office on Impeachment for and Conviction of, Treason, Bribery, or other high Crimes and Misdemeanors.

ARTICLE III
The Judicial Branch

Section 1.

The judicial Power of the United States, shall be vested in one supreme Court, and in such inferior Courts as the Congress may from time to time ordain and establish. The Judges, both of the supreme and inferior Courts, shall hold their Offices during good Behavior, and shall, at stated Times, receive for their Services, a Compensation, which shall not be diminished during their Continuance in Office.

Section 2.

1. The judicial Power shall extend to all Cases, in Law and Equity, arising under this Constitution, the Laws of the United States, and Treaties made, or which shall be made, under their Authority;— to all Cases affecting Ambassadors, other public ministers, and Consuls;— to all Cases of Admiralty and maritime Jurisdiction;— to Controversies to which the United States shall be a Party;— to Controversies between two or more States;— between a State and Citizens of another State;— between Citizens of different States;— between Citizens of the same State claiming Lands under Grants of different States, and between a State, or the Citizens thereof, and foreign States, Citizens, or Subjects.

2. In all Cases affecting Ambassadors, other public Ministers and Consuls, and those in which a State shall be a Party, the supreme Court shall have original Jurisdiction. In all the other Cases before mentioned, the supreme Court shall have appellate Jurisdiction, both as to Law and Fact, with such Exceptions, and under such Regulations as the Congress shall make.

3. The trial of all Crimes, except in Cases of Impeachment, shall be by Jury; and such Trial shall be held in the State where the said Crimes shall have been committed; but when not committed within any State, the Trial shall be at such Place or Places as the Congress may by Law have directed.

Article 3 deals with the judicial branch.

SECTION 1. Federal Courts
The judges of the Supreme Court and other federal courts have the power to make decisions in courts of law. If they act properly, federal judges hold their offices for life.

9. Do you think it's a good idea that federal judges hold their offices for life? **Explain** your answer.

....

....

....

....

....

....

SECTION 2. Powers of Federal Courts
Federal Courts have legal power over
- laws made under the Constitution
- treaties made with foreign nations
- cases occurring at sea
- cases involving the federal government
- cases involving states or citizens of different states
- cases involving foreign citizens or governments

Only the Supreme Court can judge cases involving ambassadors, government officials, or states. Other cases begin in lower courts, but they can be appealed, or reviewed, by the Supreme Court.

In criminal cases other than impeachment, trials are held in the state in which the crime took place. A jury decides the case.

SECTION 3. The Crime of Treason

Treason is waging war against the United States or helping its enemies. To be found guilty of treason, a person must confess to the crime; or, two people must have seen the crime committed.

10. Identify the three branches of the federal government described in Articles 1, 2, and 3.

....

....

....

Congress decides the punishment for a traitor. The traitor's family cannot also be punished for the crime if they are innocent.

Article 4 deals with relationships between the states.

SECTION 1. Recognition by Each State

Each state must respect the laws and court decisions of the other states.

SECTION 2. Rights of Citizens in Other States

Citizens keep all their rights when visiting other states.

A person charged with a crime who flees to another state must be returned to the state in which the crime took place.

A slave who escapes to another state must be returned to his or her owner. (The Thirteenth Amendment outlawed slavery.)

SECTION 3. New States

Congress may let new states join the United States. New states cannot be formed from the land of existing states unless Congress approves.

Congress has the power to make laws to govern territories of the United States.

Section 3.

1. Treason against the United States shall consist only in levying War against them, or in adhering to their Enemies, giving them Aid and Comfort. No Person shall be convicted of Treason unless on the Testimony of two Witnesses to the same overt Act, or on Confession in open Court.
2. The Congress shall have Power to declare the Punishment of Treason, but no Attainder of Treason shall work Corruption of Blood, or Forfeiture except during the Life of the Person attainted.

ARTICLE IV
Relations Among the States

Section 1.

Full Faith and Credit shall be given in each State to the public Acts, Records, and judicial Proceedings of every other State. And the Congress may by general Laws prescribe the Manner in which such Acts, Records and Proceedings shall be proved, and the Effect thereof.

Section 2.

1. The Citizens of each State shall be entitled to all Privileges and Immunities of Citizens in the several States.
2. A Person charged in any State with Treason, Felony, or other Crime, who shall flee from justice, and be found in another State, shall on Demand of the executive Authority of the State from which he fled, be delivered up, to be removed to the State having Jurisdiction of the Crime.
3. No Person held to Service or Labor in one State, under the Laws thereof, escaping into another, shall, in Consequence of any Law or Regulation therein, be discharged from Service or Labor, but shall be delivered up on Claim of the Party to whom such Service or Labor may be due.

Section 3.

1. New States may be admitted by the Congress into this Union; but no new State shall be formed or erected within the Jurisdiction of any other State; nor any State be formed by the Junction of two or more States, or Parts of States, without the Consent of the Legislatures of the States concerned as well as of the Congress.

2. The Congress shall have Power to dispose of and make all needful Rules and Regulations respecting the Territory or other Property belonging to the United States; and nothing in this Constitution shall be so construed as to Prejudice any Claims of the United States, or of any particular State.

Section 4.

The United States shall guarantee to every State in this Union a Republican Form of Government, and shall protect each of them against Invasion; and on Application of the Legislature, or of the Executive (when the Legislature cannot be convened) against domestic Violence.

ARTICLE V
Amending the Constitution

The Congress, whenever two thirds of both Houses shall deem it necessary, shall propose Amendments to this Constitution, or, on the Application of the Legislatures of two thirds of the several States, shall call a Convention for proposing Amendments, which, in either Case, shall be valid to all Intents and Purposes, as Part of this Constitution, when ratified by the Legislatures of three fourths of the several States, or by Conventions in three fourths thereof, as the one or the other Mode of Ratification may be proposed by the Congress; Provided that no Amendment which may be made prior to the Year One thousand eight hundred and eight shall in any Manner affect the first and fourth Clauses in the Ninth section of the first Article; and that no State, without its Consent, shall be deprived of its equal Suffrage in the Senate.

ARTICLE VI
Debts, Federal Supremacy, Oaths of Office

Section 1.

All Debts contracted and Engagements entered into, before the Adoption of this Constitution, shall be as valid against the United States under this Constitution, as under the Confederation.

Section 2.

This Constitution, and the Laws of the United States which shall be made in Pursuance thereof; and all Treaties made, or which shall be made, under the Authority of the United States, shall be the supreme Law of the Land; and the Judges in every State shall be bound thereby, anything in the constitution or Laws of any State to the Contrary notwithstanding.

11. There were only thirteen states when the Constitution was written. Do you think the framers expected the United States to grow in size? **Explain** your answer.

....

....

....

....

....

SECTION 3. Supporting the Constitution

Federal and state officials must promise to support the Constitution. A person's religion cannot disqualify him or her from holding office. Nine of the thirteen states must approve the Constitution for it to become the law of the land.

Article 7 deals with ratifying the Constitution. On September 17, 1787, twelve years after the Declaration of Independence, everyone at the Constitutional Convention agreed that the Constitution was complete.

The delegates to the Constitutional Convention signed their names below the Constitution to show they approved of it.

12. "The power under the Constitution will always be in the people," wrote George Washington in 1787. **Explain** what you think he meant.

....
....
....
....
....
....
....

Section 3.

The Senators and Representatives before mentioned, and the Members of the several State legislatures, and all executive and judicial Officers, both of the United States and of the several States, shall be bound by Oath or Affirmation, to support this Constitution; but no religious Test shall ever be required as a Qualification to any Office or public Trust under the United States.

ARTICLE VII
Ratifying the Constitution

The ratification of the Conventions of nine States, shall be sufficient for the Establishment of this Constitution between the States so ratifying the same.

Done in Convention by the Unanimous Consent of the States present the Seventeenth Day of September in the Year of our Lord one thousand seven hundred and Eighty-seven and of the Independence of the United States of America the twelfth. In witness whereof We have hereunto subscribed our Names.

Attest:
William Jackson, *Secretary*
George Washington, *President and Deputy from Virginia*

New Hampshire
John Langdon
Nicholas Gilman

Massachusetts
Nathaniel Gorham
Rufus King

Connecticut
William Samuel Johnson
Roger Sherman

New York
Alexander Hamilton

New Jersey
William Livingston
David Brearley
William Paterson
Jonathan Dayton

Pennsylvania
Benjamin Franklin
Thomas Mifflin
Robert Morris
George Clymer
Thomas FitzSimons
Jared Ingersoll
James Wilson
Gouverneur Morris

Delaware
George Read
Gunning Bedford, Jr.
John Dickinson
Richard Bassett
Jacob Broom

Maryland
James McHenry
Dan of St. Thomas Jenifer
Daniel Carroll

Virginia
John Blair
James Madison, Jr.

North Carolina
William Blount
Richard Dobbs Spaight
Hugh Williamson

South Carolina
John Rutledge
Charles Cotesworth Pinckney
Charles Pinckney
Pierce Butler

Georgia
William Few
Abraham Baldwin

AMENDMENTS

Amendment 1

Congress shall make no law respecting an establishment of religion, or prohibiting the free exercise thereof, or abridging the freedom of speech, or of the press; or the right of the people peaceably to assemble, and to petition the Government for a redress of grievances.

Amendment 2

A well-regulated Militia being necessary to the security of a free State, the right of the people to keep and bear Arms, shall not be infringed.

Amendment 3

No Soldier shall, in time of peace be quartered in any house, without the consent of the Owner, nor, in time of war, but in a manner to be prescribed by law.

Amendment 4

The right of the people to be secure in their persons, houses, papers, and effects, against unreasonable searches and seizures, shall not be violated, and no Warrants shall issue, but upon probable cause, supported by Oath or affirmation, and particularly describing the place to be searched, and the persons or things to be seized.

Amendment 5

No person shall be held to answer for a capital, or otherwise infamous crime, unless on a presentment or indictment of a Grand Jury, except in cases arising in the land or naval forces, or in the Militia, when in actual service in time of War, or public danger; nor shall any person be subject for the same offence to be twice put in jeopardy of life or limb; nor shall be compelled in any criminal case to be a witness against himself, nor be deprived of life, liberty, or property, without due process of law; nor shall private property be taken for public use, without just compensation.

The first ten amendments to the Constitution are called the Bill of Rights.

First Amendment—1791
Freedom of Religion and Speech
Congress cannot set up an official religion or stop people from practicing a religion. Congress cannot stop people or newspapers from saying what they want. People can gather peacefully to complain to the government.

Second Amendment—1791
Right to Have Firearms
People have the right to own and carry guns.

Third Amendment—1791
Right Not to House Soldiers
During peacetime, citizens do not have to house soldiers.

Fourth Amendment—1791
Search and Arrest Warrant
People or homes cannot be searched without reason. A search warrant is needed to search a house.

Fifth Amendment—1791
Rights of People Accused of Crimes
Only a grand jury can accuse people of a serious crime. No one can be tried twice for the same crime if found not guilty. People cannot be forced to testify against themselves.

13. Identify the amendment number that protects each right.

_____ to speak freely

_____ to be protected against unreasonable searches

_____ to not be put on trial twice for the same crime

Sixth Amendment—1791
Right to a Jury Trial

People have the right to a fast trial by a jury and to hear the charges and evidence against them. They also have the right to a lawyer and to call witnesses in their own defense.

Seventh Amendment—1791
Right to a Jury Trial in a Civil Case

In a civil, or noncriminal case, a person also has the right to a trial by jury.

Eighth Amendment—1791
Protection from Unfair Punishment

A person accused of a crime cannot be forced to pay a very high bail. A person convicted of a crime cannot be asked to pay an unfairly high fine or be punished in a cruel or unusual way.

Ninth Amendment—1791
Other Rights

People have other rights that are not specifically mentioned in the Constitution.

Tenth Amendment—1791
Powers of the States and the People

Some powers are not given to the federal government or denied to states. These rights belong to the states or to the people.

Eleventh Amendment—1795
Limits on Rights to Sue States

People from another state or foreign country cannot sue a state.

Amendment 6

In all criminal prosecutions, the accused shall enjoy the right to a speedy and public trial, by an impartial jury of the State and district wherein the crime shall have been committed, which district shall have been previously ascertained by law, and to be informed of the nature and cause of the accusation; to be confronted with the witnesses against him; to have compulsory process for obtaining witnesses in his favor, and to have the Assistance of Counsel for his defense.

Amendment 7

In Suits at common law, where the value in controversy shall exceed twenty dollars, the right of trial by jury shall be preserved, and no fact tried by a jury, shall be otherwise re-examined in any Court of the United States, than according to the rules of the common law.

Amendment 8

Excessive bail shall not be required, nor excessive fines imposed, nor cruel and unusual punishment inflicted.

Amendment 9

The enumeration in the Constitution, of certain rights, shall not be construed to deny or disparage others retained by the people.

Amendment 10

The powers not delegated to the United States by the Constitution, nor prohibited by it to the States, are reserved to the States respectively, or to the people.

Amendment 11

The Judicial power of the United States shall not be construed to extend to any suit in law or equity, commenced or prosecuted against one of the United States by Citizens of another State, or by Citizens or Subjects of any Foreign State.

Amendment 12

The Electors shall meet in their respective States and vote by ballot for President and Vice President, one of whom, at least, shall not be an inhabitant of the same State with themselves; they shall name in their ballots the person voted for as President, and in distinct ballots the person voted for as Vice President, and they shall make distinct lists of all persons voted for as President, and of all persons voted for as Vice President, and of the number of votes for each, which lists they shall sign and certify, and transmit sealed to the seat of the government of the United States, directed to the President of the Senate;— The President of the Senate shall, in the presence of the Senate and the House of Representatives, open all the certificates and the votes shall then be counted;— the person having the greatest Number of votes for President shall be the President, if such number be a majority of the whole number of Electors appointed; and if no person have such a majority, then, from the persons having the highest numbers not exceeding three on the list of those voted for as President, the House of Representatives shall choose immediately, by ballot, the President. But in choosing the President, the votes shall be taken by States, the representation from each State having one vote; a quorum for this purpose shall consist of a member or members from two thirds of the States, and a majority of all the States shall be necessary to a choice. And if the House of Representatives shall not choose a President whenever the right of choice shall devolve upon them, before the fourth day of March next following, then the Vice President shall act as President, as in case of death or other constitutional disability of the President. The person having the greatest number of votes as Vice President, shall be the Vice President, if such number be a majority of the whole number of Electors appointed, and if no person have a majority, then from the two highest numbers on the list, the Senate shall choose the Vice President; a quorum for the purpose shall consist of two thirds of the whole number of Senators, a majority of the whole number shall be necessary to a choice. But no person constitutionally ineligible to the office of President shall be eligible to that of Vice-President of the United States.

Twelfth Amendment—1804
Election of President and Vice President

This Amendment changed the way the Electoral College chooses the President and Vice President. Before this amendment, candidates for President and Vice President ran separately, and each elector had two votes—one for President and one for Vice President. The candidate receiving the most votes became President, and the runner-up became Vice President.

Under this Amendment, a candidate for President and a candidate for Vice President must run together. Each elector has only one vote, and the pair of candidates that receives more than half the electoral votes become the President and Vice President. If no one receives a majority of the electoral votes, the House of Representatives votes for the President from a list of the top three vote-getters. In this situation, each state has one vote, and the candidate must receive more than half of the votes to become President.

If the Representatives fail to elect a President by March 4 (later changed to January 20), the Vice President serves as President. If no candidate receives at least half the electoral votes for Vice President, the names of the two top vote getters are sent to the Senate. The Senators then vote on the names, and the person receiving more than half the votes becomes Vice President.

Thirteenth Amendment—1865
Abolition of Slavery

The United States outlaws slavery.

Congress can pass any laws that are needed to carry out this amendment.

Fourteenth Amendment—1868
Rights of Citizens

People born in the United States are citizens of both the United States and of the state in which they live. States must treat their citizens equally. States cannot deny their citizens the rights outlined in the Bill of Rights.

This section of the amendment made former slaves citizens of both the United States and their home state.

Based on its population, each state has a certain number of Representatives in Congress. The number of Representatives from a state might be lowered, however, if the state does not let certain citizens vote.

This section tried to force states in the South to let former slaves vote.

14. Explain why a state would not want to have its number of Representatives in Congress cut.

....

....

....

....

....

Amendment 13

Section 1. Neither slavery nor involuntary servitude, except as a punishment for crime whereof the party shall have been duly convicted, shall exist within the United States, or any place subject to their jurisdiction.

Section 2. Congress shall have power to enforce this article by appropriate legislation.

Amendment 14

Section 1. All persons born or naturalized in the United States and subject to the jurisdiction thereof, are citizens of the United States and of the State wherein they reside. No State shall make or enforce any law which shall abridge the privileges or immunities of citizens of the United States; nor shall any State deprive any person of life, liberty, or property, without due process of law; nor deny to any person within its jurisdiction the equal protection of the laws.

Section 2. Representatives shall be apportioned among the several States according to their respective numbers, counting the whole number of persons in each State, excluding Indians not taxed. But when the right to vote at any election for the choice of electors for President and Vice President of the United States, Representatives in Congress, the Executive and Judicial officers of a State, or the members of the Legislature thereof, is denied to any of the male inhabitants of such State, being twenty-one years of age and citizens of the United States, or in any way abridged, except for participation in rebellion, or other crime, the basis of representation therein shall be reduced in the proportion which the number of such male citizens shall bear to the whole number of male citizens twenty-one years of age in such State.

Section 3. No person shall be a Senator or Representative in Congress, or elector of President and Vice President, or hold any office, civil or military, under the United States, or under any State, who, having previously taken an oath, as a member of Congress, or as an officer of the United States, or as a member of any State legislature, or as an executive or judicial officer of any State, to support the Constitution of the United States, shall have engaged in insurrection or rebellion against the same, or given aid or comfort to the enemies thereof. But Congress may, by a vote of two thirds of each House, remove such disability.

Section 4. The validity of the public debt of the United States, authorized by law, including debts incurred for payment of pensions and bounties for services in suppressing insurrection or rebellion, shall not be questioned. But neither the United States nor any State shall assume or pay any debt or obligation incurred in aid of insurrection or rebellion against the United States, or any claim for the loss or emancipation of any slave; but all such debts, obligations and claims shall be held illegal and void.

Section 5. The Congress shall have power to enforce, by appropriate legislation, the provisions of this article.

Amendment 15

Section 1. The right of citizens of the United States to vote shall not be denied or abridged by the United States or by any State on account of race, color, or previous condition of servitude.

Section 2. The Congress shall have power to enforce this article by appropriate legislation.

Officials who took part in the Civil War against the United States cannot hold federal or state office. Congress can remove this provision by a two-thirds vote.

The United States will pay back the money it borrowed to fight the Civil War. The money that the South borrowed to fight the Civil War will not be paid back to lenders. The former owners of slaves will not be paid for the slaves that were set free.

Congress can pass any necessary laws to enforce this article.

15. Identify two ways in which the Fourteenth Amendment tended to punish those who rebelled against the United States.

....

....

....

....

....

....

....

....

....

**Fifteenth Amendment—1870
Voting Rights**
The federal and state government cannot stop people from voting based on race or color. Former slaves must be allowed to vote.

Sixteenth Amendment—1913
Income Tax

Congress has the power to collect an income tax regardless of the population of a state. (Originally, Section 9 of Article 1 of the Constitution had denied this power to Congress.)

Seventeenth Amendment—1913
Direct Election of Senators

The voters of each state will elect their senators directly. (Originally, Article 1, Section 3 said state legislatures would elect senators.)

A state can hold a special election to fill an empty Senate seat. Until then, the governor can appoint a senator to fill an empty seat.

Eighteenth Amendment—1919
Prohibition

Making, importing, or selling alcoholic drinks is illegal in the United States. This was called Prohibition because the Amendment prohibited, or outlawed, the use of alcohol.

Congress and the states can make any laws to prohibit alcohol.

This amendment becomes part of the Constitution if it is approved within seven years.

This Amendment was repealed, or cancelled, in 1933 by the Twenty-first Amendment.

16. **Identify** the amendment number that did each of the following:

_____ let the Federal Government collect income tax

_____ guaranteed voting rights for African Americans

_____ outlawed the sale of alcohol

_____ abolished slavery

_____ let voters elect their senators

Amendment 16

The Congress shall have power to lay and collect taxes on incomes, from whatever source derived, without apportionment among the several States, and without regard to any census or enumeration.

Amendment 17

The Senate of the United States shall be composed of two Senators from each State, elected by the people thereof, for six years; and each Senator shall have one vote. The electors in each State shall have the qualifications requisite for electors of the most numerous branch of the State legislatures.

When vacancies happen in the representation of any State in the Senate, the executive authority of such State shall issue writs of election to fill such vacancies: Provided, That the legislature of any State may empower the executive thereof to make temporary appointments until the people fill the vacancies by election as the legislature may direct.

This amendment shall not be so construed as to affect the election or term of any Senator chosen before it becomes valid as part of the Constitution.

Amendment 18

Section 1. After one year from the ratification of this article the manufacture, sale, or transportation of intoxicating liquors within, the importation thereof into, or the exportation thereof from the United States and all territory subject to the jurisdiction thereof for beverage purposes is hereby prohibited.

Section 2. The Congress and the several States shall have concurrent power to enforce this article by appropriate legislation.

Section 3. This article shall be inoperative unless it shall have been ratified as an amendment to the Constitution by the legislatures of the several States, as provided in the Constitution, within seven years of the date of the submission hereof to the States by Congress.

Amendment 19

The right of citizens of the United States to vote shall not be denied or abridged by the United States or by any State on account of sex.

Congress shall have power to enforce this article by appropriate legislation.

Amendment 20

Section 1. The terms of the President and Vice President shall end at noon on the 20th day of January, and the terms of Senators and Representatives at noon on the 3d day of January, of the years in which such terms would have ended if this article had not been ratified; and the terms of their successors shall then begin.

Section 2. The Congress shall assemble at least once in every year, and such meeting shall begin at noon on the 3d day of January, unless they shall by law appoint a different day.

Section 3. If, at the time fixed for the beginning of the term of the President, the President elect shall have died, the Vice President elect shall become President. If a President shall not have been chosen before the time fixed for the beginning of his term, or if the President-elect shall have failed to qualify, then the Vice President elect shall act as President until a President shall have qualified; and the Congress may by law provide for the case wherein neither a President elect nor a Vice President elect shall have qualified, declaring who shall then act as President, or the manner in which one who is to act shall be selected, and such person shall act accordingly until a President or Vice President shall have qualified.

Section 4. The Congress may by law provide for the case of the death of any of the persons from whom the House of Representatives may choose a President whenever the right of choice shall have devolved upon them, and for the case of the death of any of the persons from whom the Senate may choose a Vice President whenever the right of choice shall have devolved upon them.

Section 5. Sections 1 and 2 shall take effect on the 15th day of October following the ratification of this article.

Section 6. This article shall be inoperative unless it shall have been ratified as an amendment to the Constitution by the legislatures of three fourths of the several States within seven years from the date of its submission.

Twenty-first Amendment—1933
Repeal of Prohibition

The Eighteenth Amendment, which outlawed alcohol, is no longer in effect.

Any state may pass laws to prohibit alcohol.

17. How long was the Eighteenth Amendment in effect in the United States?

....

Twenty-second Amendment—1951
Limit on Terms of the President

A President can only be elected to the office for two terms (eight years). If a President serves more than two years of the last President's term, then the President may only be reelected once.

18. Do you think a President should be limited to just two terms in office? **Explain** why or why not.

....

....

....

....

....

....

....

Amendment 21

Section 1. The eighteenth article of amendment to the Constitution of the United States is hereby repealed.

Section 2. The transportation or importation into any State, Territory, or possession of the United States for delivery or use therein of intoxicating liquors, in violation of the laws thereof, is hereby prohibited.

Section 3. This article shall be inoperative unless it shall have been ratified as an amendment to the Constitution by conventions in the several States, as provided in the Constitution, within seven years from the date of the submission hereof to the States by the Congress.

Amendment 22

Section 1. No person shall be elected to the office of the President more than twice, and no person who has held the office of President, or acted as President, for more than two years of a term to which some other person was elected President shall be elected to the office of the President more than once. But this Article shall not apply to any person holding the office of President, when this Article was proposed by the Congress, and shall not prevent any person who may be holding the office of President, or acting as President, during the term within which this Article becomes operative from holding the office of President or acting as President during the remainder of such term.

Section 2. This article shall be inoperative unless it shall have been ratified as an amendment to the Constitution by the legislatures of three fourths of the several states within seven years from the date of its submission to the States by the Congress.

Amendment 23

Section 1. The District constituting the seat of Government of the United States shall appoint in such manner as the Congress may direct:

A number of electors of President and Vice President equal to the whole number of Senators and Representatives in Congress to which the District would be entitled if it were a State, but in no event more than the least populous State; they shall be in addition to those appointed by the States, they shall be considered, for the purposes of the election of President and Vice President, to be electors appointed by a State; and they shall meet in the District and perform such duties as provided by the twelfth article of amendment.

Amendment 24

Section 1. The right of citizens of the United States to vote in any primary or other election for President or Vice President, for electors for President or Vice President, or for Senator or Representative in Congress, shall not be denied or abridged by the United States or any State by reason of failure to pay any poll tax or other tax.

Section 2. The Congress shall have power to enforce this article by appropriate legislation.

Amendment 25

Section 1. In case of the removal of the President from office or of his death or resignation, the Vice President shall become President.

Section 2. Whenever there is a vacancy in the office of the Vice President, the President shall nominate a Vice President who shall take office upon confirmation by a majority vote of both Houses of Congress.

Section 3. Whenever the President transmits to the President pro tempore of the Senate and the Speaker of the House of Representatives his written declaration that he is unable to discharge the powers and duties of his office, and until he transmits to them a written declaration to the contrary, such powers and duties shall be discharged by the Vice President as Acting President.

Twenty-third Amendment—1961
Presidential Elections for District of Columbia

People living in Washington, D.C., have the right to vote in presidential elections. Washington, D.C., can never have more electoral votes than the state with the smallest number of people.

Twenty-fourth Amendment—1964
Outlawing of Poll Tax

No one can be stopped from voting in a federal election because he or she has not paid a poll tax or any other kind of tax.

Congress can make laws to carry out this amendment.

Twenty-fifth Amendment—1967
Presidential Succession

If the President dies or resigns, the Vice President becomes President.

If the office of Vice President is empty, the President appoints a new Vice President.

When the President is unable to carry out the duties of the office, Congress should be informed. The Vice President then serves as Acting President. The President may resume the duties of the office after informing Congress.

If the Vice President and half the President's top advisers, or Cabinet, inform Congress that the President cannot carry out his or her duties, the Vice President becomes Acting President. If the President informs Congress that he or she is able to carry out these duties, the President returns to office. However, after four days, if the Vice President and half the Cabinet again tell Congress that the President cannot carry out his or her duties, the President does not return to office. Instead, Congress must decide within 21 days whether the President is able to carry out his or her duties. If two thirds of Congress votes that the President cannot continue in office, the Vice President becomes Acting President. If two thirds do not vote in this way, the President remains in office.

People who are eighteen years old have the right to vote in federal and state elections.

Congress can pass laws to carry out this amendment.

Over the years, amendments to the Constitution have improved our democracy by expanding voting rights to more and more citizens.

19. Identify the number of the amendment that:

_____ gave votes to women

_____ gave votes to citizens in Washington, D.C.

_____ gave votes to eighteen-year-olds

_____ outlawed taxes that blocked voting

**Twenty-seventh Amendment—1992
Limits on Congressional Salary Changes**

Laws that increase the salaries of Senators and Representatives do not take effect immediately. They take effect after the next election of the House of Representatives.

Section 4. Whenever the Vice President and a majority of either the principal officers of the executive departments or of such other body as Congress may by law provide, transmit to the President pro tempore of the Senate and the Speaker of the House of Representatives their written declaration that the President is unable to discharge the powers and duties of his office, the Vice President shall immediately assume the powers and duties of the office as Acting President.

Thereafter, when the President transmits to the President pro tempore of the Senate and the Speaker of the House of Representatives his written declaration that no inability exists, he shall resume the powers and duties of his office unless the Vice President and a majority of either the principal officers of the executive department or of such other body as Congress may by law provide, transmit within four days to the President pro tempore of the Senate and the Speaker of the House of Representatives their written declaration that the President is unable to discharge the powers and duties of his office. Thereupon Congress shall decide the issue, assembling within forty-eight hours for that purpose if not in session. If the Congress, within twenty-one days after receipt of the latter written declaration, or, if Congress is not in session, within twenty-one days after Congress is required to assemble, determines by two-thirds vote of both Houses that the President is unable to discharge the powers and duties of his office, the Vice President shall continue to discharge the same as Acting President; otherwise, the President shall resume the powers and duties of his office.

Amendment 26

Section 1. The right of citizens of the United States, who are eighteen years of age or older, to vote shall not be denied or abridged by the United States or by any State on account of age.

Section 2. The Congress shall have the power to enforce this article by appropriate legislation.

27th Amendment

No law varying the compensation for the services of the Senators and Representatives, shall take effect, until an election of Representatives shall have intervened.

Texas, Physical

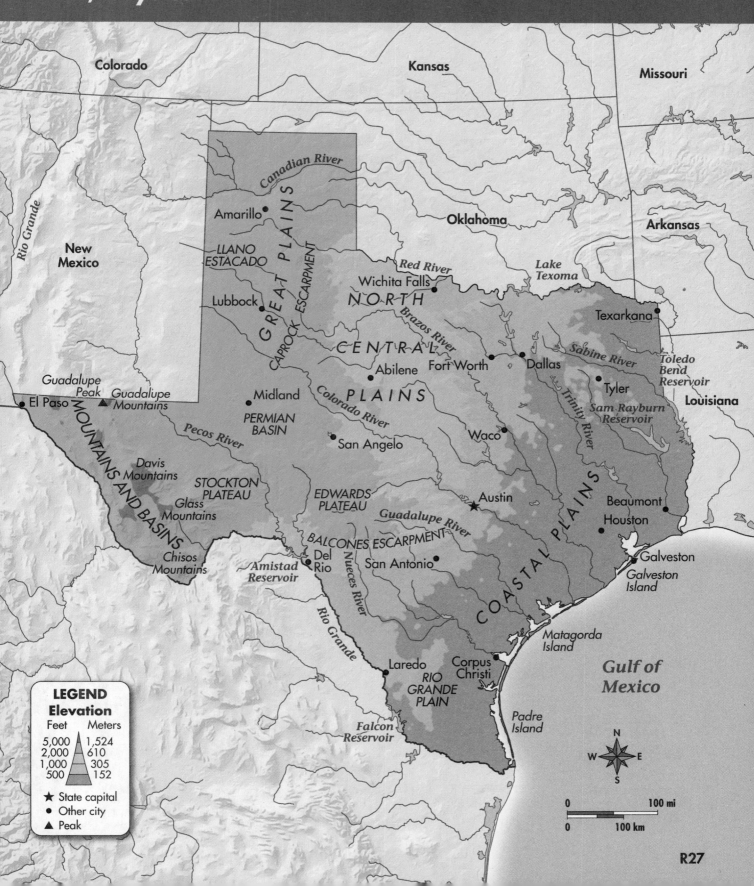

Colorado

Kansas

Missouri

Rio Grande

New Mexico

Oklahoma

Arkansas

Canadian River

Amarillo

LLANO ESTACADO

GREAT PLAINS

Lubbock

CAPROCK ESCARPMENT

Red River

Wichita Falls

NORTH

Lake Texoma

Texarkana

Brazos River

Sabine River

Toledo Bend Reservoir

CENTRAL

Abilene

Fort Worth

Dallas

Tyler

Sam Rayburn Reservoir

Louisiana

PLAINS

Guadalupe Peak

Guadalupe Mountains

El Paso

Midland

PERMIAN BASIN

Colorado River

Trinity River

Pecos River

San Angelo

Waco

MOUNTAINS AND BASINS

Davis Mountains

STOCKTON PLATEAU

Glass Mountains

EDWARDS PLATEAU

Austin

Beaumont

Houston

COASTAL PLAINS

Chisos Mountains

Amistad Reservoir

Del Rio

BALCONES ESCARPMENT

Guadalupe River

San Antonio

Galveston

Galveston Island

Nueces River

Rio Grande

Laredo

Corpus Christi

Matagorda Island

RIO GRANDE PLAIN

Gulf of Mexico

Falcon Reservoir

Padre Island

LEGEND
Elevation

Feet	Meters
5,000	1,524
2,000	610
1,000	305
500	152

★ State capital
● Other city
▲ Peak

N
W   E
S

0   100 mi

0   100 km

R27

Texas, Counties

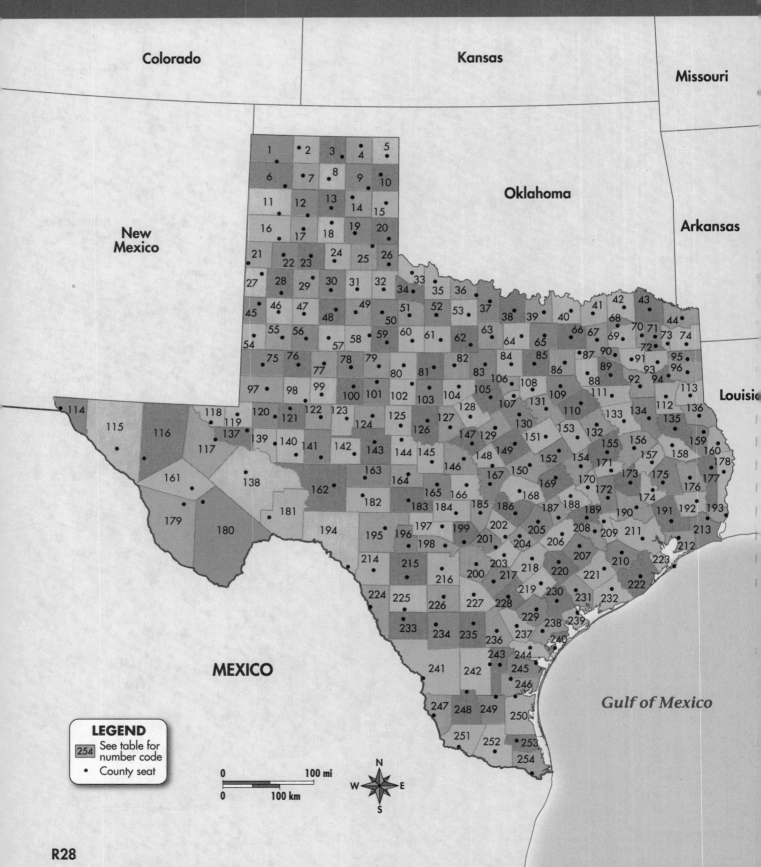

County	County Seat	Number
Anderson	Palestine	133
Andrews	Andrews	97
Angelina	Lufkin	158
Aransas	Rockport	240
Archer	Archer City	53
Armstrong	Claude	18
Atascosa	Jourdanton	227
Austin	Bellville	208
Bailey	Muleshoe	27
Bandera	Bandera	198
Bastrop	Bastrop	205
Baylor	Seymour	52
Bee	Beeville	237
Bell	Belton	150
Bexar	San Antonio	200
Blanco	Johnson City	185
Borden	Gail	77
Bosque	Meridian	130
Bowie	Boston	44
Brazoria	Angleton	222
Brazos	Bryan	170
Brewster	Alpine	180
Briscoe	Silverton	24
Brooks	Falfurrias	249
Brown	Brownwood	127
Burleson	Caldwell	188
Burnet	Burnet	167
Caldwell	Lockhart	204
Calhoun	Port Lavaca	239
Callahan	Baird	103
Cameron	Brownsville	254
Camp	Pittsburg	72
Carson	Panhandle	13
Cass	Linden	74
Castro	Dimmitt	22
Chambers	Anahuac	212
Cherokee	Rusk	134
Childress	Childress	26
Clay	Henrietta	37
Cochran	Morton	45
Coke	Robert Lee	124
Coleman	Coleman	126
Collin	McKinney	66
Collingsworth	Wellington	20
Colorado	Columbus	207
Comal	New Braunfels	201
Comanche	Comanche	128
Concho	Paint Rock	144
Cooke	Gainesville	39
Coryell	Gatesville	149
Cottle	Paducah	32
Crane	Crane	139
Crockett	Ozona	162
Crosby	Crosbyton	48
Culberson	Van Horn	116
Dallam	Dalhart	1
Dallas	Dallas	86
Dawson	Lamesa	76
Deaf Smith	Hereford	16
Delta	Cooper	68
Denton	Denton	65
DeWitt	Cuero	219
Dickens	Dickens	49
Dimmit	Carrizo Springs	233
Donley	Clarendon	19
Duval	San Diego	242
Eastland	Eastland	104
Ector	Odessa	120
Edwards	Rocksprings	195
Ellis	Waxahachie	109
El Paso	El Paso	114
Erath	Stephenville	105
Falls	Marlin	152
Fannin	Bonham	41
Fayette	La Grange	206
Fisher	Roby	79
Floyd	Floydada	30
Foard	Crowell	34
Fort Bend	Richmond	210
Franklin	Mount Vernon	70
Freestone	Fairfield	132
Frio	Pearsall	226
Gaines	Seminole	75
Galveston	Galveston	223
Garza	Post	57
Gillespie	Fredericksburg	184
Glasscock	Garden City	122
Goliad	Goliad	229
Gonzales	Gonzales	218
Gray	Pampa	14
Grayson	Sherman	40
Gregg	Longview	94
Grimes	Anderson	172
Guadalupe	Seguin	203
Hale	Plainview	29
Hall	Memphis	25
Hamilton	Hamilton	129
Hansford	Spearman	3
Hardeman	Quanah	33
Hardin	Kountze	192
Harris	Houston	211
Harrison	Marshall	96
Hartley	Channing	6
Haskell	Haskell	60
Hays	San Marcos	202
Hemphill	Canadian	10
Henderson	Athens	111
Hidalgo	Edinburg	252
Hill	Hillsboro	131
Hockley	Levelland	46
Hood	Granbury	106
Hopkins	Sulphur Springs	69
Houston	Crockett	156
Howard	Big Spring	99
Hudspeth	Sierra Blanca	115
Hunt	Greenville	67
Hutchinson	Stinnett	8
Irion	Mertzon	142
Jack	Jacksboro	63
Jackson	Edna	231
Jasper	Jasper	177
Jeff Davis	Fort Davis	161
Jefferson	Beaumont	213
Jim Hogg	Hebbronville	248
Jim Wells	Alice	243
Johnson	Cleburne	108
Jones	Anson	80
Karnes	Karnes City	228
Kaufman	Kaufman	88
Kendall	Boerne	199
Kenedy	Sarita	250
Kent	Jayton	58
Kerr	Kerrville	197
Kimble	Junction	183
King	Guthrie	50
Kinney	Brackettville	214
Kleberg	Kingsville	246
Knox	Benjamin	51
Lamar	Paris	42
Lamb	Littlefield	28
Lampasas	Lampasas	148
La Salle	Cotulla	234
Lavaca	Hallettsville	220
Lee	Giddings	187
Leon	Centerville	155
Liberty	Liberty	191
Limestone	Groesbeck	153
Lipscomb	Lipscomb	5
Live Oak	George West	236
Llano	Llano	166
Loving	Mentone	118
Lubbock	Lubbock	47
Lynn	Tahoka	56
Madison	Madisonville	171
Marion	Jefferson	95
Martin	Stanton	98
Mason	Mason	165
Matagorda	Bay City	232
Maverick	Eagle Pass	224
McCulloch	Brady	145
McLennan	Waco	151
McMullen	Tilden	235
Medina	Hondo	216
Menard	Menard	164
Midland	Midland	121
Milam	Cameron	169
Mills	Goldthwaite	147
Mitchell	Colorado City	100
Montague	Montague	38
Montgomery	Conroe	190
Moore	Dumas	7
Morris	Daingerfield	73
Motley	Matador	31
Nacogdoches	Nacogdoches	135
Navarro	Corsicana	110
Newton	Newton	178
Nolan	Sweetwater	101
Nueces	Corpus Christi	245
Ochiltree	Perryton	4
Oldham	Vega	11
Orange	Orange	193
Palo Pinto	Palo Pinto	83
Panola	Carthage	113
Parker	Weatherford	84
Parmer	Farwell	21
Pecos	Fort Stockton	138
Polk	Livingston	175
Potter	Amarillo	12
Presidio	Marfa	179
Rains	Emory	90
Randall	Canyon	17
Reagan	Big Lake	141
Real	Leakey	196
Red River	Clarksville	43
Reeves	Pecos	117
Refugio	Refugio	238
Roberts	Miami	9
Robertson	Franklin	154
Rockwall	Rockwall	87
Runnels	Ballinger	125
Rusk	Henderson	112
Sabine	Hemphill	160
San Augustine	San Augustine	159
San Jacinto	Coldspring	174
San Patricio	Sinton	244
San Saba	San Saba	146
Schleicher	Eldorado	163
Scurry	Snyder	78
Shackelford	Albany	81
Shelby	Center	136
Sherman	Stratford	2
Smith	Tyler	92
Somervell	Glen Rose	107
Starr	Rio Grande City	251
Stephens	Breckenridge	82
Sterling	Sterling City	123
Stonewall	Aspermont	59
Sutton	Sonora	182
Swisher	Tulia	23
Tarrant	Fort Worth	85
Taylor	Abilene	102
Terrell	Sanderson	181
Terry	Brownfield	55
Throckmorton	Throckmorton	61
Titus	Mount Pleasant	71
Tom Green	San Angelo	143
Travis	Austin	186
Trinity	Groveton	157
Tyler	Woodville	176
Upshur	Gilmer	93
Upton	Rankin	140
Uvalde	Uvalde	215
Val Verde	Del Rio	194
Van Zandt	Canton	89
Victoria	Victoria	230
Walker	Huntsville	173
Waller	Hempstead	209
Ward	Monahans	137
Washington	Brenham	189
Webb	Laredo	241
Wharton	Wharton	221
Wheeler	Wheeler	15
Wichita	Wichita Falls	36
Wilbarger	Vernon	35
Willacy	Raymondville	253
Williamson	Georgetown	168
Wilson	Floresville	217
Winkler	Kermit	119
Wise	Decatur	64
Wood	Quitman	91
Yoakum	Plains	54
Young	Graham	62
Zapata	Zapata	247
Zavala	Crystal City	225

The United States of America, Political

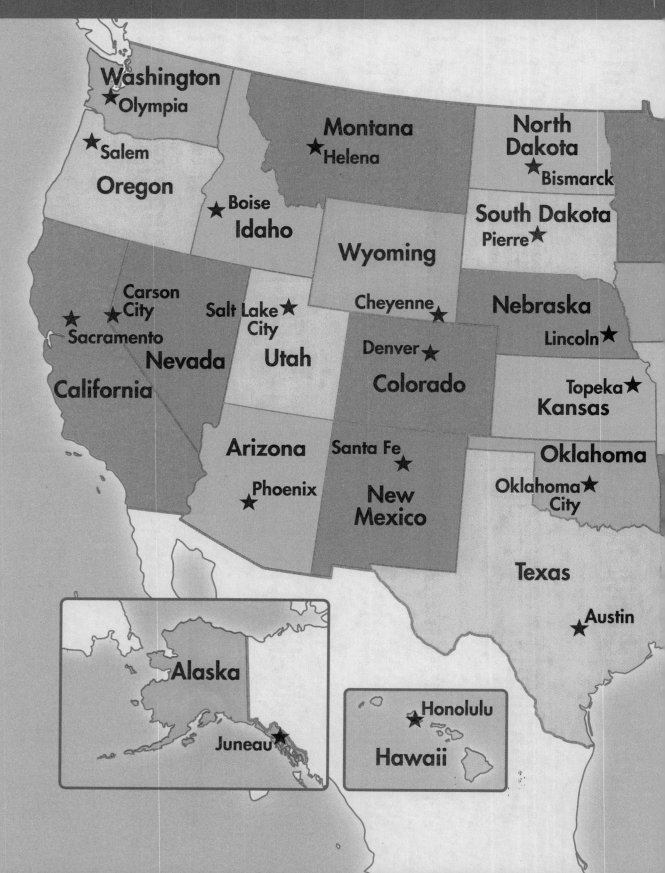

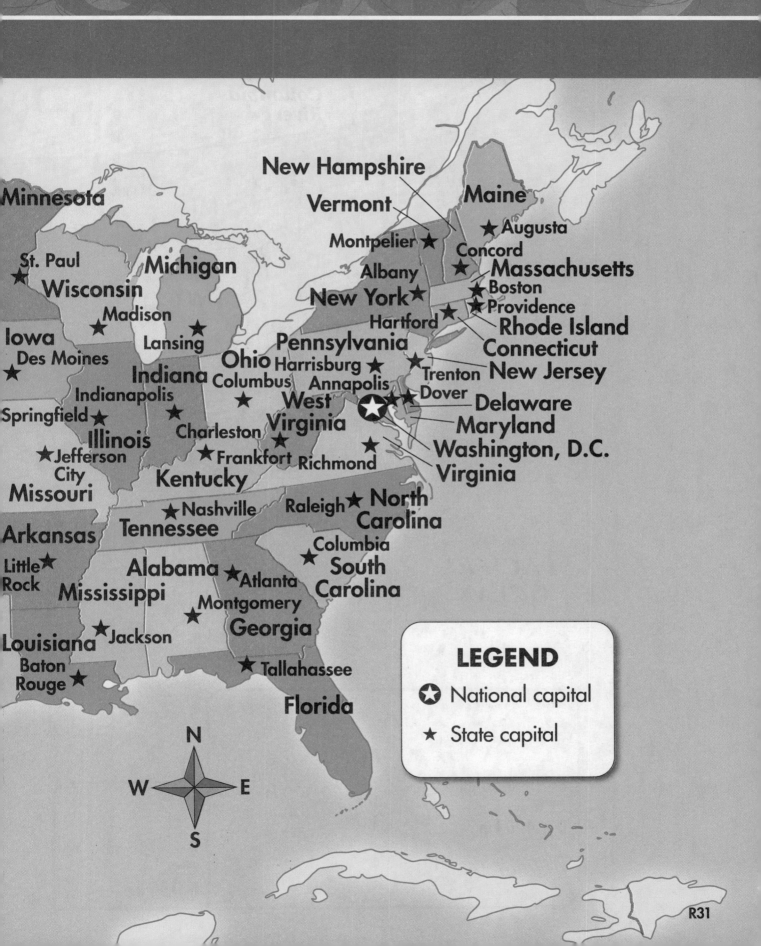

New Hampshire

Vermont

Maine

★ Augusta

Concord

Montpelier ★

Massachusetts

Minnesota

St. Paul

Michigan

Albany

★

Boston

Wisconsin

Madison

New York

★

★ Providence

Hartford

Rhode Island

Iowa

Lansing

Pennsylvania

★

Connecticut

Des Moines

Ohio

Harrisburg ★

Trenton

New Jersey

★

Indiana

Columbus

Annapolis

Dover

Delaware

Springfield

Indianapolis

West

Maryland

★

Virginia

Washington, D.C.

Illinois

Charleston

Virginia

Jefferson
City

★ Frankfort

Richmond

★

Missouri

Kentucky

Raleigh ★ North

★ Nashville

Carolina

Arkansas

Tennessee

Columbia

Little
Rock

Alabama

★ Atlanta

South
Carolina

Mississippi

Montgomery

Jackson

Georgia

★

Louisiana

Baton
Rouge

★ Tallahassee

Florida

N

W   E

S

LEGEND

⭐ National capital

★ State capital

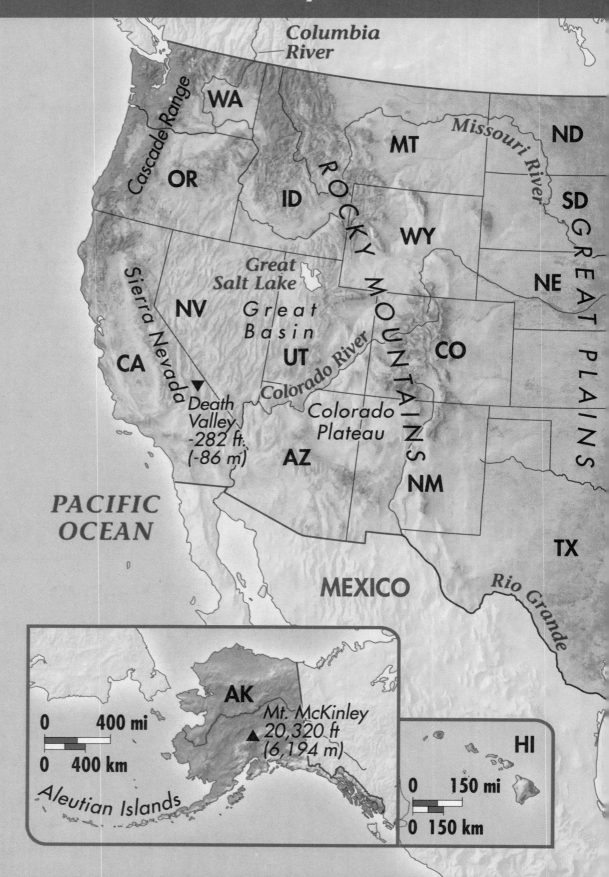

Columbia River

WA

Cascade Range

OR

MT

Missouri River

ND

ID

R O C K Y

SD

WY

G R E A T

Great Salt Lake

NE

Sierra Nevada

NV

Great Basin

M O U N T A I N S

CO

P L A I N S

CA

UT

Colorado River

▼ Death Valley -282 ft. (-86 m)

Colorado Plateau

AZ

NM

PACIFIC OCEAN

MEXICO

TX

Rio Grande

AK

Mt. McKinley
▲ 20,320 ft
(6,194 m)

0   400 mi

0   400 km

Aleutian Islands

HI

0   150 mi

0   150 km

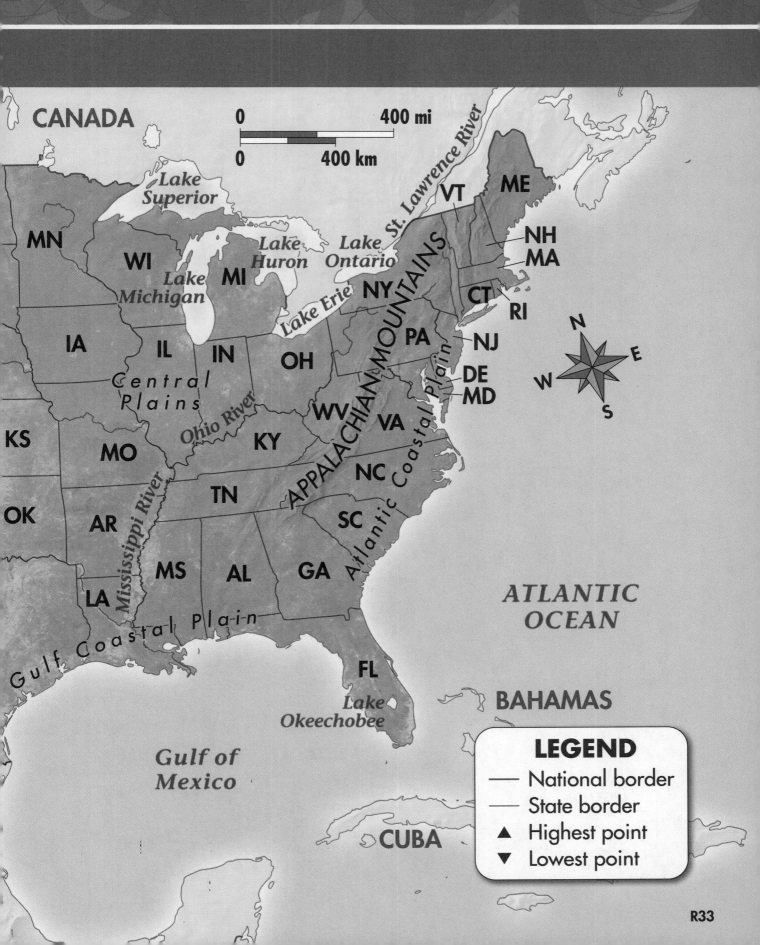

CANADA

0   400 mi

0   400 km

Lake Superior

MN

WI

Lake Huron

MI

Lake Michigan

St. Lawrence River

Lake Ontario

VT

ME

NH

MA

NY

CT

RI

IA

IL

IN

OH

Lake Erie

PA

NJ

DE

MD

Central Plains

Ohio River

WV

VA

KS

MO

KY

APPALACHIAN MOUNTAINS

NC

Atlantic Coastal Plain

OK

AR

TN

SC

Mississippi River

MS

AL

GA

LA

Gulf Coastal Plain

FL

Lake Okeechobee

ATLANTIC OCEAN

BAHAMAS

Gulf of Mexico

CUBA

N

W   E

S

LEGEND

—— National border

—— State border

▲ Highest point

▼ Lowest point

North America, Political

ARCTIC OCEAN

Bering Strait

Bering Sea

Beaufort Sea

Viscount Melville Sound

GREENLAND (Denmark)

Baffin Bay

Davis Strait

ALASKA (U.S.)
Fairbanks
Anchorage

Gulf of Alaska

Great Bear Lake

Great Slave Lake

Foxe Basin

Hudson Strait

Labrador Sea

Juneau

CANADA

Hudson Bay

Lake Athabasca

James Bay

Gulf of St. Lawrence

Edmonton
Calgary

Lake Winnipeg

Quebec

ATLANTIC OCEAN

Vancouver
Puget Sound
Seattle

Regina
Winnipeg

Ottawa ★ Montreal
Boston

Portland

Toronto
Detroit

New York City
Philadelphia
Washington, D.C. ★

Great Salt Lake
Salt Lake City

Great Lakes

Chicago

San Francisco

Denver

St. Louis

UNITED STATES

30° N

Las Vegas

Los Angeles
San Diego

Phoenix

Atlanta

Savannah

PACIFIC OCEAN

San Antonio

Dallas

New Orleans

Houston

Miami

BAHAMAS

DOMINICAN REPUBLIC

TROPIC OF CANCER

Gulf of Mexico

★ Nassau

PUERTO RICO (U.S.

MEXICO

Havana
CUBA

Santo Domingo ★
Port-au-Prince

Mexico City ★

BELIZE
Belmopan

Kingston
JAMAICA ★ HAITI

Caribbean Sea

GUATEMALA

Guatemala City ★
San Salvador ★ ★ Tegucigalpa

HONDURAS

★ Managua

EL SALVADOR
NICARAGUA
San José

★ Panama City

COSTA RICA

PANAMA

LEGEND
— National border
★ National capital
• Other city

North America, Physical

ARCTIC OCEAN

Bering Strait

Point Barrow

Ellesmere Island

Greenland

Bering Sea

Brooks Range

Beaufort Sea

Queen Elizabeth Islands

Viscount Melville Sound

Melville I. Devon I.

Baffin Bay

Mt. McKinley 20,237 ft (6,168 m)

Aleutian Islands

Alaska Range

Banks Island

Davis Strait

Cape Farewell

30° W

Alaska Peninsula

Kodiak Island

Yukon River

Victoria Island

Baffin Island

Yukon Plateau

Mackenzie R.

Foxe Basin

Labrador Sea

ATLANTIC OCEAN

Mt. Logan 19,524 ft (5,951 m)

Gulf of Alaska

Liard R.

Great Bear Lake

C A N A D I A N

Hudson Strait

Peace R.

Athabasca R.

Great Slave L.

Hudson Bay

Labrador

Newfoundland

Queen Charlotte Islands

Lake Athabasca

S H I E L D

James Bay

Gulf of St. Lawrence

Vancouver Island

Saskatchewan R.

Lake Winnipeg

G R E A T

Great Lakes

St. Lawrence R.

Nova Scotia

Puget Sound

Mississippi R.

Bay of Fundy

Coast Ranges

Cascade Range

Snake R.

Missouri R.

Ohio R.

APPALACHIAN MOUNTAINS

Cape Cod

Long Island

R O C K Y

M O U N T A I N S

Black Hills

INTERIOR PLAINS

Cape Hatteras

Great Salt Lake

Platte R.

P L A I N S

30° N

Sierra Nevada

GREAT BASIN

Arkansas R.

Ozark Plateau

Mt. Whitney 14,495 ft (4,418 m)

Colorado R.

C O A S T A L   P L A I N

Death Valley (lowest point in N.A.) –282 ft (–86 m)

Baja California

Sonoran Desert

Rio Grande

Bahamas

Puerto Rico

Lesser Antilles

TROPIC OF CANCER

Sierra Madre Occidental

Sierra Madre Oriental

Gulf of Mexico

Cuba

Greater Antilles

Hispaniola

Citlaltépetl 18,701 ft (5,700 m)

Yucatán Peninsula

Jamaica

Caribbean Sea

LEGEND
Elevation
Feet	Meters
10,000	3,048
6,000	1,829
3,000	914
1,000	305
500	152
0	0

▲ Peak

▼ Below sea level

Isthmus of Panama

Lake Nicaragua

PACIFIC OCEAN

EQUATOR

120° W

90° W

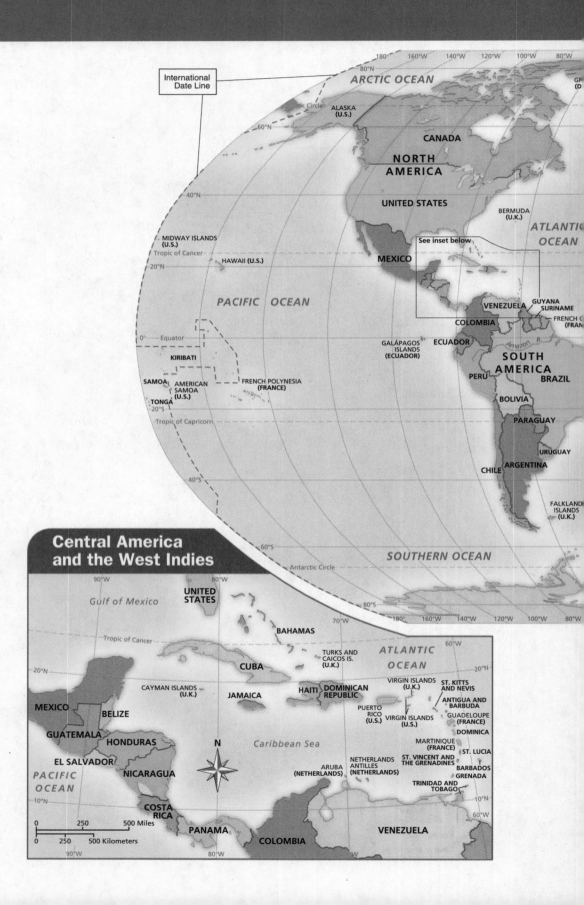

Central America and the West Indies

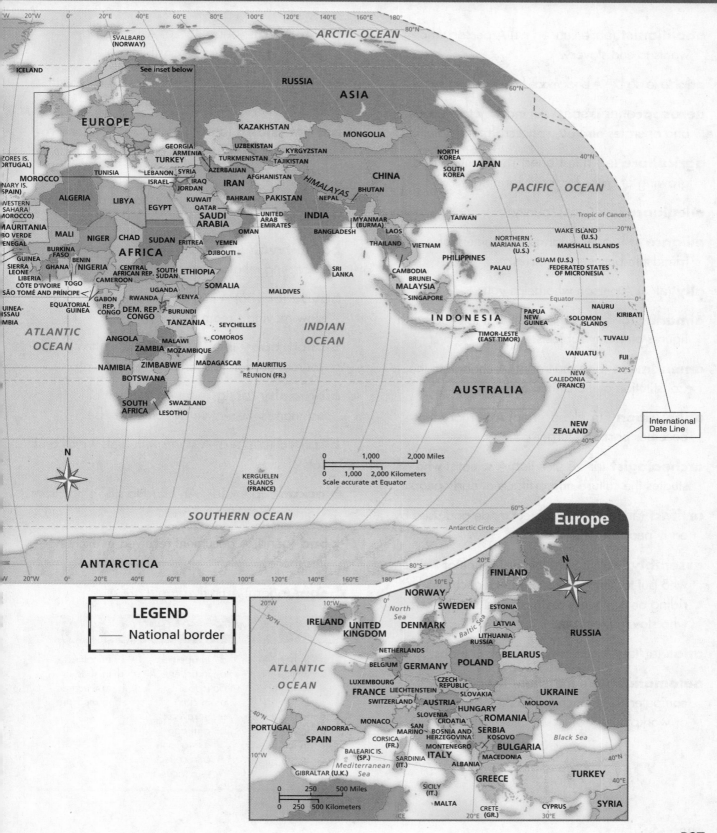

ARCTIC OCEAN
80°N

SVALBARD
(NORWAY)

ICELAND

See inset below

RUSSIA

ASIA

60°N

EUROPE

KAZAKHSTAN

MONGOLIA

GEORGIA
ARMENIA
TURKEY
TUNISIA
AZERBAIJAN
LEBANON   SYRIA
ISRAEL   IRAQ
JORDAN
IRAN
BAHRAIN
KUWAIT
QATAR
UNITED
ARAB
EMIRATES
OMAN

UZBEKISTAN
KYRGYZSTAN
TURKMENISTAN   TAJIKISTAN
AFGHANISTAN

PAKISTAN

HIMALAYAS
NEPAL   BHUTAN

CHINA

NORTH
KOREA
SOUTH
KOREA

JAPAN

PACIFIC   OCEAN

40°N

AZORES IS.
(PORTUGAL)

CANARY IS.
(SPAIN)

MOROCCO

WESTERN
SAHARA
(MOROCCO)

ALGERIA   LIBYA   EGYPT

SAUDI
ARABIA

MAURITANIA
CABO VERDE
SENEGAL

MALI   NIGER   CHAD   SUDAN   ERITREA   YEMEN

AFRICA   SOUTH
SUDAN   DJIBOUTI

GUINEA
BURKINA
FASO
SIERRA
LEONE   GHANA   BENIN
LIBERIA   TOGO
CÔTE D'IVOIRE
SÃO TOMÉ AND PRÍNCIPE

NIGERIA
CENTRAL
AFRICAN REP.
CAMEROON

EQUATORIAL
GUINEA
GABON
REP.
CONGO
DEM. REP.
CONGO   UGANDA
RWANDA   KENYA
BURUNDI

ETHIOPIA

SOMALIA

INDIA

BANGLADESH

SRI
LANKA

MYANMAR
(BURMA)

LAOS

THAILAND

MALDIVES

Tropic of Cancer
20°N

TAIWAN

WAKE ISLAND
(U.S.)

NORTHERN
MARIANA IS.
(U.S.)

MARSHALL ISLANDS

GUAM (U.S.)
FEDERATED STATES
OF MICRONESIA

PHILIPPINES   PALAU

CAMBODIA
VIETNAM
BRUNEI
MALAYSIA
SINGAPORE

Equator   0°

NAURU   KIRIBATI

GUINEA-
BISSAU
GAMBIA

ATLANTIC
OCEAN

ANGOLA

NAMIBIA

TANZANIA

MALAWI
ZAMBIA   MOZAMBIQUE

ZIMBABWE
BOTSWANA

SOUTH
AFRICA   SWAZILAND
LESOTHO

SEYCHELLES

COMOROS

MADAGASCAR

INDIAN
OCEAN

MAURITIUS

RÉUNION (FR.)

INDONESIA

TIMOR-LESTE
(EAST TIMOR)

PAPUA
NEW
GUINEA

SOLOMON
ISLANDS

VANUATU

NEW
CALEDONIA
(FRANCE)

TUVALU

FIJI

20°S

AUSTRALIA

NEW
ZEALAND

40°S

International
Date Line

N

KERGUELEN
ISLANDS
(FRANCE)

0   1,000   2,000 Miles
0   1,000   2,000 Kilometers
Scale accurate at Equator

60°S

SOUTHERN OCEAN

Antarctic Circle

80°S

ANTARCTICA

20°W   0°   20°E   40°E   60°E   80°E   100°E   120°E   140°E   160°E   180°

LEGEND

National border

Europe

N

FINLAND

NORWAY   SWEDEN   ESTONIA

North
Sea
Baltic
Sea   LATVIA

RUSSIA

IRELAND   UNITED
KINGDOM   DENMARK
LITHUANIA
RUSSIA

BELARUS

NETHERLANDS
BELGIUM   GERMANY   POLAND

ATLANTIC
OCEAN

LUXEMBOURG
FRANCE   LIECHTENSTEIN
CZECH
REPUBLIC
SLOVAKIA
UKRAINE

SWITZERLAND   AUSTRIA   HUNGARY
MONACO   SLOVENIA   CROATIA   ROMANIA   MOLDOVA

PORTUGAL   ANDORRA
SAN
MARINO
BOSNIA AND
HERZEGOVINA
SERBIA
KOSOVO
Black Sea

SPAIN   CORSICA
(FR.)
MONTENEGRO
ITALY   BULGARIA
MACEDONIA

BALEARIC IS.
(SP.)
SARDINIA
(IT.)
ALBANIA

GIBRALTAR (U.K.)
Mediterranean
Sea
SICILY
(IT.)

GREECE   TURKEY

MALTA   CRETE
(GR.)
CYPRUS   SYRIA

0   250   500 Miles
0   250   500 Kilometers

Glossary

A

abolitionist (ab′ə lish′ən ist) A person who wants to end slavery.

adobe (ə dō′bē) A brick made from mud and straw.

aerospace (er′ō spās) An industry that builds and operates aircraft, spacecraft, and satellites.

agriculture (ag′ri kul′chər) The planting and growing of crops for food; farming.

allegiance (ə lē′jəns) Loyalty.

alliance (ə lī′əns) A formal agreement of friendship between countries.

ally (al′ ī) A person who helps you.

almanac (ôl′mə nak) A book that lists facts and figures on many subjects.

amendment (ə mend′mənt) A change to the Constitution of the United States.

annexation (an′ek sā′shən) A territory that becomes part of a larger country.

archeologist (är′kē äl′ə jist) A scientist who studies the culture and artifacts of early people.

artifact (ärt′ə fakt) An object made and used by early people in the past.

assembly line (ə sem′blē līn) A line of workers who put together just one part of each product riding on a moving platform past the workers who stay in place.

atlas (at′ləs) A collection or book of maps.

automation (ôt′ə mā′shən) The use of computers and machines to do jobs in a factory or workplace.

B

bar mitzvah (bär mits′və) A Jewish boy accepting religious responsibilities.

barbed wire (bärbd wīr) A twisted wire with sharp points, or barbs, along it.

barrier island (bar′ē ər ī′lənd) A long, narrow island that lies just off the coast and protects the mainland.

basin (bā′sin) A large bowl-shaped depression in Earth's surface.

bat mitzvah (bät mits′və) A Jewish girl accepting religious responsibilities.

bayou (bī′yōō) A marshy outlet of a bay or a slow-moving stream.

bibliography (bib′lē äg′rə fē) A written list of sources used in preparing a research report.

biography (bī äg′rə fē) An account of someone's life written by someone else.

blizzard (bliz′ərd) A storm with high winds and lots of snow.

blockade (blä kād′) An effort to stop ships from going in or out of a port.

bond (bänd) A document received in exchange for money.

boom (bōōm) A time of rapid growth.

Pronunciation Key

a in hat	ō in open	'l in cattle
ā in age	ô in order	'n in sudden
ä in father	ōō in tool	th in weather
e in let	u in cup	zh in measure
ē in equal	ʉ in reverse	
i in it	ə a in ago	
ī in ice	e in agent	
o in hot	o in collect	
	u in focus	

border (bôr′dər) A boundary line.

boundary (boun′drē) A line that separates one place from another.

brand (brand) A design burned into the hide of a cow.

Buffalo Soldiers (buf′ə lō sôl′jərz) African American soldiers who fought against the Plains Indians in the late 1800s.

C

cardinal directions (kärd′′n əl də rek′ənz) The directions of north, south, east and west.

cash crop (kash kräp) A crop grown to sell at a market.

cavalry (kav′əl rē) A group of soldiers who fight battles on horseback.

charity (char′i tē) An organization that helps people in need.

citizen (sit′ə zən) A member of a city, state, or town who has legal rights and responsibilities.

civil rights (siv′əl rīts) The rights of people to enjoy freedom and equality.

civilization (siv′əl i zā′shən) A highly developed human society.

climate (klī′mət) The patterns of weather in a place over a long period of time.

colonist (käl′ə nist) A person who lives in a settlement far from the country that rules it.

colony (käl′ə nē) A settlement of people who have moved to another country but are still ruled by their home country.

communism (käm′yoo niz′əm) A system in which the government owns all the property in a country.

compass rose (kum′pəs rōz) A symbol that shows directions on a map.

confederacy (kən fed′ər ə sē) A union of people or groups who work together for a common goal.

conquistador (kän kwis′tə dôr) A conqueror, especially one of Spanish descent from the sixteenth century.

conserve (kən surv′) To limit the use of something in order to protect from waste or overuse.

constitution (kän′ stə too′shən) A written plan for the nation's government.

constitutional republic (kän′ stə too′shən əl ri pub′lik) A form of government in which representatives get their authority from the people, serve an established amount of time, and have sworn to uphold the United States Constitution.

consumer (kən soom′ər) A person or company that buys or uses goods and services.

convention (kən ven′shən) A formal meeting.

county (kount′ē) One of the sections into which a state is divided.

cultivate (kul′tə vāt) To use to raise crops.

culture (kul′chər) The way of life of a group of people.

custom (kus′təm) A way a group of people do something.

D

debt (det) Something, usually money, owed to others.

degree (di grē′) A unit of measure; there are 360 degrees of latitude and longitude used to locate places on Earth.

delegate (del′ə git) Someone who represents other people.

demand (di mand′) A consumer's, or buyer's, willingness to buy a good or service at a certain price.

depression (dē presh′ən) A time when business slows and prices fall.

descendant (dē sen′dənt) A relative.

desert (dez′ərt) An area that gets less than 10 inches of rain per year.

dictator (dik′tāt′ər) A ruler who does not answer to the people.

dictionary (dik′shə ner′ē) A book that lists the meanings, pronunciations, and spellings of words.

discrimination (di skrim′i nā′shən) The unequal treatment of people.

drought (drout) A period of time with little rain.

dugout canoe (dug′out kə nōō′) A boat made by hollowing out long logs, traditionally made by American Indians.

duty (dōō′tē) Something that you must do.

E

economic (ek′ənäm′ik) Of or relating to things that involve money and paying bills.

elevation (el′ə vā′shən) The height above sea level.

empire (em′pīr) A group of countries under the control of one ruler.

empresario (em prə sar′ē ō) A land agent who recruits new settlers, divides up property, and keeps the law.

encyclopedia (en sī′klə pē′dē ə) A set of books that gives facts about people, places, things, and events.

endangered (en dān′jərd) Something that is in danger of disappearing forever such as plants or animals.

equator (ē kwāt′ər) A line drawn around Earth halfway between the North Pole and the South Pole.

escarpment (e skärp′mənt) A long, steep slope or cliff.

ethnic group (eth′nik grōōp) A group of people with similar national origin and culture.

executive branch (eg zek′yōō tiv branch) The branch of government that enforces laws.

expand (eks′ pand′) To spread out.

expedition (eks′pə dish′ən) A journey made for a special purpose.

F

fort (fôrt) A strongly constructed building used to house soldiers and weapons.

free enterprise (frē ent′ər prīz) An economic system in which people are free to buy and sell goods and services with little control by the government.

frontier (frun tir′) The limit of settled land beyond which lies wilderness.

globe (glōb) A small round model of Earth.

government (guv′ərn mənt) A system by which a group of people are ruled.

grid (grid) A system of lines that cross each other forming a pattern of squares.

groundwater (ground′wat ər) Water that is located below the surface.

habitat (hab′i tat) A place in nature where plants and animals live.

helium (hē′lē əm) A gas that is lighter than air with no color or smell.

hemisphere (hem′i sfir′) A half of a sphere; Earth's hemispheres are formed by the equator and the prime meridian.

heritage (her′ə tij) A shared history.

hunter-gatherer (hunt′ər gath′ər ər) A person who collects plants and hunts wild animals for food.

Ice Age (īs āj) A time when huge sheets of ice and snow cover parts of Earth's land and sea.

immigrant (im′ə grənt) A person who moves to a new country.

import (im′pôrt) A product brought from a different place to trade or sell.

Indian Territory (in′dē ən ter′ə tôr′ē) Land that was set aside as territory for the American Indians in 1830.

industry (in′dəs trē) A group of businesses that make a type of product or provide a type of service.

inland (in′lənd) Away from the coast toward land.

interdependent (in′tər dē pen′dənt) Reliant on one another to meet ones needs and wants.

interest (in′trist) Money earned at a regular rate for the use of money lent.

intermediate directions (in′tər mē′dē it də rek′shənz) The directions of northeast, southeast, northwest, and southwest.

Internet (in′tər net′) A global network connecting billions of computers around the world.

invention (in ven′shən) A newly created product.

jazz (jaz) A type of music started in African American communities.

judicial branch (jōō dish′əl branch) The branch of government made up of courts and judges that make sure that state and national laws are applied fairly and correctly.

junction (junk′shən) A place where two or more rail lines meet.

Juneteenth (jōōn′tēnth) A state celebration which started on June 19, 1866, of the day remembering when slaves in Texas learned that they were free.

jury (jōōr′ē) A group of people who listen to evidence and decide the outcome of a trial.

K

kayak (kī′ak′) A canoe with a watertight covering.

L

landmark (land′märk) An object, such as a mountain, that stands out from the area around it.

latitude (lat′ə tōōd) Lines that measure the distance north and south of the equator.

legend (lej′ənd) The wording on a map that tells what each symbol on the map stands for.

legislative branch (lej′is lā′tiv branch) The branch of government that makes laws.

legislature (lej′is lā′chər) A group of elected people who make new laws.

lignite (lig′nīt′) A type of soft coal.

line rider (līn rīd′ər) A cowboy that rides along the borders of a ranch to watch the cattle.

livestock (līv′stäk′) Animals that are raised by farmers.

locomotive (lō′kə mō′tiv) A steam engine used to pull a train.

longitude (län′jə tōōd) Lines that measure the distances east and west of the prime meridian.

M

mainland (mān′land) The main part of the continent.

manufacture (man′yōō fak′chər) To make or process goods especially by machine in large quantities.

militia (mə lish′ə) Volunteer soldiers.

mission (mish′ən) A settlement where religion is taught.

mohair (mō′her) The hair of angora goats.

monument (män′yōō mənt) A structure built to show respect for a past event.

municipal (myōō nis′ə pəl) Of a city or town.

N

natural resource (nach′ər əl rē′sôrs) Anything found in nature that is useful to people.

natural vegetation (nach′ər əl vej′ə tā′shən) Plants that have grown naturally in an area for a long time without being planted or watered.

neutral (nōō′trəl) To not support one side or the other, especially in a conflict.

nomad (nō′mad) Someone who travels from place to place at different seasons.

non-combatant (nän′kəm bat′′nt) A person at a war who does not fight.

nonrenewable resource (nän ri nōō′ə bəl rē′sôrs) A natural resource that is available in limited supply. It cannot be replaced or renewed.

norther (nôr′thər) A powerful mass of cold air.

nullify (nul′ə fī) To cancel.

O

oil refinery (oil ri fīn′ər ē) A factory that cleans and processes oil into products such as gasoline or kerosene.

open range (ō′pən rānj) Grassy plains of Texas.

outline (out′līn) A written plan to interpret information.

_____ **P** _____

pesticide (pes′tə sīd) A chemical that kills the pests that damage crops.

petition (pə tish′ən) An official request to the government signed by many citizens.

petrochemical industry (pe′trō kem′i kəl in′dəs trē) Industries, refineries, and factories that use gas and oil to make products such as plastics, fertilizer, chemicals, and fabrics.

petroleum (pə trō′lē əm) Natural oil.

philanthropist (fə lan′thrə pist) A person who gives away money to help others.

physical map (fiz′i kəl map) A map that shows geographic features of a place, such as landforms and bodies of water.

plain (plān) A large area of flat land with gently rolling hills and few trees.

plantation (plan tā′shən) A large farm that produces crops to sell.

plateau (pla tō′) A level area higher than the surrounding land.

political map (pə lit′i kəl map) A map that shows political boundaries for counties, states, or nations, as well as capital cities.

political party (pə lit′i kəl pärt′ē) An organized group of people who share similar ideas about how to run a government.

pollution (pə loo′shən) Chemicals and other harmful substances that can damage the water, air, or land.

port (pôrt) A place where ships can dock to load or unload cargo.

precipitation (prē sip′ə tā′shən) Moisture that falls to the ground as rain, snow, sleet, or hail.

prejudice (prej′ə dis) A strong opinion formed without facts.

preserve (prē zurv′) To keep in its original state.

presidio (pri sid′ē ō′) A Spanish military fort.

primary source (prī′mer′ē sôrs) A piece of evidence created by someone who was part of an event.

prime meridian (prīm mə rid′ē ən) A line drawn from the North Pole to the South Pole that passes through Europe and Africa.

producer (prə doos′ər) A person or company that makes or sells goods or offers a service.

profit (präf′it) Money left over after the costs of running a business are paid for.

pueblo (pweb′lō) A Spanish word meaning "village" that refers to some American Indian groups in the Southwest.

_____ **Q** _____

quarry (kwôr′ē) An open pit where people mine, or dig up rocks.

quinceañera (kin′se ä nyer′a) A Hispanic celebration that a girl might have on her fifteenth birthday to mark the transition from childhood to adult status.

recession (ri sesh′ən) A period of reduced economic activity.

Reconstruction (rē′kən struk′shən) The time of rebuilding and change in the South after the Civil War.

region (rē′jən) An area with common features that set it apart from other areas.

renewable resource (ri noo′ə bəl rē′sôrs) A resource that can be restored naturally over time, such as a forest.

republic (ri pub′lik) A type of government in which citizens choose leaders to represent them.

research report (rē′surch ri port′) An in-depth essay, based on detailed information on a topic.

reservation (rez′ər vā′shən) Land set aside as a place for American Indians to live.

reservoir (rez′ər vwär) A natural or artificial lake used to reserve or store water.

resolution (rez′ə loo′shən) A decision.

responsibility (ri span′sə bil′ə tē) Something that a person should do.

retreat (ri trēt′) To leave the battlefield and not fight.

revolution (rev′ə loo′shən) The overthrow of one government and its replacement with another.

right (rīt) A freedom that belongs to citizens.

Roman numerals (rō′mən noo′mər əlz) A combination of letters from the Latin alphabet to show values; first used in ancient Rome.

roundup (round′up′) A systematic gathering of things, such as cattle.

rural (roor′əl) In the countryside.

scale (skāl) A tool that shows the relationship between distance on the map and distance on Earth.

scout (skout) A person who gathers clues about an enemy or location.

scrape (skrāp) A tricky situation or a problem.

secede (si sēd′) To officially leave or separate from a group.

secondary source (sek′ən der′ē sôrs) Information or research made after an event has happened.

segregation (seg′rə gā′shən) An unfair separation, based on race.

sharecropper (sher′kräp′ər) A farmer who pays part of what he or she grows to a landowner.

siege (sēj) The surrounding of a place by enemy forces trying to capture it.

skirmish (skur′mish) A small battle.

slavery (slā′ər ē) The practice of owning people and forcing them to work without pay.

software (sôft′wer′) Special programs that tell computers what to do.

spring (spring) A place where groundwater comes to the surface.

stampede (stam pēd′) A sudden rush of a herd of frightened animals, such as cattle.

stock (stäk) A share of ownership in a company.

suburb (sub′ərb) A community next to or near a city.

suffrage (suf′rij) The right to vote.

supply (sə plī′) The number of items that producers offer for sale at a certain price.

symbol (sim′bəl) A thing that stands for or represents something else.

T

tariff ('tarif) A tax paid on goods that come from another country.

tax (taks) Money a government charges in exchange for services.

technology (tek näl′ə jē) The use of scientific knowledge, skills, and tools to help people meet their needs.

teepee (tē′pē) A large tent made of hide, traditionally used by American Indians.

term (turm) The time a person serves in office after each election.

threatened (thret′′nd) When a plant or animal species is likely to become endangered.

time zone (tīm zōn) An area in which all clocks are set to the same time.

title (tīt′′l) The name of something that tells you what that thing is about.

tornado (tôr nā′dō) A fierce swirling funnel of wind created by thunderstorms.

tourism (tōōr′iz′əm) The industry that serves people who are visiting an area for pleasure.

trading post (trād′ing pōst) A small frontier store.

travois (trə voi′) A wooden sled dragged by dogs or horses.

treaty (trē′tē) A formal agreement between two countries.

U

unemployed (un′em ploid′) To have no job.

urban (ur′bən) In the city.

urban sprawl (ur′bən sprôl) The rapid growth of areas just outside a city.

urbanization (ur′bən i zā′shən) The process by which towns and cities are formed and grow as more and more people begin living and working in central areas.

V

vaquero (vä ker′ō) A Spanish cowboy.

vegetation (vej′ə tā′shən) All the trees and plants growing in an area, even farmers' crops.

veto (vē′tō) To refuse to sign a bill into law.

viceroy (vīs′roi) A person who rules a country as a representative of his king and is empowered to act in the king's name.

villa (vil′ə) A Spanish town.

visual materials (vizh′ōō əl mə tir′ē əlz) Pictures, maps, charts, and graphic organizers.

volunteer (väl′ən tir′) To give of one's time.

W

weather (weth′ər) The condition of the air at one time and place, including temperature, precipitation, and wind.

Index

This index lists the pages on which topics appear in this book. Page numbers followed by *m* refer to maps. Page numbers followed by *p* refer to photographs. Page numbers followed by *c* refer to charts or graphs. Page numbers followed by *t* refer to timelines. Bold page numbers indicate vocabulary definitions. The terms *See* and *See also* direct the reader to alternate entries.

F

Credits

Text Acknowledgments

Grateful acknowledgement is made to the following for copyrighted material:

Pages 4–5
Song "Texas, Our Texas," music by William J. Marsh, lyrics by Gladys Yoakum Wright & William J. Marsh.

Page 119
Penguin Books
Chronicle of the Narvaez Expedition by Alvar Nunez Cabeza de Vaca, translated by Fanny Bandelier. Copyright © Penguin Books.

Page 199
Texas Monthly
"Texas Primer: The Runaway Scrape" by Jan Reid from Texas Monthly, May 1989. Copyright © Texas Monthly.

Page 155
University of Texas
Music in Texas: A Survey of One Aspect of Cultural Progress by Lota M Spell. Copyright © University of Texas.

Page 158
Wallace L. McKeehan
"Rubí's Expedition 1767" from Entradas and Royal Inspection Expeditions Future DeWitt Colony 1550–1800. Copyright © Wallace L. McKeehan.

Maps
XNR Productions, Inc.

Photographs
Photo locators denoted as follows: Top (T), Center (C), Bottom (B), Left (L), Right (R), Background (Bkgd)

Cover
Front Cover (TL) Texas flag, David Lee/Shutterstock; (TR) Sam Houston Monument, Witold Skrypczak/Getty Images; (CL) Battleship Texas, Jorg Hackemann/Shutterstock; (CC) Texas Ranger badge, Geoff Brightling/DK Images; (B) Fort Worth street scene, Al Argueta/Alamy.
Back Cover (TC) Mission Concepción, BentheRN/Fotolia; (C) San Jacinto Monument, Library of Congress Prints and Photographs Division [LC_DIG_highsm 14179]; (BL) Texas state seal, Peter Tsai Photography/Alamy; (BL) Congress Avenue Bridge, Kushal Bose/Shutterstock; (BC) Palo Duro Canyon State Park, mikenorton/Shutterstock.

Text
Front Matter
x: Rolf Nussbaumer Photography/Alamy; xi: Walter Bibikow/Getty Images; xii: Richard Cummins/SuperStock; xiii: Private Collection/Boltin Picture Librar, Bridgeman Art Library; xiv: Witold Skrypczak/Lonely Planet Images/Getty Images; xix: Interfoto, Alamy; xv: Stephanie Friedman, Alamy; xvi: Library of Congress Prints and Photographs Division [LC-DIG-ppmsca-19442]; xvii: Jetta/Fotolia; xviii: Underwood Archives/Archive Photos/Getty Images; xx: Bob Daemmrich/Alamy

Celebrate Texas and the Nation
00: Matt York/AP Images; 001: Bob Daemmrich/Alamy; 002: Andersen Ross/Stockbyte/Getty Images; 003: David Lee/Shutterstock; 004: Rusty Dodson/Fotolia; 006: VanHart/Fotolia; 006: Fotogal/Fotolia; 006: Richard Cummins/RGB Ventures LLC dba SuperStock/Alamy; 006: Witold Skrypczak/Alamy; 007: Daniel Gillies/Fotolia; 007: Patrick Ray Dunn/Alamy; 007: Walter Bibikow/JAI/Corbis; 007: Witold Skrypczak/Alamy; 008: Bill Florence/Shutterstock; 008: Joannapalys/Fotolia; 008: Michael J Thompson/Shutterstock; 008: Peter Wilson/Dorling Kindersley; 008: SunnyS/Fotolia; 008: Tom Suarez/Fotolia; 008: Viktoriya Field/Shutterstock; 010: Album/Oronoz/Newscom; 010: Chris Howes/Wild Places Photography/Alamy; 010: Jt Vintage/Glasshouse Images/Alamy; 010: W. Langdon Kihn/National Geographic Society/Corbis; 010: Wm. Baker/GhostWorx Images/Alamy; 011: Library of Congress Prints and Photographs Division [LC-USZ62-110029]; 011: North Wind Picture Archives/Alamy; 012: Corbis; 012: Library of Congress Prints and Photographs Division [LC-USZ62-4723]; 012: Library of Congress Prints and Photographs Division, [LC-USZC4-960]; 012: Library of Congress Prints and Photographs Division [LC-DIG-ppmsca-19241]; 013: Art Directors & Trip/Alamy; 013: Charles Tasnadi/AP Images; 013: Library of Congress Prints and Photographs Division Washington, D.C.[LC-USW361-1054]; 013: Roger L. Wollenberg/Upi/Newscom; 013: White House Photo/Alamy; 014: David Hensley/Flickr/Getty Images; 015: Chris Howes/Wild Places Photography/Alamy; 015: Ian Dagnall/Alamy; 029: Digital Media Pro/Shutterstock; 031: Tetra Images/Getty Images; Album/Oronoz/Newscom

Chapter 01
034: Rudolf Friederich/Fotolia; 035: oliclimb/fotolia; 036: Witold Skrypczak/Alamy; 036: Worldspec/NASA/Alamy; 038: Gary Retherford/Science Source; 040: Bill Heinsohn/Alamy; 040: John Elk III/Alamy; 040: Prisma/SuperStock; 040: Superstock/Glow Images; 046: Witold

Photographs Division [LC USZ62 21276]; Library of Congress Prints and Photographs Division [LC USZ62 110029]; Niday Picture Library/Alamy; Sotheby's/AP Images; The New York Public Library/Art Resource, NY; World History Archive/Image Asset Management Ltd./Alamy

Chapter 06

215: Norman Sciple/iStock/Thinkstock; 218: George Stephenson/Alamy; 218: phil gould/Alamy; 218: Picture History/Newscom; 221: Witold Skrypczak/Alamy; 222: Stephen Saks Photography/Alamy; 223: University of Texas at San Antonio Libraries Special Collections; 224: Stephanie Friedman/Alamy; 225: LS Photos/Alamy; 228: University of Texas at San Antonio Libraries Special Collections; 230: Geoff Brightling/Dorling Kindersley, Ltd; 230: Rangers (gouache on paper), ./Private Collection/© Look and Learn/The Bridgeman Art Library; 230: The Art Archive/Art Resource, NY; 231: Bettmann/Corbis; Stephanie Friedman/Alamy

Chapter 07

240: onelifearts/Fotolia; 242: Album/Art Resource, NY; 242: Library of Congress Prints and Photographs Division; 242: The Library of Congress; 244: Library of Congress Prints and Photographs Division; 247: Jerry Larson/AP Images; 249: National Geographic/SuperStock; 250: Library of Congress Prints and Photographs Division, [LC DIG ppmsca 26824]; 252: Ralph Barrera/Austin American Statesman/WpN/Photoshot; 252: The Granger Collection, New York; 253: National Archives and Records Administration; 256: North Wind Picture Archives/Alamy; 258: University of Texas at San Antonio Libraries Special Collections; 259: Luc Novovitch/Alamy; 260: Train Passengers on the Kansas Pacific Railroad, shooting buffalo for sport in the 1870's (colour litho), American School, (19th century)/Private Collection/Peter Newark Western Americana/The Bridgeman Art Library; 263: WorldPhotos/Alamy; 264: Historical/Corbis; 266: The Metropolitan Museum of Art/Art Resource, NY; 270: Train Passengers on the Kansas Pacific Railroad, shooting buffalo for sport in the 1870's (colour litho), American School, (19th century)/Private Collection/Peter Newark Western Americana/The Bridgeman Art Library

Chapter 08

276: Jetta/Fotolia; 276: Terry Eggers/Corbis; 277: Marie Read/NHPA/Photoshot; 278: Emmett Shelton, 908 Capitol National Bank Building, Austin, Texas; 278: University of Texas at San Antonio Libraries Special Collections; 279: University of Texas at San Antonio Libraries Special Collections; 281: Carol Wood/Flickr Open/Getty Images; 282: Farm Security Administration-Office of War Information Photograph Collection (Library of Congress); 283: W.Scott/Fotolia; 286: Nancy Greifenhagen/Nancy G Western Photography/Alamy; 286: Stephen Saks Photography/Alamy; 287: Picture History/Newscom; 289: University of Texas at San Antonio Libraries Special Collections; 291: General Electric Company's Interurban Car Number 700, Driving For The Dallas Street Railway/Museum of Science and Industry, Chicago, USA/The Bridgeman Art Library; 292:

University of Texas at San Antonio Libraries Special Collections; 296: HO/AP Images; 296: Texas Energy Museum/AP Images; 299: Farm Security Administration   Office of War Information Photograph Collection (Library of Congress); 302: Alfred Schauhuber Image Broker/Newscom; 302: David Kent/MCT/Newscom; 304: Carl Mydans/Time & Life Pictures/Getty Images; 305: Curt Teich Postcard Archives/Heritage Image Partnership Ltd/Alamy; 305: Everett Collection/Newscom; byjenjen/Shutterstock; Carl Mydans/Time & Life Pictures/Getty Images; Dave Hughes/E+/Getty Images; Farm Security Administration-Office of War Information Photograph Collection (Library of Congress); Leena Robinson/Shutterstock; Margo Harrison/Fotolia; max voran/Shutterstock; outdoorsman/Fotolia; Stephen Beaumont/Shutterstock; Texas Energy Museum/AP Images; Vicki Beaver/Alamy

Chapter 09

313: spiritofamerica/Fotolia; 314: Bettmann/Corbis; 315: Everett Collection/Newscom; 316: University of Texas at San Antonio Libraries Special Collections; 317: Library of Congress Prints and Photographs Division [LC DIG npcc 01705]; 318: Mary Evans/Michael Cole Automobilia Collection/Everett Collection; 318: Shaunl/Getty Images; 319: Archive Photos/Getty Images; 320: University of Texas at San Antonio Libraries Special Collections; 320: William Lovelace/Express/Getty Images; 321: Keystone France/Getty Images; 322: Michael Ochs Archives/Getty Images; 324: National Geographic Image Collection/Alamy; 324: Underwood Archives/Archive Photos/Getty Images; 325: nsf/Alamy; 326: Library of Congress Prints and Photographs Division [LC USF34 032310 D]; 327: AP/Corbis; 329: Bettmann/Corbis; 330: Drought Stricken Area, 1934 (oil on canvas), Hogue, Alexandre (1898 1994)/Dallas Museum of Art, Texas, USA/The Bridgeman Art Library; 330: Marino, Olivia; 332: Library of Congress Prints and Photographs Division [LC USZC4 2328]; 332: University of Texas at San Antonio Libraries Special Collections; 333: Bettmann/Corbis; 334: nsf/Alamy; 335: Library of Congress Prints and Photographs Division [LC USE6 D 006777]; 336: Robert Harding Picture Library Ltd/Alamy; 337: Lake County Museum/Getty Images; 339: Library of Congress Prints and Photographs Division [LC U9 32937 32A/33]; 342: PF (bygone1)/Alamy

Chapter 10

346: tave_luigi/Fotolia; 347: 3dsculptor/Fotolia; 347: Daniel Gillies/Fotolia; 347: Ian Dagnall/Alamy; 347: lexaarts/Fotolia; 348: Jim Parkin/Fotolia; 349: Rachel Denny Clow/AP Images; 350: NASA/DVIDS; 350: NASA/ZUMA Press/Newscom; 351: Bettmann/Corbis; 351: Interfoto/Alamy; 351: Itar Tass Photos/Newscom; 351: MADDRAT/Shutterstock; 351: wwwebmeister/Shutterstock; 352: Bill Barksdale/AgStock Images, Inc./Alamy; 353: Everett Collection Historical/Alamy; 353: Yoshikazu Tsuno/AFP/Newscom; 354: Terry Underwood Evans/Shutterstock; 356: OJO Images Ltd/Alamy; 357: Ljupco Smokovski/Fotolia; 358: chomnancoffee/Fotolia; 358: Dana White/PhotoEdit, Inc; 358: ZUMA Press, Inc./Alamy; 359: lunamarina/Fotolia; 360: Deborah Cannon/American Statesman/AP Images; 361: Kevin